PENGUIN

CHINESE LOVE

ANNE BIRRELL (University of Cambridge, Clare Hall) read Russian, French and Latin at Manchester University. She then read Chinese at the School of Oriental and African Studies, University of London, continuing her studies at the University of Michigan, where she obtained her MA in Chinese Literature and Language. She obtained her M.Phil. and Ph.D. degrees at Columbia University in the City of New York. Her doctoral dissertation focused on the new love poetry of early medieval China preserved in *New Songs from a Jade Terrace*. Besides her complete translation of this anthology, the first in any Western language, she has published several related articles, 'Erotic Decor', 'The Dusty Mirror' and 'Courtly Love Poetry in Early Medieval China'. She then published the first in-depth study of the earliest repertoire of folk-songs and ballads in ancient China, *Popular Songs and Ballads of Han China* (1988, reprinted in paperback 1993). She published another pioneering research work, *Chinese Mythology: An Introduction* (1993), with two related scholarly articles. Professor Birrell has been on several official visits to China, sponsored by the British Academy and the Chinese Academy of Social Science. The British Academy have also funded much of her research work. Her teaching posts include City University, New York, and the University of Cambridge. Her research paper written from the Gender Studies approach, 'In the Voice of Women: Chinese Love Poetry in the Early Middle Ages', was presented at the Centenary Conference on *Women and the Book*, St Hilda's College, University of Oxford, appearing in print in 1995.

CHINESE LOVE POETRY

NEW SONGS
FROM A JADE TERRACE

A Medieval Anthology

TRANSLATED WITH ANNOTATIONS
AND AN INTRODUCTION
BY ANNE BIRRELL

PENGUIN BOOKS

PENGUIN BOOKS

Published by the Penguin Group
Penguin Books Ltd, 27 Wrights Lane, London w8 5tz, England
Penguin Books USA Inc., 375 Hudson Street, New York, New York 10014, USA
Penguin Books Australia Ltd, Ringwood, Victoria, Australia
Penguin Books Canada Ltd, 10 Alcorn Avenue, Toronto, Ontario, Canada m4v 3b2
Penguin Books (NZ) Ltd, 182–190 Wairau Road, Auckland 10, New Zealand

Penguin Books Ltd, Registered Offices: Harmondsworth, Middlesex, England

First published by George Allen & Unwin 1982
Published in Penguin Classics 1986
Second edition, extensively revised 1995
3 5 7 9 10 8 6 4 2

Typeset by Datix International Limited, Bungay, Suffolk
Filmset in 9.5/10.75 pt Monophoto Baskerville
Printed in England by Clays Ltd, St Ives plc

To the memory of
my dear departed mother
Margaret Brigid

ACKNOWLEDGEMENTS

I wish to thank the following colleagues who have made valuable suggestions for this new edition: Professor Hans H. Frankel, Professor Victor H. Mair, Professor David R. Knechtges, Professor Mu K'o-hung and Professor David McCraw. I am grateful to the Editor-in-Chief of Penguin Books, Peter Carson, and to Mark Handsley for their generous and far-sighted decision to issue this new revised edition, and to Josine Meijer for her expert assistance with the new cover illustration. I am particularly indebted to Paul Keegan, editor of the Penguin Classics, for his intelligent and constructive advice and for his sympathetic encouragement of new research. The new edition has benefited from the expert literary guidance of Peter Ford. I am also thankful for the friendly interest of Fra' Ewen G. Cameron, Carolyn Cather, Liz Blair, John Cayley, Rémi Mathieu, Piers and Poh Sim Plowright, Hok-lam Chan, Bob and Marian Tignor, Enid and Stan Adelson, and to Mrs Alison Waley.

CONTENTS

xi

CHAPTER SIX   Poets of the Southern Dynasties   185
(EARLY SIXTH CENTURY)

xv

CHAPTER SEVEN Royal Poets of the Liang 211
(THE HSIAO FAMILY)

xvi

xvii

CHAPTER EIGHT   Twenty Poets of the Liang Dynasty   241
(SIXTH CENTURY)

CHAPTER NINE   Love-songs in Irregular Metres   269
(FROM SECOND CENTURY BC TO SIXTH CENTURY AD)

CHRONOLOGICAL TABLE

<small>(DATES AND NAMES PRIOR TO 841 BC ARE TRADITIONAL)</small>

The Age of the Gods, Culture Heroes and Sage Kings   ?2852–?2206 BC

    Yellow Emperor (Yellow God)
    Yao
    Shun

The Golden Age of the Three Dynasties

?Hsia Dynasty	?2205–?1767
Shang (Yin) Dynasty	?1766–?1123
Chou Dynasty	?1123–221
Western Chou	?1123–771
Eastern Chou	771–256
Spring and Autumn Era	722–481
Warring States Era	403–221
Ch'in Dynasty	221–207
The Han Empire	202 BC–AD 220
Former (or Western) Han	202–AD 8
Hsin Dynasty (Interregnum)	9–23
Later (or Eastern) Han	25–220
The Three Kingdoms	221–280
Minor Han Dynasty	221–265
Wei Dynasty	220–265
Wu Dynasty	222–280
Chin Dynasty	265–419
Western Chin	265–316
Eastern Chin	317–419

The Period of Disunion   317–589
    (also known as the Six Dynasties, namely
    Wu, Eastern Chin, Liu-Sung, Ch'i, Liang, Ch'en,
    or the Northern and Southern Dynasties)
    The Northern Dynasties   386–580

INTRODUCTION

'Who can stop love once love happens?' (Yen Yen-chih). 'Autumn will come when all things must wither, / And touch her body with nature's stealth' (Hsü Ling). 'A bed of love reflects an orphan shadow' (Hsiao Yen). 'I offer my love to the kohl across her eyebrows, / Send my heart to the lipstick on her mouth' (Shen Yüeh). 'The reason your sad wife is wasting away / Is not that you like slim waists!' (Wang Seng-ju). Such are the voices of love, contradictory yet credible. They might belong to any time or place. In fact Chinese poets wrote these lines some fourteen centuries or more ago. This will surprise people who have read that Chinese poets prefer to write about their friends, not their lovers. The idea that Chinese poetry does not deal with love is a myth. Love, that unfailing interest of man, has also captured the Chinese imagination. The evidence lies in the broad range of love expressed within these pages: wooing, marriage, divorce; celebrations, obsessions, laments; new love, old love, dead love.

This book is a translation of a medieval Chinese anthology of love poems called *New Songs from a Jade Terrace*. It was compiled by a court poet, Hsü Ling, between the years 534–45. It consists of 656 poems in 10 volumes arranged in chronological sequence. What prompted me to undertake this translation is the fact that it embodies representative love poems from the second century BC to the mid-sixth century AD. As such the anthology testifies to the rich vein of love poetry in the Chinese tradition. Another factor that influenced me is that, except for some of its earliest pieces (notably translated by Arthur Waley and Burton Watson), and some later ones (notably translated by John D. Frodsham), this anthology has never been fully rendered into a Western language before. More important, however, apart from spanning seven and a half centuries *New Songs from a Jade Terrace* represents selected love poems from an entire era, the hundred or so years from the early fifth century to the middle of the sixth century AD. This era is known as the Southern Dynasties, the dynasties of the Sung, Ch'i, Liang, and, the last, the Ch'en. Numerically, Southern Dynasties love poems dominate the anthology. It was in this period that a new poetic style crystallized from the royal patronage of Southern Dynasties courts, especially of the Liang Dynasty. The new vogue was dubbed at the time 'Palace Style Poetry', what we would term today the love poetry of Southern Dynasties court poets.

This volume of translations, therefore, serves a manifold purpose.

First, it will demonstrate the advanced level of literature in early medieval China. It will also show the development of a major literary theme over several centuries. Furthermore, it will demonstrate the mature features of the new Southern Dynasties 'Palace Style Poetry'. As a corollary, forgotten poets and' their poetry will be rediscovered. Lastly, this anthology will provide a necessary link between the more familiar landmarks of ancient China and the later medieval period of the T'ang Dynasty. Clearly, much of the originality claimed for T'ang poetry has to be put back where it rightly belongs – to poets of the Southern Dynasties.

Historical Perspective

Poets in general speak the language of their time and reflect something of the changing nature of their society. *New Songs from a Jade Terrace* appeared at a favourable juncture in time, during a period of relative present peace poised between past war and future political strife. This collection was a literary product of the Liang Dynasty, ruled by Emperor Wu from the southern capital of Chienk'ang, modern Nanking. It was the literary inspiration of his son, the Crown Prince Hsiao Kang. Between the years 534–45 Hsiao Kang commissioned the court poet, Hsü Ling, to compile these love poems. The majority of them date from the fifth and early sixth centuries AD, when China was ruled in the south by a succession of Chinese dynasties, and in the north by foreign invaders. Men of the Liang Dynasty looked back on three hundred years of divisive warfare. Their ancient Han empire which for four centuries had dominated the Orient east to Korea, west to Turkestan, and south to Indo-China, collapsed in the year AD 220. China became a divided country. Reunification was only achieved after the passing of the Ch'en Dynasty in AD 589. The three and a half centuries between AD 220 and 589 were characterized by rivalry among regional warlords and foreign invaders. The crisis came in the year AD 317 when foreign tribes conquered the ancient Chinese capitals of Ch'angan and Loyang and drove the Chinese rulers and their court south into exile. Until reunification in AD 589 Chinese territorial power was eclipsed to a shadow of its former size and grandeur.

A major source of continued strife was the lack of coherence within the ruling groups of China. Powerful family warred against family for supremacy in the political sphere. Even within the great families internecine rivalry for power superseded the desire to achieve concerted dynastic aims. During these centuries there were twenty-nine different dynasties in north China and six in the south. This historical period is variously known as the Period of Division, or the Six Dynasties, or the

Northern and Southern Dynasties. The result of this inter-family and intra-clan struggle was the proliferation of power bases among a number of great families, rather than the concentration of power in one central dynastic house. The southern dynasty of the Liang itself was founded by an act of usurpation by Hsiao Yen when he destroyed the Liu-Sung royal house of which he was a member and proclaimed himself Emperor Wu of the Liang. He went on to enjoy a long and peaceful reign lasting fifty years. His son and heir, Hsiao Kang, was not so fortunate. He ruled for a mere two years before being assassinated by a Tartar general from the north.

The historical era of *New Songs from a Jade Terrace* was aristocratic. The southern Liang court was based at Chienk'ang and Emperor Wu conferred upon his numerous sons and relatives aristocratic rank and administrative power. The twenty-three provinces of his domain were ruled by civil and military governors related to him. Often they were figureheads enjoying the wealth, status and privilege that went with their noble rank and official title. Actual governmental duties were carried out by educated men of the middle ranks of society. These imperial policies of conferring hereditary rank on members of the royal family and of recruiting officials from lower bureaucratic echelons meant that many men from great and illustrious aristocratic families were bypassed in political life. In some cases they directed their energies to the literary life of the capital and provincial courts.

Court Patronage of Literature

One of the striking features of southern aristocratic society was the system of literary patronage that operated in the imperial court at Chienk'ang and the minor courts of princes in the provinces. Much of the literary efflorescence of this era was lost when the capital was sacked and its libraries and cultural treasures destroyed in AD 555. *New Songs from a Jade Terrace* survived the holocaust. It owes its creation to one of the great men of early medieval China. Promoted to Crown Prince in AD 531, Hsiao Kang succeeded to the throne in 549, and is known to history as Emperor Chienwen. Like many Chinese dynastic rulers he managed to combine a political career with literary and intellectual interests. While he was Crown Prince he assumed the role of patron of the arts in his own court at Yung, west of the capital. His literary circle was attended by nobles, courtiers, and educated men of the gentry class. The composition of the anthology testifies to his royal patronage: of its 10 volumes one whole volume is devoted to poets of the Liang royal house, and, of the 502 poems by 51 Southern Dynasties poets, Hsiao Kang is represented by 76 poems, his father Hsiao Yen by 41, and the

3

Liang royal house as a whole by 166 poems. A nice case of flattery on the part of Hsü Ling, the compiler, who modestly included only four of his own poems.

In this aristocratic society the poet was not a special class of person. He was very different from the romantic Western image of a wild-eyed, unbuttoned, tousle-haired poet, an independent spirit moved by the divine muse to express himself in original verse. The Chinese poet of this era was more like a Victorian poet laureate who was also a civil servant. In order to be recognized the Chinese writer had to gain entry into the central or provincial court through family connections, imperial preferment and literary talent. Once admitted, he was required to perform official duties and attend numerous court functions. On such occasions as formal banquets he was not only commanded to participate in poetry competitions, but also presented with a mandatory theme for competitive extempore composition. A number of poems have tagged on to their titles the formal phrase 'By royal command', or 'At the command of His Royal Highness', or 'Composed at His Majesty's Banquet on Such-and-Such a Theme'. In this sense poetry was not simply an art, but also a form of social intercourse, and more importantly a means for official promotion and literary recognition.

In such an environment where literary success was dependent upon royal patronage it was natural for courtier poets to offer their compositions to their social superiors, albeit artistic peers. The honorific tag 'Respectfully Submitted to His Highness' appears in many poem titles of this period. Another way the court poet consolidated his official and literary career was to imitate the poems of his superior. Not only was the theme imitated, but more often the rhyme-scheme of his superior's admired poem was matched, or 'harmonized with'. That this technique was extremely popular is evident in the large number of poems in this collection bearing the tag 'Respectfully Submitted to His Highness, Harmonizing with the Rhymes of His Poem'. The proliferation of these dedicatory titles in the anthology indicates the extent to which court poets felt the literary weight of royal patronage.

The Anthologist's Purpose

T. S. Eliot claimed with understandable poetic licence: 'Few things that can happen to a nation are more important than the invention of a new form of verse.' Certainly, poets of the Liang era would have glumly agreed as they witnessed their dynasty disappear into ashes. The most significant factor of court patronage of poetry was the development of a new form of love poetry. Historical annals credit various people with the invention of 'Palace Style Poetry' – Hsiao Kang, Hsü

4

Ch'ih (Hsü Ling's father), Yü Chien-wu and his son Yü Hsin. Regardless of who the actual innovator was, the last three names were associated with Hsiao Kang's literary court. In his capacity of patron it was Hsiao Kang who set his seal of approval upon the new poetic vogue and thus ensured its success. The prevalence of imitation in poetry circles and the trend towards dedicatory verse meant that the fashion legitimized by a royal patron was destined to become popular. By commissioning Hsü Ling to garner the gems of the earlier tradition of love poetry and glean the finest contemporary models, Hsiao Kang was instrumental in immortalizing this new form of verse.

Anthologies by their nature are in some respects ephemeral literary things. They are often based on literary views and sets of values which sum up an attitude to the past and present held at a particular moment by a particular person or group. Of the 656 poems in the Chinese anthology 75 per cent are of the century or so before and up to its compilation. That is to say they were modern in their own day. Modernity is but one aspect of the word 'New' (*hsin*) in the anthology's title. Another is the compiler's personal predilection for poems representing the new poetic vogue. Linking these two aspects of modernity and fashion is the new aesthetic preoccupation of Hsü Ling and of his patron Hsiao Kang.

Although at first glance it seems that Hsü Ling selected love poems from the vast time span of seven and a half centuries in order to demonstrate the richness of Chinese love poetry down through the ages to his own day, he did in fact make two important omissions in his selection. One was the body of love poetry among the 305 poems in *The Book of Songs*, traditionally believed to date from the ninth to the seventh centuries BC. The other was the corpus of erotic and elegiac rhapsodies of *The Songs of Ch'u*, dating from the fourth century BC to the second century AD. The reason for these glaring omissions cannot be said to be metrical, for both their metres, the archaic tetrasyllabic and the *sao*-song metres respectively, appear in Hsü Ling's anthology. The reason has more to do with a radical change in literary values in the sixth century AD.

In the early part of the Han dynasty (202 BC–AD 220) *The Book of Songs* was elevated to the status of a classic, together with four other works associated with the teachings of Confucius, and Confucianism was espoused by the state as official doctrine. The idea gained currency that Confucius had edited the 305 poems of this classic from an earlier collection of over three thousand poems. Authorities were appointed to supervise each of the five *Confucian Classics* and Han scholars began to write commentaries on them. Adhering to the belief that Confucius had edited the songs, these writers insisted that the sage had implicitly editorialized in making his selection. Consequently, these scholars

5

evolved elaborate explanations and interpretations of quite innocent songs, giving them a didactic tone. Thus a marriage song becomes an allegory for the exemplary marital relationship between a ruler and his consort. Or a lovers' elopement becomes an allegory for dissident peasants fleeing to another country. *The Songs of Ch'u* suffered a similar fate at the hands of exegetical writers. Its early poems written in a highly complex symbolic language were reduced to mere prosaic allegory of a political, moralizing nature.

The result was that later generations of scholars and writers extended the didactic values attached to these works, especially *The Book of Songs* as a state classic, to literature in general. The function of literature, they persuaded, was to edify and improve; literature was to provide a mirror of personal conduct. It was only some fourteen centuries later, when the forthright philosopher Chu Hsi (AD 1130–1200) punctured the pious excesses of Han and post-Han scholarship, that these allegorical distortions of classical poetry and literature in general were deflated and Confucian doctrine on the didactic value of literature was diminished.

In this context Hsü Ling and Hsiao Kang were avant-garde writers. When Hsü Ling compiled his anthology of love poems, didactic views of literature had long held sway. In his Preface to the anthology, however, he makes it quite clear that his purpose in literature is to give pleasure rather than instruction. Tilting obliquely at dour academics who managed to find moral meaning everywhere, Hsü Ling mischievously pictures his readers as women indolently passing days and nights in luxurious harem boudoirs. He archly states: 'The palace lady takes no delight in idle hours, / But devotes her mind to the latest verse.' Tongue-in-cheek, Hsü Ling brags about the popularity of his volumes of poetry among this female audience, who after preening themselves in their boudoir nonchalantly tuck his volumes under their pillow: they 'will always be tucked away in vermilion pillows'. He claims that ladies will 'for long hours be diverted behind their reading drapes, / My book always open in slim hands.' Hsü Ling ends his Preface with a series of humorous disclaimers: 'Certainly my book will be quite different / From Empress Teng's study of *The Spring and Autumn Classic*, / For a scholar's attainments are too hard to acquire!' Empress Teng was famous in the Han Dynasty for her single-minded pursuit of knowledge, conning the *Confucian Classics* all day long, solemnly and earnestly. Finally, to make sure that his view of literature as entertainment is perfectly understood, Hsü Ling sardonically notes that poetry is better than drugs, such as 'the flower of oblivion', for alleviating boredom: 'For poetry can / Be a substitute for the flower of oblivion / And can banish the disease of ennui.' This ambience of boudoirs, cosmetics, pillows and palace ladies is a world apart from the solemnities of exegetical scholarship. It is an urbane acknowledgement that art is lightly to be pursued for art's sake.

Conventions of the Love Poem

Art and artifice were the hallmark of literary products in the Southern Dynasties era. To be successful the courtier had to be an accomplished artist in many different forms of literature. Not only must he compose correct memorials to the throne, obituary notices and eulogies for his superiors, treatises and epistles, but also works in various forms of verse for specific occasions. The diverse functions and forms of writing were appreciated quite early in the literary tradition. In the third century AD the poet Ts'ao P'ei, known to history as Emperor Wen of the Wei Dynasty, made a list of eight genres in his *Essay on Literature* (*Lung wen*). By the sixth century Hsiao T'ung, Hsiao Kang's older brother, had compiled an *Anthology of Literature* (*Wen hsüan*) which contained examples of no fewer than thirty-seven different forms of literature. Each of these literary forms had recognizable rhetorical, structural and stylistic differences. Many of them were composed for a special social or official occasion. Success or failure depended to a large extent on whether the writer conformed to a particular literary model and had displayed technical virtuosity in its execution. It was no good confusing the diction and allusions of a prose obituary with those of a treatise, still less muddling the diction and allusions of a poem about a hermit with those about a lover. The genre was the thing in the writer's composition and in his critics' appreciation.

Depending on the different genres and sub-genres, therefore, the writer employed different systems of rhetoric. When he composed in the love-poem genre, and especially in the sub-genre of 'Palace Style Poetry', the court poet not only respected the appropriate devices of rhetoric, but also observed a strict code of poetic convention governing subject, theme, mood and attitude. This well-defined system of conventions was an implicit agreement between the poet and his literary circle to impose certain restrictions upon and to take certain liberties with his treatment of the theme of love. These courtly conventions were strongly influenced by earlier love poems in the literary tradition – anonymous folk-songs, ballads, so-called ancient-style poems, and the poems and rhapsodies of *The Book of Songs* and *The Songs of Ch'u*. Many features of these types of poetry were borrowed and adapted according to the dictates of Southern Dynasties literary fashion. Originally existing as disparate elements in varying literary sources stretching back over several centuries, they were welded together in the hands of later court poets into a unified, distinctive, well-developed pattern of love poetry. The fascination of *New Songs from a Jade Terrace* lies partly in the fact that those earlier love poems best fitted to the purposes of the collection (excluding those of the two aforementioned collections) appear together with the later artefact. That the poems are arranged in the anthology in chronological order within metrical divisions heightens the reader's awareness of how the Southern Dynasties love poem developed from pastoral simplicity to courtly sophistication.

When the court poet composed a love poem, he would usually select as his subject a woman in love, rather than a man in love with a woman. When a man is featured in the poems, he is mostly portrayed as a homosexual love object akin to the way a woman is presented, or as a man mourning the death of his wife or mistress. The poet, usually male, takes on the literary persona of a woman in love, expressing in descriptive and lyrical terms her deep emotions. This literary pose had a long tradition before the Southern Dynasties era and derived mainly from the ballad, folk-song and ancient-style poem. What is significant in the new poetic vogue is that the female subject of the love poem conforms to a noble ideal of femininity. She would appear to be well-born and living in luxurious surroundings, preferably palatial. Even when the poet is clearly borrowing stock characters from the earlier tradition, such as a merchant's wife, a soldier's sweetheart, a courtesan, a country girl or a barmaid, he gives them a courtly treatment in so far as their environment and appearance are concerned. His poetic portrait of a woman in love conveys impressions of noble breeding and pampered living through her physical appearance: she is slender, graceful, elegantly dressed, adorned with costly jewels and heavily made up with cosmetics. This accent on glamour and wealth is a feature of the earlier ballad tradition, but in 'Palace Style Poetry' it is given a distinctly new emphasis.

Another obligatory convention of the love poem of this era is that the woman's lover must be absent from the love scenario. The court poet must depict her pining for him with unrelieved sadness. This melancholy mood pervades much of the ancient-style poetic repertoire, and probably derives from the older poetic tradition of *The Songs of Ch'u*. This collection contains a pivotal poem dating from about the fourth century BC, 'Encountering Sorrow', and its later imitations, besides a suite of shamanistic songs. All these pieces are commonly characterized by the persona's pursuit of love – a mortal for a goddess, a shaman for his god or goddess, a courtier for his lord – and the ultimate frustration of such desire. Overshadowed by its literary precursor, the Southern Dynasties courtly love poem is imbued with a profound sense of obligatory melancholy. The woman portrayed therein should seem depressed but submissive in her acceptance of doomed love. Because of her literary role as a victim of love, she should strike a pose of appealing emotional vulnerability and pathetic physical weakness. Her time must be spent conventionally waiting in the palatial ambience of her boudoir or its environs for her absent lover. The poet should describe certain items there with sensuous and metaphorical detail. His portrait of a woman in love is usually framed in an interior setting where nature is not too far off. For the natural world outside and the interior world within are poetically deployed to contrast with the beauty and fate of a woman in love, to pinpoint the ephemeral aspect of time, and to underscore poetic statements on the meaning of love and of life. The general tenor of the court poet's portrait is one of touchingly pretty pathos.

Images of Woman

As this degree of conventionality suggests, woman is depicted by the court poet as a type rather than as a realistically observed individual. The poet does not seek to inject into the fictionalized image of a woman in love some semblance of his own personal experience. Courtly love was never intended to be autobiography, or biography in verse. Western readers who set a high premium on originality in poetic creation should resist the temptation to construct a consistent autobiographical or biographical framework around these poems. One has only to compare a handful of poems with similar titles in the anthology, such as 'Green, green riverside grass', to realize that they share so many resemblances that the poets cannot be describing details drawn from the crucible of their own amatory agonies. On the other hand the 656 love poems of *New Songs from a Jade Terrace* do not by any means conform to an identical pattern of conventions in a narrow sense. That would be too monotonous, even for the most determined poetaster! One line of demarcation between the more loosely structured love poem and the stricter conventional love poem is temporal. About 150 poems dating from the second century BC to the late third century AD have a fairly flexible design, while the five hundred or so dating from the fourth to the early sixth century follow a recognizably conventional pattern.

This divergence between the old and new poetic styles is never more noticeable than in the physical portrait of a woman in love. In the older poems a woman is presented in an idealized way. Much of this mode of presentation derives from even earlier models in the literary tradition, such as the fourth century BC shamanistic poems, the 'Nine Songs', of *The Songs of Ch'u*. This image of divine eroticism develops into an idealized portrayal of palace ladies, an example of which appears in a poem by Lu Chi of the third century AD:

> Sweet looks glister in white sun,
> Kind hearts soft and pure.
> Lovely eyes spread gleams of jade,
> Moth eyebrows like kingfisher plumes.

9

Fresh skin, oh so smooth,
Vivid bloom it seems one could nibble.
Meek, mild, full of grace,
Enchantingly clever wit.

This serene image of female beauty changes radically under the brush of later court poets. They prefer to show a woman not in terms of divinely perfect beauty but as the tarnished image of feminine loveliness. The flawless mask described in the earlier love poems surrenders to pathetic facial ruin. What has happened here is that the court poets have adopted the trend in earlier love poems towards expressing unhappy love and have extended it to its ultimate limits of personal neglect. A passage by Wu Chün (AD 469–520) illustrates this new mode of presentation:

From grief green-glinting hair has changed,
Pink cheeks from tears are ruined.
Tears not only form into pearls,
But I see pearls turn to blood.

This change in perception marks a shift in sensibility from the earlier interest in woman as a divine image to the later preoccupation with woman as a victim of love's disease.

Furthermore, there is a marked contrast between the old and new love poetry in the manner of describing dress and adornments of a woman in love. In the older poems cosmetics, jewellery and dress are described, to be sure, but not to the same lavish degree as in the new style of love poetry. The court poets reveal a fascination for the opulent minutiae of feminine fashion. The typical portrait shows woman adorned with fine jewels, costly silk clothes and elaborate make-up. She indicates her beauty and worth in a very material way through the sheer opulence of her personal décor. So closely and persistently is a woman's rich attire associated with her personal attractiveness that her portrayal as a desirable woman depends on the financial and status value of her costume. What this amounts to is an aesthetic convention of courtly love poetry: woman is adored when adorned. The effect of such an emphasis on material rather than personal, individual qualities is that human values seem to be less important than material values in the aesthetic consciousness of the court poets. A passage from a poem by Shen Yüeh (AD 441–512), one of the most popular poets of his day, typifies this way of presenting a woman in love:

She is lovely and pretty in face and figure,
Courteous and clever the way she talks.

Her waist and limbs are graceful,
Her clothes so sweet and fresh.
Her round red cape reflects early chill,
Her painted fan welcomes the first spell of heat.
On brocade slippers is a 'like flower' pattern,
On broidered sash is a 'same heart' lettuce design.
Gold-leaf brooches fasten her silk bolero,
Flower jewel pins hold up her cloudy hair.

Of the thirty-four lines of this poem only the second line here describes the woman's personality, whereas fifteen lines are devoted to her appearance. The female figure is redolent with sensuous luxury and an erotic, but impersonal, ornamentation.

A further distinction between the image of woman in old and new poetic styles is that earlier poetic settings of rustic simplicity were replaced by the new poetic charm of sophisticated urban life. It was inevitable that as life in the city, especially at the courts of the capital city and provinces, grew more genteel, affluent and fashionable, it would become separate from the pastoral naivety of the countryside. The love poems of *The Book of Songs* have outdoor settings: rivers, mulberry patches or city walls. The erotic poems of *The Songs of Ch'u* have settings that range from the terrestrial to the celestial and supernatural. The early folk-songs and ancient-style poems continue this outdoor, mostly rural tradition, and such models are represented in this anthology. The courtly love poem, however, makes a significant break with this tradition: love moves indoors. The vertiginous, wild mountain eyrie of a goddess or the dusty, bustling corner of a city wall where a poor country girl waits for her lover becomes the polite boudoir of a court lady with nature domesticated in her cultivated garden. Hsü Ling set the tone for this shift of emphasis in his Preface. There he clearly established the boudoir of a woman in a palace harem as the typical setting of the new style of love poem:

And so,
Through labyrinthine spirals of pepper palaces,
Up mysterious elevations of thorn-tree halls,
Scarlet Crane keys impose privacy at dawn,
Bronze Clam knockers fall silent at noon.
Before the Three Stars twilight hour
The ladies are not summoned to bring their quilt.

Southern Dynasties poets depict the boudoir as a closed erotic world. The normal elements of a lady's daily life, such as servants, children, friends, family and, most important, her husband or lover, are pruned away from the scenario. In the full flowering of the love poetry of this era woman becomes confined to symbolic isolation in her luxury boudoir. This desolate, claustrophobic setting is an essential feature of the courtly love poem.

The most curious aspect of these love poems is the lack of physical contact between lovers. Superficially, this may be explained by the convention in love poetry that the male lover must be absent from the scene. At a deeper level, what informs this literary convention and court love poetry as a whole is a sense of decorum, or a taboo on explicit references to human sexuality. Birds mating tail to tail are the nearest the reader will approach to any form of sexual relations in the animal world. Comparisons are made between the inanimate and the animate to suggest intercourse. But in poetry lovers are only permitted to hold hands on the rare occasions when they are shown together. That the poets' literary evasion of carnal love was not due to personal bashfulness is indicated by the fact that in this period, and long before, there existed arcane erotic texts and illustrated sexual manuals, the function of which was to describe sexual intercourse in terms that the inexperienced would clearly understand. The omission of sexual references such as existed in these manuals from the love poetry of early China means that sex and human reproduction were considered unfit subjects for poetry. This erotic decorum accords with the general sense of refinement and restrained courtly grace that permeates even the most daring and avant-garde poems of that era.

Compulsorily deflected from the themes of procreation, reproduction, fertility and virility which inform many occidental love poems, and Sanskrit love poetry in the Orient, the Southern Dynasties court poet had to modestly turn his attention away from related aspects of the female physique. Breasts, buttocks, hips, thighs and genitalia are conspicuously absent from these poems. Instead the poet focuses his attention on key erogenous zones permissible within the bounds of poetic decorum. These might seem innocent at first glance, but in the absence of overt sexuality they act as compensatory erotic signals to the reader. Thus when the poet imagines a beautiful woman he sees her clothed outline, her face, waist, arms, sometimes her feet. Although the nude form is never described, the presence of flesh is suggested through diaphanous gowns. The bare waist is not seen, but is implied through a jewelled belt lovingly described. This is one of the more important of the various erotic signals the poet employs, for when the belt is unfastened, the woman's gown falls open. Such an act is a euphemism for sexual pleasure. Similarly, the arm is an erogenous zone, and is suggested often through descriptions of filmy sleeves. Since the sleeve is of a piece with the woman's dress, to describe a woman's sleeves and her arms suggests entrée to more intimate parts of her body. When a woman's foot is mentioned in these poems it is either bare or in an expensive shoe, and it has fetishistic overtones. The sexual appeal of a woman's foot has a long history in China. One example of it is an ancient dynastic myth which tells of the legendary ruler, Hou Chi, being conceived after his barren mother 'trod on the big toe of God's footprint'. More frequent in these poems is the description of a male lover's footprints leading up the path to a woman's boudoir. This is a negative image in the poems, for the woman in her boudoir usually keeps a lonely vigil and wishes she did see her lover's footprints. A good example of this occurs in lines of a poem by the third-century AD poet Chang Hua:

> My sweetheart roams, alive to me no more,
> Far, far, distantly sundered.
> Through bedroom lattice uninvited comes the wind.
> Doorway and garden bear no footprints.
> Reeds grow beneath my bed,
> Spiders spin round the four walls.

Much of the amorous intent and erotic appeal of these images of woman lies in the reader's ability to detect, analyse and savour this kind of inverted, negative insinuation and innuendo.

Attitudes to Love

Courtly love poetry conveys indirectly through metaphorical language and directly through words voiced by the poet or his feminine persona various attitudes to love. Some of them are the universal and familiar expressions of lovers in any era or culture. Others are unfamiliar, the particular expressions of love which reflect currents of thought, cultural history and literature in traditional China. One of the most frequent representations of a woman in these poems is as a divorced or deserted wife. When a Chinese girl married, she bound her hair, said goodbye to her parents and entered her husband's parents' house. There she accepted the norms of fidelity, obedience, subordination, dignified respectability and chastity in his absence. Though her husband might prefer one of his concubines, his wife was not in a position to complain. If he found fault with her on the grounds of childlessness or any other legal or trumped-up charge, she would be sent back home to her parents. They would not welcome the social stigma of her divorce, nor the economic burden of an extra mouth to feed. They would try to make her remarry. In poetic portraits such divorced wives always remain in love with their indifferent husbands.

Another recurring role is that of a discarded courtesan. Called a singing-girl, or dancer, or artiste, she is said euphemistically to live in a house of song, and be visited by honoured guests. The typical situation is that a courtesan or female entertainer has been lavishly fêted by a wealthy merchant or honoured guest at the house of song, or brothel. After his sojourn there, the man continues on his way until his next tour in the area. The courtesan is left behind, hopelessly in love with him and desperate for his promised return.

There are many similar relationships in these poems: country girl and wayfarer, wife and wastrel husband, city mistress and casual lover or playboy, palace lady and lord, barmaid and page, grass widow and enlisted soldier. What they have in common is that the woman remains behind while the man moves on. The woman usually waits in hopeless longing within her boudoir; the man walks down the road of life, often eager for his next amorous encounter. These love relationships not only conjure up polar images of female immobility and male mobility, but they also underscore woman's dependency on man. This is more than an emotional dependency, the poets seek to persuade. Without a man's saving love, it is implied, a woman will languish in emotional malaise to the extent that her health will suffer. Recurring images in the poems emphasize the frailty of a woman's emotional hold on her male lover. She is likened to alga clinging to the surface of water, to a plant reaching out for the sun, or to shadow pursuing form. Water, sun and form are all images of male love. He is seen to confer love and life itself upon a woman. Many courtly-love poems extend this kind of metaphor to its ultimate conclusion by depicting woman's malaise in images of surprising morbidity.

Love is not celebrated by the court poet. He is not usually in love, nor does his literary pose of a woman in love express love in the present tense of happy fulfilment. Rather the passing of love is mourned. The temporal sense is the past. Interwoven into this elegiac mood are several strands of thought and feeling which originated in philosophical works. One prevalent idea deriving from *The Way and Its Power* (*Tao Te ching*, third century BC) concerns the process of change. Like other phenomena, love inevitably progresses slowly and gradually to its peak of happiness and fulfilment, then lapses into swift, abrupt, ineluctable decline. This process is essentially linear, not cyclical. Love, once lost, can never be recaptured – this is the repeated refrain of the poems. Women cast their eyes backward and upward in longing to the ideal happy time of the past, and look down towards the present and future with pessimism and foreboding. Nostalgia reigns in boudoir poems.

The idea of natural determinism is another strand of thought that imparts a haunting mood of melancholy to the poems. The notion that the cycle of nature and the span of human life are linked already had a long tradition in ancient Chinese philosophy and literature. Human life is analogous to the seasons and subject to a similar pattern of transformation. It is a convention of Chinese poetry in general, and of love poetry in particular, that two seasons predominate in this type of analogy – spring and autumn. For these are seasons when nature is in the process of fundamental change and most clearly manifests its movements. The pathos of the human condition, these poems suggest, is not just that human life is finite, but that, whereas in nature life and beauty are reborn in an eternal cycle of return, human beauty and love terminate irrevocably long before the natural span of life ends. A woman is an object of desire mainly because of her physical attraction. In the poetic cameos of women, poets do project some personal qualities, but these are idealized stereotypes and are subordinated to descriptions of appearance. Feminine beauty is often likened to a flower's bloom and scent, lovely in springtime, pathetic in autumn. According to the sentiment expressed in these poems, a girl is most desirable when she is between the ages of fifteen and twenty. Some poems mention girls of ten years as objects of desire and of pathos. So strong is the poetic convention of amorous melancholy that even this tender age engenders pathetic thoughts of how its beauty is neglected. These lines by Liu Hsiao-wei (d. AD 548) illustrate this feature:

A beauty, teenaged, perhaps ten or more,
Turns shyly smiling, smooths her windblown skirt.
He's off shooting pearl pellets, can't be found.
Left alone, who will comfort her, poor darling?

It is not surprising that when court poets elaborate the facets of natural determinism in poetic terms they depict women who are so anxious to keep the love of their wayward men that they become obsessed with their own physical appearance. Youth and age create a cruel dialectic. Vanity and daydreams are major themes. The logical outcome of such an analogy between nature and human love is that unremitting pessimism penetrates the very fabric of the love poems.

Akin to these attitudes to love is the temporal concept of the brevity of life, and by extension of love. Life is likened to the evanescence of a fleet horse glimpsed through a crack in a wall, of a lightning flash, of evaporating dawn dew, of a traveller's sojourn, or of a flower's exquisite, ephemeral beauty. These similes and metaphors conventionally appear in the early Chinese literary and philosophical tradition. Such a sombre concept of the transience of life stands out stark and grim amid poems on love, for the bleak reminders of life's finite nature only serve to emphasize the fleeting nature of romance. These closing lines of a poem by Wu Man-yüan (*c.* AD 471) are a typical example of this attitude:

> Let's cling to this hundred-year span,
> Let's chase after each inch of time's shadow,
> As the grass on an empty hill
> Knows in its heart it will wither and die.

Age, an aspect of time physically perceived, links the universal elements of beauty's bloom and decay, love's birth and death, the changes of which are wrought by the devastation of time.

Another characteristic of Southern Dynasties love poetry is the obsessiveness of a woman's love. Luxuriously immured in her claustrophobic boudoir and dependent emotionally on a lover who prefers to withhold his love, a woman's thoughts turn to amorous reverie, daydreams, fantasy and morbid brooding. It is the very intensity of this obsessiveness that makes many poems unique in the literature of love. Poets project into their portraits extremes of feeling based on idealistic concepts of love. A woman sees herself as pure, chaste and faithful in her lover's absence. She demands that he observe her own rigid code of morality. When he fails to do so, by staying away, taking on a new love or rejecting her, she is shown in these poems to be quite unprepared for such a catastrophe. She rails against his wrongs, his other women and life's inequities in general. While there is a great deal of subjective introspection in the love poems, there is rather less self-perception. This is coupled with a reluctance to soften unrealistically strict moral codes and to accept life and love on their own terms. Such an inflexible attitude towards love brings in its wake a succession of pathetic reactions among women. Cast in the role of love's victim, a rejected woman responds by going into total seclusion, by ceasing all activity (including personal grooming), by weeping unquenchable tears, by litanizing life's futilities and disappointments, and finally by letting health of mind and body deteriorate. The court poets are fascinated by unfulfilled love. With unerring vividness they picture the stages of a woman's psychological and physical disintegration when her relationship with her lover founders. Through the literary pose of a woman the court poet expresses love in terms of a malaise, describing in a unique way the pathology of love. Thus, while the poets of the anthology explore the light and dark sides of love, they prefer especially in the later court poems to describe lovingly the descent into the shadows.

Imagery

The structure of the poems is an interplay of lyrical expression and of imagery, which reinforces and develops the emotions of love. The logic of the poem progresses through the interpenetration of emotional statements and presentations of imagery. Individual images are rarely elaborated or sustained. Rather a series of images is presented. At first glance the sequence of images in a given poem might seem aimless and baffling. In fact the imagery is not a rag-bag of word-pictures, but a finely spun thread of connections and suggestions. The imaginative pattern of the poet may sometimes seem to be roundabout, inconsequential, even abrupt. Yet his use of images is associative, not discursive. One image makes a subtle transition to the next. Fortunately, the poets use a shared repertoire of imagery and its associative meaning. This is particularly true of the later court poets. Theirs was not a private, subjective imaginative code, a 'miracle of unintelligibility', as Edmund Gosse called Stéphane Mallarmé's *L'Après-midi d'un faune*.

The main reason why the meaning of images in Chinese love poetry in this period is clearly intelligible is that they are drawn from a common repertoire. The court poets did not pick randomly from any and every facet of experience. They were highly selective. They rigorously chose details to depict scenes, figures and objects which would convey impressions and sensations agreeably recognizable to the cultural élite of their contemporary society. The imaginative world of their poems is courtly, palatial and luxurious. It is infused, too, with images borrowed from earlier sources of love literature filtered through a courtly sensibility. Within the bounds of these two spheres of palatial reality and literary quotation, the poets created with their assemblage of details settings that are richly and vividly concrete. Their poems have an opulent aura in which luxury objects are lovingly displayed. The style of describing this interior décor is ornamental and sensuous. The impulse of the poet is decoratively artistic; hardly a surface exists that is not embellished with flourishes and curlicues. This kind of descriptive imagery operates at a simple, literal level. The most frequent is the visual and many poems have a pleasing pictorial quality.

On closer inspection, however, the majority of images in the poems prove to be not so much literal realism as figurative fantasy. Scenes, characters and objects, while superficially appearing as sensitive vignettes of wealthy women in affluent surroundings, also create an emotional aura in the poems. In fact the framework of the poems is mainly analogical, either directly through simile, or obliquely through metaphor or symbol. States of mind, attributes, ideas and feelings are conveyed through these vividly concrete images. A palatial boudoir with its ivory bed, silk bedcurtains, bronze lamps and jade mirror-stand, occupied by an exotic, richly dressed beauty, evokes aesthetic besides erotic pleasure. A woman's finely carved ivory bed is pleasing to the eye of the reader; but at the same time, when it is shown to be empty and covered with dust under rays of moonlight, this visual and tactile image also suggests the woman's sexual frustration due to her lover's conventional absence. Her bed so described also hints at sensuality – were it to be occupied. Thus the image of the bed acts as an emotive metaphor charged with aesthetic nuance. Similarly, an elaborately decorated bronze censer for perfuming clothes is pleasing to imagine with its flaring fire, coiling smoke, metallic sheen and heavy scent; but it also serves as an analogy for the wanton destructiveness of passion's consuming fire and the volatile nature of love.

There are several complications about understanding some images and therefore the meaning of the poems where they occur. The first concerns the cultural response of the non-Chinese reader. If Western readers, for example, come across an image of two pheasants in a poem, they are likely to associate them with a brace to be bagged. In Chinese love poetry they in fact suggest marital devotion. Similarly, to the Western mind the image of a dragon is one of a virgin-devourer which needs to be slain by a hero on a white horse. In these love poems a dragon is an image of fertility and regeneration since it is the harbinger of fructifying water. A second difficulty the non-Chinese reader is likely to experience is the significance of images based on unfamiliar cultural objects. For example it was highly fashionable in the Southern Dynasties era for women to attach to their forehead a yellow beauty-spot in the shape of a flower, moon or mountain. There was also the custom of giving one's beloved an incense candle marked with jewelled rings as a love-token. As the incense candle burned down the rings would slip and appear to sink, evoking images of time's passage and of ardent love that cannot be recaptured once it is consumed. The poets felt no need to explain such familiar items of fashion or custom in their poems. Often they referred to them in an elliptical way confusing to the uninitiated reader. A third complication is that many images have more than one meaning, some of them contradictory. The reader has to determine if all the meanings are valid in a given poem, and if not which of them is the valid one for this poem. The dragon image, for example, has contradictory meanings: it can denote the emperor, sexual favours, fructifying power or coursers of sky deities. Another example of multiplicity occurs in the image of the jade terrace (*yü-t'ai*), which occurs in this anthology's title. It could mean concretely a platform for performances of dance, music and song, or allusively the haunt of a seductive mountain goddess, or concretely a mirror-stand. Customary item of a woman's boudoir, the mirror-stand must have acquired fetishistic overtones. Like many courtly images, the jade terrace is no doubt an enigmatic pun combining all three complementary associations to create a unique erotic resonance.

One of the most fascinating aspects of imagery in the Southern Dynasties is the use of a string of images to form a cluster bound together by a single unifying theme. A complex and sophisticated example of this is what might be called the neglect-cluster. The poems generally suggest that when a woman is left alone for whatever reason by her lover she feels so emotionally neglected that she is driven to neglect her physical appearance and surroundings. Her hair grows matted, her face grimy with stale make-up, and her clothes drab. In sympathy with her predicament her jewels become lacklustre, her gold objects tarnished, hairpins disconsolately drooping. Dust palls her bed and mirror-stand; cobwebs, lichen and grass film the house and bed-room. She grows pale, sickens and appears moribund. So many poets draw on this cluster of neglect images, each adding his own artistic detail, that the mode of presenting neglected love becomes stylized.

Many images go beyond immediate metaphorical association and shade off into symbols. The most central of these is the symbol of the boudoir with its counterpart of the road. A woman in love is typically shown to be in her boudoir not only isolated from her lover but also from all human contact. She waits for him with a deep sense of loss and despair. She spends her idle hours in luxury reminiscing about the past, dwelling on memories stimulated by certain boudoir objects. Her environment, her thoughts and her activities are directed towards one goal: the pursuit of love. Cooped up in her magnificent boudoir she is neither free to leave, nor free to love another man, nor free to rid her mind of obsessive love. Images of immobility, inactivity and futility abound in this poetic atmosphere. The boudoir symbolizes imprisonment. This enclosed setting is underscored by the poetic highlighting of certain architectural features, such as doors and windows which usually suggest access or egress. The lattice around a boudoir's outer wall is a pun for a cage (*lung*). A passage by Ho Sun (d. *c.* AD 517) illustrates this use of architectural features of a boudoir to suggest a physical and emotional prison:

> Fallen leaves cross the window sill,
> Beyond the blind flitting fireflies are trapped.
> Full of love she lowers kingfisher drapes,
> Soaked with tears she closes the golden screen.

The boudoir is successful as a symbol of emotional withdrawal and imprisonment because it is so naturally wedded to the familiar world of the courtier and his cultivated audience.

Diametrically opposed to this symbol of the boudoir is the 'male' symbol of the road. The absent male who is the object of a woman's eternal longing is usually described as a wanderer on a road, either as a campaigner on the march, or an official on circuit, or a merchant, and so forth. His travels and destination are but vaguely mentioned in the poems. He figures as a shadow on the horizon. In contrast to the private, interior world of a woman's boudoir, the road is outdoors, connected with public life. Man is free to walk down the highways and byways of life while woman remains closeted. Just as a woman's world is full of architectural barriers, such as doors, windows, screens and lattice, so the world of the male is inaccessible because of topological barriers, such as steep mountains, wide rivers without bridge or boat and vast distances of ten thousand leagues. These two primary symbols play in ironic counterpoint throughout the love poems, evoking the emotional depths of discord and estrangement in woman's relationship with man.

The Hidden Witness

The most original feature of Southern Dynasties love poetry in the context of its tradition is the technique of erotic personification. Prohibited by taboo and poetic decorum from portraying sexual love, the court poets found an ingenious way to circumvent these restraints. If a man was forbidden to enter a woman's boudoir in a love poem, except in a dream sequence, then a permissible alternative was to animate boudoir objects with a male personality. The vehicle the court poets chose for this technique was the blandly named *yung-wu* poem, or composition on an object, which had probably evolved from the descriptive prose poem genre (*fu*) popular in the Han dynasty. (The reader's attention is directed to this sort of generic poem by the use of capitals for the object.) The hand of the court poet exposed beneath this discreet title a whole new world of sighing bedcurtains, seductive lamps, flirtatious incense smoke, passionate beds, and jealous pillows. These animated objects speak in voices breathless with desire. An example of this type of erotic personification occurs in a poem by Liu Yün (AD 465–511) in which he allows a mattress made of fine blue-green rush to suggestively peep about a lady's bedroom and make lascivious comments:

> Island in a stream rimmed with light,
> Rippling breezes down green waters.
> Though I'm not so light as a bed of one cocoon,
> I am happy with my blue-robe colour.

Specks of dust on my lady's silk sleeves,
On this ivory bed are many lovely ornaments.
What I want is, when you drink on orchid nights,
My lovely one, feast and rest on me sometimes.

The curious aspect of these personifications is that the object personified as a male adopts a pleading, subordinate, cajoling tone that is quite different from the absent male lover who features so dominantly, capriciously, even cruelly in the imagination of the woman in love. The voice of the personified lover finds its closest echo in the plaintive voice of the troubadour of medieval Europe who confesses hopeless love to an indifferent lady. Both are the voices of a vassal enthralled by a feudal sovereign, offering homage with no hope of requital. In the Chinese case the peculiarity is that the objects owned by a woman defer to her as their mistress, addressing her as a grovelling slave fawns on the mistress of the house who mistreats him.

The court poets devised other obviating methods to circumvent the rules of poetic decorum. The most popular was punning, together with the use of erotic emblems. The most common pun is on the word silk (*ssu*), which also means love. Lotus (*lien*) might just seem an exotic botanical image, but it is also a pun for passion. The willow tree (*liu*) is a pun for keeping someone, a lover, behind so that he will not leave on his journey. The word for the fulling tool used to pound silk fibres (love) was a complicated pun for a husband or lover. This hidden language is used with great finesse, as in a poem about fulling cloth by Wang Seng-ju (465–522):

I leave my loom, the slanting moon speeds west,
Pound my block, the glowing sun hurries east.
My sweet sweat is like an orchid rinse.
The carved gilt of dragon candles I avoid.

Since pounding has the erotic connotation of a lover and the woman in this poem is beating the silk/love all night, inevitably associations of lovemaking arise in the mind of the reader. The sweat is the link between the prosaic action of fulling and the suggested activity of love. It is not surprising that the fourth line states that the image of sexual favours, the dragon, is avoided because of the (conventional) absence of the woman's lover.

Another device favoured by the court poets was that of the poet's roving eye peeping into bedrooms through curtains, under blinds, across silk window-panes, and even through chinks in the wall. To the poets these insinuating tactics were a great game, and some indulged in joyous elaborations and complications of the poetic sport. Many poems are, if read correctly, taut with a nervously negated eroticism. All is nuance, hint, suggestion. The reward of conventionally oblique expression and hidden meaning in the poetry of love was that they acted as a spur to the poets' fertile and fevered imagination. The dictum 'Let nothing remain unsaid' would have been anathema to these decorous, playful poets in the court of love.

Prosodic Features

The title of the anthology, *Yü-t'ai hsin-yung*, indicates that this is a collection of *yung*, a catch-all term for different kinds of poetry. If any definite meaning can be attached to this term it is that when used as a noun it vaguely means poetry which comes from the heart, and as a verb it means to compose. In fact it is generally true to say that with the exception of a few narrative pieces, ditties, punning songs and so forth, *New Songs from a Jade Terrace* is a collection of lyrics. As Francis T. Palgrave defines the term in his Preface to *The Golden Treasury of Songs and Lyrics* (1861), 'Lyrical has here been held essentially to imply that each poem shall turn on some single thought, feeling, or situation.' It is also interesting to note in comparison that just as Palgrave restricts his anthology to shorter lyrical poems, so does Hsü Ling in the main. Of the 656 Chinese poems here, 515 are no more than 20 lines long. The majority of the poems have only 4 lines (157 poems), then 8 lines (129 poems), then 10 lines (85 poems).

A superficial survey of the poems suggests that there is great metrical and generic variety in the anthology, for there are 5-word and 7-word *shih* or lyrics, 5-word *chüeh-chü* or short pieces, 5-word *yüeh-fu* or folk-songs and ballads, 5-word ancient style poems, besides modern poems, *ch'ü*-songs, *sao*-songs, archaic tetrasyllabic *shih* and poems of irregular metre. Despite this apparent diversity the anthology is metrically homogeneous. Of the ten volumes comprising the anthology, nine volumes (1–8, and 10) are in the 5-word metre, and Volume 9 is in irregular metres. Volume 1 contains a good number of ancient-style poems, and Volume 10 is entirely devoted to 5-word, 4-line poems. The principle operating in this context is that genre is not always tied up with metre. The typical *shih* or lyric form embraces such diverse themes as the didactic, martial, reclusive and love poetry, and ranges from 5- to 7-word metres of 4 to 355 lines in length. The *yüeh-fu* or folk-song form had originally been irregular in metre, simple and direct in expression, and anonymous; it varied in theme from protest poem to love poem and in form from narrative to lyric. In the later years of the Han dynasty named poets began to imitate this humble poetic form, transforming it into polished, metrically regular pieces. By the date this anthology was compiled, it had become increasingly hard to distinguish between poems entitled *shih*, *yüeh-fu* or *ch'ü* in terms of metre and style, at least when they dealt with the same theme of love. To sum up the metrical categories, there are 569 poems in the anthology in the 5-word metre (from 4 to 355 lines long), 50 in the 7-word metre (from 2 to 20 lines), 1 in the archaic 4-word metre (16 lines long), 4 poems in the 6-word or *sao*-song metre (from 6 to 60 lines), and 32 poems of mixed metres (from 4 to 50 lines), making 656 poems in all.

It is clear from the different types of literature prevalent in the sixth century AD that writers conformed to miscellaneous literary conventions. The prose style was markedly different from the poetic, and both these written styles were divorced from colloquial speech. Classical Chinese poetry has many unique prosodic features which partly arise from the special nature of the literary language, and partly from consciously observed poetic conventions. The classical language is generally mono-syllabic except for a few disyllabic words such as *chih-chu*, spider, and some descriptive binomes similar to pell-mell. There are no grammatical inflections of declension, conjugation, case, number or gender: the monosyllabic word remains unchanged in the syntax of the sentence. A word can have different syntactical functions; it can act as a verb, noun, adjective, adverb or predicate. Verbs, being uninflected, can carry no idea of tense. Occasionally in poetry a particle acting as an adverb of time is inserted into the line. Also the subject or object of a verb is often omitted from poetry, especially when these are pronouns. A poem can quite happily exist in the Chinese without any indication of subject, tense, object, verbal mood, number, gender, definite or indefinite article, and so forth. To compensate for the phonetic limitations of the monosyl-labic language, words are further differentiated in meaning by tones, four in the classical system (different from the four of modern Man-darin). These impart a quality of lilting euphony to the verse.

As such a prosodic system suggests, there tends to be a great deal of ambiguity in the poems, especially for the untutored reader. Some types of ambiguity are deliberately employed by the poet. Others occur when the reader is unable because of cultural differences to infer correctly what the poet intends. The usual ambiguities arise in cases such as the number of noun – is it a lone bird (pathetic) or a flock (felicitous)? Or gender – is it a male or female I-persona? Or tense – when the poetic stream of consciousness shifts, is it to the subjunctive mood from the past tense or to the future tense from the present? Or subject – when the speaker seems to change in the poem, from which persona is there a change and to which persona? This elliptical style brings to the poetry the advantages of verbal compression, linguistic versatility, universality and artistic ambiguity. Against the disadvantages of such a style, particularly a certain confusion of meaning, several prosodic elements operate to hold the poem together. First, in most cases each line is an independent unit in terms of sense; it is called an end-stopped line. Then each last word of a couplet, or every even line, has either verbal or tonal rhyme; often the same class of rhyme continues throughout the poem. Furthermore, parallel couplets are frequent; one line compares or contrasts with the next in terms of sense or syntax, or both. The metre, usually the five-word line, is uniform throughout the poem, with rare exceptions. To this regular metrical scaffolding is welded the image, or series of images, unifying the poem in terms of sense and mood. Thus metre, rhyme, parallelism and imagery form the basic structure of the poem, carrying the burden of meaning.

Of these prosodic features parallelism and imagery translate best from the Chinese into English. It is fortunate, therefore, that they are both fundamental pivots of the poem. It is also fortunate that the Chinese word order is similar to the English. The metre is more of a problem in translation. Where the lapidary Chinese original maintains a staccato rhythm of five syllables per line for, say, twenty end-stopped lines stripped of non-functional words, the result when translated word for word degenerates into a weird telegram or list of headlines at best, and into pidgin English at worst. The literary idiom of classical Chinese poetry cannot be left to flounder in a literal *reductio ad absurdum*. Since in English poetry conventional grammar and syntax are the nuts and bolts, things have to be spelled out in translation in order that the sense is not obfuscated. Sometimes, however, the density and ambiguity of the Chinese original may be retained in English, especially where a litany of epithets and nouns is used. In general, what all this means is that by adding so much in translation the unique stringent metre of the Chinese original is lost.

A further problem arising from rendering into English such a style of linguistic compression and consciously artistic ambiguity is that multiple meanings rarely survive the process of translation. Like all poetic language, some words are culturally bound and have resonances not shared by other countries. 'To return' (*kuei*) in Chinese not only means to go back, go home, retire and rotate cyclically, but also to die, to return to one's source of origin, and for a woman to be divorced. In many poems such an evocative word conveys some of the multiple meanings simultaneously. Then again in a culture where certain objects such as chopsticks are a special indigenous invention, the image of jade chopsticks for tears will not seem totally odd. Chopsticks, like streams of tears, come in pairs and are translucent when made of jade. In such cases of cultural specialities it is wrong for the translator to paraphrase such an image in the misguided notion that the reader will not understand what is going on in the poem, or will be

24

aesthetically offended. By such criteria translations would be more emasculated than they are. The image being the soul of poetry is sacrosanct.

Finally, how will the translator differentiate the styles of various writers? Obviously the conventional system of the love poem as a genre and the linguistic conformity inherent in classical Chinese poetry mean that the style of many poets in this anthology, especially those dating from between AD 400 and AD 545, bears several resemblances. It has been possible to keep a good number of stylistic techniques in my translation, whether they are inversions, novel placements of words, bizarre appositions or padding. The more general stylistic question of who the finer poets are is partially solved, in Hsü Ling's view, by the proportion of their poems in the anthology. Thus his patron, Hsiao Kang, reigns supreme among the 105 known poets there with 76 poems, followed by his father and emperor at the time of the compilation, Hsiao Yen, with 41 poems, then Shen Yüeh with 30, Wu Chün with 26, Wang Seng-ju with 19, Pao Chao with 17, Ho Sun and Hsieh T'iao with 16 each. To Hsü Ling's list, with which I concur, I would add Wang Yün and Fei Ch'ang. These ten poets are the major poets of China in the Southern Dynasties era of the fifth and early sixth centuries. Tastes vary. The placement of poets, their rank in order of merit, has been a favourite literary game in China. The sixth-century AD critic, Chung Hung, ranked 122 poets in three classes of excellence in his book, *The Classification of Poets (Shih p'in)*. He marked down Shen Yüeh, Hsü Ling's favourite non-royal poet, besides Pao Chao and Hsieh T'iao, as poets of the second rank. Subjective though he was, even Chung Hung had to grudgingly admit that Shen Yüeh's poetry was popular in his own day. Today Pao Chao is the darling of the literary critics in mainland China because his poetry is deemed to voice the protests of the people and to monitor their hardships. In the West, Pao Chao is admired for quite different, artistic reasons. But the question of who sits higher at the table remains with the final arbiter, the reader.

The Courtly Love Poem as Artefact

Compared with other collections of love poetry in world literature *New Songs from a Jade Terrace* has suffered a curious fate. Chinese down through the centuries have tended to look askance at it, dismissing much of it as 'all flowers and moonlight', or hiding it from public view as a delectable object of shame. Had it not been commissioned by a crown prince who later became an emperor, it might well have been consigned to oblivion. For in the succeeding era of the Sui Dynasty (AD 589–618) there began a barrage of abuse against the anthology, echoes of which reverberate still today. Furthermore, had it not been read and enjoyed by the Japanese, and in more recent years studied by the great

25

sinologist, Suzuki Torao (1878–1963), this anthology would still be languishing under the dust of time.

Southern Dynasties love poetry seems to me remarkable, but it has been made the target of a great deal of undeserved criticism. The usual accusations against it include mannerism, shallow conventionality, tedious cleverness, excessive allusion, pretension and ornateness. It is charged with being poetry of the head, not of the heart. All this is very strange when one thinks of poetry of different countries and eras which is prized while being mannered, or allusive, or clever, or ornate. *New Songs from a Jade Terrace* has also borne the dubious distinction for centuries of being regarded as morally decadent. 'Not for gentlemen!' was the verdict of Hsiao Kang's biographer. 'The sound of a state in collapse!' was the opinion of a later historian. 'A poetic disgrace!' is the view of critics in Mainland China, who argue that courtly love poetry is worthless because it was the product of an aristocratic society. Through this roar of prudery and polemic Hsü Ling's invitation to his reader echoes with urbane charm: 'For long hours be diverted'.

One major difficulty the Western reader may have in getting through to certain poets and poems is that our criterion of 'real' poetry is that it must be an intensely personal thing and the creative poet must write from individual experience. The love poems of *New Songs from a Jade Terrace* were never intended to be autobiographical. Court poets wrote within a well-defined system of conventions in which subject, theme, mood and diction were already established. Their poems were meant to be finely wrought professional artefacts, embodying rhetorical techniques and distilled emotion. It would be entirely wrong, therefore, to judge them by mistaken critical standards. When the poets appraised the poems of their own era their criteria were fine craftsmanship, verbal ingenuity, apt allusion, delicate imagery and harmonious rhyme and rhythm. The poems they admired were consciously artistic, sophisticated, subtly ambiguous creations, evincing a trained poetic imagination and technical virtuosity.

The Southern Dynasties was an exciting period for Chinese poetry. A new style was being developed, and poets were eager to show their mastery of it. That this meant observing certain rules of composition was immaterial. Most forms of Chinese literature had long been full of conventions. That it also meant employing an extended set of allusions was likewise no handicap. Poetry had long been allusive and full of quotations. What had changed so radically was the concept of what were legitimate subjects for poetry. Court poets certainly reaped a rich harvest here. Going far beyond the traditional repertoire, they now wrote love poems which mentioned all sorts of private details hitherto forbidden. Tinted notepaper, a coiffure net, ladies' slippers, a camisole, a powder-puff, all became fit for poetic parlance. Although these were items drawn from daily life in noble circles, it did not mean that anything and everything was suitable subject-matter for poetry. It was all right to mention eyebrows, wine-cups and silkworms, but indecorous to mention the nose, a carving knife and a cat. A strict system of high and low diction was in effect. On the other hand the language of love experienced an enrichment of vocabulary. Just in the category of words for a lover, male and female, there were seventy-four possibilities, ranging from 'mop-and-broom', 'idol', 'quilt-sharer', 'lovely date', to 'my delight', slightly more than the list in Roget's *Thesaurus*.

In addition the technique of the court poets rested on selecting and arranging words expressively within each line. This involved sound and sense. In the fifth century AD the Chinese poet's latent interest in euphony was awakened to a new consciousness. While euphonic effects had appeared in earlier poetry, it was random and unconscious. Now poets elaborated patterns of sound and tonal harmony to create a pleasing play of music in the poem. Like the originator of the new wave of 'Palace Style Poetry', the inventor of the new tonal principles is not properly known. Liu Yün and Shen Yüeh are usually said to be their inventors. As Shen Yüeh puts it, egotistically thrilled with their novelty: 'Only the men of my generation who can appreciate music properly are able to understand – I do not exaggerate! If you don't believe me, wait for the verdict of future sages.' Some of his contemporaries claimed to be mystified by Shen Yüeh's comments on euphony, such as his reigning monarch, Kao-tsu, who asked haughtily, 'What *are* these four tones?' Still, a number of poets began to apply his rules in a rudimentary way. Coupled with a sense of the right word and the right placement of the word this musicality resulted in lines of haunting beauty.

Another technical development was the great artistry with which court poets described ways of seeing things in the world around them. Their sensuous, aristocratic imagination revelled in descriptions of fashionable luxury. Images appealing to the five senses suffuse their poetry with richly decorative and voluptuous detail. Their poems have bejewelled surfaces. Yet it was not simply the furnishings and objects of palatial interiors, the erotic décor, that caught the eye of the court poets. Their artistic imagination was also stimulated by the way these objects looked in a certain light, or in movement, or in reflection. The oblique presentation of reality became a fascinating new game. They described not a crowd of people by a river, but the shadows of their hats on the river's surface; not just rouge on a woman's cheek, but sunset red deepening her rouge; not just dust shifting, but dust changing colour as it moves from surface to surface; and not just a silk scarf, but a woman's made-up face reflected on a silk scarf. The impulse of the poet was decorative and painterly. It is probably no coincidence that at the same time as Southern Dynasties poets became interested in the architectonic qualities of poetic composition, such as tonal musicality, they also became fascinated with aspects of design, such as colour, shape and patterns of light and shade.

The courtly love poem of the Southern Dynasties has a distinctively elaborate, formal and rhetorical style. Rich in evocative imagery, symbolism, decorative pathos and verbal virtuosity, the poems open a new world of amatory art. They reveal an unusual interpenetration of the material and the emotional, of the natural and the human spheres of experience – a literary phenomenon taken to even greater heights by poets of the T'ang Dynasty, acknowledged as the Golden Age of Chinese poetry. The court poets of the Southern Dynasties enriched the framework of love poetry by dint of embellishing their borrowings from the literary heritage and weaving new imaginative material into their artefacts. In subject, setting and diction, they extended the repertoire of love. Until now, the legacy of these court poets has by no means been fully appreciated or acknowledged. When their poems have been read, much of what seemed original in later poetry will be recognized as derivative. Many claims for the creativity of later poets will have to be pruned back to allow the full flowering of Southern Dynasties love poetry to be admired in its own rightful setting. If today there is a quickening of the pulse, a frisson when these love poems of erotic décor, decorously erotic, are read, then Hsü Ling's purpose, 'For long hours be diverted', will have been fulfilled.

Now,
Cloud-conqueror and Sun-high
Were palaces such as Yu Yü never glimpsed.
Their ten thousand gates, one thousand doors
Were once rhapsodized by Chang Heng.
On King Mu of Chou's jade-disc terrace,
In Emperor Wu of Han's House of Gold
There were jade trees with coral boughs,
Pearl blinds on tortoiseshell frames,
And within them lived beautiful women.

These beauties
Were aristocrats of Wu-ling,
Chosen for the imperial harem
From the best families of the Four Clans,
Celebrities of the seraglio.

There were also beauties from Ying-ch'uan and Hsinshih,
Lovelies from Hochien and Kuanchin
Who have long been called 'gracefully fair',
And named 'charming smiles'.

They were like ladies of King Ling of Ch'u's palace
Whose slender waists none failed to admire;
Or like beautiful girls of Wei kingdom
Whose delicate hands all marvelled at.
Our beauties were well-read in *The Book of Songs*, polished in
    Rites,
Quite different from the east neighbour who did her own
    matchmaking!
And they were nice, refined,
No different from Hsi Shih after she had been trained.
One beauty had a brother who harmonized the pipes,
So she studied singing from an early age;
Another grew up in Yang-o,
So from the first she was skilled in dance.

29

One beauty's new song for the lute
Did not wait for the poet Shih Ch'ung.
Another lady's lute medley
Did not look to Ts'ao Chih.
One lady inherited her drumming on the guitar from the Yang
    clan,
Another learned to blow the flute from the daughter of Ch'in.

So it seems that
When a favourite became well-known to Eternal Joy Palace
Empress Ch'en knew and grew disturbed.
And when a painting revealed a goddess,
The *Yen-chih* stared at it in distant envy.
The east girl with her charming smiles
Came to serve the royal bed at the Robe-changing.
Hsi Shih, puckering her eyebrows,
Was bedded within luxurious curtains.
Another lady accompanied the emperor to Saso Palace
Where she moved her slim waist sinuously to *Whirlwind Music*.
Forever happy at Mandarin Duck Palace,
A lady played new music to rhythmic tunes.

A beauty dresses her hair into wispy 'chirping cicada' side-curls,
Sees reflected her tumbling 'fallen colt' locks,
Inserts gold hairpins at the back,
Fixes a jewelled comb slantwise.
Black kohl from a southern city
Accentuates twin eyebrows,
Yen rouge from a northern place
Brings fine colour to two cheeks.

Gold stars rival the brilliance of the Fair Maid star,
Musk moons compete with Ch'ang O's sweet light.
From the flirtatious sleeves of a startled phoenix
There once hovered incense from Secretary Han.
The long skirts of a flying swallow
Were meant to be clasped by the Prince of Ch'en's girdle.
Though never painted in a portrait,
Our beauties are no different from that of the lady which hangs
    in Sweet Springs Palace.

Also there were
A divine youth on a mountain peak
Who shared his drug pills with the Wei Emperor;
And one with a precious phoenix at his waist
Who presented his calendar to Hsüanyüan.

So, although they are far from being goddesses,
They are indistinguishable from her who played at Sun Terrace.
They may truly be called
Beauties who destroy realms and cities,
Matchless and unique.

Besides,
Divine is their brilliance,
Exquisite their mind.
They superbly appreciate literature,
Are skilled in the craft of poetry.
Their coloured glass inkstone-case
Is beside them all day long,
Their kingfisher jade pen-case
Never for one moment leaves their hands.
The fine literary pieces cramming their cabinets
Are not just about peony blooms!
Their new compositions, verse after verse,
Are a marked advance on *The grapevine ode*!
When they climb a height on the Double Ninth
They often produce a poem of feeling.
On the Princess of Ten Thousand Years
They would not be shy of eulogistic phrases.
Our ladies' beauty is as I have described before,
Our ladies' gifted natures, too, are as I have just described.

And so,
Through labyrinthine spirals of pepper palaces,
Up mysterious elevations of thorn-tree halls,
Scarlet Crane keys impose privacy at dawn,
Bronze Clam knockers fall silent at noon.
Before the Three Stars twilight hour
The ladies are not summoned to bring their quilt.
Even five days seem too long –
For whom will they comb untidy hair?

Languidly idle with few distractions,
In quiet tranquillity with hours of leisure
They loathe Eternal Joy Palace's tardy bell,
Are weary of Central Hall's slow arrow of time.
So weak are their slender waists
They are daunted at washing clothes in Nanyang.
Brought up in secluded palaces
They delight in the Fufeng woven brocade.

Also, suppose
A palace lady is Jade Girl playing tosspot –
Her interest will flag by the hundredth throw!
Or she is a girl of Ch'i competing at draughts –
Her interest will die on the sixth move!
The palace lady takes no delight in idle hours,
But devotes her mind to the latest verse.
For poetry can
Be a substitute for the flower of oblivion,
And can banish the disease of ennui.

Yet
The famous works of former eras
And the artistic compositions of today,
Being as they are variously deposited in Unicorn Gallery
Or scattered in Hung city,
Unless I anthologize these literary pieces,
Our beauties will have no means to peruse them.

Therefore
Have I written, burning the midnight oil,
Wielding my pen over tomes at dawn.
I have selected love-songs,
Ten books in all.
They could never compare with the *Odes* and *Hymns*,
But they do reach the strict standard set by poets of the *Airs*.
Like the hiatus between Ching and Wei rivers
Is my method of selecting good from bad among love-songs.

Afterwards
These books were put under golden casing
And bound on luxury rollers.
Like the magnificent calligraphy of the Three Chancelleries,
Their script is in Dragon-coiling and Wriggling-caterpillar styles,

Written on coloured floral sheets
Of paper from Hopei and Chiaotung.
In lofty rooms red rouge
Revised copyist errors in the script.
Musk and the freshest incense
Will ward off Yüling bookworms.
Together with *Divine Flight* and *Titular Six*
My book will be kept in a jade box;
Together with *Brilliance Vast: The Art of Immortality*
It will always be tucked away in vermilion pillows.

So it seems that
Inside our ladies' black-ox curtains,
When their lingering lyrics have ended,
Beside the Vermilion Bird Window
When their cosmetics have been applied,
This is when they will first undo the bright book wrappers,
Scatter braided ribbons
And for long hours be diverted behind their reading drapes,
My book always open in slim hands.
Certainly my book will be quite different
From Empress Teng's study of *The Spring and Autumn Classic*,
For a scholar's attainments are too hard to acquire!
And my book will differ from Empress Tou's specialization in
    Huang-Lao —
The art of gold-and-cinnabar can never be mastered!
Then, of course, my book will be superior to the case of
The well-born man of Western Shu
Who devoted his feeling to exhaustive recitation of *Lu Palace*!
And to the case of the Crown Prince at his imperial lodge
Whose repertoire of chant was limited to *The Cloistral Flute*!

Lovely the ladies of Ch'i!
They will always help to chase away the hours.
Pretty her red pen holder!
Beautiful her scented vanity-case!

CHAPTER ONE

EARLY FOLK-SONGS
AND BALLADS
(FIRST AND SECOND CENTURIES AD)

ANON.

Eight Old Poems

No. 1

Uphill I picked sweet herbs,
Downhill I met my former husband.
Kneeling I asked my former husband,
'Your new one, what is she like then?'
'My new one is good, I suppose,
But not as fine as my old one.
In looks they are like each other,
But their fingernails are not the same.
My new one comes in through the main gates,
My old one would leave through the back door.
My new one is skilled at weaving finespun,
My old one was skilled at weaving homespun.
Finespun is forty foot a day,
Homespun was fifty foot or more.
Comparing fineweave and plainweave,
My new one won't match the old!'

No. 2

Chill, chill, the year now fades.
Mole-crickets at dusk sadly chant.
Cold winds suddenly blow fierce,
The traveller feels chill with no cloak.

A brocade quilt he sent to Lo shore,
My bed-sharer has betrayed me.
Alone I sleep endless long nights.
In dreams I think I see his bright face:
My darling remembers past rapture,
Drives towards me, offers his coach strap.
I long for eternal charmed laughter,
Holding hands share his carriage home.
He did come, but for a moment,
Not to live within my many doors.

37

Truly without the wings of Dawn Wind
How can I soar on the wind?
I glance sidelong to send my thoughts,
Lean forward staring far after him.
Uncertain, I nurse wounded feelings,
Trickling tears soak twin door-leaves.

No. 3

Bit by bit grows an orphan bamboo,
Marries its roots to Mount T'ai's flank.
To you am I newly wed,
Dodder attached to creeping vine.
There is a season for dodder to grow,
There is a right time for man and wife to join.
A thousand leagues distant are we married,
Far, far by mountain slopes divided.

Longing for a lover makes one grow old.
How late does your high carriage come!
I'm wounded by the orchid's rich bloom,
In full glory it displays its bright lustre;
Though past its season it is not plucked,
With weeds of autumn to wither.
It's clear you hold to your lofty vow,
So what could be better for poor me?

No. 4

Fierce winter's cold air has come,
North winds so bitter and cruel.
Sorrow keener knows the lasting night.
I gaze up at hosts of serried stars.
The fifteenth's bright moon is full,
The twentieth's toad and hare are waning.

A traveller came from faraway,
He brought me a letter.
Above it says 'I'll always love you'.
Below it says 'Long must we part'.

I put the letter in my bosom sleeve.
Three years no word has faded.
My single heart that keeps to itself true
I fear you'll never know.

No. 5

A traveller came from a far place;
He brought me a length of damask.
Gone from me more than ten thousand leagues,
My old love's heart is still the same.

Its pattern of a pair of mandarin ducks
I make into a 'joy of love' quilt,
Stuff it with 'always love you' padding,
Bind it tight, never to sunder.
Throw glue into lacquer –
Who could ever break them apart?

No. 6

Dear audience, not so loud!
I want you to hear me sing a song,
Let me tell of a bronze censer.
It is craggy like Mount Chungnan,
On top its boughs are of pine and cypress,
Below its roots spread over a brazen dish.

Carved patterns of all different kinds,
Twisted and intertwined.
Who could create such a vessel?
Master Shu, Pan of Lu state.

Scarlet flames flicker within,
Green smoke billows around,
Borne on a breeze it slips inside your breast.

Of her audience there was none but sighed.
Perfumed breezes do not linger long,
Only to make the orchid waste away.

No. 7

Sad to part from a dear friend,
Distraught, I cannot speak.
I would give myself to you in love,
The road is far, we cannot meet.

Human life lasts no time at all,
Trouble keeps on coming along.
I remember you cast me off,
New love now holds you enchanted.
Your mind is set on blue clouds up above,
When will you come back home?

No. 8

Soft, softly a pure breeze rises,
Blowing my silken skirt.
His green shirt is like spring grass,
Long blades with the wind a'waving.

At dawn I go to the top of the ford bridge,
Lift my hem and watch for the one I love.
How to be true unto 'clasping the bridgepost'?
By the white sun I make my vow.

ANON.

Six Old Folk-Songs

Sunrise at the south-east corner, a folk-song

Sunrise at the south-east corner
Shines on our Ch'in clan house.
The Ch'in clan has a fair daughter,
She is called Lofu.

Lofu is good at silkworm mulberry,
She picks mulberry at the wall's south corner.
Green silk is her basket strap,
Cassia her basket and pole.

On her head a twisting-fall hairdo,
At her ears bright moon pearls.
Green silk is her lower skirt,
Purple silk is her upper shirt.

Passers-by see Lofu,
Drop their load, stroke their beard.
Young men see Lofu,
Take off caps, put on headbands.
The ploughman forgets his plough,
The hoer forgets his hoe.
They come home cross and happy –
All from seeing Lofu.

A prefect from the south is here,
His five horses stand pawing the ground.
The prefect sends his servant forward
To ask, 'Whose is the pretty girl?'
'The Ch'in clan has a fair daughter,
Her name is Lofu.'
'Lofu, how old is she?'
'Not yet quite twenty,
A bit more than fifteen.'

The prefect invites Lofu,
'Wouldn't you like a ride with me?'
Lofu steps forward and refuses:
'You are so silly, Prefect!
You have your own wife, Prefect,
Lofu has her own husband!
In the east more than a thousand horsemen,
My husband is in the lead.
How would you recognize my husband?
His white horse follows black colts,
Green silk plaits his horse's tail,
Yellow gold braids his horse's head.
At his waist a Lulu dagger –
Worth maybe more than ten million cash.

'At fifteen he was a county clerk,
At twenty a court official,
At thirty a chancellor,
At forty lord of his own city.

'As a man he has a pure white complexion,
Bushy whiskers on both cheeks.
Majestic he steps into his office,
Dignified he strides to the courtroom,
Where several thousand in audience
All say my husband has no rival!'

We met in a narrow alley

We met in a narrow alley,
A path so tight would not take carriages.
Well, the two boys,
Hubs aligned, asked 'What about your house?'

'Your house is so easy to recognize,
Easy to recognize, hard to forget.
Yellow gold are your gates,
White jade your hall.

'Up in the hall stand jugs of wine
Served by Hantan singers.
In the garden grow cassia trees,
Flowery lamps how they blaze!

'Brothers you have, two or three.
The middle one is a chancellor.
One in five days he comes home.
On his way he creates a bright light.
Yellow gold braids his horse's head.
Spectators crowd the roadsides.

'You enter the gates, and when you look left,
All you see are pairs of mandarin ducks,
Mandarin ducks seventy-two,
Lined up in formation.
Their song how murmurous!
Storks chant on east and west houses.

'The eldest wife weaves fine silk,
The middle wife weaves flowing yellow,
The youngest wife has nothing to do,
She hugs her lute, goes up the high hall:
"Dear husband, please sit quiet,
My tuneful strings are not midway!"''

Lunghsi, a folk-song

What's that up there in the sky?
Twinkling White Elm star is planted there,
Cassia trees grow down each roadside,
Green dragons face across road corners,
Male and female phoenix sing lullabies,
A mother hen leads her nine chicks.
And as I look back upon the human world
There's a scene of joy quite unique.

A fair wife goes out to greet her guests,
Her face happy and cheerful.
She bows and kneels twice in greeting,
Asks the guests, 'Was your journey pleasant?'
She invites the guests up the north hall,
Seats the guests on woollen cushions.
Clear wine, white wine, for each a separate tankard,
Beaded bubbles full at the brim.
She pours wine, hands it to her guests,
The guests say, 'Hostess, you have some!'
She declines, kneels down twice,
Then accepts one cup.
Before talk and laughter are ended,
She looks back to the left, gives orders in the kitchen:
'Hurry up and make a fine meal,
Mind you don't dilly-dally!'

Cordially she shows her guests out,
Majestic they stride into the office.
In showing the guests out she doesn't go too far,
Her foot won't cross the gate-pivot!

When choosing a wife, if you get one as good as this –
Even Ch'i Chiang would not be as good.
A hearty wife who keeps a good house and home
Is worth more than one great husband.

Song of beauty, a folk-song

Flit, flitting swallows by the hall
Show winter hides, summer appears.
My brothers, two or three
Have fun and romp in another town.
Old clothes who must mend?
New clothes who must sew?
I'm lucky to have a just mistress,
She takes them to stitch for me.

Her husband through the gates comes,
He peeps slyly and peers in from the north-west.
I say to Master, 'Don't peep in at me!
Water runs clear, pebbles show,
Pebbles show in heaps and heaps.
Going far is not as good as going home!'

White as mountaintop snow

White as mountaintop snow,
Pale as the moon between clouds.
I hear you have two loves,
That's why you broke up with me.
Today a keg of wine at a party,
Tomorrow dawn the top of the canal.
I trudge and trail along the royal canal,
Canal water east then westward flows.
How bleak, bleak it is, it's so bleak, bleak.
A bride at her wedding must not weep.
I long to get a man of one heart,
Till our white-hair years he would not leave me.

Fishing rod so supple, supple!
Fishtail so glossy, glossy!

When a man prizes the spirit of love,
Who needs dagger-coins?

A pair of white swans

There came flying a pair of white swans,
They are from the north-west come.
In their ten tens and five fives
They spread uneven in straggling lines.

Suddenly one falls ill:
'I can't keep up flying with you.'
Five leagues and one looks back,
Six leagues and one has faltered.
'I would carry you away in my beak,
But my beak is sealed and can't open.
I would carry you away on my back,
But my feathers and tail each day would be crushed.'

How happy they were to fall in love!
Sadness comes with lifetime separation.
It stops and looks back at its flock mate,
Tears drop trickling criss-cross.
Today we delight in our mutual love,
For a lifetime, ten thousand years we vow.

ANON.

Nine miscellanous poems
(*attributed to Mei Sheng*)

No. 1

North-west there is a tall house,
Its top is level with floating clouds.
Delicate tracery set in silken windows,
Roofs in three-tiered storeys.

Up above there's the sound of strings and song,
The melody echoes so sadly.
Who could compose such a tune?
No one but Ch'i Liang's wife.

Autumn's Clear Note carries on the breeze,
But midway the tune falters.
One chord, two or three sighs,
Yearning grief has a deeper sorrow.
I don't pity the singer's bitterness,
But I'm hurt so few appreciate her music.
I wish we were a pair of wild swans
With rushing wings to soar up high.

No. 2

The east city wall high and long
Twists and turns in a continuous line.
Whirlwinds stir the earth to rise,
Autumn grass lush and green.
The four seasons in succession change,
The year fades all too swift.
Dawn Wind nurses a bitter heart,
Crickets pine in prison pent.
I'm wiped pure, released from all passion,
What need have I of self-control?

Yen and Chao are full of lovely women,
Beauties with faces like jade,
Wearing silken filmy clothes.
They face the doorway arranging clear tunes,
The melody echoes so sadly.
When her strings quicken, I know her frets are tighter.
My feelings race, and I straighten my inside belt,
Hum low, hesitate a while.
Imagine we are two flying swallows
With mud in our beaks to nest in your home.

No. 3

On, on, ever on and on,
From you a lifetime separation,
Away from one another ten thousand leagues,
We each live on the other horizon.
The pathway is steep and long,
Who can tell if we shall meet again?
The Hu horse neighs into the north wind,
The Yüeh bird nests in southern boughs.
Away from one another each day ever further,
Robe and belt each day ever looser.
Floating clouds screen the white sun,
The wanderer never looks back.

Longing for you makes one grow old,
Years, months are suddenly grown late.
Of rejection say no more.
We must try and eat up somehow.

No. 4

Wading the river I pluck lotus blooms,
Orchid marsh full of sweet grass.
I pick hoping to send them to someone.
The one I love lives down a far road.
I look back and stare at our old village,
The long path stretches far and away.
Sweethearts, yet we live apart,
The pain of despair will last till we're old.

No. 5

Green, green riverside grass,
Bushy, bushy willow in the garden.
Sleek, sleek a girl upstairs,
White, white faces her window.
Fair, fair her rouge and powder face,
Slim, slim extends a white hand.

Once I was a singing-house girl,
Now I am a playboy's wife.
A playboy roves, never comes home,
My empty bed is hard to keep alone.

No. 6

Orchid, flag-iris grow in spring sunshine,
Passing to winter, still they're in full bloom.
Wistful, I search for past love,
My faithful heart moved by the four seasons.
My lovely one lives on the cloud's edge,
A skypath remote, without promise.
Night's glimmer shines through dark shadow,
Long sighs, desire for the one I love.
Who says I feel no despair?
Stored memories bring on madness!

No. 7

In the forecourt there is a wondrous tree,
Green leaves burgeon with blossoms moist.
Pulling a twig I break off its glory
To send to the one I love.
Sweet perfume fills my bosom sleeve,
The road is far, it will not reach him.
This thing of nature – why is it worth sending?
It's just that I'm moved how time has passed since parting.

No. 8

Far, far Herdboy star,
Pale, pale girl of River Han,
Slim, slim rise white hands,
Clack, clack, plying her loom shuttle.
All day long she never ends her pattern,
Tears she sheds fall like rain.

River Han clear and shallow,
Away from each other how much longer?
Swelling, swelling, the whole river widens.
Staring, staring, she can't say a word.

No. 9

The bright moon white, so white
Shines on my silk bedcurtains.
In sad despair I cannot sleep,
I take my robe, get up and pace.
To travel, they say, is pleasant,
But not as good as going home soon.
I go out alone and walk round alone.
My sad longing to whom can I tell?
I lean forward, go back to my room,
Tears fall soaking my robe.

LI YEN-NIEN

A song poem, with a preface

Preface: Li Yen-nien was a specialist in music, and he was a superb singer and dancer. Every time he composed modern songs and new-style tunes, his listeners were all deeply moved. Once when Yen-nien was in attendance on the throne, he got up to perform a dance, to which he sang these words:

In the north there is a lovely woman,
She is sublime and supreme.
One look and she destroys a man's city,
A second look and she destroys a man's kingdom.
A city-destroying and kingdom-destroying
Beauty can't be found twice!

?SU WU

A poem on the wife I left behind

We bind our hair, become man and wife,
True love sundered we never suspect.
Pleasure is ours tonight,
Happiness lasts the good times.

A campaigner yearns for the distant road,
Gets up to view how fares the night.
Antares and Orion both now sinking,
Away, away from here they depart.

The campaigner on the battlefield
Never promises to meet.
With clenched fists he sighs one long sigh,
Tears glisten from this parting in life.

Try hard to cherish spring flowers,
Don't forget our hour of rapture.
If I survive, I'll come back to you again,
If I die, then always love me.

?HSIN YEN-NIEN

The Imperial Guards officer

Once there was a slave in Huo's household,
Surnamed Feng, his name was Tzu-tu.
Exploiting General Huo's power,
He flirted with a Tartar winemaid.
The Tartar girl, aged fifteen,
One spring day keeps shop all alone.
Her long skirt with 'embracing boughs' belt,

Her wide sleeves with 'joy of love' bolero.
In her hair jade from Indigo Field,
Behind her ears pearls from Greater Ch'in.
Two coils of hair so dainty,
In all the world none so fine.
One coil over five million cash,
Two coils over ten million!

By chance this guardsman
Suave, sleek, passes by the wineshop.
His silver saddle so dazzling,
Kingfisher canopy lazily dawdling.
He comes up to me, asks for clear wine.
By its silk cord I lift the jade jug.
He comes up to me, asks for delicacies.
On a gold plate I slice carp.
He gives me a green bronze mirror,
Fastens my red silk waistband.

I don't mind red silk torn,
Why bother if he scorns my poor body?
A man loves his new wife,
A woman always thinks of her former husband.
In life there's the new and the old,
The noble, the commoner don't trespass on each other.
Many thanks, Gold Guardsman, Sir,
But your selfish love is just a dud!

?LADY PAN

A poem on regret, with a preface

Preface: Long ago in the court of Emperor Wu of the Han, Lady Pan
lost her position as the emperor's favourite, and she was demoted to
serve at Eternal Trust Palace. Then she composed a prose poem telling
of her hurt and loss, and she also made this poem:

Newly torn off fine Ch'i silk
Fresh, pure as frosted snow,
I cut into a 'joy of love' fan,
Round, round like the bright moon,
To go in and out of your bosom sleeve
And stir a gentle breeze.
Yet I always fear when autumn season comes
And cold winds plunder flaming heat,
It will be cast aside in a box,
Sweet love severed midway.

SUNG TZU-HOU

A poem on Graceful Tung

Down Loyang's east city road
Peach and plum grow by the wayside,
Blossom to blossom facing each other,
Leaf and leaf turning to the other.
Spring winds from the north-east rise,
Flowers, leaves fall and lift.

I don't know whose daughter
Carries her basket off to pick mulberry.
Her slim hands break twigs of blossom,
Flowers fall, whirling and swirling.

May I ask this pretty maid,
'Why are they being damaged?
In high autumn's eighth and ninth months
White dew will turn to frost.
At year's end they'll come whirling down,
How will their sweet scent last?'

'In autumn time it's theirs to shed and fall,
In spring months there's fragrance renewed.
Isn't that better than beauty's best years passing,
Love's rapture forgotten eternally?'

I want to end this song,
This song that saddens one's guts.
Let me go home and pour fine wine,
Hug my lute and go up the high hall.

ANON.

A Children's Rhyme of the Han Era

In the city they like a tall coiffure –
In the country they go one foot high!
In the city they like long eyebrows –
In the country they go half across the forehead!
In the city they like wide sleeves –
In the country they go the whole bolt!

CHANG HENG

Like sounds, a song

By chance I met you, my lord,
Favoured to serve in your harem.
When we fell in love, first came together,
I trembled as if I held boiling water.
I tried my sorry best
To do what I ought as your spouse.
I tuck my sleeves up, order your kitchen,
Attend with reverence winter and autumn sacrifice.

I long to be a rush mat
Underneath covering your square bed.
I wish I were a silk canopy and quilt
Up above warding off windy frost.
I sprinkle and sweep, cleanse your pillow and mat,
Perfume slippers with savage scents.

The doors I lock with golden bars,
High and low I light flowery lamps.
I slip off my robe, put on net and powder,
Lay out pictures, draw our pillows close.
White Girl is my teacher
For doing the myriad positions!
What every husband hopes to see
Old Man of Heaven taught the Yellow Emperor.
No rapture was sweeter than the rapture of this night,
To the end of my days I will never forget!

CH'IN CHIA

Three poems to my wife, with a preface

Preface: Ch'in Chia, whose courtesy name was Shih-hui, came from
Lunghsi. When he was promoted to commandery inspector at the
capital, his wife, Hsü Shu, fell ill and returned home. Unable to say
goodbye to her personally, Ch'in Chia had these poems sent on to her:

No. 1

Human life is like the morning dew,
Existence is full of cares –
Hardship that ever comes too soon,
Happiness ever sadly late.
I remember when I took my present post
Leaving you further each day.
I sent a carriage to welcome you home,
Empty it went, and empty it returned.
I study your letter, feel disheartened,
At meals I cannot eat,
I sit alone in our empty room.
Who will give me good cheer?
Long nights I cannot sleep,
Lean on my pillow, toss and turn alone.
Despair comes like a circling ring,
My 'not a mat' heart can't be rolled away.

The holy gods feel no selfish love,
The good they do is bearing Heaven's blessings.
Pity yourself and me!
As very small children we suffered from loneliness.
Then we came to be joined in marriage,
Love's rapture was sadly unfulfilled.
I remember I had to go far from you,
Fondly remember I told you my heart was true.
The river is wide without boat or bridge,
The path is near but cut off by hills.
I look down the road, disappointed,
Drive halfway, then halt undecided.
Drifting clouds rise from tall mountains,
Doleful winds fret in deep vales.
My good horse won't be saddled for home,
My light coach won't wheel its hubs round.
Though needle and drugs can often help,
Sad love unending is hard to bear.
This faithful man is steady from first to last,
Love and marriage cannot fail.

Briskly the drivers set out,
Jingle-jangle sound the merry bells.
At daybreak I must start off.
I fasten my belt, wait for cockcrow.
I look back in our empty room,
Dim, dark, I imagine your face and form.
Once parted I nursed ten thousand regrets.
I get up, sit down, cannot settle.
How shall I describe my heart?
I send my love, pledge fidelity.
The jewelled pin can sparkle in your hair,
The bright mirror can reflect your image.
The sweet scent will banish stale aromas,
The plain lute has clear tones.
A poet once moved by his lady's quince token
Wanted to respond with jasper.

I'm ashamed at your generous gifts to me,
Embarrassed these my presents are so slight.
Though I know they are inadequate gifts,
Their value lies in the message of my love.

CH'IN CHIA'S WIFE, HSÜ SHU

A poem in reply

My poor body felt so unwell,
Weighed down with illness I came home.
I lie limp indoors,
Seasons pass, I don't improve.
I am remiss not being at your side,
Neglectful in love and respect.

You have now received your commission,
Gone far away to the capital.
A vast gulf divides us,
There is no way to tell you my feelings.
Hoping to see you I dance for joy,
Then stand still, perplexed.
I long for you, my feelings tangle,
I dream I see your radiant face.

You set out on your journey
From me more remote each day.
I hate not having feather wings
To fly up high in pursuit of you.
Long I moan, for ever I sigh,
Tears fall and soak my blouse.

Watering horses at a Long Wall hole

Green, green riverside grass.
Skeins, skeins of longing for the far road,
The far road I cannot bear to long for.
In bed once I saw him in a dream,
I dream I see him by my side.
Suddenly I wake in another town,
Another town, each in different parts.
I toss and turn, see him no more.

Withered mulberry senses wind from the skies,
Ocean water senses chill from the skies.
I go indoors, everyone self-absorbed,
Who wants to speak for me?

A traveller came from far away,
He brought me a double-carp.
I call my children and 'cook the carp'.
Inside it is a foot-long white silk letter.
I kneel down and read the white silk letter.
What does it say in the letter, then?
Above it has, 'Try to eat!'
Below it has, 'I'll always love you.'

Watering horses at a Long Wall hole

I water my horse at a Long Wall hole,
The water's chill hurts my horse's bones.
I go and tell the Long Wall officer,
'Mind you don't keep us T'aiyüan men for good!'
'Corvée has a set time to run!
Swing your sledge! lend your voice!'
'We men would rather die fighting!
Why be bored to death building the Long Wall?'

The Long Wall, how it winds and winds,
Winds and winds three thousand leagues.
Border towns full of strong young men,
Homesteads full of widowed wives.

I write a letter to my wife at home:
'Better remarry, don't stay on at my home.
Better to serve new in-laws.
From time to time think of your old husband.'
Her reply reached the border:
'What you came up with is so silly!
You are in the thick of disaster –
How could I stay in another man's house?'

'If a son is born, mind you don't raise him!
If a girl is born, feed her dried meat.
Don't you just see below the Long Wall
Dead men's skeletons prop each other up?'

'With bound hair I went to serve you,
My aching heart sealed with care.
I know full well your border grief –
How can your wife survive for long?'

HSÜ KAN

Bedroom longing

Deep shadow grips sorrow's despair,
Sorrow's despair, for whom does it arise?
I brood on parting from you in this life,
Each living on another horizon.
Happy reunion will never have its day,
Deep in my heart the crushed and wounded feeling
Is not from anxiety over the evening meal
But I feel hopeless craving.
I sit straight, practise Inaction,
Faint is the light of your face.

Sheer, sheer mountain peaks high,
Vast, vast ten-thousand-league road.
You left, each day going further,
The grip of despair makes one grow old.
Man's life, his whole existence,
Is swift as spring grass dying.
Time cannot be had again,
So why do we fret and fume?
Whenever I repeat your past kind vows,
How will my poor self repay you?

Drifting clouds are so distant and remote,
Though I long to confide my message,
Whirling, swirling they can bear none.
Hesitant, I long in vain for you.
When people part they always meet again,
You alone give no promise of return.
Ever since you went away
My bright mirror darkens neglected.
Thoughts of you are like a flowing river,
When will they ever cease?

Cruel, cruel the season dies away,
Orchid blooms shed and fall.
I gasp and sigh long sighs,
Your promise soothes my passion.
I toss and turn sleepless,
Long nights are skeins and skeins.
I put on slippers, rise, go outside,
Look up at Three Stars.
Hating myself for desire unfulfilled,
I weep tears like a gushing stream.

Longing to see your turban and comb
Increases my weary burden.
How will I get huge phoenix wings
To see this man of my heart?
True love will clearly not be won.
I scratch my head, stand dismayed.
How to admit I no longer see him
And there'll be no way to meet him again?
Long ago we were like fish eye to eye,
Now we're divorced like Antares from Orion.

'There is no one who has no beginning',
I dream you can make this last.
Since parting years have passed,
Old kindness how can you promise?
Favour the new, forget the old!
That's my lover's wrongful way.
I trust myself to him though far,
How to forget you one moment?
Since you are generous, not mean,
I dream I am sometimes in your thoughts.

A love poem

The high palace looms sheer, sheer,
Broad roofs freeze chill, chill.
Faint winds stir by a boudoir door,
The setting sun shines on steps and garden.

I linger beneath cloudy roofs,
Whistle and sing against flowery pillars.
You set out, not yet returning.
Why bother to adorn myself?

Censer incense lies closed, unused,
On my mirror-case dust is spreading.
Silks fine have lost their colour,
Gold, kingfisher are dull, lacklustre,
Choice foods I've long forgotten to taste,
Fine wines also forgone.

I look back and stare: empty, hushed,
All I hear is swallow and sparrow noise.
Despairing thoughts linked in a chain,
My heart within is like a hangover.

FAN CH'IN

A poem on suppressing love

I left the east gate to roam
And chanced to receive your bright dust.
I long for you to come to my hidden room,
I would help you to bed, take your robe and turban.
Nowadays no courting in mulberry,
But seduced by this passer-by!
I fell in love with your figure,
And you were charmed by my face.

How does he convey doting affection?
He clasps my arm with twin gold bands.
How does he convey deep devotion?
He slips on my finger a double ring.
How does he convey touching care?
At my ears twin bright pearls.

How does he convey firm fidelity?
A scent pouch he ties at my elbow.
How does he convey courteous warmth?
He encircles my wrists with twin bangles.

How does he seal loving passion?
Jade pendants stitched to my silk belt fringe.
How does he seal deep love?
Pure white thread joins twin needles.
How does he seal mutual intimacy?
A gold-leaf painted head-scratcher.

How does he comfort me in separation?
Behind my ears tortoiseshell pins.
How does he respond to pleasure?
Of pure white silk three skirts.
How does he seal sorrow's comfort?
White silk twin under-robes.

He promised to meet me where?
He promised by the east hill nook.
It was sunrise! he didn't come.
East vale breezes blew my jacket,
I stared far, saw nothing,
Shed tears, got up in reluctance.

He promised to meet me where?
He promised in the hill's south sunshine.
It was noon! he didn't come.
South winds soft blew my blouse.
I wandered, glimpsed nothing.
Hoping for you saddens my guts.

He promised to meet me where?
He promised by the west hill slope.
It was dusk! he didn't come.
I dawdled, sighed long sighs.
I stared far, chill winds came.
I looked up and down, tidied my clothes.

He promised to meet me where?
He promised on the hill's north ridge.
It was sunset! he didn't come.
Bitter winds blew my collar.
I hoped for him, could not sit still.
Despair, anguish made my heart grieve.

I kept myself for him – why?
I regret my flowered season.
Our deep passion had been true, true,
Then we made our pledge.
I lifted my hem, trod mown grass,
Saying you'd never deceive me.
Now I mix with the depraved kind,
Here and there, nowhere to go.
Wounded for loss of my heart's desire,
Tears fall like twin silk threads.

ANON.

*An old poem written for Chiao Chung-ch'ing's wife,
with a preface*

Preface: At the close of the Han Dynasty, during the years 196–220 AD,
the wife of Chiao Chung-ch'ing, the magistrate of Luchiang prefecture,
whose maiden name was Liu, was dismissed from home by her husband's
mother. She swore to herself that she would never remarry, but her own
parents and family brought a great deal of pressure to bear on her. So
she committed suicide by drowning herself. When her husband, Chung-
ch'ing, learned of this, he also committed suicide by hanging himself
from a tree in the garden. A contemporary poet felt deep sympathy for
these two and composed a poem about them. It goes as follows:

A peacock south-east flew,
After five leagues it faltered.

'At thirteen I could weave white silk,
At fourteen I learned to make clothes.
At fifteen I played the many-stringed lute,
At sixteen recited *Songs* and *History*.
At seventeen I became your wife
And my heart was full of constant pain and sorrow.

'You became a government clerk,
I kept chaste, my love never straying.
At cockcrow I went in to weave at the loom,
Night after night found no rest.
In three days I cut five lengths of cloth,
Mother-in-law still nagged that I was lazy.
It wasn't my weaving that was too slow,
But it's hard to be a wife in your home.
I don't want to be driven out,
But there's no way I can stay on here.
So please speak to your mother
To let me be sent home in good time.'

The clerk heard these words
And up in the hall spoke with his mother.
'As a boy my physiognomy chart was unlucky,
I was fortunate to get such a wife as she.
We bound our hair, shared pillow and mat,
Vowed to be lovers till Yellow Springs.
We both have served you two years or three,
From the start not so long a time,
Yet the girl's conduct is not remiss,
Why do you treat her so unkindly?'

His mother said to the clerk,
'How can you be so soft!
This wife has no sense of decorum,
Whatever she does she goes her own way.
I've borne my anger for a long time now,
You must not just suit yourself!
Our east neighbours have a good daughter,
Her name is Ch'in Lofu.
So pretty her body, beyond compare,
Your mother will seek her for your wife.
It's best to dismiss this one as soon as we can,
Dismiss her, we won't let her stay!'

The government clerk knelt down in reply,
'Now I only have this to say, Mother.
If you dismiss this wife today,
For the rest of my life I will not remarry!'
His mother heard these words,
Thumped her bed, then in a fierce rage:
'My son, have you no respect?
How dare you speak in your wife's defence!
I have lost all feeling for you,
On no account will I let you disobey me!'

The government clerk silent, without a word,
Bowed twice and went back within their doors.
He started to speak to his new wife,
Stammered, unable to talk.
'I myself would not drive you away,
But there's my mother, scolding and nagging.
You just go home for a little while,
Today I must report to the office.
It won't be for long, I'll soon be coming home,
And when I come back I'll be sure to fetch you.
So let this put your mind at rest.
Please don't contradict me!'

His new wife said to the clerk:
'No more of this nonsense!
Long ago in early springtime
I left home to come to your gates.
Whatever I did I obeyed your mother,
In my behaviour never dared do as I pleased.
Day and night I tried hard at my work.
Brought low I am caught in a vice of misery.
My words have been blameless,
I fulfilled my duties diligently.
Why then, as I'm being summarily dismissed,
Do you still talk of my coming back here?
I have embroidered tunics,
Gorgeous they shine with a light of their own;
Red silk funnel bedcurtains,
At the four corners hang scent sachets;
Dressing cases sixty or seventy,
Green jasper, green silk cord;
Many, many things, each of them different,
All sorts of things in these boxes.

65

I am despised, and my things also worthless,
Not worth offering your next wife,
But I'll leave them here as gifts.
From now on we'll never meet again,
From time to time please bring me some comfort,
And never, never forget me!'

The cock crew, outside it was getting light.
The new wife got up and carefully dressed.
She puts on her broidered lined gown
And four or five different things.
On her feet she slips silk shoes;
On her head tortoiseshell combs gleam;
Round her waist she wears flowing silk white,
On her ears wears bright moon pendants.
Her hands are like pared onion stems,
Her mouth seems rich scarlet cinnabar.
Svelte, svelte she walks with tiny steps,
Perfect, matchless in all the world.

She went up the high hall, bowed to Mother.
The mother heard she was leaving, didn't stop her.
'Long ago when I was a child,
I grew up in the countryside.
I had no schooling from the start,
On both counts would shame the man of a great house.
I received from you, Mother, much money and silk,
I do not want to be summarily dismissed;
Today, though, I am going back home.
I am afraid I have brought trouble to your house.'

She withdrew and took leave of her sister-in-law.
Tears fell, beads of pearl.
'When I first came as a bride
You were beginning to lean on the bed.
Now as I am being dismissed,
You are as tall as I, Sister.
Care for Mother with all your heart,
Be nice and help all you can.
On the first seventh and last ninth of the month,
When you're enjoying yourself, don't forget me!'

She left the gates, climbed the coach, departed,
Tears fell in more than a hundred streams.
The clerk's horse was in front,
The new wife's coach behind.
Clatter-clatter, how it rumbled, rumbled!
They met at the mouth of the main road,
He dismounted, got into her coach.
With bowed head he whispered these words in her ear:
'I swear I won't be parted from you,
Just go home for a little while.
Today I am going to the office,
Not for long, I'll be back home.
I swear by Heaven I'll not betray you!'

His new wife said to the clerk:
'I feel you love me fondly,
And you seem to hold me in high esteem.
Before long I hope you will come for me.
You must be rock firm,
I must be a pliant reed.
The pliant reed is supple as silk,
The firm rock will not be rolled away.
I have my father and brothers,
Their temper is wild as thunder;
I fear they will not let me do as I wish
But oppose me, and this makes my breast seethe.'
They raised their hands in a long, long farewell,
For both loves the same wistful longing.

She entered the gates, went up the family hall,
Approaching, withdrawing with expressionless face.
Her mother beat her fist loud:
'We didn't plan for you to return on your own!
At thirteen I taught you to weave,
At fourteen you could make clothes,
At fifteen you played the many-stringed lute,
At sixteen you knew ceremonial rites,
At seventeen I sent you off in marriage,
Telling you to swear not to give offence.
What have you done wrong now that
Uninvited you come home yourself!'
'I, Lanchih, have brought shame on my mother,
But your child has truly done no wrong.'
Her mother's heart was broken with deep sorrow.

She had been home more than ten days
When the district magistrate sent a matchmaker.
He said, 'We have a third young master,
Charming beyond compare in all the world!
He is barely eighteen or nineteen,
Eloquent, very talented he is!'

Mother said to daughter:
'Go, you may answer yes.'
Her daughter choked back the tears:
'When I, Lanchih, first came home,
The clerk showed me great kindness,
Swore on oath he'd never desert me.
If I were now to betray our love,
I fear this act would be wrong.
Let's break off the betrothal talks.
In good time we'll discuss the matter again.'

Her mother explained to the matchmaker:
'In all humility, I do have such a daughter,
She went away in marriage, but is returned to our gates.
She was reluctant to be an official's wife,
How would she please a fine gentleman's son?
I hope you will be successful with other inquiries.
We cannot at present give permission.'

The matchmaker was gone many days,
Then a deputy was sent for, asked to reconsider.
'They say they have a daughter, Lanchih,
Whose forefathers for generations have held office.
Say, "My master says he has a fifth son,
Elegant, refined, not yet married.
My deputy I've sent as matchmaker,
And a secretary to bring his message."'

Immediately they put their case: 'The prefect's family
Has such a fine son,
He wishes to take solemn vows of marriage
And so we are sent to your house.'

The mother refused the matchmaker:
'My daughter has already sworn an oath.
What dare a mother say?'
When her brother learned of this

He was disappointed and furious in his heart.
He broached the matter, telling his sister:
'In these arrangements, why are you so unreasonable?
First you married a government clerk,
Later you might marry a squire.
Fortune is like Heaven and Earth,
It can bring glory to your person.
Not to wed this lord now,
What will happen in the future?'

Lanchih looked up and replied:
'In fact what my brother says is right.
I left home to serve my bridegroom.
Midway I returned to my brother's gates.
It's my place to follow my brother's wishes,
Why would I do as I please?
Though I made a vow with the government clerk,
I may never chance to meet him again.
Tell them straight away I agree to marry,
They may arrange a betrothal.'

The matchmaker got down down from the ritual couch:
'Yes, yes!' and 'Quite, quite!'
He went back to the office and explained to the prefect:
'Your servant has carried out your command.
Our discussion has met with great success!'
When the prefect heard this
He rejoiced in his heart.
He scanned the calendar, opened the almanac:
'It will be auspicious this month,
The Six Cardinal Points are in conjunction.
The luckiest day is the thirtieth.
Today it's now the twenty-seventh,
You may go and conclude the nuptials.'

Discussions on both sides hastened the wedding gifts,
In succession like floating clouds.
A green sparrow and white swan boat,
At the four corners were dragon banners
Softly curling in the wind.
A gold coach, of jade its wheels,
Prancing piebald horses,
Coloured silk threads and gold-stitched saddles.
A wedding gift of three million cash,

All strung on green cord.
Assorted silks, three hundred bolts,
From Chiaokuang a purchase of fine fish.
A retinue of four or five hundred men
Densely massed set out to the palace.

Mother said to daughter:
'I have just received a letter from the prefect,
Tomorrow he will come to invite you in marriage.
Why aren't you making your clothes?
Don't fail to start now!'
Her daughter, silent, without a word,
Sobbed with her kerchief stifling her mouth.
Tears fell as if poured.
She moved her seat of lapis lazuli,
Set it near the window.
Her left hand held shears and rule,
Her right hand took the sheer silk.
By morning she finished an embroidered robe,
Later she finished an unlined dress of silk.
Dim, dim, the sun was about to darken,
With sad thoughts she left the gates and wept.

When the government clerk heard of this affair
He asked for furlough to go home a while.
When he was still two or three leagues away
His weary horse sadly whinnied.
His new wife recognized his horse's whinny,
Slipped on her shoes and met him.
Sadly from a distance they gazed at each other,
She knew it was her long lost one coming.
She raised her hand, patted his horse's saddle,
Her loud sighs tore his heart.
'Since you parted from me
Unimaginable things have happened!
Things have turned out not as we once wished,
Nor could I make you understand.
I have had my parents – father and mother,
Bringing pressure to bear joined by my brother,
To make me consent to marry another man.
You have come back, but what hope is there for you?'

The government clerk said to his new wife:
'Congratulations for winning such high promotion!
The firm rock square and strong
Could have endured a thousand years.
The pliant reed, once so supple,
Is reduced to this in the space of dawn to dusk!
You will prosper and move up with each day,
I will face Yellow Springs alone.'

His new wife said to the government clerk:
'What do you mean by such words?
Together we have suffered this great crisis,
First you, and then your wife.
Down in Yellow Springs we will meet,
Don't betray our vow made this day!'
They held hands, then went their separate ways,
Each returning to their different gates.
For the living to make a parting unto death
Is more hateful than words can tell.
They think of their farewell from this world,
Never in a million years to be brought back to life.

The government clerk went back home,
Up in the hall he bowed to his mother:
'Today the great wind is cold,
Cold winds have crushed a tree,
Harsh frosts grip the garden orchid.
Your son today goes to darkness,
Leaving Mother to survive alone.
For I must carry out a most unhappy plan,
Torment our souls no more!
May your life be like South Mountain's rock,
Your four limbs healthy and strong!'

When his mother heard these words
Teardrops fell with each word:
'You are the son of a great family,
With official position at galleried courts.
Don't die for the sake of that wife!
About noble and base are you so naive?
Our east neighbour has a good daughter,
Meek and mild, the loveliest in town.
Your mother will seek her for your wife,
All will be arranged between dawn and dusk.'

The government clerk bowed twice and went back
Sighing long sighs in his empty rooms.
The plan he made was fixed as ever.
He turned his head towards the door,
Slowly he watched, grief's oppressive rage.

That day horses and cattle lowed,
His new wife goes into her green hut.
After dusk had fallen
A quiet hush, people start to settle down.
'My life will end today,
My soul will vanish, my corpse will linger a while.'
She lifts her skirt, removes her silk shoes,
Stands up and goes towards the clear lake.

When the government clerk hears of this act,
His heart knows it is the long separation.
He hesitates under a garden tree,
Hangs himself from a south-east branch.

The two families asked for a joint burial,
A joint burial on the side of Mount Hua.
East and west were planted pine and cypress,
Left and right catalpa were set.
Branch with branch joins to form a canopy,
Leaf with leaf meets in wedlock.
Among them are a pair of flying birds,
Called mandarin ducks, drake and hen,
Lifting their heads they call to each other,
Night after night until the fifth watch.
Passers-by stay their steps to listen,
Widows get out of bed and pace to and fro.

Be warned, men of the future,
Learn this lesson and never forget!

CHAPTER TWO

POETS OF THE
WEI AND CHIN DYNASTIES
(THIRD AND FOURTH CENTURIES)

*At Ch'ingho I saw a newly wed knight part from his bride
in an escort-boat*

To you I am newly wed
But overnight we have to part.
Cool winds stir autumn grass,
Crickets moan in trailing choir.
Chill, chill a cold cicada chirps,
Cicada chirps, hugs a dead twig.
The dead twig swings, a moment's flight,
A bodily form is suddenly moved away.

I am not sad your body moved away,
Only regret years and months have raced,
Years and months unending.
Our next meeting – how can we foretell it?
I wish we were a pair of brown geese
Wing to wing playing by crystal pools.

Another poem composed at Ch'ingho

A double boat basks on the long river,
Calm, soft it sways and rocks.
Strings, song carry midstream,
Sad echoes leave trailing music.
The sound of music enters a lover's breast,
A dull ache wounds the human heart.
My wounded heart, what do I remember?
All I want is your fond love to grow deeper,
And I want to be the Dawn Wind bird
Flying double to glide over north woods.

Another Empress Chen poem, the folk-song 'Along the embankment'

Rushes grow in my pool
Their leaves so thick and lush.
A perfect, dutiful marriage
None knows so well as your wife.
Common gossip that melts yellow gold
Has forced you to live apart.

I remember when you left me,
Alone I grieve, ever keen my sorrow.
I imagine I see your face,
Tangled feelings wound the hollow of my heart.
I remember you, ever keen my sorrow,
Night after night I can't sleep.

Don't through glory and renown
Reject one you loved before.
Don't because fish and meat are cheap
Reject the leek and shallot.
Don't because hemp and jute are cheap
Reject straw and rushes.

I go out and feel bitterly sad,
I come in and feel bitterly sad.
Many the grieving border winds,
The trees how they rush and roar.
May army life though lonely make you happy!
May your years last one thousand autumns!

Two miscellaneous poems, with a preface

Preface: Wang Sung was the wife of the P'inglu General Liu Hsün. Some twenty years after marrying her Hsün fell in love with a daughter of the Ssu-ma clan from Shanyang and because Wang Sung was childless he divorced her. On her way back to her parents she composed these two poems:

No. 1

Billowing, billowing the curtains by my bed
Flare out to shade my bright lamp.
Once I went away with you,
Now I have come back with you.
Locked up in your case
When will you lie open once more?

No. 2

Who says a divorced woman is pathetic?
A divorced woman's feelings grow more mature.
From a thousand leagues you come, don't spit in my well!
No more than you'd defile bedcurtains you once used.
Faraway gazing does not take me far,
Hesitant doubt won't move me forward.

Five miscellaneous poems

No. 1

Bright the moon shines on a tall house,
Flooding light now ebbs, now flows.
Upstairs there is a sad wife in love,
In her sad sighs there is a trace of grief.
May I ask who is sighing?
She says, 'I am a travelling man's wife.
My lover has travelled more than ten years,
His bereaved wife still nests alone.
My lover is like clear highway dust,
His wife, I'm like thick river mud.
To float, to sink, each a different impulse.
To meet, when will we agree?

'I long to be the south-west wind
Coursing far to enter my lover's breast.
If my lover's breast never lies open
Who will his loving wife rely on?'

No. 2

In the north-west there is a weaving wife,
Her fine flowered silk is so tangled.
At bright dawn she plies loom and shuttle,
But by sundown her pattern is not finished.

Great sighs last the long night,
Sad whistling pierces dark blue clouds.
His wife, I keep to our empty room,
My sweetheart marches on campaign.
He promised in three years he'd come home.
Now nine springs have passed.

Bereaved a bird circles a tree and flutters,
Sobs and cries, calls to its lost flock.
I wish I were a southward-streaming sunbeam –
I'd race light to see the man I love.

No. 3

A hint of shadow screens the sunshine,
Pure winds ruffle my gown.
Darting fish hide in emerald waters.
Soaring birds cleave to skies in flight.

A dwindling speck, the travelling man
Campaigns far away and can't come home.
When first he left harsh frost gripped,
By now white dew has dried.

The wanderer sighs at the *Millet thick* song,
While she at home sings *How few!*
Depressed I face my honoured guest,
Downcast I ache with inner grief.

No. 4

I take my coat, leave my inner room,
Aimlessly pace between two pillars.
Idle bedroom how hushed and still,
Green grass carpets steps and garden.

The empty house gives birth to winds,
All the birds glide southward bound.
Spring love how can I forget?
Despair is my companion.

My handsome man stays on the far road,
His wife, I'm alone and lonely.
Blissful meetings cannot happen twice,
Sweet iris will glory no more.

Men always cast off old love,
Won't my lover be the same in our lives?
Cleaving to pine I become dodder,
Clinging to water I am like floating alga.

I tidy myself, fix my collar and belt,
Dawn to dusk they won't slip awry.
If only you'd take one last backward glance
To help me ever in my deepest love.

No. 5

In a land south there is a lovely girl,
A glorious bloom like peach or plum.
Dawn she roams the river's northern shore,
Dusk she rests on Hsiang river isle.

Modern fashion spurns her rosy cheeks.
For whom will she flash white teeth?
She looks up and down, the year about to fade.
It's hard to wait for a lasting glorious flame.

A beautiful woman

A beautiful woman charming and graceful
Picks mulberry between forked paths.
Long twigs gaily stretch and stretch,
Tumbling leaves flurry and flurry.

She tucks up her sleeves, reveals white hands,
Pale wrists clasped by golden bands.
On her head gold sparrow pins,
Her waist is strung with kingfisher jade.
Bright pearls lace her jade body,
Coral interweaves with green pearl.
Her silken clothes swirl and swirl,
Light collar twirls with the breeze.

Her backward glance darts with flashing light,
She whistles long, the air is like orchids.
Passers-by halt their coach,
Those who rest forget their meal.

May I ask where this girl resides?
'Well, she lives by the main city gates.
Her green house overlooks the highway,
Tall gates are bolted by heavy bars.
Image of a bloom glistening in dawn sun,
Who wouldn't hope for one who looks so fine?'
'The matchmakers, what are their plans?'
'Jade and silk were importunate betrothal gifts.'
The lovely one admires lofty virtue,
Her search for a worthy man is very hard.
All men clamour for her in vain,
How can they know what will make her happy?
Through her best years she stays in her house,
At midnight she rises with long sighs.

The 'Planting beans' piece

I plant beans below the south hill,
Bean creepers form their own shade.
When I was first married to you,
We bound our hair, our wedded love was deep,
Love's pleasure reigned on pillow and mat,
We slept nights sharing a fitted quilt.
I secretly burned for the *Ch'ang-ti tree* song,
Sweet joy, harmony of lute and harp.

The year moves into darkness late,
My handsome man loves another's heart.
Fondness severed joins with me no more,
My love has foundered and sunk.

I go out, but where to look back to?
Hesitant I step through northern woods.
Below are cattle nuzzling their necks,
I look up and see a pair of nesting birds.
I hold a branch, heave long sighs,
Tears fall and soak my silk collar.
A kind bird knows my sorrow,
Stretches its neck trilling to me.

Once we were fish of the same pool,
Now we're like Antares and Orion.
In days long past all I met was joy,
Now in the present I suffer loneliness.
Discarded as I am, I'll trust the will of Heaven.
Sad heart, how will this be borne?

The 'Floating alga' piece

Floating alga clings to clear water,
With the wind east and west it flows.
With bound hair I took leave of stern parents,
Coming to be a mate for you.
Polite, busy I lived dawn till dusk,
Then for no reason incurred your blame.

In the past you covered me with fond love,
Joy harmonious like harp and lute.
Why am I now rejected?
Estranged like Antares from Orion?
Dogwood has its own scent,
But not as sweet as cassia and orchid.
New love may be lovable
But not as dear as past love.
Moving clouds have their hour of return,
Your fond love may yet return midway.

Dejected I gaze up at heaven and sigh,
Where will my sad heart appeal?
Sun and moon do not stay fixed for ever,
Human life is like a brief lodging.
Sad winds come into my breast,
Tears fall like trembling dew.
I take out a box, make you a robe,
Cut and stitch silks fine and white.

The pomegranate planted in the forecourt
With green leaves tossing celadon tints,
With cinnabar blooms ablaze in fiery flames,
Their dazzling tints that have a glorious sheen,
A glorious sheen gleaming with rare turquoise,
Is where the blessed spirits might play.
Here birds come flying in flocks
And beat their wings in mournful choir.
In mournful choir, but why?
Cinnabar blooms have not borne fruit.

She strokes her heart, sighs long sighs,
The childless wife who must go home for good.
With child she is the moon that sails the skies,
Childless she's like a falling star.
Skies and moon each wax and wane,
A falling star dies without a glimmer.
She lodged a while, failed in her duty,
She has fallen among tiles and stones.

Despair and longing surge within me,
My sighs go on till cockcrow.
I toss and turn unable to sleep,
Stray aimlessly through the forecourt.
I pause, at a loss, go back inside my room,
Wistful bedcurtains rustle.
I roll up the drapes, tidy my dress,
Stroke the strings and play my plain lute.
Anguish carries on echoing notes,
Hauntingly sad and clear.

I hold back the tears, sighing long.
How did I offend the sacred Gods?
The Troubled Star waits for frost and dew.
Must spring and summer alone bring ripeness?
Late harvests make for fine fruits –
I want – oh, lover, please stay calm and steady!

Two folk-song poems

No. 1

Shine, shine white moon bright,
Let gleaming rays lighten my bed.
One in despair cannot sleep,
Dull, dull nights so long.
Soft breezes blow the bedroom door,
Silk curtains unmoved flare and drift.

I take my robe trailing its long sash,
Put on slippers, go down from the high hall.
East, west, which way to turn?
I hesitate and falter.

A spring bird southward flies,
Soars and soars fluttering alone.
Sad its voice calling to its mate,
Mournful cries that hurt my guts.
Moved by nature, I long for the one I love,
Sudden spilling tears drench my coat.

No. 2

I planted melons by the east well,
Bit by bit they creep over the wall.
When I first married you,
Melon tendrils were locked in close embrace.
I leaned my poor frame against you,
As if clinging to Mount T'ai.

Stemless, rootless dodder
Spreads out and upward clambers.
Alga leans on clear currents
Ever fearing bodily harm.

Covered by hillock favours,
Your humble wife, I hold firm and true.
The sun shining in the sky knows this,
I imagine you'll also be the same.

JUAN CHI

Two poems from Poems from my heart

No. 1

Two nymphs play by the river bank,
Drifting aimlessly with the breeze.
Chiao-fu slips off their rings and pendants,
Seductive their charms, sweetly scented.
Soft, tender, passionate with love's rapture:
'We'll never forget you for a thousand years.'
They have destroyed cities and bewitched Hsiats'ai,
Their lovely faces tie his guts in knots.

Emotions excited breed despairing thoughts.
The flower of oblivion they plant by orchid rooms.
Hair glossed and rinsed, for whom are they groomed?
'Let it rain! We hate the dawn glow!'
Why do bonds of metal and rock
In one morning change to parting's wound?

No. 2

In days gone by the gay boys,
Anling and Lungyang,
Fresh, fresh blossom of peach and plum,
Glowing, glowing with a brilliant sheen,
Were happy as nine springtimes,
Pliant as if bowed by autumn frost.

Their melting looks soften pretty faces,
Words and laughter release sweet scent.
Holding hands they share love's rapture,
Spend nights sharing a fitted quilt.

We long to be a pair of birds flying,
Gliding wing to wing, soaring together.
Cinnabar and green paint inscribe their clear vow:
'To eternity I'll never forget you!'

FU HSÜAN

The 'Green, green riverbank grass' piece

Green, green riverbank grass.
Long, long ten-thousand-league road.
'When grass grows in spring'
He vowed to return from the far road.
Spring came, grass no longer grows,
For vows broken I sigh voiceless sighs.

Moved by nature my loving heart yearns,
In my dreams I imagine we're aroused to deep passion.
I dream of you, we're like mandarin ducks
Wing to wing gliding through the clouds;
When I wake, silence, I see your face no more,
Remote as Antares and Orion.

The Lo and Yellow rivers are safe enough,
But not as sure as Mount Sung.
Incoming tides never reach home,
Floating clouds pass and then come back.
Sad winds trouble my loving heart,
Since he's far, so far, who will know?
Suspended planets neither stop nor stay,
Swift as a team of racehorses.

I bend my ear to listen for your echo,
Avert my gaze, tears double spill.
In our lifetime there is no hope of meeting,
I'll see you down in Yellow Springs!

The 'Pity me!' piece, a 'Yü-chang' ballad

Pity me! my body is female,
My lowly state is hard to describe.
A boy faces door and gate,
Comes down to earth divinely born.
His manly heart burns for the four seas,
Ten thousand leagues he yearns for windy dust.

A girl is born, there is no celebration,
She is not her family's prized jewel.
Grown up, she hides deep in her room,
Veils her head, too shy to look on others.

The tears shed at marrying into another town
Are sudden like a cloudburst of rain.
With bowed head she calms her features,
White teeth clenched beneath red lips.
She kneels countless times in greeting
To maids and concubines like grim guests.
Happy love is like Cloudy Han,
Like mallow or bean that leans towards spring sun.
Love is much worse than water on fire,
A hundred wrongs are heaped upon her person.

Her jade face with the years alters,
Her husband takes many new loves.
Once they were form and shadow,
Now they are Hun and Chinese.
Hun and Chinese sometimes see each other.
Love once severed is remote as Antares and Orion.

The 'There is a girl' piece, a 'Song of beauty' ballad

There is a girl enfolded in sweet scent,
Fair, fair she walks through eastern rooms.
Moth eyebrows part in kingfisher wings,
Bright eyes illumine her clear brow.
Cinnabar lips screen white teeth,
Delicate her face like sceptre jade.
Ravishing smiles reveal her dimples,
The host of her charms can't be litanized.
Such a beauty rarely appears in this world,
In fact, she's the Mao Ch'iang of olden days.

On her head is set a gold 'step-quiverer',
From her ears hang bright moon orbs.
Pearl bangles clasp white wrists,
Kingfisher bird pins cascade pure gleams.
Her patterned coat is broidered with reed and axe,
Her jade body shimmers under a blouse of silk.

Besides the present glamour of her beauty,
Her chaste air is like the autumn frost.
Sweet music skims blue clouds,
Sound and echo flood the four points.
How rare her flower of virtue!
Worthy consort of a duke or king.

Sacred matches are made each myriad epoch,
Sun and moon now and then conjoin.
Matchmakers display betrothal rolls of silk,
Lamb and goose shriek in the front hall.
A hundred coaches crowd the main road,
She rises like phoenix paired in soaring flight.
Ordinary men just stamp and strut,
She fades from view remote as Antares from Orion.

The 'Hour of dawn' piece, a 'Song of regret' ballad

Shines, shines the hour of dawn sun,
Pale, pale is daybreak's bright moon.
At fifteen I entered your gate,
Once we parted my hair turned hoary white,
Sweethearts suddenly became strangers,
Estranged like Hu from Yüeh.
Yet Hu and Yüeh sometimes meet;
Antares and Orion are distant and aloof.
Of form and shadow no faint image,
Sound and echo are mute, indistinct.
Delicate strings excited on taut stops,
Touch them, sad music escapes.
Passionate thoughts like a ring full circle,
Despair visits, won't be repulsed.

The T'u-shan girl still harboured resentment.
The poet made the song of *Picking beans*.
Crickets moan near my bed,
Eddying winds stir by the dark door.
Spring glory falls with the dew,
Hibiscus blooms at the tip of the tree.

Sad am I with my unhappy life,
From fine dawn parted for ever.
How can I bear things as they are?
I'm like the torn fine white silk,
Or the orphan hen fluttering near its old nest,
Or the falling star's last dying gleam.
My soul races ten thousand leagues,
My willing heart seeks our shared grave.

The 'Bright moon' piece

Pale, pale the bright moon's light,
Flaming, aflame the dawn sun glows.
Once I was spring cocoon silk,
Now I am an autumn girl's dress.

Scarlet lips line white teeth,
Kingfisher glints dart from moth eyebrows.
A charming child, full of sweet talk,
The joy of love plays around her features.

A jade face has its hour of perfection,
A fine complexion withers with the years.
She ever fears new love supplanting old,
Disaster that stems from nothing.

Floating alga has no root or stalk,
What will it lean on, if not water?
Sorrow and joy usurp each other,
The peak of joy must revert to sorrow.

The 'Autumn orchid' piece

Autumn orchid shades a jade pool,
Pool water clear and fragrant.
Lotus blooms to the wind unfold,
Among them is a pair of mandarin ducks.
And paired fish impulsive leap and dart,
And two birds capricious wheel and glide.
You promised nine autumns past
To share with me your robe in bed.

The 'West Ch'angan' ballad

My beloved, where is he?
Well, he's out in west Ch'angan.
What does he use when asking after me?
An incense candle's paired pearl rings.
What does he use when asking again?
Plumed pins and kingfisher jade.

Now, oh! now I hear that you
Once more, oh! once more have changed heart.
So neither can I burn the incense,
Nor the rings can I let sink.
For incense burning daily is consumed,
Rings sinking each day fall the deeper.

A poem harmonizing with Mr Pan's poem

Ch'iu Hu brought his fair wife home,
In three days he was detailed to another town.
White, white his pure wife's face,
Cold, cold she keeps to her empty room.
Pleasure was not to last the evening,
They parted like Antares and Orion.
Despair comes deeper than four seas.
It's easy to be moved, hard to guard one's feelings.
People say life's day is brief,
The mourner hates the long hours of the night.

When all plants wave their springtime glory,
She tucks up her cuffs to pick soft mulberry.
White hands search for thick boughs,
Falling leaves don't fill her basket.
Silk clothes film her jade body,
Roving eyes float iridescent.

Her lord work-weary comes home,
His carriage and horse prance like dragons.
Their souls race ten thousand leagues,
Man and wife meet, neither recognizes the other.
The traveller in love with her sweet face
Begs, 'Rest awhile beside this tree.'
He tempts her with the 'meet a minister' ploy,
Then tosses down a bag of yellow gold.
Fierce, fierce the chaste girl's anger,
Her refusal harsh as autumn frost.

A long gallop brings him to house and home,
He takes his gold, goes up the north hall.
His mother stands and calls his wife to come.
Before their joyful reunion gets halfway,
Ch'iu Hu sees the other woman!
Nervous as one carrying hot water is he.
'To betray love, surely that's no disgrace?
Lasting vows aren't meant to be kept!'

Clear and cloudy always rise from different springs,
Duck and phoenix never glide together.
She withdraws, goes to the long flow.
The outcome? A chaste wife's pluck.
That man was none too moral,
Yet this wife was rather too severe!

CHANG HUA

Five love poems

No. 1

In the north there is a lovely woman,
Grave she sits drumming her tuneful guitar.
All morn she strokes her flute and strings,
By twilight has not made music.

Despair comes, ties knots that won't unfasten.
My thoughts dwell on my treasure;
My lord has gone on a tour of duty,
His secluded wife nurses a bitter heart.
First it was a three-year parting,
Till now he has dallied longer.

Lichen grows over door and window.
The garden bower has become a jungle.
Gliding birds sing escorting their mates,
Grass insects hum harmonious chant.

My saddened heart is easily aroused.
I look up and down, tears stream on my collar.
I want to ask for the Dawn Wind bird's wings
So that neatly sashed I'll serve your fitted quilt.

No. 2

The bright moon shimmers with clear rays,
Soaring light shines on a gloomy porch.
A secluded person keeps still night vigil,
Turns and enters empty bedcurtains.
His sash tied, he waits for dawn,
Sprinkled morning stars grow sparse.

As sleep embraces our kindred souls
I gaze on my lovely one's face:
Charming smiles with pretty dimples,
Twin graces her eyes and brow.
As I waken my long sighs grow keener,
Dejected my heart is lonely and sad.

No. 3

Clear winds stir curtains and blind,
The dawn moon brightens a dark room.
Her handsome one lives far away,
From orchid rooms his radiant face is absent.
Her breast collar hugs his vacant shadow,
His light quilt drapes an empty bed.

When we live in joy we mourn the speed of night,
In sorrow we resent the dim night's tedium.
She strokes her pillow, moans lonely sighs,
Skein on skein of aching deep within her heart.

No. 4

You live in north seas sunshine.
Your wife, I live in south river shadows.
Far-flung the distant route remote,
Mountains, rivers sheer and deep.
Favoured with love, drenched with lavish care,
I bound my life to serve him I adore.
I cherish your kindness, keep my marriage vows,
To ten thousand leagues entrust my tiny heart.

No. 5

I let my eyes roam beyond the four wilds,
I idly wander and pause all alone.
Marsh orchid rims a clear brook,
Rich blooms shade green banks.

My handsome one is not here.
I pick some, but to whom to give them?
Nesting creatures sense the winds whirl,
Burrowing beasts know of dark rains.
If you have never lived far apart,
How can you know desire for your mate?

Two miscellaneous poems

No. 1

Idly I wander through the springtime palace,
Enjoy a rest by the green lake bend.
White lemna with matching white leaves,
Scarlet plants lush with cinnabar blooms.
Gentle winds shake flag iris,
Rippling waves rock sweet lotus.
Glorious glints shimmer in the woods,
Drifting scents invade silky gauze.

A prince wanders without return,
Distant his road, far beyond reach.
With whom will I savour last sweetness?
I stand still alone and sigh.

Measure by measure sun and moon revolve,
Cold and heat abruptly fluctuate.
My sweetheart roams, alive to me no more,
Far, far, distantly sundered.
Through bedroom lattice uninvited comes the wind.
Doorway and garden bear no footprints.
Reeds grow beneath my bed,
Spiders spin round the four walls.

Heartfelt longings surely won't breed more?
Moved by nature they teem and hatch anew.
Roving geese wing to wing are gliding,
Homing swans know they are of a feather.
Come to me, oh man of mine!
Careless, idle, he keeps away.

P'AN YÜEH

Two 'Look homeward' poems

No. 1

I live in quiet, longing for my delight;
I climb the city wall and gaze on the four marshes.
Spring grass is lush green, green,
Mulberry and thorn dense, dense,
Fragrant forests shake scarlet splendour,
Green water hits white rocks.

When I first travelled, ice had not thawed.
Suddenly I'm shaking out summer clothes.
Wide, wide three thousand leagues,
Far, far recedes the distant traveller.

Racing passion desires her scarlet cheeks.
The inch of shadow extends beyond one foot.
Night grief lasts until clear dawn,
Morning sorrow abides into the dusk.

Mountains, rivers truly never-ending,
Desire clearly unattainable.
I lean forward, ask a homebound cloud.
Sinking thoughts find no comfort.

No. 2

Alone I pine. Where is the one I desire?
Human life is like the morning dew.
Through boundless space I cleave to my severed land,
With tender passion I remember the way we were.
Your love pursues me even here,
And my heart looks homeward to you.
Our bodies parted cannot touch,
Our souls embrace midway.

Don't you see the hilltop pine?
In dead of winter it never changes from old.
Don't you see the cypress in the glen?
In year-end chill it keeps the same appearance.
Don't say I sought this separation,
From far away the bonds of love grow firmer.

Two 'Bereavement' poems

No. 1

Sluggish winter bows out to spring,
Cold and heat suddenly fluctuate.
This child returns to Eternal Springs,
Heavy earth seals her lasting darkness.

Who can give rein to private feelings?
And what is the good of lingering on?
I try hard to perform court duties,
Turn my mind back to former tasks.

I stare at the hearth, thinking of that person,
Enter her room remembering the past.
Curtains, screen hold no fleeting image,
Pen and ink bear her last trace.
Drifting fragrance still not faded,
Her clothes are left hanging on the wall.
Ghostly faint, she seems to live on.
I feel nervous, uneasy, afraid.

Like those feathered birds of the woods,
Nesting mates bereaved one dawn.
Like those roving fish of the stream,
Eye to eye, then sundered midway.

The spring breeze visits through a crack,
Dawn moisture trickles down the eaves.
Asleep, rising, when will I forget?
Deep despair weighs heavier each day.
I crave the hour of my fading.
Chuang Chou's pot can still be drummed!

No. 2

White, white moon through a window
Shines on my room's south end.
Clear-tone winds usher autumn in,
Sultry heat ebbs with the season.
Bleak, bleak cold winds rise,
I begin to feel my summer quilt too flimsy.
I wouldn't say I have no thick clothes,
But with whom will I share year's end cold?

The year's end cold no one to share with.
The clear moon how it soars, soars!
I toss and turn, stare at pillow and mat.
The long mattress lies empty on the bed,
The bed lies empty, lost to clear dust.
To my vacant room mournful comes the wind.

97

I'm alone, have no vision of Lady Li.
Vague, faint, I glimpse your face.
I stroke my collar, sigh long sighs,
Tears unawares soak my breast,
Soak my breast, how can I stop them?
Sad longing wells deep inside me.

Asleep, awake, in my eyes your image lives on.
Your last words still echo in my ear.
First I'm shamed by Tung-men Wu the stoic,
Last I'm disgraced by Chuang Tzu of Meng.
I compose poems, try to tell of my feelings.
In bereavement it's hard to set them down.
How can fate be borne?
Prolonged grief brings ruin in its wake.

SHIH CH'UNG

Wang Chao-chün's farewell, one poem, with a preface

Preface: Originally, Wang Ming-chün's name was Wang Chao-chün, but because it violated the taboo name of Emperor Wen of the Chin Dynasty, Ssu-ma Chao, she had to be called Ming-chün. When the Huns were becoming more powerful, they demanded a Chinese bride. Emperor Yüan of the Han ordered Ming-chün, daughter of a good family and one of the ladies of the imperial harem, to become the Hun consort. Many years previously when a Chinese princess married into the Wusun tribe, the Han court arranged for music to be played on the balloon guitar while she rode away, in order to comfort her as she pined on the path from China. The escort for Ming-chün was exactly the same. The new song composed on that occasion was so full of sad regret that I set it down on paper. It goes like this:

Once I was the daughter of a Han family,
Now I go in marriage to the Shanyü court.
Before my farewell had ended,
Front riders were raising the banners.
The coachman's tears spilled down,
Shaft horses neighed with grief.
Oppressive sorrow hurt my whole body,
Falling tears soaked my pearl pomander.

On, on, each day we travelled further
Till we reached the Hsiungnu capital.
They drew me to a round tent,
Gave me the title of 'Princess'.
Their foreign race offered me no comfort,
Even their honours afforded me no glory.
By father and son I was cruelly defiled,
I felt shame and terror towards them.
Suicide would not be easy.
In silence I lived my mean life.

In my mean life what refuge had I?
Heavy thoughts always overwhelmed me.
I longed for the wings of a flying goose
To ride far away.
The flying goose would not look back.
I stood still, breathless and anxious.

Once I was jade in a jewel box,
Now I am a flower on a dungheap.
The blossom of dawn isn't worth its pleasure –
Better to lie alongside autumn grass!
These words I bequeath to men of the future:
Marriage far from home is hard on the heart.

A poem on a dainty girl

In my house there is a dainty girl,
Fair, fair, she glistens so very white,
Her nursery name is Silk Blanche.
Her mouth and teeth are finely chiselled,
Sidecurls sweep across her wide brow,
Twin ears are like the linked planets.

At daybreak she toys with cosmetic trays,
Kohl eyebrows look daubed and streaked,
Thick scarlet smears cinnabar lips,
Yellow beak is smudged with crimson gloss.

Dainty words like fine links in a chain,
She flies into a rage, then her words come clipped and clear.
Holding a pen she favours the cinnabar holder,
But her seal-script expects no prize!
Taking a book out, she admires its thick pure silk,
And in recitation she brags of what she's conned.

Her young sister's name is Orchid Sweet,
Her face and eyes glisten as if in a portrait.
Lightly dressed she frolics near the house,
Leaning near the mirror she forgets to reel thread.
She lifts a jar, copying Chang of the capital,
She applies beauty-spots, then changes them round,
Plays at sticking them between her eyebrows.

She rushes madly to work at loom and shuttle,
Calm and composed she loves the Chao dance,
Stretching out sleeves, image of wings in flight.
Whenever the string stops are raised or lowered,
Literature and history books are tucked away.

Coyly she eyes the painting on a screen,
As if she's seen something remarkable.
Cinnabar and green darken each day with dust,
Clear inscriptions become indecipherable.

They bolt and scuttle into the orchard,
Under fruit trees pick all the raw ones:
From red corollas tear purple calyx,
Alga blebs they quickly throw away.
Greedy for blossom even in a storm,
They hurtle outdoors hundreds of times.
They stamp hard, frisky in frosty snow,
Shoelaces in perpetual tangled heaps.

Twin hearts dote on choice morsels,
They sit straight and arrange tidbits on a dish.
Pen and ink gather in a box,
Often kept far out of sight.

They constantly rush out to the pedlar's gong,
Slippered feet go helter-skelter.
Impatient for tea leaves to brew,
They huff and they puff at his kettle.
Greasy fat smears white sleeves,
Soot stains fine silk.
Their clothes all a puddle of blots
Can't be scrubbed clean in water green as jade.

I'd let these kids do as they please,
They blush at adults' scolding.
But aware that a caning is due,
They swallow tears, both turned to the wall.

CHAPTER THREE

POETS OF THE CHIN DYNASTY
(THIRD AND FOURTH CENTURIES)

LU CHI

Seven poems in the style of old poems

In the style of 'North-west there is a tall house'

A tall house so sheer all round,
Far, far, sheer and serene.
Silken windows vault the dust beneath,
Flying stairs scale the cloudy horizon.

A lovely woman strokes her jasper lute
With slim fingers pure and soft.
Fragrant breath laces the breeze,
Sad echoes sweet as orchid.

Who could look back at her jade face?
For she destroys a city with one chord.
I stand still watching the sun go down,
Hesitate, give two or three sighs.
I wouldn't mind standing here longer,
I only want the singer's happiness.
I long to ride homing goose plumes,
Wing to wing we'd soar in paired flight.

In the style of 'The east city wall high and long'

The west hills, how sheer they are!
Layered folds loom rough and rugged.
Showering dew drops thickly from skies,
Orchid leaves fade, wilting in the woods.
Heat and cold succeed to one another,
Seasons vanish swift as ruins.

Ch'ü Yüan hitched his flying reins.
In old age we mourn the sinking rays.
Why be lured by worldly matters?
The heart within grieves at self-betrayal.

Ch'angan and Loyang are full of beauties,
Jade faces like jasper tendrils.
In hushed night they stroke plaintive lutes,
Harmonies clear and sad.
Crooning moves to a faster beat,
Sad notes follow heightened string-stops;
One song, ten thousand men sigh,
Two songs, rafter dust flies.
I dream we are birds of a river bend,
A roving pair along the fertile strand.

In the style of 'Orchid, flag-iris grow in spring sunshine'

The fine tree grows in dawn light,
Stiff frost enchains its boughs.
Steadfast its heart, faithful through the seasons,
Though the year grows old it refuses to wither.
A lovely woman, so remote is she,
Scintillates in cloudy mist.
Many a time I dream as years and months pass,
Whistle long to pierce the whirlwinds.
I crane my neck to stare at land's end,
Like the plant that reaches for the sun.

In the style of 'Far, far Herdboy star'

Bright, bright Han sky-river sparkles.
Radiant, radiant glitter her steps in the sky.
Herdboy turns north-west,
Weaver looks back south-east.
How silky her dainty face!
Her waving arms sway like white threads.

She hates that River without a bridge,
Mourns this year drawing to its close.
She slants across, but there's no wedded bliss;
Bright he shines, but cannot ford the River,
She cranes her neck, stares at its great flow.
Twin streams of tears like soaking dew.

In the style of 'Green, green riverside grass'

Downy, downy the sweet river grass,
Vivid spangles grow beside the river.
Pale, pale the pretty girl
Gracefully weaves at the eaves.
Glowing, glowing her bewitching face and figure,
Radiant her lovely face.
Her lover wanders with no return.
She nests apart, a lone, single wing.
To her empty room come mournful winds.
At midnight she gets up sighing sighs.

In the style of 'In the forecourt there is a wondrous tree'

My darling friend at orchid time departed,
Far, far, word of him is muted.
Yü Gulf drags down dying rays,
Four seasons pass as if in flight,
The sweet grass is long since mown.
My lovely one has not returned.

I walk in doubt by woods and shores,
Kind winds creep into my breast.
Moved by nature I desire my darling.
I pick, but who will have my gift?

In the style of 'Wading the river I pluck lotus blooms'

Uphill I pick jasper buds.
The hollow valley teems with sweet orchis.
I pick and pick, but don't have one handful,
Faraway dreaming of him I adore.

So remote our old village!
Mountains, rivers perilous and sheer.
Deep longing mantles ten thousand leagues.
Doubtful, alone, I breathe a sigh.

Two poems for Ku Yen-hsien to give his wife

No. 1

Farewell to home! I'm going far away,
Far and wide three thousand leagues.
Ch'angan and Loyang full of windy dust,
White clothes turn black.

I soothe my body's pain of bitter grief,
Moved by memories of my sweetheart.
Great longing troubles a corner of my heart,
Sunken desires slumber unwaking.

Desires sunken, never to revive,
My heart troubled, never to heal.
I long to borrow homing goose wings
To circle the streams of Chekiang.

No. 2

In the south-east there is a pining woman,
Long sighs fill her hidden bedroom.
May I ask, 'For whom do you sigh?'
'My lover is lost to the far horizon,
A circuit official long not returning.
Mountains and rivers far and wide,
Form and shadow, estranged Antares and Orion.
News from afar never comes through,
In partings and meetings, there is no constancy
Like the arrowhead with its bowstring.
I long to keep my body gold or rock firm,
To relieve my constant hunger and thirst.'

A poem for Lady Chou to give her equerry

From broken threads I weave sheer silk
To make you a single tunic.
You journey, won't you look back?
She longs for you, this woman her man.

Some time ago I got your letter,
Heard you lived in Grand Plains.
Today I get your letter,
Hear you live in the capital.

The capital is the place for flowery beauty,
Dazzling – it's a very different part.
Most men are intent on going far away,
But you must know that I, your wife, am thinking of you.

Some time ago when I parted from you
The year was fading, soon to fail.
Days, months all too swift!
White autumn sheds drenching dew.

Drenching dew steady, how steady!
Thoughts of you drag the year late.
I face my food, but cannot eat,
Lean over my winecup, but cannot drink.

Three folk-songs

Song of beauty, a ballad

From Leaning Mulberry a dawn glow risen
Shines on the brink of this high terrace.
The high terrace has many charming beauties,
From secret rooms peep bright faces.
Sweet looks glister in white sun,
Kind hearts, soft and pure.
Lovely eyes spread gleams of jade,
Moth eyebrows like kingfisher plumes.
Fresh skin, oh so smooth,
Vivid bloom it seems one could nibble.
Meek, mild, full of grace,
Enchantingly clever wit.

In late spring their spring clothes are made,
Scintillating silks and satins.
From gold sparrows hang wispy plumes,
Jasper pendants laced with fine jade.
A line of coaches raises clear dust.
They rinse their feet in Lo river ripples.

Hazy, hazy windblown clouds gather,
What a gay crowd of beauties!
South shore full of gauze veils,
North bank thick with carriages.

The clear river drinks in reed shadows,
High slopes carpeted with flower's cinnabar.
Sweet, sweet scented sleeves flutter,
Plink! plink! slim fingers strum.
Sad song breathes pure music,
Elegant dance sways to *Secret orchid*,
Cinnabar lips hum *Nine autumns*,
Delicate steps trace *Seven spirals*.
Overture tunes quicken like startled swans,
Finale rhythms are like flocking phoenix.
Exquisite poses change with their expressions,
A fathomless fountain of limpid shapes.
Up and down they look, all soft and tender,
Backward glancing steps are delightful.
Last scents blend with whirling winds,
Floating shadows mirrored in clear streams.
Their charms I have no power to praise.
For such pleasure I might well sigh!

A short opening song

Flitting sprites cluster in magic haunts,
Meet on high in layered mountain nooks.
Long winds lift ten thousand leagues,
Balmy clouds hover in sheer peaks.

Fufei appears from Lo river bank.
Wang and Han scale great Mount Hua.
The North summons the girl of Jasper Terrace,
The South demands Fairy Radiance of Hsiang river.

Swift, swift sky carriage moves,
Twirl, whirl kingfisher canopy plumes.
On feather pennants perch magic bird bells,
Jade axles murmur sonorously.

T'ai Yung plucks strings shrill,
Hung Yai bursts into clear song.
Pledgecups now pass round,
Light wheels mount purple haze.

They hitch reins on Leaning Mulberry boughs,
Rinse their feet in Bright Valley waves.
Pure rays flood the Gates of Heaven,
Blessings pour down on the royal house.

Along the embankment, a ballad

Sweet river grass grows on hidden isles,
Faint scent barely spreading.
A happy marriage of wind and rain
Has moved you to a lake's flowered bank.
Blades sprout near a jade terrace,
Cast shadows on blue grotto depths.
Now sleek with moisture rich
Your roots entwine deep and firm.

The four seasons course unresting,
Glorious blooms cannot stay fresh long.
Fair weather fails with the season,
Last scents fade with the wind.

Natural law has its shifts and turns,
Moral law lacks saving constancy.
When men seek pleasure, the smart defeat the dull;
Of women in love the withered avoid the sleek.

I do not pity my poor rejected body,
But fear the blueflies' gossip.
I long for your last broad wave of light
To shine on my sparse fading years.

Four poems, letters and replies, for Ku Yen-hsien to give his wife

No. 1

I am in Three Rivers sunshine,
You live in Five Lakes shadow.
Mountains, seas, a gulf so vast,
Like the gulf between fliers and divers.

My eyes imagine your clear kind face,
My ears hold echoes of your good sweet voice.
I sleep alone with many far-off memories,
Then waken, caressing your empty collar.
Oh beautiful heart of my heart!
Except you, who would hold my heart?   (from the husband)

No. 2

Far, far away you journey on,
Alone, all alone, your wife remains here.
How to cross mountains and rivers?
Forever cut off, road of ten thousand leagues.

Mansions in the capital are full of pretty charms,
Brilliant, brilliant are the city people.
Elegant they step with soft, slim waists,
Bewitching smiles show white teeth.
Their loveliness is so enviable,
This ugly wretch is hardly worth a mention!
I received your fond words from a distance,
I cherish the kind thought unexpected.   (from the wife)

No. 3

Flurry, flurry windblown tumbleweed travels,
Lovely, lovely cold tree glorious.
To wander, to stop, to each his own nature.
To float, to sink, surely no two natures are alike.

Great love wed us in the past,
Vows of fidelity bound us to the Three Gods.
I keep my heart metal and rock firm –
How could I be ruined by common fashion?
Lovely eyes pass by, but I don't look,
Slender waists are nubile in vain.
What shall I use to pledge my deep affection?
I look up and point at that pole-star!   (from the husband)

No. 4

He who sails the ocean finds rivers dull.
He who roams forests finds other scenes dull.
Beauty at its peak more precious grows,
The flower of dawn mourns the passing day.

Pale, pale those pretty girls,
Bright, bright, kissed by spring's sparkle.
The west side is skilled at courtly dance,
Concert halls resound with clear strumming.
Tuneful pipes ring out from cinnabar lips,
Scarlet strings vibrate beneath white wrists.
Light skirts quiver like lightning,
Twin sleeves streak like mist.
Flower faces suffuse spangled curtains,
Sad echoes pierce Cloudy Han.

Few in the world appreciate such music,
Except you, who could appraise them?
Throw aside your pole-star –
Solicit those Dark Dragon starlets.
Time grows late, no more words.
A wilting bloom must of course be worthless.   (from the wife)

CHANG HSIEH

A miscellaneous poem

Autumn night. Cold winds stir.
Pure air exiles torpid heat.
Crickets chirp beneath the steps,
Flying moths brush candles bright.

A lord serves on a distant campaign,
His lovely lady keeps to solitude.
Living apart, how much longer?
The fire-drill soon changes kindling.

Bedroom lattice, no passing footsteps,
Garden grass a wilderness of green.
Emerald moss clings to the lonely fence,
Spiders weave webs around four walls.
Troubled by nature, her passion deepens,
Sinking despair clogs the corners of her heart.

YANG FANG

Five 'Joy of love' poems

No. 1

Tigers roar, valley winds rise,
Dragons leap, iridescent clouds scud.
Like sounds accord with each other,
Like souls seek each other out.

My love is close to you
As shadow follows form.
For food we share grain from the same root,
For drink we share a kissing-bough cup.
The clothes we wear are double-thread silk,
In bed we share a seamless quilt.

At home I long to kneel by your side,
On the road hasten to hold your hand.
You rest, I do not move,
You journey, I will not stay behind.
Like those birds of one heart,
Like the fish that swim eye to eye.

My passion aroused splits metal or rock,
Is stronger than glue mixed with lacquer.
My one desire is never to part,
That we'll make our bodies one.
In life we'll be the double-body thing,
In death we'll be dust in the same grave.
The girl of Ch'in bragged of high ideals,
My love for you can find no rival.

No. 2

Magnet attracts long needle,
Speculum pours down fiery smoke,
Do and *re* notes harmonize with each other,
Sweethearts cling close together.

My love is married to you
As shadow pursues body.
In bed we share a close-weave quilt,
Padded with floss of clustered cocoons.

In the heat we flutter fans wing to wing,
In the cold we sit on rugs side by side.
You laugh, I'm sure to smile,
You're sad, I feel no joy.

Coming I tread in your footprints,
Going I walk in your dust.
We are like the fabled double creature,
No matter what, we'll never lose each other.

All I desire is never to part,
That our bodies will become one.
In life we'll share a happy home,
In death be joint-grave dwellers.
Lady Hsü bragged of high ideals,
My love can find no words.

No. 3

Alone I sit in our empty room.
Sorrow has many thousand beginnings.
Sad echoes answer sorrowful sighs,
Unhappy tears respond to bitter words.

I wander and gaze all around,
The white sun enters western hills.
I do not see my handsome one approaching,
I only see birds flying home –
Flying birds, and so joyfully
They nest at night, each to its own flock.

No. 4

Flying Chestnut champs long reins,
Winging, winging turns the light wheels.
My lover looks down as he fords green flowing torrents,
Looks up as he crosses the hill's nine folds.
The long path is winding and perilous,
Autumn plants grow on both sides.

Yellow blooms like heaps of gold,
White flowers like scattered silver,
Green buds shoot kingfisher tints,
Crimson corollas image red clouds.

And in their midst dew-laden boughs,
Purple blossoms enshrining plain scent
Hang luxurious in patterns crystalline,
Wafting fragrance and freshness.

My eyes grow dizzy with glorious designs,
My mind whirls with wondrous colours.
I soothe my heart, mourn the lone traveller,
Look down and up, feel self-pity.
I pause with a sigh by the garden wall,
Take my pen and compose this verse.

No. 5

My south neighbour has a fine tree,
It greets the sun, stretches white blooms,
Sleek fronds sheathe long boughs,
Green leaves screen red stems.
With the wind it breathes faint whispers,
Perfumed air pierces purple mist.

My heart burns for this tree,
I long to move it near my home.
At dusk I would stroll underneath,
At dawn caress its corollas.

How deep and firm the roots!
So mean and low my home!
To transplant it is a hopeless dream,
The sighs I sigh, what good are they?

A poem on watching Weaver star on Seventh Night

Herdboy is sad in his alien lodge,
Weaver mourns in her exiled home.
Once a year the promise of one night,
This promise of true pleasure.

Majestic the Dark Gates open
To flying arcades massed in crested peaks.
Rumble, rumble a thousand coaches coursing,
Rattle, rattle they cross the starry stream.
Six dragons strain at jasper reins,
Streaked serpents bear her jade carriage.

Flaming Cinnabar raises her jasper torch,
White Girl holds nephrite blooms.
Crimson banners seem to shoot lightning,
Scarlet canopies appear like swaying mist.
Cloud gate, *Nine chord*, how the fanfare roars!
Drums of the gods beat measured rhythms.

She stops her coach, turns her gaze on high,
Looks back for me on sheer cliffs.
Soaked in sweet dew moist
His favour, enriched with orchid breezes.
Till daybreak they pleasure together,
Phoenixes fluttering circle round.

Pleasure shared, but joy is not ours to share,
I remember you, and anguished grief deepens.
Humbly I implore through the Trinity Prayer,
That you may rank with Huang O the goddess.

LI CH'UNG

Parody of a lover

Sweethearts, we felt the same pleasure,
So deeply were we entwined and entangled.
Long ago you sensed my feelings,
And I knew of your love.

Serene years went by
Harmonious as lute and harp.
Good times did not keep me company,
Midway we grew distant like Antares and Orion.
You separated south of northern hills,
I was apart, south of south river.
Happy joy no longer sought,
Heavy thoughts, how to bear them?

My eyes bear the image of your lovely form,
My ears hold the sound of your clear voice.
Through the day endless memories surge,
Far into night I sigh in lonely grief.

When you were leaving on circuit
And said we must part, tears soaked my collar.
Please honour me with your jade footsteps,
One look is worth more than a thousand in gold.

TS'AO P'I

In the night I hear fulling

Cold begins, and preparing pure-white silks
Lovely women make up fitted quilts ready
For wintry nights clear and long
When the white moon shines in dark halls.

As slim hands fold light silks,
Clear the pounder bangs the thudding block.
On pure breezes drift their complex rhythms,
Gusting winds with faint humming are sprinkled.

I sigh for time's swift flow.
Alas for this swift passing!
Two objects that disturb my emotions –
Are they just sound and noise?

T'AO CH'IEN

In the style of an old poem

Sunset, cloudless skies,
Spring breezes fan faint warmth.
A beauty, lovely in clear night,
Till dawn she drinks deep and sings.
Her singing ends, she sighs long sighs,
For these disturb her more.
Bright, bright moon between clouds,
Sparkling, sparkling flowers among leaves.
Why not be fair for this hour?
In a while how then will they be?

Two folk-songs

In the style of 'We met in a narrow alley'

Dawn breaks in Hantan city.
Dusk brings quiet to Well Path.
Well Path is so very narrow,
Horse and coach cannot move.

Suddenly I happen to meet you,
We exchange a word on the rough track,
A word, no room for more.
I lean on the rail, ask about your house.

Your house is easy to recognize,
Easy to recognize and easy to find.
South it fronts on to Lord P'ingyüan's residence,
North it runs to Lin Hsiang-ju's pavilion.

Flying storeys overlook the famed city,
Avenue gates lean over flowery suburbs.
You enter the gates, not a soul to be seen,
All you see are pairs of roosting storks.
Roosting storks in several tens
And mandarin ducks flocked in rows.

Your oldest brother wears gold earrings,
Your middle brother flaunts capstring tassels.
Summer and winter feastdays they come home
And neighbouring hamlets grow in splendour.
Your youngest brother has nothing to do
But go to cockfights at east lane crossroads.

The eldest's wife weaves fine silks,
The next wife sews sheer robes,
The youngest wife has nothing to do
But hug her lute and play sonorous stops.
'Dear husband, don't leave your seat –
Rafter dust is going to fly!'

In the style of 'Green, green riverside grass'

Glow, glow fires on the hill.
Far away Lung East is remote.
Lung East I cannot reach,
Our souls become one as we sleep.

As we sleep we share quilt and bedcurtain,
Suddenly I wake in another land.
Another land, each in a strange city.
We each search, but never find each other.
Lost in the wilds, I stay staring through the smoke.
Trees have shed, I sense the ice is hard.

Up at court each man is bent on self-advancement.
Who will want to promote you?
A traveller came from the north part,
He brought me a piece of thick black silk.
I asked my maid to open the black silk,
Inside was an embossed cryptic jade disc.
I bow low and read the cryptic disc.
The words are bitter and the tone is anguished.
The top says, 'Let's both try and cheer up.'
Below it says, 'I'll always love you.'

Two miscellaneous poems

No. 1

A mulberry wife alone, what am I longing for?
In my tilted basket not yet one handful.
I tell myself my many bitter sorrows.
Though I brush them aside, they won't go away.

A wife's sorrow cannot be told,
My burden of grief will not melt away.
A cold goose going home where I would follow
Midway has lost her helpmate.

Impetuous he clapped and galloped off,
Wildly in defence of court and altar.
He ever yearned to cleanse the Han shame,
Ever wished to restore Chou glory.
Prizing fame he sought his memorial writ on stone,
Scorning life he desired a hero's epitaph.
Ten thousand leagues he crossed the sandy wastes,
With far-flung troops trod the northern wilds.

I heard tell of troops defeated,
But I saw nobody come back home.
Where did they bury the flags?
Where were horse and chariot interred?

I soothe my heart, mourn my honest man,
Falling tears drop and sheet my face.
He only said we'd be parted long,
I never looked for lasting widowhood.
Soft, soft I shut the tall gates;
Alone, alone, empty wide eaves.
I waited for you, you didn't come home at last.
Now I compose my face and go towards my coffin.

No. 2

A wife in love leans from a high terrace,
Faraway she dreams and yearns from flowery eaves.
She strums the strings but doesn't finish her tune,
In sad song bids goodbye to bitter words.

His dust-and-mop was left behind at the river,
Her fine man lives at Goose Gate Pass.
Why dwell on his robeless misery?
All she knows is white fox-fur warmth.

Day darkens, cattle and sheep move down,
Birds of the wild fill the empty orchard.
Fierce winter's cold winds stir,
East Wall star appears due south in dusk.

Scarlet flame, shine on a lonely one,
Embrace my shadow, sad with its own regret.
Who will know the tempest deep in my heart?
To my beloved I cannot speak.

HSIEH HUI-LIEN

*On the seventh day of the seventh month I write a poem
on Herdboy and the Girl stars*

The sinking sun hides behind eaves and pillars,
The soaring moon illumines bedroom lattice.
Drip, drop, the dew fills the leaves,
Creak, creak, the wind tosses branches.

I stamp my feet down the wide courtyard,
Blink as I gaze at the serried dome.
In Cloudy Han there's the divine couple,
They pass the year waning in pursuit.

The distant river thwarts their passionate love,
The long shore dims his clear image.
She works her shuttle, never ends her pattern,
She tugs the reins, gallops swiftly forward.

They parted long ago, two autumns now,
They meet tonight, a night that won't be double.
The sloping river she easily circles,
The face of desire not long enjoyed.

Glossy her coach divine glides round,
Soft veils of cloud form a void.
Forlorn love looks back to flowery sleep,
His faraway heart follows her racing dragons.
I sigh, deeply moved by you,
Profound feeling makes my love the keener.

Fulling cloth

Scales' cycle does not stay its course,
Time's motion suddenly seems to hasten.
White dew soaks orchard chrysanthemum,
Autumn winds make garden locust trees shed.
Twitch, twitch grasshopper wings,
Chill, chill cold cicada cry.
Darkness of dusk wreathes empty curtains,
Gloaming moon whitens an inner bedroom.

A lovely woman prepares clothes,
Neatly groomed she holds her friend's hand.
Hairpin jade leaves the north room,
Tinkling gold treads down south stairs.

Verandas tall with fulling-block echoes ring,
Pillars long with pounder thuds moan.
Faint perfume lifts from two sleeves,
Light sweat glistens on twin brows.

Fine white silk is now ready,
Her lord journeys, not yet home.
For cutting she uses cabinet scissors,
Sewing she makes his ten-thousand-league robe.

Snugly encased with her own hands,
Tightly sealed, patient for her lord to open.
'My waist sash measures the same as long ago –
I don't know today if that is good or bad.'

In the manner of old verse

A traveller came from a far place;
He presented me with swan-pattern damask
Stored in a 'loving you' case
Tied with 'sweethearts' string.

I cut it into a gown next to my body,
Stuff it with 'sleeping together' floss.
Since you left the yearly seasons pass,
My loving heart can journey no more.

Sprinkle some wine in a well –
Who can tell from the scooped measure?
Mix up river waters in a cup –
Who could judge the Tzu from Sheng river?

LIU SHUO

Five miscellaneous poems

In the manner of 'On, on, ever on and on'

A tiny dot, braving the far road
Way, way off, I go travelling further on.
I turn my coach away from the capital
Waving farewell to all that.

In the hall shifting dust will spread,
In the garden green grass will grow rampant.
Cold cicadas flit across the river bend,
Autumn hares hug the foothills.

In the scented season there's a flowery moon.
My lovely one gives no promise of return.
Twilight's cool wind stirs,
I face wine in love with you for ever.
Sorrow pours forth in the *South of the River* tune,
Despair is banished by *Your collar* poem.

Lying down I watch the bright lamp dimming,
Sitting up I see my light silk is dingy.
Tearful face long unadorned,
Darkened mirror I can no longer polish.
Please send down last wan rays
To brighten my Mulberry-Elm time.

In the manner of 'The bright moon white, so white'

Sinking stars halfway over far walls,
Floating clouds veil serried turrets.
From the jade vault come pure winds,
Silk curtains stretch out to the autumn moon.

Wrapped in thought she dreams of that man,
Sunk in despair she longs for day to break.
Who'd have thought a man would travel so long?
Many a time she's seen flowing fragrance fade.
Waters wide, river without a bridge,
Mountains high, paths denying passage.

In the manner of 'Fierce winter's cold air has come'

White dew, autumn winds start,
Autumn winds, the bright moon is new,
The bright moon shines on tall storeys,
White dew blanches dark porches.
Now is the time cold clouds rise.
As I walk I see chill woods bare.

A traveller came from a far place
Presenting me with a thousand-league letter.
First it said, 'I long for my old love.'
Last it stated, 'Long must we live apart.'

At the first reading its meaning wasn't fully grasped,
By the third time my heart was overwhelmed.
Please grant me a life of fond regard,
Don't let your sweet words prove hollow!

In the manner of 'Green, green riverside grass'

Bleak, bleak Sip Dew Terrace,
Brisk, brisk Welcome Breeze Lodge.
A girl in love goes out to curving eaves,
Her sad heart transfixes Cloudy Han.
Sitting straight, she strokes sad strings and weeps,
Alone she faces the bright lamp and sighs.
Her beloved has been on campaign long,
Virginal pure she passes dusk to dawn.
Sharp and clear her *Autumn river* song,
Wistful, wistful *Picking caltrop* strumming.

A poem on Herdboy and the Girl stars

Autumn rustles, clear winds fan,
Fire star veers, fiery air subsides.
Wide lattice breathes in shades of night,
Tall eaves touch the evening moon.

Gentle she steps, circling scented woods,
Upward she stares beyond cloudy turrets.
Fringed drapes rimming Han unfold,
Her dragon coach crowning the skies emerges.
Who says Long river is distant?
It's just as soon crossed as a mat!
Before their deep love has been told,
Flying dawn light suddenly flickers.
Tomorrow's meeting is remote, hopeless.
Today's joy from this hour is dead.

CHAPTER FOUR

POETS OF THE SOUTHERN DYNASTIES
(EARLY FIFTH CENTURY)

WANG SENG-TA

Beneath the moon on Seventh Night

Over faraway hills swirling mist thickens,
On a broad garden rippling moonlight streams.
Summer air subsides, winds press through cracks,
Autumn returns, dew glistens on the bough.
Now the hot season is fading
She shakes out sheer silk mid-heaven.
The joy to come only lasts one night,
Gathering tears spill on the River that divides.

YEN YEN-CHIH

For Weaver girl to give Herdboy star

Fair Maid star couples with Warp stars,
Ch'ang O nestles on the gliding moon.
I'm ashamed to be without these beauties' divine power
To offer myself to serve at Heaven's towers.
The Gates of Heaven are not shining yet,
How can I wash my hair in Hsien pool?
On Han's dark south night curtains are not drawn,
For whom will I cross Long River?
Though there's promise of a feast soon,
I must wait for cold winds to blow.
I count in vain the Two Discs' revolutions,
Idly languish while Three Stars fade.
I don't resent shuttle and spindle labours,
I just think how flowery fragrance fades.

A poem on Ch'iu Hu

Catalpa lean toward lofty phoenix,
Cold Valley waits for singing pipes.
Shadow and echo, aren't they in love?
Distant though they are, each has a mate.

Lovely the girl in her hidden room
When she became wife in her lord's home.
Strict her virtue, taut with autumn frost,
Radiant her beauty, like the morning sun.
'Good fortune is with us now,
We dearly hope it lasts all our days.'

Serenely they lived, but before it reached its best
Her beloved recalled he had to go away.
He removed his headband to go beyond ten thousand leagues,
Tied on official ribbons to go up to the royal domain.
He ordered his servants to come at break of dawn,
His followers all came to his side.
Driven in his coach he left the suburbs,
His path slow and winding.
If he lived, they would be parted long,
If he died, he would nevermore return.

Oh I hate official travel!
Three hills I suffer from dawn to dark.
Hitching coaches tight we trek through winds chill,
Unsaddling we brave frosty dew.
High plains, wet lowlands redouble our misery,
Whirlwinds roll tall trees.
Scattered beasts appear in wild trails,
Frightened birds go off in criss-cross lines.
How wretched is the official on circuit!
He struggles along paths of crag and creek.

Far away the traveller grows distant,
Smoothly roll the years away.
That happy hours turned to such a parting!
Days and months are drawing close to summer.
Who knows how many hot and cold seasons will mass up?
In a glance I see the blossoming and the withering.
The year ends, I go towards my empty room,

Cold winds stir from the corners.
In bed or rising I feel the days grow colder,
White dew grows on garden weeds.

I worked hard, then gave in to homeward longings,
The road back skirts hills and rivers.
Long ago I said goodbye before autumn whitened,
And now it is the season of flowers.
In silkworm months I see a time of rest,
In mulberry fields all is busy movement.
A lovely girl doing her work,
Graceful she draws high branches down.
Who wouldn't look back at this city-destroyer?
I slow my pace, pause halfway up the ridge.

As the years had passed he'd truly suffered for love.
His work was distant, word and image remote.
Though it was a five-year separation,
Each was a stranger to the other's normal life.
He leaves his coach, treads his old path,
A duck among water plants he gives a quick wink.
Southern gold he by no means undervalues,
But at such a time he counts it as little!
Married love brings many sorrows.
Intimate is the sound of his gold and jade.

Her high principles forbid him to dally.
At long last he leaves her, nothing won.
Slow, slow he covers the old path,
Eager, eager he reaches his gatepost.
Going up the hall he offers respectful greetings,
Entering their room he asks, 'Where is she?'
'At sunset she comes home from picking,
At nature's Mulberry-Elm time.'
A beautiful woman arrives towards dusk.
He gasps with shock – he'd been with her before!

Who can stop love once love happens?
Let's tell of this wife's own hardship.
We lived apart year in, year out.
Once parted, river and pass blocked our way.
Spring comes, perhaps he no longer enjoys it?
Autumn is falling, he must feel the cold soon?

Till daybreak I fret my sad heart away,
In my room I rise with long sighs.
Bitter is the pain with the darkening year
As the sun sinks down on my wanderer's face.

Playing high notes causes broken strings,
Intense music comes from high-pitched chords.
Long ago when I bent before your bright dust
We vowed to be true from first to last.
Aren't you who made our parting so long
To blame for all that's gone wrong?
Since you betrayed our pure marriage,
With whom will I end my days?
I'm the disgraced woman of the *Dewdrops* poem.
I'd better drown myself in the long river.

PAO CHAO

Nine miscellaneous poems

Admiring the moon from the west city gate

First seen over south-west houses,
Fine, fine as a jade hook;
Later reflected on a north-east porch,
Soft, soft like a moth eyebrow.
Moth eyebrows screened by pearl grilles,
Jade hooks set apart by silken windows.
At the time of the fifteenth and sixteenth
It shines one thousand leagues on you and me alike.
Night moves on, Scales and Han stars set,
It shimmers still through curtained doors.
Departing flowers bent by early dew,
Loosened leaves soon dismissed by winds.

A man on travels hates the hardship, and
This official is weary of windblown dust.
Happily today I'm free from work,
A time for feasting at my own pleasure.

Shu lutes play *White snow*,
Ying melodies render *Sunny spring*.
Fine food has been eaten, wine not run out,
The gold clock-jar starts its evening trickle.
I turn my coach, fix its light canopy,
Linger over drinks and wait for my darling.

In the manner of the 'Lo capital city' piece

Phoenix houses twelve deep
With four doors and eight silk windows,
Broidered rafters with golden lotus,
Cassia pillars with jade coiling dragons,
Pearl blinds that don't keep out the dew,
Sheer drapes that don't ward off the wind,
Exquisite curtains in thirty million rooms –
All for your face one morning!

Incense perfume spreads over purple smoke,
Tints drop down into green swirling clouds.
Spring piping turns the white sun back,
Frost-time songs bring frontier swans sinking down.
All I fear is autumn dust will rise,
Love's bloom will follow withered tumbleweed.
Sitting up I see green lichen's rank fullness,
Lying down I face mattress brocade emptiness.
Lutes, guitars jumbled in heaps,
Dancing dresses hanging unsewn.
Since time began love always withers,
How will your love alone thrive?
Just watch that pair of brown geese
Follow each other a thousand leagues.

In the style of the folk-song, 'The white head lament'

Straight as silk of scarlet strings,
Pure as ice in a jade jar,
Why should I be ashamed of past love?
Jealous hate wells up inside me.

People in love despise favours grown old,
Public opinion shuns failure, courts success.
Once a flaw minute as a hair appears
Even mountains won't fail to crumble.

The seedling gobbler is the big rat,
The whiteness smircher is the bluebottle.
Ducks and geese from afar become prized,
Firewood and feed are valued out of all proportion.
Queen Shen was deposed when Paossu was promoted.
Lady Pan retired when Chao Feiyen was in ascendance.
Each day the king of Chou sank deeper in obsession.
The Han emperor sang her praises ever louder.
Their doting admiration was unreliable,
A courteous veneer is not something to trust.
Since time began it's always been like this –
You aren't the only one beating your breast!

A poem on picking mulberry

Late spring plum starts falling,
Women's work turns to silkworm care.
They pick mulberry between Ch'i and Wei rivers,
Or play near Upper Palace pavilion.
Early reedmace weaves timely shade,
Late bamboo begins to shed bark.
Hazy, hazy mists fill boudoirs,
Soft, soft sunlight floods curtains.
Nursing swallows hunt for grass insects,
Bees harvest petals for their hives.
This is the season of warmest charms,
Once again beauty's dress is dazzling fresh.

I silence my sighs, face the distant road,
Pour out my song, play *Beanleaves in my patch*,
Pluck my lute, try to soothe my pining.
I offer you my girdle to show my full trust in you.
Please praise my song like the man from Ying!
In my faithful heart I'm thankful for your favour.
Wei songs have always been thought depraved,
Cheng morals long considered debauched.
I mourn Ch'ü Yüan's idle dream to ford the Hsiang,

I smile at Ts'ao Chih's rhapsody on crossing the Lo.
The peak of beauty never comes twice,
The gulf of love, for whom will it run dry?
You, my lord, why don't you strum the strings
While I, your wife, pour a measure of cassia wine.

A poem on dreaming of home

Biting back tears I leave the suburb gate,
Stroke my sword at deserted crossroads.
Sandy winds rise dark along the border,
My exiled heart stares to my village and realm.
Midnight. I go to my orphan pillow,
Imagine in my dreams I've gone home in an instant:
My widowed wife sighs at the door,
Unwinding silk she makes the loom hum again.
We talk happily of our long separation,
Return together to silk bedcurtains.
Faint, faint chill beneath the eaves,
Dim, dim gleam in the window.
Cut orchids compete with her fragrance,
Plucked chrysanthemum contends with her bloom.
From opened boxes she gathers sweet herbs,
Feels inside her sleeve, unties sachet strings.
In my sleep the long road grew nearer,
After I woke the great river cut me off.
I got up afraid, sighed futile sighs,
My fevered soul flew forward.
White river in spate menaced, menaced,
High mountains grim loomed large.
Billowing tides change from flux to ebb,
Windy frost turns bloom to decay.
This land is not my land,
In deep despair, who can I speak to?

In the style of old verse

Riverside grass has not yellowed,
Hun geese are spreading their wings,
Autumn crickets moan huddled against the door,
A chill wife weaves from dawn to dusk.

Last year a soldier came home
Bringing news of one she knew long ago.
I hear that when you climbed Lung range
You stared east sighing long sighs,
And that overnight your coat and belt turned looser,
Between dawn and dusk your colour had changed.
Imagine how anxious this makes me!
As nights lengthen, anxiety grows sharper.
My bright mirror lies in its dusty case,
My precious lute is overspread with cobwebs.

A lyric poem on swallows

A pair of swallows plays near cloudy cliffs
Feathered quills go bobbing up and down.
In and out of the south boudoir they come,
Through the north hall they go,
Longing to nest in your curtains,
But a tall pillar they cannot spy.
Panting while the scented season grows late,
Hesitant as spring glory departs,
With sad song they leave their old love,
Beaks full of mud they seek a new friend.

To my former love, two poems

No. 1

Cold ash dies, flares once more,
Evening flowers freshen at dawn once more.
Spring ice, though thawed for a while,
Hardens once again into winter ice.
My lover cast me off,
Bonds of love true broken for ever.
Happiness comes, but never stays,
Each time I'm moved it's the wounding year.

A pair of swords about to be separated
First cried out in their case.
In night smoky rain they became one,
From then on they took different forms.
The female sank in Wu river water,
The male flew into Ch'u city.
Wu river is deep, fathomless,
Ch'u city has forbidding portals.
Once the sky was separated from the earth
Wasn't that the same as light gone from darkness?
Divine things do not part for ever,
In one thousand years they'll still come back together.

WANG SU

A poem in imitation of Infantry Officer Juan Chi's style

Deep love arouses distant longing,
Coils of obsession bring dreams of my love.
Muffled notes I hear of pan-pipe and flute,
A singing phoenix welcomes Lady Ying.
They leave together on cloudy wings,
Joyfully happy, holding hands.

I say to those in the flush of beauty:
Love's favour, good fortune won't last for ever!
When Ching and Wei rivers divide they're clear and muddy –
Read that in the *Valley wind* poem!

WU MAN-YÜAN

Four poems in the folk-song style

There came flying a pair of white swans

A pretty pair of white swans
Double, double, far from dusty chaos;
Wings embracing, they play in bright sunlight,
Necks caressing roam the blue clouds.
Felled by nets or felled by corded arrow
Hen and cock are parted one dawn.
Mournful sounds drift down river bends,
Orphan cries come from river banks.
'It's not that I don't long for my former mate,
But because of you I won't reach my flock.'
Drop by drop she sheds a tear.
'A thousand years, I'll still wait for you!'
How happy to fall in love,
So sad, separation in this life.

Let's cling to this hundred-year span,
Let's chase after each inch of time's shadow,
As the grass on an empty hill
Knows in its heart it will wither and die.

Sunny spring tune

I stare at Hsienyang one hundred leagues away,
I can tell it's the imperial capital.
Green trees sway with cloud and light,
The spring city stirs with billowing colour.
A beauty loves its sparkling flowers,
Dappled shimmers beside her garden bank.
Her charming face is the gorgeous moon's image,
Her silk clothes cicada wings ruffled.
Though Sung Yü sang *Sunny spring*,
Man of Pa brought the deepest sighs.

140

The *Odes* and *Cheng airs* aren't valued the same,
Don't these last make your heart ache?
All my life I will treasure your kind love,
For my single self, is there an end to pity?

Long separation

I cannot bear to hear of lifetime parting,
Much less long separation between us.
Why be apart from you
When at the peak of beauty?
Each time the orchid bloom trembles
For your wife's heart it's an empty comfort.
My bloom lacks the rapture of plants and trees,
My wilting surpasses the gloom of frosty dew.
Wealth and status slow down the body's ageing,
Poverty and misery hurry on the year's waning.
To be comforted by that would wrench my guts,
As you might guess yourself.

At Huaiyin there was the famous general, Han Hsin;
He broke his wings rather than soar.
In Ch'u the warrior Hsiang Yü lifted heavy cauldrons;
He left his gates and never got back home.
Just for the sake of a Duke Highnose
You grip your sword, enter Tzu-wei galaxy.
Maybe your talent is like these men?
But the white sun falls with struggling gleams.

I'll always love you

At dawn there was a traveller on the road.
Wistful, wistful he neared our gateway,
Man and horse the colour of windy dust,
I knew they were from the river border.
Once I had a fellow nestler,
He joined up, wandered to Hantan,
No different from this traveller,
Sharing in his hunger and at one with him in cold.
May I trouble you with my foot-long silk letter?
My inch of heart is bared inside it:

'Left behind, your wife is always tired and thin.
How can I sing again with my face in smiles?
Eaves shadowed by trees of a thousand frosts,
Garden orchids countless decades have died.
Passing spring never lifts my sleeves,
Autumn's fall I prefer to watch no more.'
Once you see him, please tell of my love:
'Your gates are locked ninefold.
Yü Ch'ing threw away his minister's seal
To carry an umbrella for his sweetheart.
In my room's shadows there'll be an early frost;
What business makes you dilly-dally for nothing?'

PAO LING-HUI

Six miscellaneous poems

In the style of 'Green, green riverside grass'

Slim, slim bamboo bends across my window,
Thick, thick catalpa leans over the gate.
Glowing, glowing a girl by green eaves,
Icy, icy in her tall terrace.
Her bright ideals beggar autumn frost,
Her jade face enriches spring pink.
In human life who doesn't part?
I hate you for enlisting so fast!
Tinkling on my strings I'm shamed by the night moon,
Indigo kohl shames me in the spring breezes.

In the style of 'A traveller came from a far place'

A traveller came from a far place
Presenting me with a lacquered tuneful lute.
On the wood there's a 'loving you' design,
Its strings have the key of 'farewell'.

All my life I will keep this chord,
The year grown cold will not change my heart.
I long to compose a *Sunny spring* tune
With *do* and *re* for ever in pursuit.

Poem sent as a postscript to a traveller

Ever since you went away
I lean by the porch, my face is tense.
Our pounder and block no longer thud at night,
Tall gates at noon stay locked.
Into my bedcurtains drift fireflies,
In the forecourt purple orchids bloom.
Nature withers, sensing the change of season,
Swans arrive that know of travellers cold.
Your journey will take till late winter to end,
But I'll wait beyond spring for your return.

An old theme addressed to a modern person

In the cold regions there's no seasonal change of clothes,
Except wool is worn instead of our patterned silks.
Month after month I watch for you to come home,
Year after year you never untie your capstring.
In Ching and Yang spring is early and mild,
Yu and Chi still have frost and hail.
Your northern cold your wife already knows,
My southern heart you will never see.
Who will tell of my bitter pain for me?
I'll send my feelings by a pair of flying swallows:
My figure is gaunt, silk consumed in a shuttle,
My face has withered, lightning chased by winds.
Lovely looks may vanish in one morning,
But to the end my heart will never change.

Two poems in the manner of the poem presented to Ko Sha-men by his wife, Kuo Hsiao-yü

No. 1

Bright moon white, so white
Through hanging curtains shines on a silk bed,
Appearing to join our night of love,
Seeming to share my dawn of despair.
Fragrant flowers, surely you feel for my looks?
Frosty dew, you spare no one!
My love, you aren't a blue cloud passing by,
But you hover around on business in Hsien-Ch'in.
Your wife carries a lifetime of tears
Passing through autumn and passing the spring.

No. 2

When my love was about to go on distant campaign
He left me a pair of inscribed brocades.
Towards the time he was due to leave
He also left me his 'loving you' pillow.
The inscription I always have pressed to my heart,
With his pillow I dream we're sleeping together.
On, on, each day further on,
The more I feel, the worse my pining gets!

CH'IU CHÜ-YÜAN

Two miscellaneous poems

A lyric on the seven-jewel fan

For exquisite silk Tunghsia is prized,
The best artists come from Wu cities.
Cut like a white jade disc,
Sewn like the bright moon's wheel.

Its face inlaid with seven jewels,
Its heart filled with rare rhino horn.
Painting creates trees on grand mountains,
Sketching evokes Lo river goddess.

A welcome toy for the hand
It enters home, an intimate of rings and bangles,
To create a breeze by long sleeve cuffs,
To cool the bloom of rouge and powder's sheen.
It sweeps past bright eyes flirting nuance,
It steals a reflection of a humming singer.

Time moves on, a man is quick to forget old love;
Seasons change, he tirelessly courts new love.
With tender affection he takes her to his ivory bed,
With an easy mind he discards his quilted bed-mat.
Dislike, rejection – what can I say?
Respect? that lasts the span of heat!

I listen to a neighbour's singer

I loosen my robe, weary of circuit debates,
Lean on the coach-rail, tired of literary wit.
Tumbleweed gates have long been still,
Empty seats appear to have grown dust.
Overlooking the noble quarter there's a cosmetics house,
Where my east neighbour has a stage for pipes and drums.
Through the clouds rapturous song soars,
In the wake of winds floats sultry music,
Making blossoms fly on jade kingfisher curtains,
Fragrance drift from gold and jasper cups.
Long since dead, beauty of Central Plains.
So too the memories, ashes of Huhsiang.
My legacy of feeling is grief for life today.
The grandeur of Chungshan, where is it now?

Five miscellaneous poems

Two poems on an old theme

No. 1

Straying birds know dusk is the hour of return,
The wandering man alone fails to come home.
I waste unawares the flower's fragrant breath,
Pass futile time with the splendour of the moon.
A frowning face comes into my morning mirror,
Pining tears stain my springtime dress.
On Mount Wu spangled mists are fading,
Along Ch'i river green boughs grow bare.
I wait for you. In the end you don't come.
Autumn geese in pairs, in pairs are flying.

No. 2

Frosty air falls on Meng ford,
Autumn winds blow through Hanku Pass.
I remember you shivering in the early cold
As I stand on the porch wrapped in silk.
My frail hands put aside cutting and sewing,
On straggling hair I stop using gloss.
One thousand leagues, no news of you,
My inch of heart feels stifled, numb,
Especially on nights when fireflies flit
Or leaves from trees scatter in jumbled heaps.

Poem on the Balloon guitar

This cradled moon seems to glimmer,
Caressed, the breeze sounds even clearer.
To its strings I tell my feelings,
To its flowers I confide spring passion.
Depressed, it has a rare timbre,
Melancholy, it resounds with lovely music.
Scented sleeves happily brush it sometimes,
Otherwise, Dragon Gate trees grew for nothing!

Poem on the Curtain

Lucky to be sewn with pearls,
Wispy, wispy round your pillars.
No need to roll me up in moonlight,
Light am I when breezes blow.
Always gathering gold censer breath,
Ever catching jade lute whispers,
All I ask is lay out casks of wine,
Let orchid oil jars match the brilliant night!

Mount Wu high

I imagine in my fancy Mount Wu high:
Dim twilight, Sunny Terrace nooks,
Smoky mists first spreading, then furling,
Herb scents now breaking off, now threading.
Perhaps that lovely girl will make a date with me?
I wake, just see a dim vision.
I'm disappointed, yet I still love her.
Autumn winds drop on my garden green.

HSIEH T'IAO

Twelve miscellaneous poems

Presented to Master of Records Wang Chi-che, two poems

No. 1

As the sun sets she sits at her window,
Rouge cosmetic makes her face more lovely.
Dance dresses are tuck-pleated, not sewn;
Flowing yellow silk lies covered, unwoven.
Dragonflies on tips of grass hover,
Stray bees from flowertops sip.
Once they met they fell in love for ever,
She longs to take wing and soar with him.

No. 2

For fluting clear he asks for Green Jade,
For strings strumming he orders Green Pearl.
Light song disturbs silken belts,
Gurgling laughter loosens silk gowns.
The rest of their tunes, about how many?
Tall carriage, won't you linger?
For dawdling as the spring scene fades
They just have the corner of Loyang city wall.

Harmonizing with Master of Records Wang Chi-che's poem, 'Resentment'

She was summoned from the harem to a remote land.
At Eternal Gate Palace she missed happy feasts.
Her meeting him is sung in *Sweet herbs*.
Removed from favour she grieved in the *Round fan*.

On flowery tufts scatter swarming butterflies,
Through windblown blinds a pair of swallows enters.
Wasted, my spring sash gets looser,
Helpless, I mourn my pink face changing.
All my life I'd treasure his one glance –
Long ago a thousand gold was thought cheap.
My old lover's heart may still be the same,
But my old sweetheart is someone I never see.

In the night I heard a singer, two poems

No. 1

In a jasper boudoir I hear bangles tinkling,
Jade mats fill with fragrant dust.
I order a Loyang person,
Ask for Chiangnan flutes.
Full of love their languid dance movements,
Swayed by passion, they sing and tenderly play.
You'll know if you're my secret love –
Jade bracelets declare my inch of heart.

No. 2

Honoured guests lend brilliance to the four seats,
Lovely beauties are worth a thousand gold.
Dangling hairpin pledges ripped capstring,
Dropped earring answers the lute's love.
Moth eyebrows now laugh with someone,
Piquant scent goes deeper into the guest's lapel.
Happy joy grows calm into night,
Kingfisher drapes hang sunken still.

A lyric on a former palace lady from Hantan who married and became the wife of a quartermaster official

All her life she lived in galleried halls,
Going in and out to serve at cinnabar court.
In opened wardrobes her sheer dresses outshone all,
Her face in the mirror rivalled all moth eyebrows.
When first she went away her feelings lay suppressed.
Years later sorrow deepened with each dawn.
She grew imperceptibly thin and pale,
But a trace of flirting beauty still remained.
Faint images of the past flickered in her dreams
Murmuring yet: 'At royal feasts I won high favour!'

Autumn nights

Autumn nights when urgent looms hum,
My south neighbour's fulling is hurried.
I think of you nine heavens distant,
Night after night I stand still, helpless.
At north windows light curtains hang down,
Through the west door moonlight comes in.
How do I know white dew has fallen?
As I sit I see the front steps moistened.
Who can live in long separation?
Autumn ends, winter is here once more.

Five poems on objects

The Lamp

Flashing kingfisher tints in Han river slanting,
Hoarded treasure on Mount T'ang peaks,
It throws stem silhouettes like a god's palm,
Breathes flares like Torch Dragon.
Flitting moths make two or three circles,
Light flowers thicken four or five times.
Alone I face this night of loving you
That shines in vain on dance gown stitching.

The Candle

Under apricot rafters guests have not dispersed,
Cassia Lodge brilliance is about to fade.
Blurred the colours among flimsy curtains,
Lowered lights brighten a jewelled lute.
Flickers of cloudy chignon shadow,
Glitters of silk lattice gilt.
I hate you on moonlit autumn nights
For leaving me to our room's cavernous shadows.

The Bed

My first home was a tidal pool,
Falling shadows reflected in flickers,
Shallows screened by iris,
Secret isles conquered by sweet river plants.
Once you chanced to gather me,
A jade couch to offer gold cups.
All I desire is silken dress caresses,
Nor would I mind a powdering of white dust!

The Mirror-stand

Its fretwork resembles cinnabar lattice,
Its dizzy height is like the Dark Turret.
Phoenix face across, suspended on clear ice,
Dangling dragons hang over a bright moon.
Her powder reflected is brushed with rouge,
Flowers inserted are fixed in cloudy hair.
A jade face vacantly stares at itself,
Forever dreading his love might fade.

Falling plum blossom

New leaves freshly uncurl, uncurl,
Fresh blossom's newly fallen snowdrift.
I met you at a rear garden party,
Close together we went home in charmed laughter.
Since you troubled with your own jade fingers
To pick some and give to your Nanwei,
I used it to pin up my cloudy chignon
To enhance kingfisher-plume sheen.
As the day darkened its petals dropped for ever,
Your fond gift I never can regain.

LU CHÜEH

A song for Prince Ching of Chungshan and his concubine, Jutzu

Lady Ju slept in the royal bedroom.
Lady Pan sat in the imperial coach.
At Vast Wave they shared drink and bedcurtains.
At Forest Gleam, spoils of Ch'in, they feasted.
The year darkens, chill gales come.
Autumn floods, hibiscus blooms fall.
Mi Tzu-hsia took the royal harem coach without permission,
Lord Lungyang wept for the first fish.
Your wretched mistress will end like them!
And you? I'm not sure how you'll behave!

A miscellaneous poem

Chao women groom their lovely faces,
Yen girls perfect their cosmetics.
Make-up done, peach is ashamed of its pink!
Kohl applied, grass is disgraced for its colour!
Silk skirts, several tens of layers,
Yet lighter than one cicada wing.
I won't say her filmy sleeve is light,
But content myself sighing for winds too strong.
Tinkling pendants near a jade pool,
Playful laughter by a silv'ry terrace.
She breaks willow as a gift for the delight of her eyes,
Picks cat-tail as a present for one known to her heart.
When she came, her glamour had not faded;
When she goes back home, what of her glamour then?

CHAPTER FIVE

POETS OF THE SOUTHERN DYNASTIES
(THE DECADES AD 490–510)

Four poems in the old form

Separation, an old poem

Faraway places keeping you from me
Are as far as Goose Gate Pass
Where yellow clouds pall a thousand leagues.
Traveller, when will you come home?
Seeing you off seems like yesterday,
Dew on the front eaves is beading now.
I don't pity orchid plants this late –
What I mourn is the road chill.

You live on the horizon
Long sundered from your wife's body.
My longing to see your face just once
Is not unlike desire for the Jade Tree branch.
What dodder and waterplant
Rely on never moves away.

Lady Pan

A white silk fan like the round moon
Has emerged from the loom's pale silk.
Its picture shows the king of Ch'in's daughter
Riding a lovebird towards smoky mists.
Vivid colour is what the world prefers,
Yet the new will never replace the old.
In secret I fear cold winds coming
To blow on my jade-steps tree
And, before your sweet love has ended,
Will make it shed and fall midway.

On Chang Hua's poem, 'Love in separation'

Autumn moon reflected on eaves and lattice,
Cascading light enters cinnabar court.
A beauty strums her lilting lute,
Clear night, she stays by empty curtains.
On the orchid path few passing footprints,
On the jade mirror-stand cobwebs grow.
Garden trees put out vivid reds,
Bedroom plants hold in their green moisture.
Fine silks I prepare for you,
A gift for my love of ten thousand leagues.
Please pour down your favour's drenching dew,
Believe in my 'white sun' vow.

On Hsiu Shang-jen's 'Resentment in separation'

North-west autumn winds come.
Traveller of Ch'u, how far away your heart!
The sun declines, blue clouds gather.
Her handsome one has still not come.

Dewy spangles now spread in beauty,
The moon's flower starts to shimmer.
Precious books because of you are closed,
My jade lute how could I bear to uncase?

I pine for you on Mount Wu's lea,
Stare jealous at Bright Cloud Terrace.
The gold censer's sinking gleams die,
Silk mats' shifting dust spreads.
Cassia river goes a thousand leagues a day;
Because of this, I'm longing all my life.

Nostalgia on campaign, a poem respectfully offered to Liu Shih-lung by way of thanks

Her clear singing is, of course, charming,
Simply graceful her elegant dance.
From her ears she removes the bright moons,
Down her hair slip golden pins.

Sparrows fly here and there at dawn,
At dusk they go into the silk front window.
Fish sport north and south, yet
Home in the end near lotus leaves.
All I see is your travel long,
New Year is not ours of the old year.

A reply to Hsü Mien's poem, presented to a wife on her husband's behalf

Her husband shouts, 'Yes! I will!'
He takes his commission and leaves his family behind.
The dregs and a reject,
His wife's hair tangled grows like matted hemp.

Indirectly, she hears from a Loyang traveller
That escorted in high gold-canopied coaches
He has audience, occasional royal visits,
His splendour beggars description.

His private rooms are one cavernous space,
Where the twice eight girls are all fragrant flowers.
In silk skirts some long, some short,
With kingfisher sidecurls not too low, nor too wavy,
Long eyebrows sweeping over jade faces,
White arms filmed in sheer gossamer.

They idly watch butterflies alight on the well,
They all gather blossom fallen from the eaves.
How can he complain of bitter warfare?
She hugs her knees, sighing useless sighs.

SHEN YÜEH

I climb high to look at spring

I climb high to gaze on Loyang city,
Streets and lanes criss-cross far and wide.
I turn my head to look at Ch'angan;
City-wall turrets bristle in zigzag.
Sunrise glints on jewel pins and kohl,
Passing winds ruffle sheer silks.
Ch'i boys stamp their red boots.
Chao girls smooth a kingfisher brow.

The spring breeze sways dappled trees,
Rich blooms emerald and cinnabar.
Jewelled lutes, ruby stops,
Gold harness, tortoiseshell saddles.
Youth loiters, sleeps at Hsiats'ai,
Pours wine on the way through Shanglan.
When relaxed eyebrows pucker once again,
I know it's hard for them to keep a charming smile.
Beautiful lovers linger in vain,
Tearful from bliss unfulfilled.
'My honoured guest is now out of sight,
Through you I send him long sighs.'

Wang Chao-chün's farewell

At dawn she sets out from Spread Scent Hall,
By dusk she ferries the river at Fenyin.
From here she feels the 'nine death' sorrow,
From this point she puckers her twin moths.
Her damp make-up is like soaking dew,
Tears wreathe her breast like eddying waves.

Each day she sees swirling sands rise,
Gradually senses tumbleweed grows rank.
Hun gales assault her flesh and bones,
Not to mention damaging her sheer silks.

She chokes back tears, hazards a southward glance:
Passes, mountains tower menacing.
At first she composed the *Sunny spring* tune,
At the end she made a *Bitter cold* lyric.
Only on nights of the fifteenth
Is there the clear moon's brief passage.

When a young man was newly wed, I made this lyric for him

A daughter of the Shanyin Liu family
You wouldn't say is from the countryside!
She is lovely and pretty in face and figure,
Courteous and clever the way she talks.
Her waist and limbs are graceful,
Her clothes so sweet and fresh.
Her round red cape reflects early chill,
Her painted fan welcomes the first spell of heat.
On brocade slippers is a 'like flower' pattern,
On broidered sash is a 'same heart' lettuce design.
Gold-leaf brooches fasten her silk bolero,
Flower jewel-pins hold up her cloudy hair.

My heart is full of rapture,
How will I express my excitement?
I offer my love to the kohl across her eyebrows,
Send my heart to the lipstick on her mouth.
Defenceless before her precious three springtimes
I die for her thousand gold coin body.

A full-length green bronze mirror,
A one-inch diameter Hop'u pearl,
These would I give, but have no way.
I'd send them by a pair of flying ducks.

Her skirt opens, showing her jade foot,
Her blouse sheer reveals gleaming marbrous skin.
I'm ashamed to talk of Chao Feiyen,
Quite scorn Ch'in Lofu.

I check my looks. Though wretchedly thin,
Capped and canopied I'll brighten the city corner!
Her tall gates lined with coach and driver,
Broad avenues a parade of black horses.

Why blush for my Lulu dagger?
Why belittle my office swagger?
Back home let her ask in the village,
'Who's good enough to be my husband?'

Three miscellaneous melodic songs

Holding hands, a melodic song

Reins tossed aside, he leaves his carved coach.
I help him change, serve by his jade bed.
Slanting hairpins in autumn water reflected,
In the opened mirror I check my spring make-up.

My fear is red cheeks will fast fade,
Your favours cannot last long.
Pheasant-cap, make yourself comfortable!
Who cares if cassia sprays die?

The one I love

Marching west I scale Lung summit,
Look east, cannot see my home.
Trees of the pass push out purple leaves,
Frontier plants put out green shoots.

K'unming lake must be nearly brimming,
Grapevines should be forming blossom.
With streaming tears I face the Han envoy,
Trust him with my letter to her narrow lane.

Night after night, a melodic song

River Han stretches along and spreads across,
Northern Dipper spreads across, then straightens.
Starry Han, an empty void like this,
How can you know the love that's in my heart?

The orphan lamp dims, bright no more,
The cold loom at dawn still weaves.
I shed tears. To whom will I speak?
At cockcrow I just heave a sigh.

Five miscellaneous poems on objects

Spring, a lyric

Willows tangle like silk threads,
Sheer silks I can't bear on me.
Spring grass is green and emerald.
The wanderer's heart aches at such an hour.
Kingfisher lichen binds Wei river now,
Jade water brims in the Ch'i once more.
Sunny florescence brightens Chao lutes,
Windblown hues ruffle Yen skirts,
On my collar ten thousand streaming tears
Are because I love only you.

Poem on the Peach tree

Winds come blowing leaves astir,
Winds go, and I fear for flowers wounded.
Pink blossoms shining now in splendour
Shine richer in sunlight caress.

Singing boys at dusk rehearse their tunes,
Roving girls by night sew their coats.
How will I lessen the tears from facing spring
That could wrench a lover's guts?

Poem on the Moon

The moon in flower looks on silent night,
Night silent, stilled the thick dust.
Angular rays across a doorway enter,
Curving shadows through a gap visit.
In her tall house a woman is torn with love.
In West Park learned men stroll.
Webbed eaves gleam with pearl strands,
Ying Gate glimmers with emerald moss.
In cloistral rooms still no hint of dawn.
Those pure beams really are far off!

Poem on the Willow

Its light shade sweeps Chienchang Palace,
It fringes the roadsides leading to Weiyang.
With the wind it knots and then unravels,
Soaked with dew it softens and grows longer.
The lady of Ch'u will soon be consumed with love.
The girl Pan's tears turn to coursing down.
The wanderer mustn't have left yet –
For its sake, come home to your old town!

Poem on the Flute

In the land of pan-pipes and flutes, South of the River,
Sublime echoes pour from young stems.
Her interest she conveys through jade fingers.
Bearing her love, it is lifted and lowered.
Notes circle carved rafters twice, thrice,
Light dust moves four or five times.
In her tune there is profound emotion.
What do you know of cinnabar fidelity?

Four poems from the Six remembrance poems,
in a three-five syllabic metre

I remember when she came

I remember when she came,
Fair, fair as she went up the court steps,
Excited, excited to meet after parting,
Eager, eager to say she loved me.
I'd look at her and still not look enough,
Watch her and so forget to eat.

I remember when she sat

I remember when she sat,
Prim, prim before the silk bedcurtain.
Either she'd sing four or five songs,
Or she'd play two or three chords.
When she smiled, there must have been no one like her.
When she sulked she was even more adorable.

I remember when she ate

I remember when she ate,
Leaning over her dish, colouring prettily.
About to sit, then too shy to sit,
About to eat, then too shy to eat.
She'd keep the food in her mouth as if not hungry,
Lift her plate as if she had no strength.

I remember when she slept

I remember when she slept,
She struggled not to fall asleep though one slept.
She slipped off her silks without waiting to be coaxed;
She moved to the pillow and waited to be drawn close.
Then, nervous her partner might see,
All coy charm before the candle.

Two poems from Ten poems on objects

Embroidery on her collar

Slender hands have fashioned this novelty,
Made it into an adorable model.
From cross-stitching fly phoenixboys,
From double needle-weave flowerboys spring,
All seeming to stir and breathe, noiseless,
To hover with grace in windless air.
If her beauty were never to fade
This will hold a while her cloudy tumbling curls.

Slippers on her feet

Up cinnabar court fluttering,
Down jade halls swiftly tapping,
They pirouette and her pearl belt tinkles,
They are the first to make her bolero scent come out.
Her skirt open, she looks over the dance-hall seats.
Her sleeves brush by, she circles the hall in song.
What they sigh to their neglectful mistress is,
'We're tossed aside when she enters silk bedcurtains.'

In the style of 'Green, green riverside grass'

Dense, dense dust on the bed,
In my heart I remember my former man,
My former man I can't bear to remember.
At midnight I sigh long sighs.
Sighing I imagine his face and figure.
I didn't want this long separation,
A separation slowly grown longer.
My empty bed. I give in to cups of wine.

In the style of 'The three wives'

The eldest's wife dusts her jade jewel-box,
The middle wife ties silk bed-drapes.
The youngest wife alone has nothing to do,
She faces the mirror painting moth eyebrows.
'Darling, come and lie down,
The night is long and I'm left to myself.'

On an old theme

She hugs her lute near Shrub Terrace,
Lingers to cherish fair beauty,
Stands still, for the sun is now declining,
Sad, sad, it wrenches a person's guts.

Dewy mallows are now fully gathered,
Ch'i river has not wet the awning.
My brocade quilt lonely will not be warm,
My silk dress for nothing is perfumed.
The bright moon though it shines outside
Can hardly know the pain in my heart.

I dreamed I saw a beautiful woman

At night I hear long sighing
And I know your heart remembers.
Then the Gates of Heaven open wide,
Our souls kiss, I gaze on your face.
You offer me your Mount Wu pillow,
And hand me food from the level of your eyebrows.
We stand and stare, then lie across the bed.
Suddenly I wake, you are not at my side.
How do you think my spirit is wounded?
Welling tears soak my breast.

Modelled on an old poem

What an adorable cassia spray!
A lone drake longs for its old mate.
The year fades, he changes his nest;
Spring comes, still they are parted.

Mountains, rivers block the long road,
The road far eclipses her face and shape.
How could I say I don't have my own mate?
My inch of heart to the end will never stray.

Early spring

They lean together down the lane, searching for sunny spring,
Pretty women holding hands together.
Grass still a faded colour,
In the woods there's nothing there yet.
Useless to seek plum blossom,
Silly to think there'll be willow!
So let's go back home again
And whisper my passion to a cup of wine!

Bereavement

Last autumn's moon of the fifteenth
This autumn too lights her room.
This spring's orchid plant
Next spring will exhale more perfume.
Sad how different this is from human life –
Once we depart, we are for ever gone.

Screens, cushions in vain laid out,
Drapes, bed arranged just as before.
Drifting dust shrouds her empty seat,
Orphan curtains pall the empty bed.
Of all creatures none escapes extinction.
Still, this wounds us who survive.

A poem on fulling cloth

The waif quilt tugs pining heartstrings,
The lone pillow hurts limits of despair.
Deep in the garden autumn grass is green,
High on the gates white dew chills.
Pining for you I rise in clear night,
Tighten lute-stops to play *Secret orchid*.
I don't regret the flying tumbleweed's bitter lot,
But suffer the orchid's dereliction.

On campaign he weathers storms,
The traveller who delays with no return.
Outpost trees are shedding their leaves,
On the crest of Lung range autumn clouds fly.
In my chill garden evening birds flock,
By the pining window grass insects grieve.
Oh, how I pity his springtime clothes,
Where will he find clothes to ward off winter's cold?

A stork's cry troubles endless sighs,
I pick beans, sad that time is fading.
I remember when you left on far campaign,
You watched me prepare fine white silk.
Autumn winds blow on green pools,
A bright moon hangs above tall trees.
'Lovely girl, adorn your smooth face,
Come, hold hands, let's do our tasks!'

I walk down corridors dark unending,
The farewell hall now locked in grief.
To eaves high dusk pounder echoes spread,
In the keen air the night fulling block thuds.
Jasper flowers tinkle with each step,
Secret orchid quickens from sleeves;
I pause to fix gold kingfisher pins,
Calmly breathe the coolness of the night.

Flowing beauty swirls in the smoky tints,
Coiling patterns of tortoise and crane.
Chill, chill the 'joy of love' sleeves,
Faint, faint the fragrant orchid musk.
I don't resent the bitter lot of shuttle and reel,
What I mourn is this thousand-league separation.
With trembling tears I send your parcel,
And bow my head to late homeward clouds.

Two melodic songs for drum and wind

Alone, I never see him

On an islet apart a terrace faces into winds,
In a gulf of sky a hall looks upon water.
Sweet grass grown not yet thick,
Spring flowers falling like sleet.

He used to leave with Lord Chang,
Going back to visit Chao Feiyen.
I served at Eternal Trust Palace,
Who knows of me? Alone, I never see him.

Crossing passes and mountains

The girls from Ch'angan's houses of song
Come from Yen's deep south.
Though mere goodness makes them lovely,
They are known for natural good looks.

Long ago I heard of passes and mountains far away –
But why would you use gold harness?
Each day your mistress's heart is more disturbed.
Autumn winds sing through slim boughs.

A miscellaneous poem

Clouds wispy, warm changing tones,
In grasses green dawn scents revive.
Mountain wastes end their chill gloom,
Orchard ponds glitter with morning beams.
Most spring hearts are aroused,
But I look on nature and my feelings grow sadder.

Ever since you went away,
Orchid hall stopped humming with the loom.
All he knows is to campaign is right,
He never thinks separation is wrong.

Despair at Eternal Gate Palace

The jade jar at night goes drip, drip.
Ying Gate is barred and deep.
Autumn winds make cassia boughs stir,
The sailing moon casts pale quivering shadows.
Silken eaves with lucid dew drenched,
Webbed doors hum with pining insects.

Sighing a sigh, she goes down from the orchid gallery,
Full of despair she plays her elegant lute.
What would set my dawn belt tinkling?
Will I get to carry my night quilt to him again?
Since you no longer remember that House of Gold,
How could you brighten my Eternal Gate heart?

A South of the River melodic song

As I picked white artemisia on an islet
While the sun sank on spring South of the River,
There was a traveller coming home from lake Tungt'ing
Who said he'd met my former man near Hsiao-Hsiang river.
My former man – why didn't he come home?
Spring flowers are about to fade once more.
Don't admit he's happy with his new love –
Let's just say, 'The road he travels is far'!

Getting up in the night to come to me

From the city south driver and coach have ceased,
The highway is filmed with pure dust.
Dewy florets gleam on kingfisher webs,
Moonlight streams through an orchid terrace.
My secret room long left unlocked,
Perhaps Ying Gate lies open too?
Creak, creak autumn cassia echoes,
Not you getting up in the night to visit.

Threading needles on Seventh Night

His jet-black horse in autumn did not come home,
His black silk will be threadbare.
To meet the cold, she prepares the night's sewing,
Lit by the moon she works fine threads.
Lustrous eyes with sorrow glisten,
The line of pining eyebrows puckers.
Clear dew falls on silken clothes,
Autumn winds blow jade lute-stops.
Flickering shade subtly deepens,
Dwindling light will be harder to work by.

Poem on the Bed

Island in a stream rimmed with light,
Rippling breezes down green waters.
Though I'm not so light as a bed of one cocoon,
I am happy with my blue-robe colour.
Specks of dust on my lady's silk sleeves,
On this ivory bed are many lovely ornaments.
What I want is, when you drink on orchid nights,
My lovely one, feast and rest on me sometimes.

Poem on the Singer

Jewelled hairpins among pearl blooms,
And I clearly see her beauty-spots,
Near her wispy fringe faint yellow applied,
Light rouge touched on powdered cheeks.
As she speaks fragrance escapes,
Enriched by her own orchid tinge.
Soaring notes release wounded sighs,
Deep chant soft, yet rough.
An orphan, she turns, then swiftly swivels round
And her twin eyebrows swiftly pucker.
She won't show herself full face to me,
But half hides behind sheer silk.

Poem on the Dancer

Slim of waist, but not a Ch'u lady,
Light of body, but not a Chao girl,
Her sparkling collar strewn with jewel seeds,
From her elbows pearl tassels swing.
With loose sleeves she performs her pose,
Moves her feet, then holds her position.
Her eyes slant, seem not to notice you,
She goes to turn, then pretends to slow down.
Why should she blush to rise with cloudy storks?
Is she less lovely than when phoenix are alarmed?

Poem on Red notepaper

Mixed shades are hardly unusual,
But this red sets it apart.
Flaming, fiery like lotus unfolding,
Flecked with glints like streaking mist.
Embossed tissue rolled with perfumed oil,

Suffused with a hundred scents of cut blooms.
Let me record my heart in separation
Enveloped in this my love for you.
If it never reaches my sweet beloved
What will he know of my 'wind-flow' bed of romance?

Poem on the Rose

Facing the door is planted a rosebush,
Branch and leaf curving gracefully.
Unstirred, its scents still scatter,
Windless its flowers flurry at will.
In her spring bedroom, unable to relax,
She opens her case and practises *Lady Ming*.
Twisting pools float with tint on tint,
Sloping banks are tiered in clinging folds.
Now she hears sweet bird of passage music,
Then sees mud-carrying birds wend home.
Let's steep ourselves in jugs of clear wine –
For the rest, I couldn't care less!

KAO SHUANG

Poem on the Mirror

When I first went to the phoenix royal court,
This mirror reflected moth eyebrows.
Here it reflects eternal resignation,
But won't reflect eternal love for you.
Empty of love I never pick it up,
Chaste and pure, pointless to hold it.
I won't declare this object obsolete,
But resurrect it next rendezvous!

PAO TZU-CH'ING

Poem on the Painted fan

Fine threads light as light can be,
Soft tints barely visible,
Meant to offset red cheeks,
Yet used as a hand-held fan.
Instantly raised when Eternal Gates wept,
Offered once at Cypress Rafter's banquet.
Pining cosmetics once revealed it now conceals,
Singing features once hidden, it now shows.
Just paint it with a pair of yellow storks,
Never the waif flying swallow.

Poem on the Jade steps

The jade steps, already so beautiful,
Become more so overlooked by Tzu-wei Palace.
North doors open on to kingfisher drapes,
South paths lead to gilded portals.
Pounded into being by sunny rays,
Dappled into hiding with moonbeams.
Light moss stains pearl slippers,
Small puddles brush silk dresses.
I smile in loneliness at K'unlun's crevice,
Watch in vain for the bluebird flying free.

In imitation of Hsieh T'iao's style

Cassia terrace is brushed with clear dew,
Bronze steps are moist with fallen flowers.
A pretty girl, her rouge cosmetics done,
Holds the hook to roll up fine blinds.
Longing for you, she tightens a moment the lute-stops
With jade fingers slim, so slim.
Just for our break-up I mustn't
Be unreasonable and so despise you!

Harmonizing with Secretary Yü Ch'ien's 'Poem on an old theme'

A lovely woman plays in white sunlight,
Glowing, glowing in the spring doorway.
Her clear mirror counters moth eyebrows,
Fresh flowers imaged on jade hands.
Swallows swoop to gather pond mud,
Breezes come to blow slim willow.
Lover, when will you come back home
To pour a measure of wine with me?

Harmonizing with Mou Lang's poem, 'Moongazing'

Clear is the night, and not yet tired
I let the fine blinds hang free a moment.
Chime, chime the jade lake waters
Reflecting a moth-eyebrow moon.
Bead on bead the dew barely in suspense,
Shimmers, shimmers the light gently sinking.
My lovely one, more than a thousand leagues,
Last shadows vain swiftly vanish.

FAN CHING'S WIFE [SHEN MAN-YÜAN]

Poem on 'Step-quiverer' flowers

Pearl blooms ring kingfisher plumes,
Jewel leaves inset with gold jade.
Artificial lotus seemingly uncontrived
Are flowers of apparent natural life.
Lower stems stroke her broidered collar,
Tiny footsteps set the jewels aquiver.
Just let me fix it on her cloudy coiffure,
Then moth eyebrows will be soon painted.

Parody of Hsiao Niang

Bright pearl, kingfisher-plume bed-drapes,
Gold leaf, sheer green-silk door tapestries
Lifting now and then with the wind.
I imagine I see your charming face and figure
At clear dawn, when you put on your 'step-quiverer',
Towards dusk, when you slip off your silk dress.
Well, give yourself to Mr Romance –
Surely perfect love can't bear to be selfish!

Poem on the Five-tone bamboo clothes perfumer

How sweet is its frost-damp texture
Of fine spliced fibre and nicely split strands
Woven to form windblown lettuce,
Wrought into wavy silk lace.
Heavy perfume pours from a pearled quilt,
Brilliant tints tone with a celadon tunic.
Now it only sighs for beautiful ornaments,
Why hark back to its cloud-piercing past?

Poem on the Lamp

On a silk bed the sun is now darkening,
To silk drapes the moon has not returned.
Open wax florets cast a stork's glint,
Full radiance outshines Ninth Blaze.
Windy eaves fan cinnabar flickers,
Frozen skies attenuate green glimmers.
Don't pity frail moths circling,
Just dread the dawn insects' flight.

HO SUN

Day and night I stare at the river, presented to Marshal Yü

P'en city girdles P'en river,
P'en river winds like a girdle.
Day and night I stare at high city walls,
Far, far off at blue clouds beyond.

In the city there are many feasts and banquets,
Strings, bamboo blend in constant concert.
The sound of flutes liquid now with rapture,
The sound of strings sharp now with pain.
A singer's kohl contracts as if in anguish,
A dancer's waist threatens to snap.

Mid-autumn's yellow leaves have fallen,
Long winds resentfully murmur.
Early geese emerge from clouds homing,
Familiar swallows leave their nests and separate.
Sad at dawn to live in a strange town,
I dream at night of return to Lo shore.
Lo shore deserted, so deserted.
I get up to look, climb the west storey.
White, white a sail homes for the strand,
Round, round the sun eclipsed by islets.
Who can, just for once, metamorphose into wings
And lightly rise to drift away in flight?

In the style of the 'Scorned' piece

The beautiful young men from the east side
Indulge their bodies, scorning the millions spent.
Thornwood slings, Lord Sui pearl shot,
White horses, yellow gold harness.
At Ch'angan's nine-radial crossroads
Green pagoda trees stand shading the way.
Wheelhubs at dawn already clatter
Jostling without pause into dusk.
From Racedog Terrace westward for the sights,
From Herdboy Bridge southward bound,
They converge near the sports ground,
Wander around the three markets.

Ivory beds draped with broidered quilts,
Jade dishes laden with fine food.
Singing girls trill, hidden by fans,
Young wives weave behind open blinds.
Eyes meet, just a secret smile,
Seeing other people faces turn prim.

Yellow stork laments its old flock,
Hillside bough sings of first love.
Crows fly, passing travellers disappear,
Sparrows flock, coursing dragons vanish.
With plumed goblets they now relax, relax:
This hour's joy has not reached its peak.

Poem on the Reflecting mirror

When pearl blinds at dawn first roll up,
Silk on the loom lies unwoven by morning.
Its jade case open, she studies her image,
Over the jewelled stand she leans to apply make-up.
She faces her image, alone, full of laughter,
Looks at a flower, idly twists sideways.
For a moment she creates 'cocoon-emerging' eyebrows,
Cautiously glosses fresh peach tones.

Perhaps plumed hairpins could go in here?
Maybe the gold hair-clasps are too close together?
Her wayward lover goes on, he's not yet home.
Tearful cosmetics unbidden soak her breast.

Bedroom regrets

At dawn the River dies on a tall ridge-pole.
The slanting moon is half over an empty garden.
Fallen leaves cross the window sill,
Beyond the blind flitting fireflies are trapped.
Full of love she lowers kingfisher drapes,
Soaked with tears she closes the golden screen.
Long ago he promised, now he's not yet back.
Spring grass though chill is green once more.
My love for you is unswerving –
Is it any different from the north pole-star?

Poem on Seventh Night

Her coach divine halts at seven removes,
Her phoenix carriage leaves the fount of heaven.
The moon shines with a Ninth Blaze glow,
Winds waft perfume of one hundred scents.
The joy to come is a moment's charmed laughter,
Tears for her return are already on her weeping make-up.
Lost to sight, as at Lo river shore;
Sudden disenchantment, as at Kaot'ang.
They separate and cannot meet.
River Han is steadily flowing in full flood.

Poem on the Dancer

Pipes blow clear, silk seats move closer,
Strings sound anxious, snowflake sleeves adagio.
Following the chanter, slim hands turn;
Answering the melody moth eyebrows move.

Numb passion notes his dropped earring,
Narrowed eyes confide eloquent secrets.
As the sun declines she delays her honoured guest,
Looking at him in this hour of love.

I watch his new wife

A misty twilight lotus that rises from the river,
The hazy dawn sun that shines on rafters –
Lovelier yet on a night of torchlit splendour
Is her light fan covering her rosy make-up,
And her lover radiant, radiant
And on their bed appears a natural light.
What grieves me is the high coach moving
And her waist jewels leaving the veranda.

Poem on the House of singers

White, white is the tall house at dusk,
As flowery candles brighten the front curtains.
On the silk drapes a peacock pin silhouette,
From a jewelled lute *Phoenix and chicks* music.
Night blossom shows on the bough,
A new moon appears through the fog.
Who is it remembering at the window?
She watches for him, alone, sleek, sleek.

Poem on White seagulls, a satire on separated people

How sweet is the pair of white seagulls
From dawn to dusk playing on the river.
Who'd have thought it? – they change their nest,
The hen goes off, the cock stays no more.
In orphan flight, one leaves the shore and bay;
One nests alone beneath Ts'angchou.
To east, to west, they're gone from here –
From shadow, from echo for no reason severed.

In imitation of 'Green, green riverside grass'

In her spring garden looking better with each day
She picks flowers, staring at the far road.
On autumn nights bitter and long
She hugs her pillow, goes to a lonely bed.
From below the fluting house her quickened rhythms
You mustn't say are due to his parting from here.
On the song-mat she hides behind her round fan,
'When will I see you once more?'
Though strings cease, they cling still to the pegs.
Though leaves fall, they now drop against the trunk.
So while I say these things come apart,
Compared to me they aren't quite forsaken.

A satire on the poet Liu Hsiao-cho

Behind bedroom lattice the flames of night go out.
The window, the door brightens in dawn light.
A charming girl draws the drapes aside,
Tiptoes early from her bed.
Sparrow hairpins slant in her morning curls,
Moth eyebrows are beautiful with last night's make-up.
Just audible her jade bangles distant,
Still savoured her kingfisher quilt scent.
How do I know the early dawn courtiers?
A straggling line of geese!

WANG SHU

Poem on an old theme, at the command of His Lordship, Hsiao Ch'ang

Mornings she gathers hungry silkworm food,
Nights she sews a thousand-league robe.
Then again I hear her up south lane
At sunset coming home from picking lotus.

Green moss sheathes the cold well,
Red peonies grow among green fern.
The joys of life are finite,
The hour of love betrayed.
How can I match the new swallows?
In pairs, in pairs they fly home together.

Arriving at Wulin village, I saw a mulberry picker and gave her this poem

From far off I see a girl lift her basket,
Young, lithe, so exquisite.
She's ready to leave, but then her body turns;
About to speak, she first gives a smile.
Newly separated from my boudoir love
I'm not ready to seek a new friend.
But just for refastening your oleaster sash,
May I thank you with my magnolia spray!

*At Chancellor Hsü's [?Hsü Mien] banquet, I was assigned the poem title
'Adorable' for composition*

Red lotus unfolding in early dew,
Jade face reflecting mists of dawn.
Her 'Chao Feiyen in tears' make-up done,
She turns her head to fix her 'step-quiverer' flower.
She has clustered gold hairpins galore!
Her rumpled broidered collar is askew!
Sunset return to jasper-strung drapes,
To scented lamps ablaze with nine blooms.

Autumn bedroom vigil

Sparkles, sparkles wide celestial Han,
Fluffy, fluffy clouds come out from craters,
The moon aslant trees casts shadows,
Winds upon water sketch rippling patterns.
Now she weeps, a wife at her loom,
And mourns the lover of her bed.
Silk tunic ever folded at dawn,
Kingfisher quilt vainly scented at night.
'Futile to draw from the silver curb well.
For whom would I sew gold lamé skirts?'
Her beloved in the end didn't come.
She kept watch in vain half the night.

One night I dreamed I went home

I flew home in a dream to my love:
With you I draw well water chill,
The bronze bucket's white silk cord,
The lovely well's white silver curb;
Sparrows dart from dense, massed trees,
Insects flit round tortoiseshell rafters.
One apart, you do not see me;
I cannot bear to face the glory of spring.

CHAPTER SIX

POETS OF THE SOUTHERN DYNASTIES
(EARLY SIXTH CENTURY)

Six poems harmonizing with the Royal Equerry Hsiao
Tzu-hsien's poem on an old theme

No. 1

Your wretched wife, I pine unbearably
As I pick mulberry south of Weich'eng.
My sash hangs loose broidered with entwined boughs,
My hair is tangled with phoenix pins.
Flowers danced, we snuggled by the long hedge,
Moths flitted, we loved by the green lake.
I have no way to requite your kindness.
With streaming tears I turn to spring silkworms.

No. 2

Your wife, I was originally a songhouse girl,
Then I came up to Royal Wei palace.
I've since been honoured in a carved litter,
And was also among the wardrobe mistresses.
A jewel of blue peacock, a lotus in its beak,
Gold insects inlaid with precious grains,
Still, I admit they fail to satisfy.
With streaming tears I long for Liaotung.

No. 3

The spring grass I gather can be bound,
But your wife's heart has quite broken.
From grief green-glinting hair has changed,
Pink cheeks from tears are ruined.
Tears not only form into pearls,
But I see pearls turn to blood.
I long to be a flying magpie mirror
Fluttering to reflect your parted image.

No. 4

Where shall I send my answer to your letter?
Left of Lung are five forked roads.
With tears I grind *t'uchih* ink,
My brush stains the whiteness of swansdown paper.
Jade-green floats on Meng Isle water,
Fragrant falls the dew on Tungt'ing lake.
You meant to come home, then you didn't come home,
I'm spending fragrant spring uselessly.

No. 5

Your wife's home is north of Broadbank,
My beauty blossomed at Small Longbank.
Floral hairpins twist with jade arms,
Strings of pearl are threaded with gold beads.
In wispy streaks hang green phoenix plumes,
With arabesque curves flutters my white fan.
Who can bear to look at these for long?
I'm full of hate at not seeing you!

No. 6

The Hsiungnu fate will soon be sealed.
I stand by Jade Gate Pass.
Lotus blooms sheathe my dagger hilt,
An autumn moon clasps my sword pommel.
Your spring loom hums meek and mild,
Summer birds pine with long-drawn cries.
My one at home is watching for me,
Her wild husband who in the end didn't go home.

Six poems in answer to Liu Yün's letter-poems

No. 1

Golden orioles fly in royal parks,
Green plants are coming out on islets.
The sun sparkles on K'unming water,
Spring comes alive in Magpie Lodge.
Rocking, swaying white flowers dance,
Rolling, swirling purple plants flow.
My letter woven in palindrome brocade
I have no way of sending to Lungt'ou.
I love you more than the jasper tree.
Not seeing you makes me despair in separation.

No. 2

Cracking my whip I approach the great ridge,
Roped up together, we ford Chang river.
Yen girls and Chao women
Cradle lutes all through the night.
With slim waists they trail wide sleeves,
Half their forehead is painted with long moths.
The traveller of course grows travel weary,
His mop-and-broom lives on the tributary shore.
My former one, she can't be thrown away.
A new friend? It's no use – how would it turn out?

No. 3

We live apart, hurt, unhappy.
Towards dusk my heart aches and aches.
Out on the road I question a Chao envoy
And hear you're employed as a top minister.

The colours of the sweet grass are now out,
Iris blades are not yet even.
Heaped mulberry feeds silkworms into cocoons,
Swooping soaring swallows drip mud.
I long to leave with the spring wind
Fluttering to you in Liaohsi.

No. 4

The white sun is hidden by city-wall houses,
Strong winds sweep the chill trees.
We broke apart, east divorced from west,
We last held hands, cold a stranger to heat.
I long for you, breathless, mute,
My hidden room is pure and still.
Years have gone swifter than fleeting smoke,
The years to come are like rolling wheels.
The parted stork one thousand leagues will fly,
The orphan hen will find no rest at night.

No. 5

Into a bedroom still and pure
The sinking moon lets a last gleam.
Chill insects hidden by walls are pining,
Autumn moths round a candle flit.
Broken clouds streak then gather,
Scattered birds depart and then come home.
Beloved, where are you now?
Far from my river is your flowing Yih.
Once I make the *Parted stork* music play
Thousand-league tears soak my dress.

No. 6

When autumn clouds are lulled in late skies,
Then chill nights are skein after skein.
I hear you blow excited on the flute
Loving you and then *Picking lotus*.
Separation was to be a few days, no more,
Yet the high moon has formed its bowstring three times.
Shying, rearing Yellow river billows,
Plaintive wailing Lungt'ou cicadas.
I'll send you sweet herb leaves,
Pin them on beside Bushy Terrace!

Four poems in the style of old poems

Mulberry up the lane

Lithe, lithe mulberry up the lane
Shades the path and overhangs the bank,
Long twigs reflecting white sunlight,
Fine leaves hiding oriole yellow.
The hunger of silkworms turns your wife to pining again.
I wipe my tears and lift my basket.
How can my former man know of this?
The hate of separation boils in my heart.

The King of Ch'in wraps a gift robe

Hsienyang spring grass is sweet.
The Ch'in emperor wraps a set of clothes.
Studded with jade is the cord on the oleaster case,
Gilded is the clay and perfumed with storax.
Its freshest fragrance incenses double drapes.
Last gleams flicker on a jade bed.
He must wait till late levée is over
To take this gift to his Huayang.

Picking lotus

With her brocade sash and mixed floral hairpins,
Her silk dress hangs over the green stream,
As I ask, 'Where are you off to now?'
'Out picking lotus south of the river.
To Liaohsi three thousand leagues
I'd send them, but have no way.
I want my lover to turn back soon,
While these lotus still stay fresh.'

Holding hands

With happy expressions in the spring sunshine
They hold hands along the clear Lo,
At cockcrow the royal park,
At twilight Hsiaop'ing ford.
Long skirts catch the white sun,
Wide sleeves carry sweet dust.
My former mate is always like this:
A new friend – and why would he think of me?

A poem presented to Tu Jung-ch'eng

One swallow comes over the sea,
One swallow rests in a high hall.
One morning both chance to meet,
What a surprise! – they are old friends.
She asks me, 'Why are you so late?
Were pass and hill so winding or straight?'
I answer, 'The sea route was long,
Winds so fierce made me powerless to fly.'

Long ago we parted and I stitched a silk cloak,
Spring winds were first entering the curtains.
By now, as summer is getting late,
Mulberry moths disperse through trees in flight.

Spring, a lyric

Spring, where does it come from
Stroking a dress and startling plum?
Clouds block Green Chain Gate,
Winds blow Welcome Dew Terrace.
My lovely one is a thousand leagues apart;
Silk drapes are drawn and never opened.
Having no way we can talk together,
Uselessly I face a 'loving you' winecup.

From a divorcée to her former husband

A deserted wife, I live by the river bridge.
Pining for you and far away from you,
Phoenix-mate pins slip down my curls,
My lotus bloom belt sags around my waist,
My guts are wrenched from this parting place,
My face in a flood of tears is wasted.
I wish you'd remember the way we used to be –
Spare me occasional scraps of news!

Poem on a Young man

Tung Sheng has a really charming smile,
Tzu Tu has truly beautiful eyes.
A million pays for one word,
A thousand in cash buys surrender.

Don't mention hide-and-seek mallow!
Who cares about virtue meek and mild?
I want you to bring your broidered quilt,
Come lie with your man of Yüeh!

WANG SENG-JU

Spring regrets

The four seasons like torrent water
Hurtle past rushing full circle.
Birds in the night echo lorn, forlorn,
The dawn glimmers shine bright, bright.

I'm bored seeing blossom become fruit,
Have too often watched shoots turn to bamboo.
I'm ten thousand leagues cut off from news and letters,
We've had ten years of sleeping apart.

The burden of sorrow sheds my scented hair,
Prolonged weeping spoils my beautiful eyes.
My lover left to be in Yükuan,
His wife, I'm left behind to live at Hanku.
I only stare at this mossy boudoir
That looks like a spiders' room.

I drink to my echoes in solitary night
And pursue my own shadow.
My ivory bed I've changed for felt and bamboo,
Silk dresses replaced with lined clothes.
However often wind and frost go by
I'll live alone, faithful still to you.

On a moonlit night I compose a poem on Officer Ch'en of Nank'ang bringing his new mistress home

His twice-eight girl is like a flower.
The three-fives moon is like a mirror.
She parts the blinds to one and the same radiance,
When she faces the door the two reflect each other.

Expensive women come down from Ch'in and Hann,
Famous ones go up to Yen and Cheng.
Ten cities is the usual asking price,
A thousand gold often makes a bargain.
Lover, your affections can focus on them –
In her heart your wife will not compete.

On seeing a nobleman bringing his glamorous lady home for the first time, an impromptu lyric

Long had he dreamed of a private boudoir beauty,
Never had he seen one to destroy a city.
For a thousand in gold he frequented gorgeous flowers,
One morning he met perfect glamour.
Her home was beyond Sumen,
She came to flirt near Bushy Terrace.
Luckily this Hsiang-ju had no mate,
And this Wen-chün was recently widowed!

Harmonizing with Archivist Ssu-ma's poem, 'Hearing my neighbour's wife weaving at night'

In my cavernous room the winds are harsher now,
Down a long veranda the moon purer still.
Dim, dim the night garden is wide,
Billowing, billowing the dawn drapes are sheer.

Confused I hear the hundred insects murmur,
Suddenly I'm pained by one wing of song,
The birdsong long is unending,
Your wife's love, too, where is its bourn?
Still worried my lover has no cloak,
Night after night at the window I weave.

Night sadness

On the eaves the dew hardens into pearl,
On the pool the ice sets to smooth jade.
In ten thousand streams dawn tears trickle,
A thousand leagues apart, night sadness deepens.
Orphan curtains are drawn, never to open.
Cold tallow is spent, then rekindles.
Who would know my heart and eyes are bewildered?
I see sudden scarlet change to green!

Spring bedroom resentment

When sadness visits, I no longer groom my hair.
When spring comes I pucker my eyebrows again.
It's sad to see the butterfly dust;
I weep to watch the spider's threads.
The moon shines on cold locust cushions,
The wind blows on kingfisher curtains.
To skimming carp it's hard to trust my thoughts,
Nor will swift wings gently bear my words.

Fulling cloth

Many a time wounded by gold flutes quickening,
Much am I troubled by red gleams hastening.
Dew beads in the purple on the pool,
Winds scurry through the green of the garden.

I leave my loom, the slanting moon speeds west,
Pound my block, the glowing sun hurries east.
My sweet sweat is like an orchid rinse.
The carved gilt of dragon candles I avoid.

I play through the *Great mound* variations,
Drum *Angler's south* rhythms.
With *Parted stork* sadness unremitting,
Parted paradise bird breaks, then resumes.
My foot of silk lies in the fish's belly,
My inch of heart relies on the webbed goose.

Describing a dream for someone

I always knew fancies turn to dreams,
But I never believed that dreams would be like this!
Fair, fair, immaculate,
Pure, pure perfection,
Intimate by hibiscus cushions,
She turns back the 'joy of love' quilt.
Her elegant footsteps are most lovely,
She's full of whispers enchanting.

What I describe didn't seem to happen fast,
Then, strangely, became a thing of the moment.
When I woke it all turned to nothingness,
And now I know all is empty illusion.

Written for someone wounded by not meeting her, though she was near

She's the girl of Ying in her phoenix-mate house;
She's the Lady of Han in Cypress Rafter Hall;
Doesn't she eclipse [Lady Li] immortalized on her death-bed –
Whose voice and image were still perceptible?

I have a lover single-hearted,
From the same village, not from a strange town.
If a strange region, we'd still not be estranged.
From the same village we stare and stare the more.
If we stared and stared like Herdboy and Weaver,
We still wouldn't mind their one word of love a year.

*Written for Armoury Department Ho's [?Ho Chiung] former mistress, in
the style of the 'Sweet herbs' lines*

Going outside to admire orchid incense
I lifted the blind and met you.
Composing my features I managed one question,
'Your new friend, may I hear about her?'

'My new one comes full of laughter,
My old love would hide full of tears.'
'Your wife's love stays with the cold pine tree.
Your heart faints with day-lilies!'

Several rhymes composed at the Chin-an Secretary Wang Fen's wine party

Meek and mild, Sung Jung-hua
Sings solo songs of liquid melody.
She turns with a look not without meaning,
Slants her fan to stare back at me.
How is she inferior to Hsü Fei-ch'iung?
She's far superior to Liu Green Jade!
How will I send my desire so desirous?
Through the green wine in the cup I've half drunk.

For someone to give her lover

She's a Green Jade and a Green Pearl,
She's a Chang-nü and a Lady Lu, both women.
Her crooning voice has no rival in the past,
Her long sleeves have no match in all the world.
She rises as if from a phoenix-mate house,
Then appears on Hsiao-Hsiang shores.
Were she to lift the skirt of her dress
I'd whisper one word of passionate love.

The anguish of Mr Ho's [?Ho Chiung] mistress

In a cold tree perches a sheltering hen,
The moon shines, the wind blows too.
Exiled statesmen and deserted wives,
For the fallen my heart can feel.

Seven idle strings on a jewelled lute,
One hundred vain stems of an orchid lamp.
Sulky pertness I won't bother to mimic,
The weeping cheeks I wipe trickle once more.
Quilt-sharers, we've become Ch'u *versus* Yüeh,
But those different states weren't so alienated!

A melodic song for drum and lute, 'The one I love'

Night breezes puff firefly sparks,
Dawn gleams glint on lichen.
Long faded are the sweet herb leaves,
Fallen in vain are the grapevine blooms.

I cannot bear ever to weave white silk,
Who can be alone and wash sheer silk?
And time, when will it end?
I hope for you soon, but you delay your return.
You are born to wander, I know.
As for your wife, I'm just an entertainer!

To someone's favourite mistress in despair

Pitiful is the lone standing tree
With branches light and roots easily shaken;
Now it is soaked by the dew,
Then it is whirled by the wind.

Wrapped in my brocade quilt, sleepless
I sit up from night until dawn.
The reason your sad wife is wasting away
Is not that you like slim waists!

For a singer who feels hurt

I know in my heart I hate you,
Yet I'm ashamed to look in my mirror.
When things went wrong I used to mope and mope,
Now I've changed and I'm cool, quite cool.
Take back the earrings you gave me!
Give back the fox-fur I sent you!
If a bowstring snaps it can be mended.
If love goes out, it's very hard to make it stay.

Autumn bedroom regrets

Slanting rays are hidden by the west wall,
Twilight sparrows go up to southern boughs.
When winds come, autumn fans are thrown aside.
When the moon appears, night candles are snuffed.

Deep love wells up one hundred times.
Tears for faraway are not one single trickle.
Useless to worry that your wife is bitterly sad –
When all is said – you'll never know!

We met, a ballad

We met by Dusk Shadow steps,
As I drove to Peak Cap village alone.
The tall gates were all as one,
Stately mansions all of a kind.
I lean on the coach rail. The sun is just setting.
'Where would one visit my lord?'

'The lord's place of residence
Is a place easy to recognize.
The green mansion overlooks the highway,
Gentle terraces look on to winding streams.

'Up the hall fluent lute studs are caressed,
Thundercloud goblets passed round day and night.
Pomelo sweet with blossomed fruit,
Crimson flames blaze on stems of gold.

'My brothers, two or three of them,
Have tunic belts that glitter with gems.
At dawn they retire from the Forbidden Palace,
Coach and rider cantering abreast,
Golden saddles, agate bridles,
The passers-by crowd the road to watch.

'Entering our gates you see in one glance
Ducks and geese, cocks with their hens,
Many thousand each of cocks and hens
Call to each other sporting their plumage,
Stand in set formation east and west,
Their flocks in rows, in such rank and file.

The eldest's wife embroiders a square collar,
The next wife is nursing her babe.
The youngest wife, still a dear child,
Sits up and blows the bamboo flageolet.
'Husband dear, come up quick!
Divine phoenix are making an appearance!'

Sitting down to wine

Sitting down to wine is most enjoyable,
And this wine might well be the finest!
Wine clear as blossom is valuable,
This wine, sweet as milk, is invaluable!

How are the top guests detained?
Make a palm-dancing girl offer them such wine:
Gold goblets will be clear and full,
Jade tankards will slowly edge together.
Who would share my late twilight years?
I'll sit down to wine till fragrant dawn.
But, my sweet, before your song is over,
I'll leave my seat and miss the rafter dust.

Far betrothed

My far betrothed in the end didn't come home.
The season and nature are just about to change.
White dew troubles my unlined gown,
Autumn winds still my round fan.

Who can be separated for long,
In another town and in a strange district?
Drifting clouds veil the mountain folds.
I stare after you. When will we meet?
The message I send to a far wanderer:
'Empty bedroom tears like hail.'

For the one at home

At sundown I imagine your clear brow
As you slip into shoes and leave your pepper room.
Spinning spiders live in brocade rugs,
Shifting dust shrouds the jade bed.
I cannot perceive your lovely image,
Only a trace of shimmering curtain scent.
This beauty, passionately happy,
Hugs her lute, sitting in the high hall.
How could one in despair from parting forget
As he turns to the corner alone and grief-stricken?
Let me use one bamboo letter-slip
To convey the 'nine-death' anguish in my guts.

*Poem on Sweet promise, written in front of a peach tree near my room for
the one at home*

Longing for you I went up the north gallery.
As I paced and paused I glanced at the east house.
Suddenly there was a tree facing the eaves
Laden with sparkling sunlit blossom.
Its freshness I'd liken to rouge and powder,
Its whiteness I'd compare to glamorous artifice,
Making my heart's passion stronger still,
Reminding me more keenly of your narrow lane.
But I don't even have any road to hinder me
For it's wispy, wispy, like dawn-streaked clouds.
Since its grim wall can't be crossed,
I break off my poem for a hempen pledge.

In Huakuang province I hear fulling at midnight outside the city wall

On the gates of heaven are lowered heavy bars,
Cinnabar court exhales a bright moon.
Autumn air freezes in the city,
Autumn fulling blocks thud outside the city wall,
Their trailing sounds circle Sparrow Terrace,
Their hovering echoes leap over Dragon Tower,
Mellifluous, faint, so faint,
They must come from the highway,
Faint, so faint, pathos unending,
Must come from the coach-driving district.

In the coach-driving district all the world resides,
Elegantly beautiful like dawn mist.
Round jewels sparkle at their ears,
Square collars broidered lie aslant.
Clothes incensed with hundred-perfume powder,
Curls quivering with nine-stem blooms.

Last evening garden pagoda trees shed.
This morning sheer silks feel thin.
They dust their beds, roll up mandarin-duck patterns,
Draw drapes, unfold tortoise and stork motifs.
Golden ripples now serene,
Jade footsteps approach block and pounder.
Red sleeves swirl back and forth,
White arms lift in flurried jerks.

I only hear but cannot see them.
Alone in the night I stand in empty grief.
Alone in the night, when will it finally end?
Desire's involuntary wound.

Steps strung with Jade Scales dew,
The garden dances with weather-vane wings.
Spangled bright shooting stars blaze,
Glistening, radiant Long River glints.

After three winters I've truly read enough,
For five days not enough provisions.
A Yang Hsiung, now silent and alone,
Here you are, 'straight as a bowstring'!

Harmonizing with Secretary Hsiao's poem, 'In a spring dawn, to the one I love'

Fragrant trees burst into spring glory,
When Ts'ai Yung stared at her blue dress.
Water with peach blossom flows away,
Spring with the willow returns.
Willow, when will you return?
You wilt and wilt, droop and droop.
Now the sun shines on Changt'ai lane,
Now sweeps Eternal Gate doors.

He who knows the loneliness of separated hearts
Regrets in vain spring glory betrayed.
Loyang is far as the sun –
How will I meet Fufei?

In spring suburbs I watch a pretty girl

In fragrant suburbs a kingfisher-plume gatherer
Rolls up her sleeves in search of sweet spring.
Golden glints kindle from her 'step-quiverer',
Red tints dart from her blown ribbons.
Bright, bright the sun on her canopy top,
Flares the dust, flares from horses' hooves.
At dim twilight, beside the tall house,
That must mean my name is Ch'in.

Poem on Reflections in a mirror

Dawn gleams shine on apricot rafters.
A Chao Feiyen rises for her morning make-up.
Careful she spreads wide lines of kohl,
Deft fingers fix on the floral yellow.

She inserts jewelled hairpins, studies her image a moment,
Pats with her powderpuff admiring its scent.
Now she complains her kingfisher plume is too old,
Now she says her jade is lacklustre.
'In the city they all go half across the forehead,
But not as long as my eyebrows are painted!'

*Two poems harmonizing with Marshal Hsiao's poem,
'The Painted screen'*

Sunny spring brings warm air

The sun shines pure on Lady Pan's gate,
The wind blows soft on Tung Hsien's lodge.
Whorlear comes out up the steps,
A shrike squawks atop the fence.
A silkworm girl and her cassia pole-hook,
A playboy and his storax shot.
Caressing sleeves mean to delay the traveller,
'Let's meet! Let's not mope!'

On autumn nights chill winds stir

A lovely person lives at Honei,
Her army husband quells Mayi city.
Fallen dew one morning beads,
By midnight two are shedding tears.
In air crisp bedcurtains are chill,
Under skies cold needle and thread lie inert.
Red cheeks will stay the same a long, long while.
You may come home, but how can they last for you?

Picking caltrop

I live near Five Lake estuary,
I pick caltrop on Five Lake shores.
My jade face isn't interested in cosmetics,
Twin eyebrows are natural kingfisher tones.

When the sun slants, the sky is about to darken.
When winds are roused, waves are restless.
There he is midstream!
No good we two falling in love . . .

Despair at Eternal Gate Palace

Towards dusk a thousand sorrows stir.
And self-blame, when will the sighing end?
When sad memories even come back to me in bed,
My gossamer gown just stifles the weeping.
Crimson trees rock gently with the breeze,
The tunes orioles make sound worried.
When your House of Gold was to treasure A-chiao,
That didn't mean you weren't to visit!

Two melodic songs for drum and pipe music

Mount Wu high

The light on Mount Wu is growing late,
Sun Terrace colours dwindle, dwindle.
The lovely woman in her eyrie's towering height,
How to tell if her heart is true or false?

Dawn clouds knock against rocks as they rise,
Dusk rain soaks clothes sheer.
I long to loosen her thousand-gold girdle
And invite her to follow the great king back home.

The one I love

Royal Forest crows are about to nest,
Over Ch'angan the sun is going down.
The one I love I despair of ever meeting,
It's useless to dream of cinnabar-court footsteps.

Blinds stirring remind me of your visits,
Sounds of thunder resemble your carriage passing.
In the north there's a lovely, beautiful girl,
Meek and mild, she makes heads turn.
'Dear husband, go and get bedazzled!
That won't make your wife's heart jealous!'

YAO FAN

Harmonizing with Palace Secretary Kuo's poem, 'Picking mulberry'

The geese are coming back to Tallwillow,
Spring is coming home to south of Lo river.
The sun shines on an oleaster collar,
The wind sways kingfisher hairpins.

Among the mulberry I see it's getting dark,
In my rooms silkworms will soon be hungry.
I love you, so you help me gather!
Watching for you – your wife can't bear it!

K'UNG WENG-KUEI

*Harmonizing with the poem, 'Lady Pan', by the Prince of Hsiangtung
[Hsiao I] at the command of His Royal Highness*

Eternal Gate and Eternal Trust
At sundown are nine-barred and deserted.
Thunderous sounds I hear rumbling, rumbling,
Echoing coaches stop their clatter-clatter.

His favoured light courted her skilful dance,
The round fan surrenders to autumn winds.
Glamorous beauty who does not desire?
It's natural human love can't last.

HSÜ FEI'S WIFE [LIU LING-HSIEN]

Two poems in reply to my husband, who is away

No. 1

The flowering garden is lovely in the slanting rays,
Through orchid windows soft breezes cross.
In the setting sun she puts on fresh make-up again.
Opens the blinds on to spring trees.
Warbling orioles in the leaves echo,
Playful butterflies among the flowers flutter.

She strums her lute in joy's own pursuit,
Her heart for sadness will not be diverted.
Happiness together is not too distant,
But my handsome man who promised I don't meet.
Would you know how much she grieves in secret?
Her spring boudoir is withdrawn and shaded.

No. 2

'In the east house a perfect beauty'?
'Of southern realms the most exquisite face'?
'In the night moon she appears like a goddess'?
'In dawn mists she seems to be Fufei the nymph'?

But I look at my face in the mirror
And know that your fond similes are false,
Your evocations hopelessly clever,
Your allusions absolutely wrong!
Though you, an intellectual, think me lovely,
A 'city-destroyer' I hardly dare aspire to!

HO SSU-CH'ENG

*Harmonizing with the poem, 'Lady Pan', by the Prince of Hsiangtung
[Hsiao I] at the command of His Royal Highness*

Hushed, hushed Eternal Trust late.
A sparrow twitters near her secret room,
Spiders spin webs down high galleries,
Lichen carpets long verandas,
Curtains hang unmoved in empty halls,
Stamens breathe scent on still stone steps.
She watches the sun set for eternity,
Turns again to dust her lonely bed.

In the style of an old poem

A past affair can never be forgotten,
It remains like the scent of cassia or of orchid.
His new friend, though he may enjoy her,
Is no different from dogwood's weak perfume.

The melody your wife has is the *Phoenix and chicks*,
Not *Mulberry up the lane*.
I gave you my song, you refused.
Cradling my lute to myself I mourn the coldness.

In South Park I met a lovely woman

Lo shore seems like driven snow,
Wu Mount like dawn clouds.
Today I first saw a city-destroyer,
Of realm-destroyers I had heard long ago.
Her seductive eyes are married to shy charm,
Her cinnabar lips are parted in a smile,
Winds curl her grapevine sash,
The sun shines on her pomegranate skirt.
She has, of course, her dashing husband there,
So a prefect simply need not bother!

? HSÜ FEI'S WIFE, NÉE LIU [LIU LING-HSIEN]

My reply to T'ang Niang's Seventh Night needlework

Singers attend the Han river girl,
Her painted face leans into the moon's glory.
Linked needle stitching imitates double stems,
Lacework forms opening buds.

But widowed rooms have done with fine silks.
To take your gift would touch a painful wound.
Though I admit not knowing you,
I've heard it said you are well-born.

In the past Huo Kuang halted his coach here,
Liu Hsia-hui used to call in his carriage.
There is no way that we can talk together.
So for now I watch the sun rise in the mist.

CHAPTER SEVEN

ROYAL POETS OF THE LIANG
(THE HSIAO FAMILY)

Fulling cloth

He yoked his carriage north of Yi river,
I escorted him north of the Yellow river.
Dejected thoughts brood on his moving harness,
Tense dreams haunt my empty bed.
When I wake red and green blur,
I begin to sense the wound of plain silk.
From Chungchou trees leaves are falling,
The frontier wall must have early frost.
Shadowy insects grow numb, chilled day by day,
Garden flowers turn a brighter yellow.
Metal winds on clear nights pass by,
A bright moon hangs over the hollow house.

Soft, soft girls of the same palace
Help me prepare his clothes.
Evening pounders in fits and starts drag on,
Doleful autumn blocks carry wide.
Light silk billows round jade arms,
Frail plumes dip over rosy faces.
Red cheeks flush up even more,
Slanting glances sparkle ever brighter.
We pound with all our 'not a stone'
The pattern forming a pair of mandarin ducks.
The shears we hold would cut metal,
The incense we use is sweet as orchid.

Long has my betrothed not returned.
I carry this to send it to his cold town.
For whom will his wife's body be made lovely?
Longing for a lover makes one's guts bitter.

In the style of 'In Ch'angan there's a narrow passage',
in eleven rhymed couplets

In Loyang there's a winding lane,
A winding lane no courier can pass.
Suddenly two youths happen to meet.
Leaning on the reins one asks, 'Where's your lord's home?'
'My lord's home is west of Hantan,
It's easy to remember and well known.
The eldest son's badge ribbons are in a tangle,
The middle son's pendants are glittering.
The youngest still in blue silk
And topknot goes out to play at Nanp'i.

'When the three sons enter the gates together
Servants bow down near the gates.
When the three sons go up the hall together
Rich wine would fill a thousand cups.
When the three sons go indoors together
A brilliant light appears inside.

'The eldest's wife is fixing gold kingfisher plumes,
The middle wife is working a bodkin.
The youngest's wife alone has time to spare,
She tunes her pipes, plays games by winding streams.
"Dear husband, stay around for a while,
My phoenix pipe is just giving a fanfare!"'

In the style of 'Bright the moon shines on a tall house'

Its round brilliance faces an empty doorway,
Clear light streams on a bed of love.
A bed of love reflects an orphan shadow,
Bitter remorse besides self-pity.
The mirror on its stand soon gathers dust,
The lute in its case, too, has no strings.
Sad desire wounds through countless seasons,
Despair in separation lasts many flowering years.

My lover is like East Mulberry radiance,
His wife, I'm like West Willow smoke.
The road away from you is now remote,
Light and darkness also hang strangely apart.
I long to be reins of bronze and iron
To stir your heart in front of Eternal Joy Palace.

In the style of 'Green, green riverside grass'

Veiled, veiled the broidered door with spiders' silk.
Far away, far away brooding on promises past.
Promises past: long he hasn't come home.
Our town and state are bereft of your sweet news;
Sweet news that binds us both is uselessly slow.
Half asleep, I feel as if he has arrived;
When I wake there is no shadow left.
I'm cut off from you all my life.
The moon's light is buried by clouds,
Leaves' ageing hurried on by frost.
Those on the way compete for their own image;
No one will speak for your wife.

In the manner of the wife of Su Wu of the Colonies

My lovely one made me a promise.
I never dreamed time would pass by.
Autumn winds suddenly dismiss the season,
White dew hardens on the front porch.
I ache, ache on my chill, lonely pillow,
I'm hurt, hurt by the orphan moonlit drapes.
Suddenly I hear a north-west goose;
It seems to be from the cold wastes,
It's true – its beak holds a ten-thousand-league letter.
In it are words of a lifetime separation.
He only talks of long separation,
No longer says 'I love you.'

Hun sheep he plundered long ago,
Han flags he held in the past.
Before I'd finished reading his words on silk
Down my cheekbones are tears like silk threads.
It's useless to cherish our 'vow unto death',
You reward me from afar with your 'joint grave' poem.

Two poems on an old theme

No. 1

Flying birds rise in flurried lines,
Scatter in fear, sudden disarray,
Cawing, cheeping they circle the treetops,
Fluttering, hovering to flock on cold boughs.
Whenever I'm sad from our campaign long
I always feel the pain of the man on the ridge.
I send these words to my love in her boudoir:
'How can you know what this heart of mine is like?
Don't you see the dodder on the pine,
Leaves may fall, but roots will never stray!'

No. 2

To welcome spring there was a flower,
Green its blossoms and many its stems.
They say it's the 'forget despair' plant.
It grows beside the north hall.

Flit, flit a pair of butterflies
Bobbing in twos up and down,
Swerving, swooping down then up.
The essence of this scent never alters;
Flitting butterflies are now a pair, then single.
Here is a heart humans will never fathom.

Fragrant tree

A green tree starts to toss fragrance,
A fragrance sprung from not one leaf;
For over one leaf pass spring winds
Making fragrance with fragrance join in close embrace.
Colours mingle in a shifting mosaic,
Massed flowers gay with piled-up treasure,
Piled treasure I cannot bear to dwell on . . .
Who can be calm to dwell on this?

Looking from a high terrace

The high terrace is half among passing clouds.
I stare, stare from limitless height.
Grass, trees no variation,
Hills, rivers all one colour.
Hazy, hazy is the road to Loyang.
The road is far, hard to make out.
Jade steps, someone I used to desire.
Desire rekindles – does he think the same of me?

The one I love

Who said lifetime separation is long!
I remember vividly parting from you.
On my clothes your scent still remains,
In my grasp your letter not yet faded,
Round my waist the twin silk belts
I dream wind into kindred hearts.
Often I fear my love will show –
A jasper bloom I cannot bear to pick.

Purple orchid starts to bud

Orchid planted near the jade terrace,
In warm air orchid starts to bud.
Its sweet scent comes out with the hours,
Grows lovely and fair to greet the season.
It alone will bring charm to gilded kingfisher plumes,
Only it will rouse red silk to passion.
Why bother to love the two pleasure-seekers?
One look – she's not a city-destroyer.
Too shy to be coupled with lotus and iris,
Why would she dread the shrike's knell?

The weaving wife

After we separated and you left the south eaves
Thoughts of parting sank heavy in my quiet room.
The loaded shuttle lies still on cold nights,
The humming loom stops on autumn days.
My lover is ten thousand leagues away,
With whom to share my woven stuff?
I wish I could once turn light back
To brighten this sorrow and pain.
If your desire is not forgotten,
Your wife's heart will last to the end of time.

Seventh Night

White dew beneath the moon is beading,
Autumn winds over the trees are freshening.
The jasper terrace enfolds green fog,
From jade curtains purple smoke grows.
Their rare meetings are not in the sweetest season,
For these sweethearts it's not the best time of year.
The jade pitcher carries night swift,
The orchid tallow till the dawn is flaring.
Long ago I was sad how hard it was to cross,
Now I'm wounded how soon it is passed.
Breathless grief, twin rapture severed.
Disenchantment, two loves in suspense.

Bagatelle

A Fufei is born from Lo shore!
A roving nymph rises from Han south bank!
Her charms are sweeter than at Hsiats'ai,
Her mystery more divine than at Kaot'ang.
Mien Chü transformed local custom,
Wang Pao transferred his native culture.
How much the more the devas gathered here!
Surely they've managed to become great?
Their long sleeves always make guests stay behind,
Clear chant ever spins round rafters.
Yen and Chao are ashamed of their looks,
Hsi Shih and Ta Chi shamed by their fragrance.
Though it's only hearsay, that pearl being fondled,
Surely you'll be needing bright earrings?

THE HEIR-APPARENT, EMPEROR CHIEN-WEN, HSIAO KANG

Composed by His Majesty, Three folk-songs

Song of beauty, in eighteen rhymed couplets

Daybreak's glowing scene is lovely,
A singer is in her phoenix house.
Seen from the front her tapered waist is tinier,
Viewed from the side a flag rolled into nothing.
She apportions cosmetics between faint dimples,
Spreads over cheeks slanting rouge.
She plays her lute with pegs not tightened,
Her singing and piping are never fully finished.

She knows herself that her heart's beloved
Frequents the Ch'in palace on duty.
Who says he bows and scrapes to officials?
He moves instead in the highest circles!
His light coach's black awning is festooned,
Reins fly, his greys clatter along,
Gold saddles matching braided tails,

Inlaid jade glinting on plaited manes.
His lance is studded with Ching Mountain jade,
His sword is made of Tanyang bronze.
His left fist grasps storax shot,
Beside him he holds the Great Curve bow.
Drawing the bowstring he relies on Magpie Blood bow,
Wielding the strong bow he uses Oxfly.
For hunting with corded dart he often climbs Lung range,
For drinking deep and song he always goes to Feng.

Glimmer, glimmer the sinking sun hides,
With measured step he goes home to boudoir lattice.
Lamps come alive from the speculum flame,
Dust scatters in Carp winds.
Coloured plume curtains seasonally lowered,
His ivory bed is replaced in its case.

Fog darkens willow before the window,
Cold engulfs catalpa over the well.
Love-vine clings to the fringe of a pine,
Sweet melon creeps east of the well.
Tight, tight I cling to your favour.
As the year fades my hope is unending.

The kingdom of Shu, a song for stringed instruments in ten rhymed couplets

Where Bronzebridge points to Yeh valley,
Dagger Road looks to Central Plains,
Following the stars up above Shu's realm is marked.
Fixed firm is its city below.
Classical song ensues from good order in the land,
Exotic dance originated in Pa and Yü.
Yang city is the place for fun and pleasure.
With daggers boys ride, racing in swarms.
The five wives journeyed, but couldn't arrive.
One hundred carriages make fine sport.

They offer sacrifice and prayer on Emperor Wang's feast-day.
They sprinkle wine on the ground for the Lord of Shu's
    execution.
The river sprites received double betrothal gifts,
The Cho girl longed to 'lead her chicks'.

I stop my strings, strum with plectrum a while,
Cease piping to put on more lipstick.
Spring colours I rinse in Brocade river waves.
My fan I twirl against the bright bird.
I hear you come home with banners raised,
Your wretched wife will go down to the corner city wall.

The 'Woman's sad fate' piece, in ten rhymed couplets

The famous capital is full of beautiful talent
Who pride themselves on their looks.
My wastrel travels but never arrives;
A Ch'iu Hu, he won't keep his promise.
On my jade face fade pink cheeks,
Long frowns furrow my kingfisher eyebrows.
In my cosmetic mirror is a puzzled morning face,
In the sewing needle is brittle old thread.

I'm different from the scolded 'rock-the-boat' girl.
What have I to do with the 'baby-snatching' suspect?
We part for life, but who will 'pat my back'?
If I dropped dead, who would say 'How slow she comes'?
Wang Ch'iang's beauty was extraordinary,
Yet she reluctantly stepped inside felt tents.
Lady Lu married late in the day
When she was no longer in her finest season.
Moving a mountain can still be done,
I'll hope for the unlikely day crows turn white.
Your wife's heart suffers for nothing.
Onlookers must be laughing out loud!

Three poems in the manner of folk-songs

Calm Joy Palace newly built

Far away through cloud and mist I see
Carved rafters reflect cinnabar red,
Pearl blinds shot with dawn sunlight,
Gilt flowers brushed by night winds.
You want to know the place for song and pipes?
Come by Calm Joy Palace!

Twin catalpas grow by a lonely well

Late spring moon. Twin catalpas by a well,
New twigs mix with old stumps.
Late leaves hide nesting phoenix,
Dawn flowers stroke morning rooks.
Once more I glimpse Hsi Shih in splendour,
By the silver kerb she draws up the rope.

Sighs of a lady of Ch'u

In her room still the water-clock drips and drips,
Time's infinity, the hush of hushed night.
Grass insects flit through the night door,
Spiders entwine autumn walls.
She faintly smiles, but she is not happy,
She softly sighs, but it turns to sorrow.
Gold pins droop down her hair,
Jade chopsticks trickle on her dress.

*Three poems harmonizing with melodic songs for
horizontal flute by the Prince of Hsiangtung [Hsiao I]*

The road to Loyang

Loyang is the place for lovely beauty,
Its highways full of spring glory.
Sportive boys hold their first catapults,
Silkworm girls carry their first baskets.
Golden saddles blaze on dragon horses,
Silken sleeves caress spring mulberry.
Jade carriages race late into town,
P'an Yüeh's fruit fills tall hampers.

Broken willow

Willow tangled into silken strands
Is pulled and broken in early springtime.
Foliage thick bird flight hinders,
Winds gentle flower's fall prolong.

222

From city walls high short flutes sound out.
Through forests bare painted horns forlorn.
In the melodies there's no hint of parting –
Every one means 'I'll always love you'.

Sorrel horse

Your wretched wife got down from her loom at dawn,
And just then met my love coming home.
Green ribbons dangling from jade stirrups,
Scarlet sweat staining perfumed clothes,
Cantering so fast precious cowries jingled,
Prancing so much scattered dust billowed.
'Oatcakes I'm pleased to serve you,
Past love you must not betray!'

Three selections from Ten Yungchou melodic songs

South lake

On South lake water-lily leaves are floating.
There, too, sweethearts seek pleasure.
Silvery fishing lines, kingfisher-blue hooks,
Jade stern, hibiscus boat,
Lotus scent blending with musk of clothes
To the sound of oars in the water's swift flow.

North beach

Over banks shady hang willow fronds,
The smooth river carries whitewashed fences.
Women from near the city I often meet,
See girls many times in their pleasure boats,
Green water spraying long sleeves,
Floating alga staining light oars.

The great embankment

Off to Yi city I stopped midway
Where travellers usually tarry.
Divorced women skilled at plainweave,
Sirens who notch up a fortune,
Cook oatcakes to detain the best clients
Who buy wine to woo these sylphs.

Two poems matching the rhymes of Yü Chien-wu's
Four poems

In lotus boats we buy a lotus crossing

Where they pick lotus at the riverbend bank
Boat girls often dilly-dally.
Lotus pickers' dresses I can just make out,
Winds soft their scent does not carry.
You want to know where boats slip through?
Just look for lotus leaves that lie open!

I see a dropped hairpin reflected in the river's flow

Following her, her reflection in green water
Seems to crave a cooling breeze.
The flow trembles, painted image ravaged.
A hairpin drops, coiffure flowers vanish.
Where is her beloved so long?
She suffers in vain for hearts no longer one.

Two poems harmonizing with the Prince of Hsiangtung
[Hsiao I], in three rhymed couplets

Spring nights

Blossoming trees hold springtime clusters,
Silk bedcurtains are ever empty at night.
The wind's voice through bamboo sounds rhythmic,
The moon's colour harmonizes with the pool.
Tinted notepaper crumples in vain,
No news will reach Yünchung.

Winter light

The wintry dawn sun shines on rafters,
Morosely she gets down from her bed,
Lifts from the curtains her bamboo-leaf sash,
Turns to the mirror her caltrop-bloom radiance.
Certain there's no one to see her like this,
What's the use of early-morning rouge?

Bagatelle in the style of Hsieh Hui-lien, in thirteen rhymed couplets

Mosaic stamens brighten the south garden,
In the garden is a bright scene so sweet.
Prettiest blossom on the bough
Will soon win the spring wind's love.
The spring wind feels passion too:
It strokes bedcurtains, reveals pillars,
Revealing pillars, reveals emerald smoke,
Stroking bedcurtains, strokes hanging lotus,
Making red flowers scatter everywhere
To tumble and flutter, dancing before my eyes.

Before my eyes there is no want of images,
I can stare at patterns kaleidoscopic:
Pearl tassels, kingfisher curtains,
Satin drapes, hibiscus folds,
Scented smoke pouring from windows,
Sunset slanting across stairs,
Sun-rays depart slower and slower.
Seasonal blooms surround me here:
Peach blossom pink like dots,
Willow leaves tangled like silk thread,
Silken twigs twist towards darkening light,
Shadows fall, dark shades lengthen.

Spring swallows dance double, double,
Spring hearts everywhere are wounded.
Wine in plenty, the heart's moment of ease.
The branch of oblivion for sorrow not forgotten.

A singer's frustration, in twelve rhymed couplets

Silk windows look on painted galleries,
Soaring galleries encircle long corridors.
Winds scatter double heart plants,
The moon sends out a sweet light.
Shadowy inside the blinds appears
A charming beauty quite unusual.
Shyly she copies Ch'in Lofu's hairdo,
Bashfully does her upstairs-girl's cosmetics.
She slips on her rustling red shawl,
Dabs fresh chic yellow on her brow.

Slanting the lamp she goes inside brocade bedcurtains
To her jade bed glimmering with faint incense.
The six-cornered twin tortoiseshell pillows,
Their eight-panelled quilt adorned with two mandarin ducks,
These things can still long since they parted
Comfort love's grief, mementoes of him.
In tears she passes tedious days
So soon transformed from hot to cold.

Jade Gate Pass riders struggle through night snow,
Metal air hurls harsh frost.
Couriers icebound at Fleetfox Pass,
Too distant the Crossriver waterway.
Of my vagrant love there is no news,
Scarlet lips are uselessly perfumed.

Harmonizing with Court Registrar Hsü Ch'ih's poem,
'Watching my wife get ready for bed'

In her hidden room the cold sun grows late,
Declining rays cross the window sill.
Red blinds far do not prevent my view,
Light drapes hang half rolled up.
So then I know slim hands are tailoring,
Such perfection his finely sewn cloak.
Dragon shears lie across her knees,
The painted rule slips down her skirt front.
Her pressing iron is the sheen of gilt varnish,
Her needle spool is cased in ivory.

Cloth is cut into 'joy of love' pleats,
The design she makes is linked mandarin ducks.
In sewing she uses double needle thread,
For padding a silkworm's eightfold thread.

Her perfume laced with Lich'iu nectar
And musk exhaling Chungt'ai smoke
Now enters lapis lazuli bedcurtains,
Suffuses Mount T'ai rugs.
Besides she has a carved stove warm,
Unlike the round fan rejected.
She fears more keenly wartime separation:
An empty bed and futile self-pity.

Bagatelle for a lovely woman

Beautiful Ta Chi and bewitching Mao Ch'iang,
You all brush on your pretty cosmetics,
Like them fix long pins in your hair,
But unlike them you put yellow on your brow.
Your silk skirts are admired for sheer fineness,
Painted slippers prized for their high rims.

Too shy to go upstairs,
You go out faintly smiling to the veranda,
Pick flowers to offset haircombs,
Tug boughs and muse on stamen scent,
Sing to yourself one snatch of song,
On dulcet strings tireless play.
You pride yourself on your sweetheart –
At thirty a palace attendant!

Night longing in an autumn bedroom

It's nothing to do with Eternal Trust exile,
Nor that my lover is on campaign,
But sudden from nine-barred rooms he disappeared,
Ten thousand jealousies flourish in my heart.
Twilight gates locked with fish-emblazoned keys,
Nightly bed grieving behind painted screens.
A distant moon looks down through the window,

Moaning insects murmur round the steps.
Early frosts dislodge tiny leaves,
Autumn winds chase scattered fireflies.
My stale make-up is still on after several days,
My new dress is tuck-pleated but unsewn.
Do you want to know if your wife no longer sleeps?
It's the sound of fulling clothes beyond the city wall.

Harmonizing with the Prince of Hsiangtung's [Hsiao I] poem,
'A famous knight delights in his city-destroyer'

A beauty described as extraordinary
Is lovely as a posy of blooms.
Though she lives north of Li Yen-nien's city,
Her home is east of Sung Yü's house.
She models her singing on the Princess's mansion,
Copies the dances of Han Emperor Ch'eng's palace.
She often enjoys herself on Ch'i river,
And loves to stay in phoenix house.

Heels so high seem to go up steps,
Skirts flaring are so nervous of the wind.
Under sheer colours I see her arms,
Pearls amassed mixed with dragonflies.
Hanging silk tassels fringe her bedcurtains,
The setting sun goes through her bedroom lattice.
Cosmetic windows blot out willow colour,
Well water reflects peach pink.
'It's not that I regret her "river bank girdle",
But I'm ashamed her spring bedroom is empty.'

Back in town on short furlough

The water by Han river banks is an early green,
Grass south of the river is once more yellow.
In sunshine reedmace hearts grow warm,
From winds blowing plum stamens are scented.
My campaign vessel moored at the brimming moat,
I gallop home to rest by the iron moat.

228

Her dance-hall dresses are still folded away,
Her concert-song strings are yet untouched.
He holds this dear, but busily strides away.
She asks, 'Who cares if I keep an empty bed?'

Poem on someone who discarded his wife

Long ago he was charmed by her jade footsteps.
She swallows her shame by flowery candles.
Surely you aren't saying his heart has stopped loving!
She bites back tears of self-pity.
She's used to watching joy turn to grief,
But this is nothing to do with beauty grown ugly.
The lone goose gives up midway,
A waif paradise bird dead before the mirror.

Pen in hand, I write a playful letter

Dancing girls and Yen maidens,
Houses of song and women of pleasure
Make their large plectrums bob up and down in sound,
And slowly wind in 'Minor hands lowered' dance.
Fishing rod from Shu they strum,
Hsinch'eng's *Broken willow* they pipe.
On jade tables Queen of the West peaches,
In pearl-whorl cups pomegranate wine.
From houses A to Z the silk drapes are different,
From One to N front doors are splendid.
Night after night there is a bright moon,
Season after season I love their change of dresses.

Song of beauty, a melodic song

Cloudy fanlight of cassia is its frame,
Flying ridge-pole of apricot are its rafters.
Through slanting windows slips stamen's breath,
Through tiny cracks trails a dusty ray.

She cuts the cloth out with her Empress of Wei measure,
Draws water from her Prince of Huainan well-kerb.
His green-black horse should be coming home at dark.
In readiness she perfumes silk skirts.

A poem on regret

Autumn winds and round white fans
Are naturally incompatible.
A new woman and past love –
Surely an intolerable idea!
With yellow gold bells behind my elbows,
With jade dishes before the table –
Who could bear to face these uselessly?
Or else accept he's turned to 'cold season' infidelity?

In the style of Lord Yin, Shen Yüeh's melodic song, 'Night after night'.

The faint, faint frost in the night
Has nothing to do with dawn's approaching light.
She weeps on her pillow still wearing powder,
Her body won't settle down to sleep in bed.
Orchid tallow gutters, flares again.
Her incense burner goes out, rekindles its perfume.
Ask but the measure of grief –
It is known by the length of night.

Seventh Night

Their autumn promise creeps towards the present.
Through long night moves the River goddess.
Purple smoke pierces phoenix wings,
Shooting light trails after her jade coach.
Loyang wonders if she's the sword spirit,
Ch'engtu marvels at the strange star.
The sky shuttle she long wove with
She now stops at last to meet him on this night.

Matching the rhymes of Palace Adviser Liu Hsiao-cho's 'Poem on Spring snow'

A late hailstorm hurls silver pebbles,
Floating clouds darken not lifting.
Snow in the pond dissolves without settling,
Dropped and picked up with the wind.
In the flowing yellow silk of a woman in love,
By her Lady Wen jade mirror-stand,
She looks at a flower, says she might pin it up –
It's certainly not spring plum blossom.

Out for a walk in late sunlight

Slender trees engulfed in unspent sunlight,
Her spring bedroom is suffused with late perfume.
Dainty flowers slip down her curls,
Faint sweat on her powder glistens.
The *Flying ducks* tune she soon stops,
The *Sobbing crow* rhythm abruptly changes.
Shamed by the white sun darkening,
Among coach and horse crowds she hopes for him.

Assigned a folk-song theme for composition, I received the title, 'Major dance gestures'

Lowered hands suddenly soar, soar,
A Feiyen enchanting on his palm.
Her silk dress lures trailing winds,
Her light sash sways with passionate surrender.
It's not like the land of Ch'angsha
Where dance steps don't make waists whirl.

Assigned the name of a musical instrument for composition, I received the title, 'The Harp'

The plectrum slackens, fluting softly starts,
The music quickens, speeding up the dance.
Bangles jingle in time to strumming strings,
Tunics whirl, half caught in the stops.
Do you want to know if her heart is excited?
Then you watch her kohl eyebrows contract!

Poem on the Dance

How sweet, she's just twice eight!
She follows the rhythms like a gliding swan.
She's far better than Hoyang entertainers,
She's sultry like those in the Huainan dance.
As she moves into line I see her feet draw nearer;
As she turns her face I watch her chignon vanish.
On her arm moves Chao Hua jade,
Sleeves follow winds fancy-free.
'Honoured guest, why must you get up?
My *Sobbing crow* tune is not ended!'

Spring bedroom passion

Willow leaves are slim, slim.
A lovely girl lazily weaves fine silk.
She straightens her dress, turns towards the mirror,
To greet spring cautiously lifts the blinds.

To pick plum blossom she circles the trees many times;
To look for swallows peers frequently into the eaves.
She simply says, 'In the pursuit of flowers
I'm quite above suspicion!'

Three more rhymed couplets [*Poem on her late boudoir*]

Pearl blinds were lowered at dusk.
Her charming form I can pursue no more.
Flowered winds in the dark I sense,
Orchid candles through curtains waft.
Within jade windows when again
Night after night will she sew?

Extempore composition

Goddess or painting is she, may I ask,
How could such beauty exist?
She destroys cities and destroys kingdoms.
Like the rain is she and like a goddess.
The Han Empress longed for the name Yen,
The king of Chou prized the name Shen.
Cradling her lute once she went to Chao.
Blowing pipes she often entered Ch'in.

By the jade steps she stares all around at the trees;
Down verandas ever chases spring.
She applies yellow with utmost artistry,
Handles strings with novel technique.
Sometimes to the wind she will stretch her sleeves,
Screening the sun holds out her momentary scarf.
Dainty flowers she inserts to sparkle in her hair,
A fine belt clasps the tunic round her body.
Who knows when the sun will darken?
She is too shy to speak.

A lovely woman's morning make-up

At the north window she turns to her dawn mirror.
Brocade curtains she drapes in a slanting twist.
Sweet, shy, unwilling to come out
She still claims her make-up isn't done.
She spreads kohl wide along her eyebrows,
Yen rouge appears across her cheeks.
No doubt with all this she's sensational,
She deserves to be called 'Adorable'!

Assigned a poem for composition, I received the title, 'At the wine-stove'

On the fifteenth it is round, quite round;
Its streaming light floods Shanglan lodge.
At the wine-stove she serves night wine.
A lodging guest unfastens his gold saddle.
She finds it easy to greet him hugging her lute;
She finds it hard to see him off with solo song.
'Didn't I know love quickly turns to hate?
Still, it makes my dress and belt hang loose.'

Singers by the wood

Burning rays relent toward twilight.
Near the front pool a casual feast is set.
Fountain and shadow harmonize,
Flower and pretty face enhance each other.
Notes from a flute trilling like birdsong,
Dancing sleeves silhouette windy boughs.
In happy joy we drink ourselves unconscious –
Let it be so for one thousand autumns!

In the style of [Hsieh T'iao's poem] 'As the sun sets she sits at her window'

Apricot rafters gleam in slanting sun,
Waning glimmers shine on a lovely girl.
She opens her jewel-box, takes off precious bracelets,
Turns to the mirror and tidies her sheer scarf.
Playful fish stir the pond leaves,
Dancing storks scatter staircase dust.
'Why waste sighs on one thousand years?
I'd like to get as far as sunny spring!'

Poem on a lovely person studying her portrait

Up in the hall there's a painting of a goddess;
In the palace emerges a beautiful person.
Lovely in every way the latter and the painting –
Who could tell art from real life?
They have clearly defined bright eyes and eyebrows,
They have the same kind of slim-waisted body.
A special differentiation could be made:
One always has that vital spark!

His favourite boy

His favourite boy's charm is loveliness itself
That outstrips Tung Yen and surpasses Mi Tzu-hsia.
Feather drapes fill with dawn incense,
Pearl blinds muffle water-clock sounds at dusk.
His kingfisher quilt is charged with mandarin-duck tints,
His carved bed is inlaid with ivory.

Remarkably youthful like the pageboy Chou,
His pretty face resembles dawn mists.
His sleeves are made of 'twin disc' brocade,
His tunic is woven from dainty cloth-tree blossom.
When he holds his trousers a light flush mounts,
When he turns his head twin side-locks slide across.
His flirting eyes hold a momentary smile,
Jade hands pick random flowers.

He's jealous not being his lord's latest catch,
His secret love is like the erstwhile carriage.
He's enough to make Yen girls envious,
Or worse, put Cheng women to shame!

THE PRINCE OF SHAOLING, HSIAO LUN

In the manner of the poem, 'The boudoir resentment of Ch'iu Hu's wife'

A wayward man has gone on official circuit,
His longing wife keeps to bedroom lattice.
Her dusty mirror dawn by dawn is buried,
The cold bed night on night lies vacant.
If it isn't a new girl he fancies,
What work is keeping him so long out east and west?
In case he wonders if somebody loves him,
Tears are spent from weeping in my dreams.

From my carriage I see a fair lady

Captive passion stirs from her eyes and eyebrows,
Tender desire catches her waist and limbs.
Her words, her smile can cast a spell,
Her walk is extremely wigglesome!
I gape up at the sky bedazzled.
Those near the moat are all unaware.
Since love from afar is like this,
How would I feel to possess her?

In the manner of the poem, 'A former mistress feels resentment'

Oh let's be ten thousand leagues apart
Rather than this life and death separation!
How can I bear to see with my own eyes
Past love move aside for new?
Spring blossom not yet unfurled tumbles
Suddenly blown down by autumn winds.
Resentful kohl become smooth contracts again;
My tearful face is wiped but trickles once more.
Who can write persuasively for me?
With yellow gold your wife would reward him!

Going up the familiar gallery in the park of Yen [Hsieh]

A tall house on the three-fives night,
When shadows stream into cinnabar court.
Long ago you made a high-ranking guest linger –
Your bridegroom's handsome figure.
With your make-up done and cicada-wing locks combed,
Your smiles ceased, moth eyebrows puckered.
From clothes' perfume he knew your steps drew near,
From bangles moving he sensed your walk was slow.
Why did the joy of the dance-hall
Change to singing rafter grief I now see?

Still hang the north window curtains,
Unfolded the south eaves drapes.
Hushed, hushed empty streets darken.
It no longer is the season of youth.

Bagatelle, a poem on beauty

As I entered the hall I came across a young wife,
As I left by the gate I met her former husband.
Choking on her words, before she could blurt them out,
She tugged his sleeve and shifted awkwardly.
The fan she twirled was like the moon,
The tears she shed like pearls.
'My love for you now never ceased in the past,
Of your past love for me now remain the lees.'

Night visit to Cypress Studio

Candles grow dim, passers-by quieten,
Blinds open, cloud shadows come in.
In slight winds the sound of rain slackens,
On nights short the water gauge hastens.

The many times Lady Pan shed tears
Make the house of song once more weep.
How much worse for this travelling man
Who at midnight is standing pointlessly.

Harmonizing with Liu's poem, 'Shanghuang'

New orioles hidden by leaves are trilling,
New swallows toward windows are flitting.
Willow fluff leans randomly over our wine,
Plum blossom drops sudden into our clothes.
A jade bridle keeps time with the wind,
A gold saddle glitters in sunshine.
Don't let spring's beauty grow late!
Lonesome I watch for a wanderer's return.

Poem on Late nesting crows

As the sun declines, wing to fluttering wing
They flock towards Royal Forest to nest.
Winds redouble, the first birds speed forward,
Clouds darken, the last ones get lost.
The way is far, cries go unheard,
They fly off course out of formation.
'You must be back from my old town,
How often did you pass into orchid bedrooms?
May I ask, a wife in a house of song –
How does she compare with a playboy's wife?'

Cold night, in three rhymed couplets

Magpies flying south at night.
My beloved travels but hasn't come home yet.
The pool water floats a bright moon,
Cold winds carry fulling sounds away.
I long to weave a palindrome brocade
And through you send it to Wuwei.

Poem on autumn night

On autumn nights, nine-barred and deserted,
For her wastrel she is plaintive by bedroom lattice.
Lamplight enters sheer bedcurtains,
Blinds' shadows loom on the screen.
On gold studs I tune the jade pegs
To strum *Parted swans* on such a night as this.

THE PRINCE OF WULING, HSIAO CHI

Matching the rhymes of the poem, 'Watching a singer', by Chief Secretary
Hsiao Chieh

Yen girls play exotic dances,
Cheng women perform clear song.
Responsive shyness shows on glossy cheeks,
Missive flirting hides in puckered eyebrows.
Is this any different from the Falling Rain tryst?
Other than the Crested Wave vision?
I imagine as you mourn the sunset
You must envy Lord Yang of Lu's lance!

Harmonizing with the Prince of Hsiangtung's poem, 'Dream in the night',
at the command of His Royal Highness

Last night I dreamed you came home:
Your wretched wife, I came down from my humming loom
Remotely aware your love had lessened:
You did not wear the clothes you left home in.
Why do I say 'Just like my dream'?
Because a letter-goose has flown to me here.

Dawning love

Daybreak birds compete to copy their warbling.
Dawn flowers tousled are about to open.
Censer smoke creeps under conical curtains,
A screen conceals her mirror-stand:
Rouge cosmetics are spoilt by tears.
Drifter, when will you come home?

From a boudoir lady to a man on campaign

Her frowning beauty's gold star winces,
Grief-shrouded jade chopsticks flow.
I wish you would see a mirage
And remember your wife up in her tall house.

CHAPTER EIGHT

TWENTY POETS OF THE LIANG DYNASTY
(SIXTH CENTURY)

Two folk-songs

Sunrise at the south-east corner, a ballad

A great glow rises far, far away,
Yang city strikes the soaring mists.
Sunlight shines on a wife at her window;
She's extraordinary, like A-chiao.
Her bright mirror with coiling dragons carved,
Hairpin plumes with phoenix attached,
Twisting-fall her Lady Liang coiffure,
Soft and slim her Ch'u palace waist.
Light silk mixed with brocade layers,
Sheer silk layered with billowing gauze.
Three sixes was she at the close of last year;
Four fives is she at the start of this year.

In the silkworm yard she gathers sweet cocoons,
Up mulberry lanes picks tender stems.
She comes and goes to the east city quarter,
Walks up and down Lo river's west bridge.
Suddenly she meets a stranger in horse and carriage,
Fluttering canopy sways with tossing blinds.
His seamless robe is of musquash weave,
His precious sword has a cast-iron ramhead.
This officer is anxious to speak to her,
The coachman reins in the jingling bit.
Through pillars he stares, stares in vain,
Over the parapet he leans, leans a long while.

'I am a girl from a west side house.
You, sir, court me from a palace.
With Han horse, thirty thousand pairs,
My husband serves in the Ministry of War.
His leather belt-bag broidered with a tiger head,
His left earring fastened with sable tail,
He blows a traverse Dragon-bell flute,
Drums his ivory pan-pipes.

At fifteen a palace page like Chang Pi-ch'iang,
At eighteen an academician like Chia I.
Everyone laughed at Yen Ssu's wizened looks;
All shout my husband is more handsome than Tung Sheng!'

In the manner of the 'Beautiful woman' piece

Hantan, stop dancing one moment!
Singers of Pa, please rest your strings!
The loveliest ones near Ch'i and Wei rivers
Are more glamorous than Chao and outshine Yen girls.
Their radiance is of plum blossom,
Reflected in water they become lotus.
Mornings they sell wine at Ch'engtu,
Evenings they make a fortune at Hochien.
Though they don't suffer the misery of candle stubs,
Their orchid tallow uselessly flames.

WANG YÜN

Six poems harmonizing with Master of Records Wu
[Chün]

Spring months, two poems

No. 1

The sun sparkles on mandarin-duck halls,
Alga grows on a waterfowl pond;
Drifting dust enters on shafts of light,
Frail willow bends with the wind.
The black hawk hunts the yellow-beaks;
A lone stork mourns its beloved hen.
My quilt-sharer pursues distant pleasure,
From wedded love parted lifelong.
At present it's just swift death for me –
Why bother with the day-lily stem?

The cockleburr's heart hasn't yet come out;
Sweet herb leaves are ready to unfurl.
Spring silkworms start trailing thread,
New swallows are just carrying mud in their beaks;
Pheasants of the fields call squawking to their hens;
Garden birds brood over their nesting young.
After you left for Liang
I just shut myself in the spring bedroom at noon.
Mountains and rivers block my road and village.
Sweet flowers bloom in idle luxury.

Autumn nights, two poems

No. 1

Nine-barred abiding in the palace lodge by night,
Four walls cruel without light.
Troubled Star turns to sink in the west,
Magpies fly towards the east.
Gliding fireflies slowly garner their flame,
Grasshoppers will soon speed up their looms.
At such an hour I think of the palindrome brocade,
And keep to it, making clothes for my traveller,
Hoping my cinnabar heart will reach there
So my fine guest might come back home.

No. 2

Florets of dew start to glisten, glisten,
Cassia twigs go rustling, rustling.
The spirit of death falls from storeyed eaves,
Light shadows flood four bedroom walls.
Parted favour lengthens distant night,
Far campaign saddens lonely sleep.
Despair wreathes kingfisher-wing eyebrows,
Tears flood sidelong rippling eyes.
Eternal Gate visits are cut off.
Full of passion I turn back to shuttle and spindle dull.

Roving gaze, two poems

No. 1

The setting sun brightens her rouge
As cradling her zither she faces the window.
I'd rather not sing *Sweet herbs* again,
All I hear are sighing willows.
In wedded bliss we lived as sweethearts,
Our separation was due to common mouths.
Useless for me to serve dewy mallow broth,
Who will pour the orchidaceous wine?
The day we'll meet is remote, without promise.
However will dawn hibiscus last?

No. 2

Restless in bed for love of you
I soon find myself east of narrow lanes.
Despairing eyebrows imitate Lady Liang's village,
A tall hairdo copies city fashion.
Twin door-leaves catch slanting sunlight,
A solitary stamen enjoys eddying winds.
My lover wrote down the longing in his heart,
Presented his poem to Sweet Springs Palace.
I hear they say he now eats from bronze vessels.
How would he remember me in my spring room?

LIU HSIAO-CHO

Five miscellaneous poems

From a distance I noticed my host in a nearby boat throw something into the water. All his singing-girls struggled to retrieve it. One of the guests asked me to write a poem about it.

The river flow is calm, calm;
Waterfowl still cry quack-quack!
Fallen blossom floats away from the banks;
Flying pheasants cross the islet and back.
On such a day as this girls from the house of song
Have faces to rival charms of peach and plum.
Their master is sorry to waste a gorgeous earring,
But wishes to pledge it for sweet rushes.
Of new fineweave old homespun was uncertain;
Chao Feiyen in the ascendant caused Lady Pan's downfall.
Flaunted silks compete with hidden plainweave,
Swinging pendants rob the ring-jingler.
The guests' hearts all throb in vain –
The loftiest boughs never can be plucked!

I point out to my companion a man flirting with a wanderer's wife on the bank of Ch'i river

Among the mulberry it starts to show leaf on leaf;
On the Ch'i it's not yet in spate, in spate.
A pretty girl seeks a patterned belt,
An honoured guest tempts her with bright earrings.
Day darkens, human sounds quieten.
Soft footsteps leave an orchid room.
For dewy mallows she doesn't need prompting,
Her lilting lute isn't slow to play.
Her kingfisher hairpin fastened now slides down,
Her silk dress stroked releases more scent.

247

'Why did I marry a playboy?
On spring nights I keep an empty bed.
I will never see my green silk rider,
So why bother with my rouged and powdered face?'

Assigned a composition, I received the poem title, 'The gleaming games-board', to be completed in the time it took the candle to burn five notches

Strings and piping of Nanp'i stop,
The final gambling keeps the guests a while.
The sun sinks, the room's lattice darkens,
Lovely girls are sent for flowery candles.
Oblique light illumines the whole board.
Refracted beams half conceal their bodies:
'We aren't complaining our slim hands are tired.
It's just a shame that night-time turns to dawn.'

At night when we heard a girl singing, I was assigned a poem for composition entitled 'A crow weeps in the night'

At the *Junglefowl* string music she stops playing a moment;
At the *Parted stork* lute tune she ceases a while the lute-studs.
Next there is the melody *A crow weeps*,
Of flying east and west, each turning its back.
The singer in despair keeps to herself alone,
Her wastrel wanders, not yet home.
If she comes across a lifetime's parting tune
She weeps the long night through in clothes of silk.

Assigned a composition, I received the poem title, 'Left behind for the one I love'

He left behind hairpins carved in tortoiseshell,
And a gift of silk woven with mandarin ducks.
These still aren't as good as moist trees in blossom,
Branches embracing across my playboy's bedroom.
Before he went away autumn had fallen,
After he went away spring grew sweet once more.
The one he loves can send him nothing –
Just wistful heady perfume in her sleeves.

Two miscellaneous poems

Gay, composed by royal command

How pretty he is, the young boy Chou,
As faintly smiling he picks orchid bunches.
His fresh skin is far better than powder white,
His smooth cheeks are like peach-blossom pink.
He hugs his catapult near Tiaoling,
Casts his rod east of Lotusleaves.
His arms move and make his perfume pouch swing;
His clothes so light are at the kind wind's mercy.

Lucky to be chosen to dust the pillow,
To be the one to serve in painted halls.
Gilt screens enclose his kingfisher quilt,
Indigo cloth drapes his incense clothes-frame.
From an early age he knew the pain of scorn,
Kept the words in, ashamed to speak.
Ripped sleeve favours though generous,
Leftover peach love still not ended . . .
What's the use of envying her moth eyebrows?
New made-up girls stream steadily through the palace.

Back from camp to the city, by royal command

Han river so deep, it's hard to ford,
Through the lowest deep I see its clear bed.
Brocade rope moors my duck-prow skiff,
Nacreous poles are strung with kingfisher pennants.
On shrill whistles the *Fragrant tree* melody,
In liquid song *Picking lotus* music.
Divine the cavalcade sweeps past fleetingly,
Return at sunset to assembled camps.
Why look back in an empty bedroom
Where green moss spreads over the steps?

WANG HSÜN

Submitted to His Royal Highness [Hsiao Kang], harmonizing with his poem, 'Extempore composition'

In the hall the many divine girls
Till now were hard to compare —
Except there's an exquisite at the window,
She has the prettiest face of all.
Her studied dance outrivals Chao Feiyen,
Powder she applies makes Nanyang's inferior.
A scattering of yellow, two lines of kohl colour,
Clothes with incense, a blend of jujube scents,
She selects hairpins, freshly pressing their kingfisher plumes;
She examines her slippers and mends their broken sides.
All morning she counts on her appearance
Or else she'll keep an empty bedroom.
'If only I could count on your love . . .
I wish we could be a pair of mandarin ducks!'

YÜ CHIEN-WU

Seven miscellaneous poems

Assigned a poem on an object, I received the title, 'The one I love'

My sweet promise in the end has not come home.
Springtime nature. I sit in scented fragrance.
Dusting a box, I see your fan of departure;
Opening a case, I look at my dress of parting.
Catalpa by the well grows not in full leaf,
The palace pagoda-tree unfurls but sparse.
I will never match mud-bearing swallows,
Together they come, in pursuit they fly.

Poem on a 'Beauty admiring herself in a painting', composed by royal command

Would you like to know how clever the painting is?
Call in real life, let her reflect it!
Appearing together, they're like bodies of the same mould.
Seen together they look like a mirror reflection.
Arranged hairpins equally spaced,
Collars worn both neat and tidy.
If the Huns had not lifted the siege at P'ingch'eng,
Who'd have survived to rival cinnabar and green paint?

Assigned a composition, I received the title, 'The road to Ch'angan', a melodic song for traverse flute

To Cassia Palace double avenues lead;
To Yellow Mount Lodge a broad road cuts through.
I hear faraway bells of P'ingling,
Discern distant trees of Hsinfeng.
The assembly hall creates a brilliant glow,
Scattered palaces raise hazy mists.
Sunset song and piping float back to me.
Dust glides from horse and coach passing.

Seeing a woman come back from South Park

A spring flower vies with a jade face,
Both are picked and both are plucked.
Her slim waist suits the tight dress,
Long hairpins add chic to her pinned-up chignon.
Torches start crossing Lo bridge,
Barriers are about to rise at Black Gate.
The woman inside probably keeps vigil:
'Will my honoured guest come back before dusk?'

Seeing someone off at Chienhsing Park, I met you

I met you north of the smaller park,
You stopped your coach, asked for the park centre.
Plum blossom new consorted with older willow,
Powder white shone on silk-scarf redness.
Your departing shadow moved against the slanting sun,
So scented air there turned windward.
Clouds drifting the steps slowly darkened,
Ice-cracking pools half thawed.
'Your departing horse, my boat that won't delay . . .'
The weeping-crow melody is not yet ended.
We part wistful from here,
Your coach westward and my horse east.

Two poems harmonizing with the Prince of Hsiangtung
[*Hsiao I*]

Spring night, composed by royal command

Long since my soldier parted from me
The season's scents once more look into my window.
Beneath candles I sew his clothes at night,
Spring's chill sharply catches my fingers.
I long to reach a homeward-flying goose,
Give it my letter to take to Tallwillow.

Winter light, composed by royal command

When the neighbour's cock heralds its sound,
A sorrowful person has had no sleep.
Moonlight creeps upon her even after dawn,
The frost's glare subsides before daybreak.
With tousled hair she rises to look in the mirror:
'Who can bother to fix flow'ry hairpins?'

Three miscellaneous poems

*Attending a banquet, I was assigned a composition and received the title,
'In the wilds of Lung on a moonlit night'*

Magpies fly idly round the trees;
The moon's wheel is not yet quite full.
Ch'ang O stares, unable to leave.
Her cassia branch is secretly hidden.
The sunset glow shifts the house shadows,
Streaming moon rays stir the moat's gleams.
Stabled horses grieve at Ch'iang flutes,
City wall rooks weep from the border cold.

I hear that my wife at loom and shuttle
Grieves that my clothes are unlined,
That come autumn my silks will be too light,
And, choked with tears, she cannot go on weaving
And frowns, no doubt unhappy.
With sword-dance I try to cheer myself up.
'Please let me speak, Hanku officer,
Must we keep on with "a plug of mud"?'

*Submitted to His Highness, the Prince of Hsiangtung [Hsiao I], harmonizing
with his poem, 'Winter light', by royal command*

From your wife's home beside Lo city
I often hear the sound of dawn bells tolling.
The sound of bells had still not died away
When a Han envoy announced that you must leave.
The sky grew cold, water in my inkwell froze.
My heart grew sad, my letter lay unfinished.

*At Jo District I happened to see a woman weaving, so I wrote this
extempore composition and sent it to my wife*

A charming girl, full of dejected love,
Weaves plain silk as autumn sounds stir.
Passing the yarn-guide her bracelet jade trembles,
Pressing the shears her belt pearls tinkle.
Warp so fine threatens to jam the shuttle,
Woof snaps, she's cross the silk is too thin.
The grapevine begins to look finished,
The mandarin ducks have yet to emerge.

Under cloudy ridge-poles they dawdle together,
Silk windows opened to each other;
Through window grilles eyebrow whispers pass;
Through silk so light come smiling eyes.
Blurred, screened by thinnest silk,
In sharp detail I see a cosmetic flower:
Sweetheart lotus roots studded with jade,
Loveknot flowers strung with jewels,
Her red gown fastened at the back,
Gold pins slant over her side-locks.
From the loom top hangs gay braid,
From the loom's side cascade strings of pearls.
Green silk threads draw in the pivot's crouching hare,
Yellow gold encircles the pulley's Lulu knob.
Gorgeous tints come from her skirt hem,
Scented gloss glistens on her lips.
One-hundred-city barons ask after her,
Five-horse teams paw the ground before her.

There is only me in my bedroom,
Faithful to past love, not seeking new amours.
In dreams weeping soaks my flowery pillow,
Waking tears drench my silk kerchief.
Sleeping alone is so hard for me,
My double quilt still feels cold.
Even more I desire your skin's marbrous warmth,
More than ever long for horizontal pleasures.

I urge on my mount with its gold bridle,
Homeward bound for the city's south end.
The city south, how slow the promised hour!
I imagine you also throb with love.
Your silk bodice must have worn out long ago,
Flower hairpins ready for repair.
On your fresh make-up don't apply the kohl –
I'll come home to paint your eyebrows myself!

HSÜ CHÜN-CH'IEN

Sitting up on New Year's Night with the one at home

With many pleasures, and love still not at its peak,
Our joy is sublime – don't stop the winecups!
From wine we fish daddy-long-legs,
In rice dumplings we search for wild plum.
Blinds open, winds come through the curtains,
Candles die, charcoal burns to ash.
'No wonder pins feel heavy in your curls –
It's from waiting till dawn light comes.'

Going out and holding hands with the one at home for fun in early spring

Coiffure ornaments are the very latest fashion,
The clothes she wears are all new this season.
Through grass short she steps still in slippers,
Plum scent comes slow to touch one.
Trees jut out to snag her brocade shawl,
Winds veer round to go in her red scarf.
Pour to the brim orchidaceous wine,
To look on this makes the soul delirious!

PAO CH'ÜAN

Two miscellaneous poems

Watching pleasure-seekers in South Park

In Loyang's Small Park grounds
Coach and horse drive past in swarms.
Along the canal she halts her trotting chaise,
Beside a willow he turns his jingling harness.
Heels so high set pendants all atinkle,
Stockings sheer half hidden by flimsy silk.
'Scudding clouds have no fixed address –
What's the use of making eyes at him!'

At sunset I watch people going home

Sweet charm competing with early spring
Races to the famous festival at Heights Park.
Films of alga change the water's colour,
Mists thicken to screen the sun's disc.
Carved roof-tiles deflect sunset rays,
Painted fans brush drifting dust.
The far scent of a dress already reaches me;
The distant redness of a skirt grows even fresher.
Whose wife are you, girl of the rocking boat?
Where's your place, weaver of fine silk?

Four miscellaneous poems

Presented with my compliments to Chief Secretary Liu, this poem on
'A famous knight delights in his city-destroyer'

I don't believe in the Mount Wu sylph,
I don't believe in the Lo river sprite!
But whether other kinds of beings exist –
Still, there are those city-destroyers:
Once she flirted with the Prince of Ch'en,
Long ago she came close to Mr Sung,
Before she married her name was Yü,
More recently her maiden name was Ch'in.

Powder's sheen seems very like her face;
The colour scarlet is inferior to her lips.
I see her from afar, a flower about to open;
I sense her scent and know it's different from spring.
Pins long match coiffure wigs,
Pannier skirt short suits her waistline.
Night after night she exhausts the language of love.
Day after day her behaviour's still quite novel!
Her talent would destroy Hsün Feng-ch'ien,
Her skill would dazzle Shih Chi-lun.
Honoured guests may waste time ogling –
They'll never get to see her horizontal!

Three poems harmonizing with the Prince of Hsiangtung
[*Hsiao I*]

Cold bedroom

After we separated, the spring pool looked different;
Lotus died, ice seemed to form.
In my sewing-box the shears felt cold,
On the mirror-stand my face-cream froze.
My slender waist become so frail
Can hardly bear the coldness of the clothes.

Autumn night

Over a house stir autumn winds,
Disillusion in an autumn bedroom.
Trickling candles stream into floral clusters,
Incense flares, the censer will soon be spent.
Vain tears cross in two streams
And float the rouge on her cosmetics.

Winter dark

I cannot bear cold nights long
Night after night keeping an empty bed.
Skirt pleats as I sit up look sharper,
Hairpin shadows near the lamp grow longer.
No one pities my four-width brocade quilt –
Why bother to get rid of stale air?

TENG K'ENG

Two miscellaneous poems

Harmonizing with the Liang-chou Prefect Yin Tzu-ch'un's Miscellaneous Regret poems

We separated, and though not so long ago
Still, it seems we've long been separated.
Massed cassia has many a time been stripped of leaves,
From garden trees I've picked countless sprays.
My lover says his wife's looks have altered –
His wife, I fear my lover's heart is wayward.
Finally, we must meet each other just once more,
So together we two can get to know each other.

Submitted to my superior, harmonizing with his poem, 'At night we heard a girl singing'

The candle's florescence is like the brilliant moon.
A chignon shadow is higher than a soaring bridge.
The singers in formation dance the Cheng dance,
Rivals in beauty, they copy the Ch'u waist.
For new songs they compose their own melodies,
Familiar zithers need no tuning.
In the chorus no singer smiles:
'Gentlemen, please don't tease!'

CHEN KU

Submitted to His Royal Highness [Hsiao Kang], harmonizing with the Heir-apparent's poem, 'Spring [bedroom] passion'

Late last night I raised the blinds to look out
And met my first pair of swallows returning.
Then this morning I saw peach and plum,
And not just a few flying blossoms.
Now I'm sad spring will soon pass,
No more to send him its fragrance.

YÜ HSIN

Three miscellaneous poems

Submitted to His Royal Highness [Hsiao Kang], harmonizing with his 'Poem on the Dance'

In a cavernous room flowery candles are bright.
Spoils of Yen, a pair of dancers light
Stamp their heels in time to staccato rhythms,
Lower coiffures on the high notes.
Half a pirouette, step back to position one,
They whirl their dresses, the melody not yet done.
Paradise birds turn, the mirror will soon be full,
Geese look back, the town must be destroyed.
Long ago they mimed dance in Heaven above –
How could they be like dancers born of this world?

Seventh Night

Herdboy shines in the distant river,
Weaver is just mounting her carriage.
The Bridge of Stars admitted the Han envoy
Who bore away her loom-stone on a magic raft.
Parted by the River they stare at each other so near.
With autumn's passing their separation grows longer.
They mourn this very night so hated
That makes them wait for next year's flowers.

*Submitted with compliments to Deputy Director of the Department of State,
Ho [Ching-jung], my poem, 'I go home to mourn my late mistress'*

In Purple Gallery dawn levée ends,
At Central Terrace evening memorials lessen.
No more her thousand-gold smile!
No use taking a five-day leave home.
The veranda at dawn will be unswept,
Orchid rooms at dusk will have closed doors.
Moss grows where she practised music,
Cobwebs gather on her palindrome loom.
Her old zither's remaining strings are broken,
Through singing rafters autumn swallows flit.
Dawn clouds I can bear to watch, and yet
The night bedcurtains are truly hard to be near.
I long to ascend into Sweet Dew Gate
And borrow the dazzling Lamp of Wisdom.
No wonder late in Loyang city
Lone homeward tears soak my robe.

Four miscellaneous poems

At Mount Wan I saw a mulberry picker

A singer wife, in invincible despair,
Descends neatly dressed from her green house
To go with friends west down silkworm paths,
Go hand-in-hand east to the top of the lane.
When leaves are done she moves to another tree,
If boughs are high, now and then she eases them with her hook.
Silk ribbons dangle and slip off,
Gilded baskets are emptied then gathered.
Silkworms are hungry now the sun sets,
Why be detained by a prefect?

Seeing someone weave, I wrote this impromptu for her

Slim, slim her jade fingers move around,
Her throbbing, throbbing moth eyebrows straighten.
Flashing scissors undo crossed yarn,
She stops the shuttle to knot broken thread.
Flowers of the eaves shine with a new moon,
On wide-open doors the drapes are not yet lowered.
She works her loom, stifling streams of tears,
Slower than ever weaves plain silk.

Autumn bedroom

Fireflies flit beyond silk windows,
A wife pines for General Huo.
Before her lamp she measures fauna brocade,
Beneath the eaves floral motif weaves.

The falling dew resembles light rain,
Long River is like thin clouds.
Autumn brings back a hundred different cares.
No time to perfume his finished robe.

Broken willow, a melodic song for drum and pipe

In this tall house ten years ago we parted
When willow was sprouting silky twigs.
Some leaves you picked, amazed they'd opened so soon,
Broke a twig, hating the long absence.
Year in, year out bereft of all news,
Month by month my appearance is fading.
Spring comes, who doesn't feel hope?
That I love you, you know by intuition.

CHI SHAO-YÜ

Three miscellaneous poems

Chienhsing Park

Cinnabar hills embrace the imperial city,
Purple pools enhance Royal Forest Park.
Silver terraces are suspended eight hundred feet,
Jade trees rise one thousand yards,
Water flows with shadows of canopy and hat,
Winds unfurl music of song and piping.
I stand and pause to pity a dropped kingfisher plume,
I turn my step to lament a lost hairpin.
At sunset the garden flowers fold in,
Square coach-blinds teem with flickering shade.
In the end, let's say 'Our joy had not yet peaked';
Let's never admit you begrudged your yellow gold!

In the style of Wu Chün's poetic form, by royal command

When garden trees put out their springtime radiance,
Fun-loving girls race down from their looms,
Rummage through boxes to pick out concert fans,
Open cases to choose dance dresses.
'Let mulberry leaves shrivel, we no longer care!'
They see sunbeams hurry into dusk:
'We have our private city owners, of course,
No need to dazzle honoured guests!'

Spring sun

A sorrowful one timidly leans from her window;
Spring beauty is by no means eternal:
Near the nets fitful steals the sun,
Trembling through blinds creeps the wind.
Fallen flowers whirled back to their trees
Fly light away to vanish in the sky
Leaving a vain trace of jade chopsticks
To hang double in her mirror bright.

WEN-JEN CH'IEN

Spring sun

The tall terrace stirs with spring's flush,
Clear pools reflect sunlit splendour,
Green mallow twists towards sunlight,
Kingfisher willow slants with the wind.
In the woods a bird startles my heart,
Orchard's massed blooms captivate my eyes.
Like me they all know this season,
Sigh that you alone keep far from home.
The traveller will not come back today,
Why bother to pick a vain hempen pledge?

Four miscellaneous poems

Taking up my pen, I write this bagatelle, by royal command

Today, your being so considerate
Offends me, but less than had it been spring.
Candle-trickling tears I shed this night
Are not because you bring her home at dark.
Her dance mat come autumn will fold away,
Her concert fan will gather sheets of dust.
Since time began new love supplants the old,
So why does old love hate to greet the new?
A sliver of moon peeps into her flowery bed,
Slight chill creeps under her shawl and scarf.
Autumn will come when all things must wither,
And touch her body with nature's stealth.

Submitted to His Royal Highness [?Hsiao Kang], harmonizing with his
'Poem on the Dance'

At fifteen she belonged to the Princess of P'ingyang
And so came to enter Chienchang Palace.
The Princess's house taught well the art of dance,
The city perfected the craft of dawn make-up.
With lowered coiffure she nears the silk mat,
With raised sleeves brushes on floral yellow.
Candles cast shadows near the window,
Her dress spreads perfume in her wardrobe.
The reason she attracts guests so well must be
That she makes her dance gown deliberately long.

Harmonizing with Member of the Royal Suite Wang's poem,
'Before I had come home from seeing a guest off, she was in her bedroom
watching for me'

The singer's song and piping over,
She checks her rouged face in the mirror,
Touches up powder, removes fancy flowers,
Takes out pins to make a small chignon.
Lovely lamps left to burn don't go out,
Tall doors stay closed not yet locked.
'Darling, where are you staying?'
But she only sees a moonbeam come home.

Written on behalf of the maid of the Yen-chou Prefect Yang Kan,
thanking him for his gift of a mirror to her

Your messenger came with your gift of a jewelled mirror,
Grand, grand as the round moon.
When a mirror ages it shines the brighter,
When a person ages so passions decline.
I accept your mirror, hang it on the empty stand,
To this day never reopened.
Don't you see the orphan paradise bird?
From where will lost love's soul appear?

A miscellaneous poem

Spring bedroom despair

Jade Gate Pass messengers have ceased.
May I ask, Don't you know me?
Spring sunshine so indifferent
Peeps through my window to visit.
Long cut off from your news and image
Suddenly I find the sun veers south-east.
Willow silk strands all tease the swallows,
Mulberry leaves hurry on the silkworms.
Nature's glory in a flash is like this:
A widowhood I can't bear.

T'ANG SENG-CHI

Poem on the title, 'In a stagnant well I found a golden hairpin'

Long ago a girl from the house of song
Was picking flowers by an open well,
And while picking flowers she fixed one in her hair,
Admiring her own reflection in the well.
She peers and peers at her image endlessly,
She laughs and laughs, aware of her charms.
But then her jewelled hairpin fell in here –
Years not one have passed since her loss.
Though kingfisher plumes dissolved into slime,
The glint of gold is still as it was before.
This person today is alive no more.
This object today is her legacy vain.

HSÜ FEI'S WIFE, NÉE LIU (WANG SHU-YING'S WIFE) [?LIU LING-HSIEN]

A miscellaneous poem

Harmonizing with Lady Pan's 'Regret'

At sunset Ying Gates are shut.
Despairing love breeds a hundred cares.
All the more since Chaoyang Palace is close,
And winds carry song and piping sounds.
His fickle favour in the end she doesn't hate,
Just her rival's wild slander so malicious.
She only admits she strove for ideals of duty,
But never envies that light dancer's waist.

WANG SHU-YING'S WIFE, NÉE LIU [?LIU LING-HSIEN]

Harmonizing with Wang Chao-chün's 'Regret'

Of life, what is certain in the end?
The world can never be really secure.
His cinnabar and green missed out her known grace,
A jade coffer turned to autumn grass.
The spilling tears that flowed at the Pass farewell
Even today are still not dried.
'Han envoy, when you go home south,
I beg you, speak eloquently for me?'

CHAPTER NINE

LOVE-SONGS IN IRREGULAR METRES
(FROM SECOND CENTURY BC TO SIXTH CENTURY AD)

ANON.

Two song lyrics

No. 1

Eastward flies the shrike, westward flies the swallow.
Yellow Slack [Herdboy] and Weaver only meet at times.
Who is the girl living across the gates?
An open bud showing beauty, she dazzles the village portals.
At south windows, north doors she hangs her bright light,
From sheer curtains, silk drapes are scents of lipstick and powder.
This girl, how old is she? Fifteen or sixteen.
Meek and mild, unique, her face is like jade.
Spring's three months ended, the flower is gone with the wind.
Left all alone, darling, who'll be your mate?

No. 2

The water midstream flows towards the east,
A Loyang girl is called Nevergrieve:
Nevergrieve at thirteen could weave fine silk,
At fourteen picked mulberry at the top of south lane,
At fifteen she married, became a wife in the Lu family.
At sixteen she gave birth to a boy named A-hou.
The Lu family have orchid rooms, of cassia are the rafters,
Everywhere the scent of Yüchin and storax.
On her head are twelve golden hairpins,
On her feet silk slippers of five patterns.
From coral hangs her mirror, radiant its light grows.
Her slave in a bandeau holds up her shoe box.
A life of wealth and status, what more would she want?
She hates not being married to the Wang family on the east side!

ANON.

Song of the Yüeh boatman

Preface: The ruler of Ngo kingdom in the state of Ch'u, Tzu-hsi, was travelling in a blue-plumed boat with a kingfisher awning. The Yüeh oarsman fell in love with Tzu-hsi, and sang a Yüeh song as he plied the oars. The ruler of Ngo was touched. Full of desire he raised his embroidered quilt and covered the boatman. His song went like this:

> Tonight, what sort of night?
> I tug my boat midstream.
> Today, what sort of day?
> I share my boat with a prince.
> Though ashamed, I am loved.
> Don't think of slander or disgrace!
> My heart will never fail,
> For I have known my prince.
> On a hill is a tree, on the tree is a bough.
> My heart is in love with you, but you will never know.

SSU-MA HSIANG-JU

Two songs for the lute

Preface: While Ssu-ma Hsiang-ju was travelling through Linch'iung, a rich man there named Cho Wang-sun had a daughter, Wen-chün, who had recently been widowed. She hid behind a screen and peeped at him. Hsiang-ju won her heart with these songs for drum and lute:

No. 1

Cock-phoenix, cock-phoenix, he goes home to his old town
From roaming the four seas in search of his hen-phoenix.
Unlucky days – he found no way to meet her.
What a surprise! This very night he goes up this hall,
In this very place there's a girl so sweet and pretty.
My bedroom so near, she so far – it poisons my guts.
How can we be mandarin ducks caressing neck to neck?

No. 2

Hen-phoenix, oh hen-phoenix, come nest with me!
Tail to tail we'll breed, be my bride for ever!
Passionately entwined, bodies one, hearts united,
At midnight come with me! Who will ever know?
Let's start up a pair, rise together, soaring high we'll fly.
If you're unmoved by my love you'll make me pine!

THE WUSUN PRINCESS [HSI-CHÜN]

A song poem

Preface: In the reign of Emperor Wu of the Han Dynasty during the
years 110–104 BC the emperor made Hsi-chün, daughter of the king of
Chiangtu, a princess and married her off to Kunmi, the ruler of the
Wusun tribe. When she reached their land, she settled in Kunmi's
palace. Through all those years she only met him once or twice, but did
not speak to him. The princess became melancholy and composed a
song which went like this:

My family married me off somewhere on the horizon,
Sent me far away to the Wusun king's strange land.
A canvas hut is my mansion, of felt its walls,
Flesh for food, mare's milk to drink.
Longing ever for my homeland, my heart within is wounded.
I wish I were the brown goose that goes back to the old town.

ANON.

Two children's rhymes of the Han Emperor Ch'eng's era

Preface: Emperor Ch'eng's consort, Chao, named Feiyen, had enjoyed his sexual favours in the harem and was with the emperor when he came to and fro from the imperial palace. At that time there was a man, the Marquess of Fup'ing, Chang Fang, who was a clever talker and was graciously permitted to ride with the emperor to Ch'i Gate. Hence in the song it says, 'Lord Chang / Is always having audience.' Feiyen was insanely jealous; she had not borne a son to the emperor. Hence the lines in the song, 'Pecks at princes', and 'flowers, but bears no fruit'. Wang Mang himself said that the man who supplanted the Han Dynasty would have the power of Earth and would prize the colour yellow. Hence the words 'yellow sparrow'. In the end Feiyen was demoted from the rank of empress and died. Hence the line 'she's pitied by all'. [Feiyen's name means Flying Swallow.]

No. 1

Swallow, swallow,
Sleek, sleek is your tail!
Lord Chang
Is always having audience
At timbered gates with green bronze rings.
Swallow flies in,
Pecks at princes.

No. 2

The cassia tree flowers, but bears no fruit.
A yellow sparrow nests in its crown.
Once the envy of others,
Now she's pitied by all.

Two children's rhymes of the Han Emperor Huan's era

No. 1

Tall wheat green, so green, short wheat shrivelled.
Who must be reapers? His wife and her mother.
And where is her husband? Out west fighting Huns.
Officers purchased his horse,
The lord confiscated his cart.
Ask the officer to make the drum roll!

No. 2

Crows on city walls,
Tails down in retreat.
Father became an officer,
Son became a soldier.
One soldier dies,
One hundred chariots,
Chariots rumble, rumble.
They reach Hochien,
They reach Hochien where a pretty girl makes a fortune,
And with her fortune builds a hall,
Of gold is her hall.
Over the door is crushed millet,
Under the millet there's a drum hanging –
I'd like to strike it, but the minister will be angry.

Four sorrows, four poems

My first reverie says:

The one I love lives on Mount T'ai.
I long to go after him, but Mount Liangfu is rugged.
Leaning forward I look east, tears soak my pen.
My handsome one gave me gold dagger coins.
How will I requite him? With fine jade.
The road is far, it won't arrive. I give in to restless idling.
How anxious I am, my heart so distressed.

My second reverie says:

The one I love lives in Cassia Forest.
I long to go after him, but Hsiang waters are deep.
Leaning forward I look south, tears soak my collar.
My handsome one gave me rare gold gems.
How will I requite him? With a pair of jade plates.
The road is far, they won't arrive. I give in to reproaches.
How anxious I am, my heart so tormented.

My third reverie says:

The one I love lives at Hanyang.
I long to go after him, but Lung range is long.
Leaning forward I look west, tears soak my coat.
My handsome one gave me a sable wrap.
How will I requite him? With bright moon pearls.
The road is far, they won't arrive. I give in to anxiety.
How anxious I am, my heart so disturbed.

My fourth reverie says:

The one I love lives at Goose Gate Pass.
I long to go after him, but snow falls thick and fast.
Leaning forward I look north, tears soak my headband.
My handsome one gave me a roll of broidered brocade.
How will I requite him? With a green jade tray.
The road is far, it won't arrive. I give in to increasing sighs.
How anxious I am, my heart so tortured.

CH'IN CHIA

A tetrasyllabic poem presented to my wife

Hazy, hazy the white sun
Trails glimmers west declining.
Sobbing, sobbing cocks and sparrows
Fly in flocks to the pillars.
White, white is the bright moon,
Twinkling, twinkling are the serried stars.
The harsh frost is biting chill,
Flurrying snow carpets the garden.
Hushed, hushed, I'm living alone,
Bleak, bleak, in the empty house.
Billow, billow the door curtains,
Gleam, gleam the flowery candles.
You don't live within them –
Why should I neatly hang door curtains?
You don't make them shine –
What's the use of flowery candles?

Two folk-songs, 'Song of beauty'

No. 1

Autumn wind's plaintive lute, the sky's air is chill.
Grass, trees tremble and shed, dew turns to frost.
Flocking swallows take their leave, geese wheel south.
I think of you travelling and love tears my guts,
As you ache, ache with homeward longing, with desire for your
　　old town.
Why do you tarry, linger in other parts?

Your poor wife, forlorn, keeps an empty room.
Despair comes. I pine for you and cannot forget.
Tears fall unawares, soaking my clothes.
I take up my lute and singing strings release the Clear Note.
A snatch of song, soft humming, I cannot go on.
The bright moon, white, white, shines upon my bed.
Starry Han flows west before the midnight hour.
Herdboy and Weaver stare at each other far.
What crime is yours, alone denied the River bridge?

No. 2

Day to part so easy! day to meet so hard!
Mountains and rivers far away, the road is lost to sight.
My full cup of love for you I dare not confide.
I send words to floating clouds; they move on, never come back.
Tears fall, rain down my face, spoiling my appearance.
Who can nurse despair alone with never a sigh?
I open poems, sing clear song, try to relax.
Joy goes, grief comes dashing against my breast.
Restless, I lean on my pillow but can't sleep.

I throw on my cloak, go outdoors, pacing east and west,
I look up at stars and moon, gaze at rifts in clouds.
Flying storks cry at dawn, pitiful sounds.
Numb with remembrance I lose the will to live.

TS'AO CHIH

A folk-song, 'A wife's mean fate', hexasyllabic

The sun now departed hides in the west.
They meet once more in an orchid house, secluded room.
Flowery lamps suffuse screens with light,
White as the sun rising from Leaning Mulberry.
Winecups hasten, everyone seated, goblets pass round.
Our host gets up to dance the *Sop'an* dance.
Artistes feel the wrench of parting.
Raised goblets, flying tankards brimful.
Equal measure, same flush, like expression,
Impulse to change cups with a lover.
Scarlet cheeks reveal the orchid's image,
Sleeves move with bodies, faces full of passion.
Skilfully they dance, with ethereal bodies light.
Clothes loosen, shoes slip off, capstrings untie;
Glances up and down, laughter, shouts, abandon.
Fixed stares at lovely women's jade faces.
All alike served from gold tankards, kingfisher plates.
Silhouettes of hands under sheer sleeves barely visible,
Arms too frail to hold pearl bangles.
The seated guests all breathe sighs, soft looks on faces,
With kerchiefs girls put powder on beside them.
Drifting scents of Huona, Tuliang,
Chishe – the five savours blended into perfume.
A girl moves forward, who is she? Ch'i Chiang?
Generous, deeply in love, unforgettable.
Our host invites his best friends to his private party,
Chants solo, 'Bring the cups! why so slow?'
Guests recite 'Unless we're drunk why go home?'
Our host responds with 'The dew will not dry'.

FU HSÜAN

Three poems in the style of northern folk-songs

The 'Past autumn's nine' piece, the 'Tung flees' ballad

Past autumn's nine, spring's three,
Our kind host greets guests from afar:
'Knowing what you dearly love in your heart,
I ordered fine talented singers,
Who glitter like sun, moon and stars!'
Laid out are gold jugs, jade goblets.
Guest and host rise together, geese in formation.
Cups fly like lightning flashes,
Pledges made, cups exchanged, clothes in a tangle.
Merry joyful laughter ten thousandfold.
Our host chants a new poem for the gentlemen,
Brilliant as a tiger's marks that change to dragon's streaks,
Mysterious as the time before sky and earth separated.

Ch'i lyrics, Ch'u dance bright and gay,
Song and music swell towards blue clouds.
Eight kinds of music all different styles,
Rare music, rapturous, every one novel.
Soft smiles, white teeth, cinnabar lips,
Elusive echoes fly and scatter rafter dust.
Souls are subtly transported to be among the gods.
The guests all drunk, steeped in joy,
Draw winecasks close, push seats together, move near the eaves,
Bring pledgecups thick and fast, drink each other's health.
With one chorus to you, 'May you live a thousand autumns!'

Let your love be immovable as a mountain!
May your kindness never fail,
Like morning sun, evening moon,
Their light unending for ten thousand leagues.
If you keep for ever our vows of first wine and bound hair,
Why should I fret lest we live as Hu and Yüeh?
Holding my soft hand with its gold bracelets
You'll roam with me through flying turrets in the clouds,
Splendid as mandarin ducks, a pair of paradise birds.
We'll settle happy in orchid rooms,
Hearts content, joy sublime, fathomless!
Yet I brood on joy that is now sublime,
That my finest season will vanish sudden like a ruin.
Chill conquers heat, drives light back,
Spring glory chased by blustery winds.
Moved by nature my troubled heart grows sadder.

The fate a wife receives is an orphan's destitution.
A son comes down on earth called 'darling',
A girl, though weak, seems scarcely to survive.
Flesh-and-blood relations, they are kept apart.
Busy and useful I attach myself to others.
You are like form which shadow follows,
Your wretched wife is like alga floating on a river.
The bright moon cannot always wax full,
Who can keep blossoming without any roots?
The good times bit by bit give way to bad.
I look back at my broidered collar radiant,
But the white sun turns its slanted rays.
The red flower sudden withers unaware,
Shadow seems to flee form, fly away on high.
Who will say past favours can be recaptured?
Shepherd's purse falls with wheat in summer.
Orchid, cassia pinched by frost grow sweeter.
Destiny depends on inscrutable Heaven.
My heart's bonds of love are true as red and green.
Why do I despair your love will fail midway?

The 'Your carriage is far, far' piece

Your carriage is far, far horses prancing, prancing.
My thoughts pursue you, cannot forget.
Where do you travel? Westward leads to Ch'in.
I long to be shadow and follow your body,
But you live in shade where shadow can't be seen.
You lean into the light where I want you to be!

The 'Yen women are lovely' piece

Yen women are lovely, Chao girls pretty.
That house so close is bound by towering cliffs.
If clouds were my carriage, the wind my steed,
I'd reach my jade of the hills, my orchid of the wilds.
Clouds don't keep promises, winds have dropped.
Who can cure so many cares in my pining heart?

In the style of 'Four sorrows', four poems

Preface: Chang Heng previously composed his *Four sorrows*. They are small pieces and popular, classified as heptasyllabic. I have composed impromptu imitations of these, calling them *In the style of 'Four sorrows'*. They are as follows:

No. 1

The one I love lives in Yingchou.
I wish we were a pair of swans playing midstream.
Herdboy and Weaver's tryst is in autumn.
Mountains high, rivers deep, no way to pass.
Miserable, unlucky am I, overcome by despair.
My lovely one gave me a bright moon pearl.
How will I pledge him? With eye-to-eye fish.
The sea is wide, I have no boat. Bitter torment.
I send my message to flying dragons, coursers of the skies.
Winds rise, clouds divide, flying dragons vanish.
Waves in panic dash against skies, coursers not in pairs.
Why do many memories make the heart world-weary?

No. 2

The one I love lives in Chuyai.
I wish we were wing to wing skimming clear pools.
Hard and soft wed powers, conjoin as Heaven and Earth.
Form and shadow once severed will separate for ever.
Miserable, unlucky am I, my feelings seem numb.
My lovely one gave me orchid plants.
How will I pledge him? With birds of like heart.
Flames are hot, water deep. Overwhelming despair,
My love I show with fine jade, night-gleaming gems.
When Pien Ho died jade was judged no more.
I live like a falling star, sudden lightning expired.
Why do many memories lock loneliness tight?

No. 3

The one I love lives on Mount K'un.
I wish we were the double-bodied creature gazing on Yü Gulf.
Sun and moon return dazzling light, rays brighten the sky.
Antares and Orion wide apart have no way to meet.
Miserable, unlucky am I, burdensome my problems.
My lovely one gave me storax perfume.
How will I pledge him? With kingfisher mandarin ducks.
Hsientu, Jo river, river without a bridge.
My love I show with brocade robes, broidery traced skirts.
The Three Lights course by, rays never lingering.
How mean is human life, swift as if floating by.
Why do many memories only bring sorrow?

No. 4

The one I love lives in the north.
I wish we were flying geese winging south together.
I long to appear like the Three Lights shining on humankind.
But Hu and Yüeh are hostile, live in separate parts.
Miserable, unlucky am I, trapped by many cares.
My lovely one gave me feather-pennant tassels.
How will I pledge him? With form and shadow.
Thick ice seals despair that rich blooms will fall.

I send my message through sun and moon, vow by bright stars.
But stars darken, sun and moon move on.
My weary horse sadly neighs, ashamed it cannot race forward.
Why do many memories bring disenchantment?

?SU PO-YÜ'S WIFE

A palindrome

In a hillock tree tall a bird sings of sorrow.
In spring water deep carp are fat.
Sparrows in empty barns always feel pangs of hunger.
An officer's wife rarely meets her husband.
She leaves the gate to watch, sees a white robe,
Says, 'That must be him!' But then it isn't,
She goes back indoors sad at heart,
Up the north hall, along the west stairs.
Swift her loom winds silk, the shuttle sounds urgent.
She sighs long sighs, who will she speak to?
'Your going away, your wife remembers it.
There was a day of departure, no promise of return.
You tied my inside belt, saying, "I'll always love you."
If you forget your wife, only Heaven would know.
If your wife forgets you, punishment is sure to follow.
Your wife is being virtuous, surely you know that?'

What's yellow is gold, what's white is jade,
What's tall is a mountain, what's low is a vale.
Your name is Su, courtesy name Po-yü.
As a man you're gifted, very intelligent.
Your family lives in Ch'angan, your body is in Shu.
How I regret your horse's hooves come home so seldom!
One thousand pounds of mutton, one hundred vats of wine.
You make your horse fat on wheat and millet.
People today are not wise enough,
Give them a letter – they can't read it!
Start mine from the middle then turn its four corners.

In the style of the 'Four sorrows', four poems

No. 1

The one I love lives in southern Ch'ao.
I long to go after him, but Mount Wu is too high.
Climbing a cliff I look far off, tears and snivel criss-cross.
My breast, my heart feel deeply wounded.
My lovely one left me cloth wrapped in a case.
What will I give him? Flowing yellow silk.
I want to cross the far road on a buoyant wind,
In the end it never comes. Desire grows keener.

No. 2

The one I love lives by northern waters.
I long to go after him, but white snow falls in blizzards.
Climbing a cliff I stare for ever, tears and snivel spill.
My breast, my heart feel painfully sad.
My lovely one left me a wing feather from the clouds.
What will I give him? Jade discs of linked cities.
I want to cross distant barriers on a homing goose,
In the end it never comes. Despair grows deeper.

No. 3

The one I love lives at Lung's west plain.
I long to go after him, but Mount T'ai cuts me off.
Climbing a cliff I look far off, tears and snivel trickle.
My breast, my heart ache with frustration.
My lovely one left me a pair of horned beasts.
What will I give him? Carved jade rings.
I want to cross ranging peaks on a cloud of passage,
In the end it never comes. Sighs grow longer.

No. 4

The one I love lives east in Yingchow.
I long to go after him, but the long road is perilous.
Climbing a cliff I look far off, tears and snivel flow.
My breast, my heart feel painful despair.
My lovely one left me a Greensilk lute.
What will I give him? A pair of southern gold bars.
I want to cross the bottomless deep on a surging wave,
In the end it never comes. Moans grow ever louder.

ANON.

A children's rhyme of the Chin Emperor Hui's era

A Yehchung girl, Mo Ch'ien-yao,
Will hug Hun waists three months from now!

LU CHI

The 'Song of beauty' ballad

The four seasons follow in turn, depart beyond recall.
Cold winds soft, soft falling leaves fly.
Crickets stay in the hall, dew floods the steps.
Remembrance of your far journey is always cruelly sad.
Why do you keep far away, long not coming home?
Your wretched wife's sad, sad heart never falters.
When the white sun expires, bright lamps glow.
Cold birds go to the woods nesting in pairs.
A pair of ospreys, Caw! Caw! nestle on the river's edge.
Despair comes stirred by nature, tears are not a few.
But for remembrance of you, who would I dream of?
How soon comes the day of parting, but reunion comes so slow!

PAO CHAO

Eight miscellaneous poems

Two poems in the manner of the King of Huainan

No. 1

The king of Huainan,
Craving eternal life,
Drank potions, purified his Humours, read magic lore.
Of lapis lazuli his drug bowls, of ivory his plates,
With gold vats and jade ladles he mixed divine cinnabar,
Mixed divine cinnabar,
Pleasured in purple rooms,
In purple rooms where vivid girls fondle bright earrings.
Paradise birdsong, phoenix dance wrenched his guts.

No. 2

Vermilion city's nine gates lie ninefold open.
With the bright moon I long to enter my lord's breast,
Enter my lord's breast,
Fasten my lord's jewelled belt.
I resent you, hate you, need your love!
To build a city look for strength, in a dagger look for sharpness.
Let's flourish as one, decay as one, neither deserting the other.

Two poems in the manner of lyrics for the 'White hemp dance'

No. 1

Scarlet lips move,
White arms lift,
Loyang boys, Hantan girls.
The ancients sang *Green river*, moderns sing *White hemp*.
Quicken the strings! Faster play the pipes! I'll dance for you.
In deep autumn, the ninth month, lotus leaves go yellow;
North winds chase geese away, skies rain frost.
Long is the night, wine in plenty, joy's course not run.

No. 2

Spring winds rock and sway, make me love the more,
The sky's colour is pure blue, the air is soft and sweet.
The peach tree is laden with pink petals, the orchid with purple
    buds,
The dawn sun glittering makes garden flowers come out.
Roll up the blinds, draw the drapes, spread jade mats.
Ch'i song, Ch'in piping, Lu girls' strings.
A thousand in gold for one smile? I'll buy the sweet season!

Four poems from the set, It's hard travelling the road

No. 1

Of five peach trees in the middle court
One tree puts out blossom early.
After two or three months of charming sunny spring
Windswept flurries of petals fall on the west house.
In the west house a girl in love watches wistfully.
Falling tears dampen her dress, she sighs, soothing her heart.
When first I said goodbye to you outside the door,
Did you tell me you'd delay through changing seasons?
On my bed dust grows, my bright mirror is stained.
My slim waist has whittled away, my hair is a tangled mat.
Life can never go as we plan!
I'm disillusioned, doubting for half the night.

No. 2

Chopped cork stains silk yellow,
Yellow silk tangled cannot be unravelled.
Long ago you and I first met,
I thought then perhaps you loved me.
Tying my belt you whispered to me,
'In death as in life, for better or worse, I won't leave you.'
Today I see my looks fade,
Your passion sadly different from before.
Take back your jade hairpin and tortoiseshell ornament!
I can't bear to see them add to my sad love.

No. 3

I offer you fine wine in a golden cup,
A carved lute in tortoiseshell and jade case,
Feather curtains with seven-tone hibiscus,
A brocade quilt with nine-bloom grapevine.
Pink cheeks wither, the year is about to close.
Cold light draws round, the season soon to fail.
I want you to trim my grief and snuff out pining.
Listen to my drumbeat, my *Hard road* song.
Don't you see up in Cypress Rafter, Bronze Sparrow –
Wouldn't you rather hear the clear flutes, music of days gone by?

No. 4

Jasper room and jade court lead to the pepper gallery,
To a patterned window, broidered door hung with gauze drapes.
Inside there is a person called Golden Orchid
Dressed in finest silk suffused with sweet storax.
Spring swallows bob and dart, winds scatter plum petals.
She opens a curtain, looks at the scene, twirls bird pins,
Hums a song, wipes a tear, unable to speak.
In life for how long can we be happy?
Wouldn't you rather become a pair of ducks flying in the wild?
I don't want to be the separated stork wheeling in the sky.

It's hard travelling the road, a poem

Don't you see the orphan goose set out beyond the pass,
Cross plaintive over Yang and Yüeh?
In a lonely town a traveller's guts are torn, he's heart-broken.
In a hidden room a pining wife nearly expires.
Crisp frost falls by night, brushing her silk dress.
Floating clouds have broken apart, opening to a clear moon.
Night after night, far far away, I love you in vain,
Year after year, hope upon hope, my passion never fails.
He sent me a green bronze mirror in a case.
My servant for your sake plucks out white hairs.
It's hard travelling the road,
It's hard travelling the road.
At night to hear Han envoys pass south of town
Makes me stream with tears – I so long for Ch'angan.

LU CHÜEH

The song of Lady Li and her palace attendant

In the royal suite coach the seat hangs dusty;
Incense on the panther's tail is fading.
Cinnabar hall reverts to bittersweet herb.
Green rush cushions crumble away.
A throne crumbles away.
Facing the bittersweet,
I look down at cinnabar steps,
And weep on pepper paths.
A widow stork, a fettered hen fly then hover.
On carved rafters and kingfisher walls spiders are spinning.
Deep in my room on a clear moonlit night
I face this, my tears like pearls.

Two pieces from Eight thematic poems

Gazing at the autumn moon

I gaze at the autumn moon.
The light of the autumn moon like sheer silk
Shines gleaming on Three Sparrow Terrace,
Shimmers on Nineflower Hall,
Nineflower's tortoiseshell rafters,
Its flowery beams with jade disc pendants.
The loveliness of these ornaments
Is enhanced by the clear moon's light.

A frozen flower, it goes inside axe-print drapes,
Its pure lustre cascades through secret bedrooms.
Long ago it passed by Feiyen's door,
Or lit up Lady Pan's bed.
At Cassia Palace pitter-patter shed cassia boughs,
At Dew Chill Hall, numb, numb freezes the white dew.
Royal Forest Park's late leaves rustling, rustling echo;
Goose Gate Pass's early geese cross in formation.

Curved perfectly round as if by a compass,
Its pure light darts like white silk,
Shining on thatched shadows of despairing eaves,
Glinting on light footsteps up stairs of gold.
Someone at home sings laughingly to it.
A separated traveller feels the pain of desire beneath it.

It crosses withered orchards,
Glints on cold shrubs,
Freezes in the pure night
Trailing autumn winds.
It lends whiteness to garden snow,
Borrows the pink of pond lotus,
Glances on jade court, pallid, pallid,
Breathes on frosty fog, blurred, blurred.

It blazes down Sky Trails, rocking with the void,
Streaks down Long Han, flying through space,
Steals behind sheer cliffs, yet half reappears,
Screened by curtains it barely filters through.
It spreads pomp and glory over a crimson garden,
Enters green chains with a tinkling clink.

By still steps it saddens a widow swan,
On a sandbar makes a separated goose lament.
The Lady of Letters wept in her barbarian hall;
Ming-chün longed for her Han palace.
As for me, what am I doing
Staying on here in the hilly east?

Greeting the spring wind

I greet the spring wind.
When the spring wind stirs spring trees,
Drifting fluff veils like cobwebs,
Falling flowers thicken like fog.
First it skims gulf of heaven pools,
Then slips through slim willow fronds,
Catching butterflies whirled into tossing flight,
Meeting swallows to ruffle their feathers.
It unfurls cassia streamers,
Shakes mushroom canopies,
Opens Yen skirts,
Blows Chao sashes.
Chao sashes fly ruffled up,
Yen skirts fold and part.
It twists hairpins and twirls kohl,
So they stop and turn, dismayed at their appearance.
Their appearance once so glamorous
The spring wind reduces now to ruins.

With thick flurries of peach and plum blossom,
Green calyx enshrining white corolla,
All that the wind lays open
Is by that very wind felled.

Tossing green stems,
Swinging purple stalks,
It makes spring snow dance,
Gliding orioles scatter.

Labyrinthine rooms open, gold knobs rattle,
Gold knobs rattle, a wife's reverie shattered.
Before the catalpa's shadow falls,
As Ch'i river starts turning jade green,
It welcomes falling rain on Kaot'ang,
Escorts migrant geese at Chiehshih,
Passes secret bedrooms,
Rustles white silk,
Troubles hidden boudoirs,
Breathes love on draped veils.

Imagine how it can roam through sweet orchards!
Think of it gently plucking outstretched orchid!
It brushes winter dust from clear mirrors,
Smooths autumn creases from silk gowns.
When it swings a girdle jingle-jangle,
Thick heavy scents pour from sachets.
First it enters bedrooms with nervous excitement,
Then slides through cracks and loiters,
Tinkles pearl blinds on broidered doors,
Scatters scented dust on silken bed-mats.
This season depresses pining women.
How can they endure their soldiers' campaign?
Yet if lovely women were not here,
For whom would the spring wind feel pity?

A spring day, melodic song for the 'White hemp dance'

Orchid leaves in a tizzy, peach half pink,
Winging scent, waltzing gauze, flirts the spring wind.
   [Shen Yüeh]
Kingfisher plumes flock in flight unceasing,
I wish we were in the clouds always wing to wing.
   [Hsiao Yen]

An autumn day, melodic song for the 'White hemp dance'

White dew is about to set, the grass colour is yellow.
Gold pipes, jade lute-stops echo through secret rooms.
A pair of hearts, one shadow glide round together,
The whispered love I send you, you mustn't forget.

WU CHÜN

Two poems from the set, It's hard travelling the road

No. 1

Don't you see the guests in Royal Forest Park?
Frosty gauze, misty silks, ivory seats.
Completely contented, oblivious to words,
Proud, esteemed, none held in pity.
Their white wine is pleasant, sweet as milk;
Green goblets, pale mirrors, lustrous as green jade.
A young man on his dignity is slow to savour.
How could he know the white courser must gallop past the
    crack?

In a Po Hill censer the hundred-blended fragrance –
Yüchin, storax and Tuliang –
Coils sinuous in sweet air round lovely faces,
Slips through green chains, past purple rooms,
Creeps now under bed-drapes of Empress Yin of Chungshan,
Then climbs into Lady Pan's imperial bed.
When Lady Pan lost favour her face never relaxed;
As Ceremonial Broom at Eternal Trust Palace,
Wide awake at sunset, she cannot sleep.
Autumn winds come biting, biting from the four sides.
Jade steps, the paths are overgrown with fine grass.
The gold censer's scented coals are turned to ash.
Love's won, love's lost in the twinkling of an eye –
But this your 'square inch' heart can't judge in advance.

No. 2

By Tungt'ing's water a single catalpa
Suffers frost, is lashed by waves and buffeted by harsh gales.
Long ago it bared its heart to bask in white sunshine,
This morning it lies down to die in yellow sands.
A famed Loyang craftsman looks on it and sighs.
In a single hack, a single slice he makes a balloon guitar.
On its heart cut from white jade discs he traces a bright moon,
On its face inlaid with tortoiseshell creates windblown blooms.
By an emperor it is treasured, never to be forgotten;
He cradles it in his arms, ascending Chienchang Palace.
It sounds terse and piteous played by a girl musician;
She quickens tense stops, a Ch'u Ming-kuang virtuoso.
Year by year, month by month it looks upon its lord;
Far, far into night on night it sleeps at Weiyang Palace.
Colourful girls from the Weiyang play pipes shrill;
Rival glances, timid strokes create a lovely radiance.
Oleaster brocade is its wrapping, of jade its case –
Why hark back to former days as a withered branch?
Don't be like the cassia on Mount Heng's southern range:
For a thousand years to this day it's still unknown.

Four miscellaneous poems

In the style of the folk-song, 'I'll always love you', two poems

No. 1

I'll always love you
However long we're parted.
My beloved's distance is like a drought.
Alone, standing still,
My heart taut inside me,
I stare at clouds gone, gone far away,
Stare at birds flown, flown into nothingness.
Useless staring always ends like this:
Pearl tears that won't be wiped dry.

No. 2

I'll always love you
However long we're parted.
Where is my love? Under looming skies he feels bitter.
My heavy heart does not know where to look for you.
On jade steps the moon at dusk is glinting.
Through filmy drapes the wind at night is blowing.
Always so in love I can't sleep;
I sit and stare as Sky River moves on.

Two poems from lyrics for the 'White hemp dance'

No. 1

A girl singer pours out song, her voice near sublime.
A dancer keeps in rhythm, her body light as can be.
The song and the dance both wonderfully match someone's
　　passion;
The response to strings, to change of key is subtly graceful.
With smooth moth brow she poses – who is she making eyes at?

No. 2

Wonderful voices in song after song, light bodies fly.
Trickling sweat stains faces, blending with sweet scents.
They move as one, stop in unison, none out of step,
Making these fine guests so rapt they forget to go home.
They have fun at night for long hours as the bright stars dwindle.

FEI CH'ANG

It's hard travelling the road, two poems

No. 1

Don't you see at Ch'angan's tavern gate
A young girl called Peachroot from the house of song?
So poverty-stricken she spins by night without lamp or candle –
What a surprise! She gets to serve His Majesty!
In His Majesty's various palaces are a hundred or more
　　residences,
The thousand gates, ten thousand doors never know the dawn.
All she hears is the Caw! Caw! of crows on city walls,
As she draws the pulley cord by a gold well's jade rail.

Up cinnabar rafters and kingfisher pillars flowing storax scent
    flies.
Over scented log cassia smoke she cooks wild rice.
That year was topsy-turvy, there were no set rules.
'It's a mean fate being a woman' – but not to be despised!

No. 2

Don't you see how human life's one hundred years are like a
    lightning flash?
With tumult raging in the heart – don't you see?
Long ago when I first entered pepper rooms,
Was I less lovely than Lady Pan or Feiyen?
At dawn I trod gold stairs up to my phoenix-cote,
At dusk lowered the jade hook to rest in lovebird hall.
Cypress Rafter day and night was perfumed,
Brocade curtains unprompted flared and furled,
While to pipes I sang the *Under the jujube tree* tune,
And to the balloon guitar I sang *Mulberry up the lane*.

Mine was the gift of the emperor's kind love,
I basked in flooding light.
When Empress Yin met with favour, she sought no preferment.
Lady Ch'eng, a favourite, had something taboo.
Once in a thousand years the Yellow river runs clear.
Whether my poor self is lucky again remains an enigma.
Moth eyebrows, half-moon mouches, these vain charms,
We apply powder, put on red gloss – but for whom?
Better to be wild ducks on gulf of heaven waters
Away in pairs, home in pairs, always wing to wing.

Imperial compositions, sixteen [eleven] poems

Four poems on 'A crow perched', melodic song

No. 1

Of hibiscus my boat, of silk my mooring rope.
Northern Dipper lies across the sky, the moon's going to sink.
Where I pick lotus up at the ferry, it would pass for the Yellow
   river.
My love would cross today, but fears the tempest waves.

No. 2

Floating clouds are like curtains, the moon becomes their hook,
How can I night after night bear it up south lane?
In Yi city the mulled wine is now getting warm.
Unsaddle and tether your horse, nestle for a while overnight.

No. 3

With your black ox, cinnabar hubs and seven-perfume coach,
How lovely it is tonight lodging at the house of song.
In the house of song's tall trees crows are going to nest.
Silk curtains, kingfisher drapes are lowered in front of you.

No. 4

By a wool-weave screen hinged with silver,
Scarlet lips and a jade face appear before the lamp.
I look at you and sigh sighs, hoping for your affection.
Who could be so bashful she won't come closer?

Off to war, a ballad in mixed metres

Yünchung's watchtower, when winged dispatches sound the
    alarm,
Sweet Springs beacons blaze through the night.
General Li of Erh-shih fame pitches a new camp,
Supreme Commander Huo starts his first campaign.
And there is our Shansi general,
Of extraordinary valour and renown.
Three battalions drilled in occult tactics,
Five brigades modelled on heavenly armies,
White clouds follow regimental colours,
Blue hills echo to the drumroll.
Sinuous goose-wing array he reviews,
Zigzag goose formation he inspects.
First he will quell Hsiaoyüeh hordes,
Then he will crush Ferghana cities.
Fine horse he'll bring back to Eternal Joy Palace,
Yellow gold he'll pay in to Shuiheng office.
His young Chao wife is skilled on drum and harp,
Maids in first hairpins will render Cheng music.
The garden peach-blossom flown into heaps –
They must surely be pink cheeks all raised to greet him!

*Four heptasyllabic poems harmonizing with Palace Attendant Hsiao
Tzu-hsien's 'A spring separation'*

No. 1

At the separate lodge the grapevines hang down with laden
    fruit.
South of the River cardamom boughs grow into an embrace.
They have no feelings or passions, they're always the same.
The person who loves or hates must needs be separate.

No. 2

The thread spiders make spreads through the curtains.
Sweet grasses' knotted blades cover the pathways.
Pink cheeks throbbing with love weep all through her life.
Golden orioles fly and fly, sometimes passing by.
Old love, though old, once was new.
New love, though new, also must grow old.

No. 3

How lovely Huai river tides flow in and out.
On its spring banks the willows cover the river bridge.
Traces of tears still not dry, can they last till noon?
As she walks I hear jade belt jewels coming to meet me.

No. 4

Peach pink, plum white are like dawn cosmetics.
I disgrace my wrecked self next to fresh willow.
I wouldn't mind living a while, then dying before you –
But I'd be in despair without my west Reincarnation scent!

Spring passion, a poem in mixed metres

Butterfly yellow, blossom purple, swallows playing tag,
Willows bowing, willows kissing, highway dust in flight.
Now that I see a dangling hook hang from green trees,
I know for sure Ch'i river is soaking silk clothes.
Two boys parked alongside ask endless questions,
Five horses south of the city are not yet turned for home.
Orioles weep that spring soon hastens away.
Nothing for it but to shut my futile doors!

In the style of an old poem

She peeps at rouge in the mirror, winces paired eyebrows.
Sorrowful she wipes her tears, unconscious thoughts of him.
She remembers how much time passed once someone had left.
With eloquent eyes, dimpling smiles her love would greet him,
In heartfelt longing, heartfelt passion so plain to see.
Desiring him she cannot bear to speak,
Smothering hate, she stifles her lonely voice.

Resentment in the house of song, a hexasyllabic stanza

The dawn sun comes slanting up to brighten my door.
Spring birds race in flight out of the woods.
Line of light, line of shadow, both lovely,
One echo, one warble inflame my heart.
Royal Forest is thick, thick with blossoms falling.
Ch'i river is veiled, veiled with alga floating.
Years race, seasons flow gentle unto death.
How to bear desire, or nurse shame?

THE PRINCE OF HSIANGTUNG, HSIAO I

Four poems on 'Spring separation', by royal command

No. 1

K'unming lake's night moon gleams like glossed silk,
Royal Forest's dawn blossom has the sheen of sleet.
The blossom of dawn, moon at night excite spring hearts.
Who can bear to love you and not meet you?

No. 2

I steal a look at the embracing dragon brocade on the loom,
Glance back at 'joy of love' boughs in the garden.
Reflected windborne sunlight throws shadows on red cushions,
Tossed flowers, upswept leaves skim gilded pools.
I've never heard those separated must often meet,
I'm only sad our meetings end: to meet becomes to part.

No. 3

The willows before the gate tangling like silk thread
Promptly make a beauty lose self-control.
She's just said she'll compose a new *Torn silk* poem.
Who'd have thought it would now turn into the *Homespun* lyric?

No. 4

As I dawdle at sunset west of Wei bridge
I just glimpse the moon sail even with clouds.
Suppose I could make moonlight equidistant
So it has to shine on those parted weeping tonight?

HSIAO TZU-HSIEN

Seven miscellaneous poems

Four poems on ' Spring separation'

No. 1

Fluttering orioles, passing swallows in pairs are wing to wing,
Willow's thousand twigs share the same colour.
And all I see is hands held homeward up the lane.
Who can face this feeling hopeless love for you?

No. 2

A secret palace where banked grass has its own sweet scent,
Golden orioles in sweet trees stay near each other in love;
They speed with the wind, race against the sun – now I hear
    their echoes;
Massed flowers, folded leaves won't admit their flight.
You should know this season stirs pining in your wife –
Making my silken sleeve stroke one moment your cloak.

No. 3

On the highway to South of the River it's sunny flowery spring,
Drooping willow, hanging willow sweep light dust.
Yesterday's farewell at Ch'i river made tears soak my kerchief.
The rouged face he slept with must be his new love.

No. 4

Stifling grief, wiping the tears – the separated heart knows.
Peach blossom, plum blossom suffer blowing winds.
Though I always knew human hearts aren't like trees,
I wonder, why do people separate like parted blossom?

*Two poems on the folk-song, 'A crow perched', a melodic song, by royal
command*

No. 1

In my hand a winecup with onyx bells,
On my skirt hem clustered pendants of amber dragons.
I would send these to you with no regrets
While pointing to Three Stars, 'What a night is this!'

No. 2

Tearstained mascara, diluted rouge blotch her petal beauty,
Almost making people fail to recognize her.
In the gold waterclock tonight, how could there still be so much
    water?
Yet it's never so full as the River hanging up in the sky!

Song of beauty, a ballad

Windy glimmer's slow dance draws out green mugwort.
Kingfisher birds on orchid stalks carol advent of spring.
In Loyang the pear blossom falls like snow.
The riverside grass is fine, fine and green like a cushion.
Catalpas at the foot of the well cross their leafy boughs.
Now I see a pair of swallows suddenly separate.

Five-storey flying mansions pierce Han river,
Nine-flower arcaded roads darken crystal pools.
Far away I see a soldier near Whitehorse ford,
He tells of men attacking Huanglung tribes.

The bright moon's gold glimmer shines vain on me,
Floating clouds' jade leaves you will never know.
I muse on when you left long ago, willows leaned, leaned near us.
Now at the eighth month you'll come home to avoid the heat.
Bright pearl silkworm cocoons struggle up the loom.
Yüchin scented petals specially sweeten his robe.

Up in Loyang city the cocks are about to crow,
Ministerial office crows have not yet flown.
I dream at night of a soldier as I stitch fox-badger,
And feel sorry for myself, a weaver tailoring scarlet and brocade.
Wu shears, Cheng wadding,
The cold bedroom quilt at night feels thin.
In the scented season the lake ducks are in the water.
Sunset. Cold night. Empty city swallows.

It's hard travelling the road, one poem

The thousand gates are all closed even before midnight;
A hundred cares flock to cut at my guts.
I delve into boxes, take out shears and rule,
Brush and wipe my loom top, and cut the flowing yellow.
Though I hate my lover for loving someone else,
Even so, I dread his having no far frontier clothes.

I have spun silk from one cocoon to make his urgent cloak,
Have pounded mixed scents to perfume his folded robe.
I still remember the size of his waist at parting time,
But I don't know his body measurements today.

I've fastened a waistband to his tunic's pair of hearts,
Inserted eight pleats both sides of his jacket.
The inside cord fits, I can't bear to sew it!
My needle eye is clear, still the silk won't go through.
Half-moons two I've joined together on your breast –
They may light up your breast, but won't light up the sky.
I want you to get their meaning clear:
Don't play around any more! Don't go on as you've been doing!
Mournful, regretful love undying.
Numb, repressed with longing, I'll wait until next year.

A poem on Liu Hsiao-cho meeting his former mistress, a singer, at Yüan Ching-chung's party

I delayed my former husband,
Had no qualms.
Deserted by him, I waited up the spring hill
And met him as I picked the sweet herbs.

LIU HSIAO-WEI

In the style of an old poem, by royal command

They nest, a pair of kingfisher-tinted mandarin ducks.
Under Mount Wu clouds, Lo river moon, I suddenly stare:
Whose house is the lovely charmer from, breaking a branch of
　　blossom?
Her moth eyebrows, flirting glance transfer my affections.
Green knobs, emerald chains, lapis lazuli doors,
Jasper mats, jade cabinets, gold lamé clothes,
A beauty, teenaged, perhaps ten or more,
Turns shyly smiling, smooths her windblown skirt.
He's off shooting pearl pellets, can't be found.
Left alone, who will comfort her, poor darling?

HSÜ CHÜN-CH'IEN

Two poems on leaving Iyang commandery

No. 1

The soaring phoenix mansion
Seen from far floats with clouds.
Echoing song lilts over trees,
Dancing shadows blend with the river's flow.
Leaves fall, I see the village closer.
Skies are high, it must soon be autumn.

No. 2

In the cosmetic beauty house
Her make-up complete, she adds a star mouche.
The rouge on my cheeks is perhaps a bit too faint?
Maybe the kohl on my eyebrows is not green enough?
Deliberately she leaves her used powderpuff
Dangling on the blind hook.

WANG SHU-YING'S WIFE [?LIU LING-HSIEN]

A poem presented in reply

Cosmetic film, dab of kohl, light brush of rouge.
Bangles jingling, belt swinging she leaves bedroom lattice.
She looks at plum and then looks at willow.
Tears well over in brilliant spring.

CHAPTER TEN

A TREASURY OF SHORT LOVE POEMS
(FROM THIRD TO SIXTH CENTURIES AD)

ANON.

Four old chueh-chü *poems*

No. 1

Pounder, where are you now?
Over the hill there lies another hill.
When will you dagger-hilt?
When broken mirror flies up in the sky.

[This poem is a series of puns, which translated read as follows:]

'Lover, where are you now?'
'I have gone away.'
'When will you come back?'
'When the waning moon flies up in the sky.'

No. 2

Sunset. Autumn clouds darken.
The Yangtze river is clear and deep.
What will bear my message?
On my tortoiseshell pin – a lotus.

No. 3

Dodder is bent by distant winds,
But its roots and stem never break apart.
If insensate things will never part,
How can sentient beings separate?

No. 4

One cassia tree on a southern hill,
A pair of mandarin ducks upon its crown.
One thousand years their necks in long caress:
'Happy love, I'll never forget you.'

CHIA CH'UNG

Three linked verses composed with my wife, Lady Li

No. 1

Who is this in her room
Sighing sighs that echo sad? (Chia Ch'ung's verse)
And why do I sigh these sighs?
I just dread our marriage failing! (Lady Li)

No. 2

Our marriage is like glue and lacquer.
My 'not a stone' heart won't stray. (Chia Ch'ung)
Who does not fear the end?
Even sun and moon join but to part! (Lady Li)

No. 3

My heart you fully understand,
And your heart is well known to me. (Chia Ch'ung)
If you don't wish to eat your words –
Let me share what is pleasing to you. (Lady Li)

SUN CHO

Two songs for my beloved Green Jade

No. 1

Green Jade, a lower-class girl,
Doesn't dare cling to kind favour:
'I'm moved by my darling's thousand-gold love,
But I'm ashamed to lack city-destroyer beauty!'

No. 2

When Green Jade was of broken-melon age
Her lover was head-over-heels in love.
Aroused by him, she didn't feel shy,
But whirled into her lover's embrace.

?WANG HSIEN-CHIH

Two songs for my beloved Peachleaf

No. 1

Peachleaf, oh Peachleaf!
To ferry your river I won't need oars,
Just to ferry, then no more pain,
For I'll be joined to you!

Peachleaf, oh Peachleaf!
Peachleaf joined to peach root.
I adore you, but it takes two to make love –
Don't make me the only one to try!

?T'AO-YEH (PEACHLEAF)

Three songs in answer to Wang Hsien-chih's 'Round fan'

No. 1

A seven-jewel painted round fan
Glittering in the bright moon's light
I send to you to chase away dull heat.
So love me, don't forget me!

No. 2

Green, green the bamboo in a grove
Could make a round white fan
To move and stir in my love's jade hand –
Through the wind I'll trust it to work wonders.

No. 3

Round fan, oh round fan!
I'll hold this to hide my face,
Care-worn and without make-up –
I'm ashamed I might meet my lover.

Two letter-poems, a letter and reply, written at Tungyang Vale

No. 1

How sweet! someone else's wife
Paddling white feet in green water.
Is the bright moon between the clouds
Far, far away and unattainable?

No. 2

How sweet! someone else's husband
Sailing his white boat on green water.
But since you ask if I'm in love –
That moon sinks into those clouds!

EMPEROR HSIAO-WU OF THE LIU-SUNG DYNASTY, LIU CHÜN

Three poems

Two songs on Viceroy Tung Kan

No. 1

When the viceroy first went on campaign,
How I hated to hear the news!
I longed to create a Shih-Yu gale contrary
And halt troops everywhere!

No. 2

Yellow river's flow is endless.
Loyang's many thousand leagues away!
The snares and pitfalls on campaign . . .
How will I meet my darling?

In the style of Hsü Kan's poem ['Bedroom longing', stanza 3, last quatrain]

Ever since you went away
Gold, kingfisher grew dull, lacklustre,
Thoughts of you like sun and moon
Go round and round as day grows into night.

HSÜ YAO

Two poems

Poem on the 'Gnarled pillow'

A straight tree growing by a river
Fell ill, so became a thing of beauty.
At dawn from cloudy hair it parts,
At night to moth eyebrows draws close.

A poem from a woman in her boudoir in reply to her neighbour

Once we were like shadow and form,
Now we're like north Hu and south Yüeh.
I don't know if you journey near or far,
I've quite forgotten what year or month we parted.

PAO LING-HUI

A poem sent to someone on his travels

Cassia breathes out two or three sprays,
Orchid unfurls four or five leaves.
At such a time you're not back home –
The spring breeze smiles at your wife in vain.

ANON.

Five modern Western melodic songs

Stone City music

I grew up near Stone City,
Our gates open on to city-wall houses.
Handsome young men in the city
Stop over as they come and go.

Merchant music

There's a merchant who often sends me letters,
No news makes my heart pine for him.
Don't be a bucket fallen down the well –
Once gone, lost without trace!

A crow weeps in the night

Sing and dance, all you young men,
Your dazzle won't impress me!
So pretty was that iris flower,
I heard her name, but never knew her.

Hsiangyang music

At dawn I set out from Hsiangyang city,
At dusk I reached Tat'i and stayed overnight.
In Tat'i the girls are all
Fresh flowers to stun a man's eyes!

Old Mother Yang's boy

I went out in front of White Gate a moment,
Where willows could hide a crow.
My boyfriend does his 'sinking-in-water scent' act,
While I do the 'Po-Hill censer' act!*

* [The euphemisms in the last two lines mean, 'I want to lie down with you', and 'I
want to go to bed with you'.]

ANON.

Nine modern Wu songs

Spring song

The morning sun shines on northern woods,
Early blossoms are of tapestry hues.
In spring who cannot fall in love,
But stay all alone weaving at her loom?

Summer song

Muggy, torpid hot midsummer months.
I give a long whistle, set out for the lakeside.
Hibiscus starts to form stamens,
Pureness enshrined, not yet become passion flower.

Autumn song

Autumn winds come in through the window,
And filmy curtains lift to sway and billow.
I raise my head, gaze at the bright moon
And send my love on thousand-league beams.

Winter song

Ice on the pool three feet thick,
White snow blanket a thousand leagues wide.
My heart is like the pine and cypress –
And your heart, what is it like?

Ch'iench'i river

Yellow vines weave a covering cage
As they grow beside Lo river creek.
Flowers fall carried by its current away.
Will I ever see its current carry back to me?

Top-key

Her pomegranate blouse with two broidered panels
Fits snug inside her silk jacket.
Her faint footsteps stir the light dust,
Her silk clothes are lifted up with the wind.

Rejoice to hear music

Far, far away the sky has no pillar;
Wide-drifting alga has no root.
My single self is like the firefly's spark –
What can I do to repay your love?

The beauty of Ch'anglo

Red silk funnel bedcurtains,
Four corners hung with scarlet pearl,
Jade pillow, Lunghsü grass mattress . . .
'When you sleep, sir, where's *your* bed?'

Hummed melodic song

A willow tree catches the spring breeze:
One swing up then one swing down.
Who can love you with hopeless longing
Yet spend three sunny months sleeping alone?

ANON.

Three modern miscellanous songs

Hsünyang music

From Chi pavilion my former lover left.
To Mount Chiuli his new love comes home.
Divorcing one means he married two –
In not a very long space of time!

A 'Greening spring' melodic song

Green lotus leaves canopy the emerald water.
Hibiscus sticks up red and fresh.
Forked lotus roots lie side by side beneath,
On top grow lotus blooms with twin hearts.

The silkworm silk song

Spring silkworms should not grow old,
Yet day and night they pine always spinning silk.
Why feel sorry for their tiny spent form?
Tangled affairs have their natural season.

ANON.

A modern miscellanous poem

Is it her jade bangle colour? I can't decide.
Or her gown sheer seeming to show her arm?
She lifts a sleeve as if to defend her shyness,
Keeps turned away, combing tousled hair.

MENG CHU OF TANYANG

A song

In sunny spring's second and third months
Grass and river are one colour.
On the road I met a kind man roving –
A pity I didn't know him sooner!

SU HSIAO [-HSIAO] OF CH'IENT'ANG

A song

Your wife, I drive a glossy panelled coach;
My lover rides a piebald horse.
Where will we sweethearts be joined together?
At West Mound 'neath pine and cypress.

WANG YÜAN-CHANG

Four poems

In the style of an old poem

Flower-root, where are you now?
This no longer grows by the woods.
When will two topknots hang down?
When the round fan is bright between the clouds.*

*[This poem is a series of visual puns, homophone puns and euphemisms, which translated read as follows:]

'Lover, where are you now?'
'I live at my old home no more.'
'When will my mirror show our two topknots untied?'
'When the full moon is bright through clouds.'

In the manner of Hsü Kan's poem ['*Bedroom longing*', *stanza 3, last quatrain*]

Ever since you went away,
My gold censer has not burned incense.
I love you like the candle bright
Consumed by vain midnight passion.

Autumn nights

Autumn nights are long, so long,
Though nights are long, pleasure's not run mid-course.
Dancing sleeves brush bright candles,
Singing echoes spin round phoenix rafters.

Poem on the Fire

My icy face is disgraced by that far disc,
My aquarian nature retires before the bright blaze.
These shine tonight while I pine for you this evening.
I hope my travelling man comes home soon.

HSIEH T'IAO

Four poems

The jade steps lament

In the evening palace pearl blinds are lowered.
Drifting fireflies fly then come to rest.
The long night through she sews his clothes of silk,*
My longing for you, when will it ever end?

*['Silk is a pun for longing.]

A party at Golden Vale

Mother-of-pearl goblets are sent round by pretty girls,
Jade cups are ordered by honoured guests.
Once horse and coach go singly east and west
And we part, let's remember this night!

A prince went wandering

The green grass is plushy like silk,
Dappled trees are putting out pink blooms.
No matter that you didn't come home –
If you had, their scent is now gone.

Matching the rhymes of Master of Records Wang's poem ['*The one I love*']

My handsome date made a date but didn't come home.
Hoping against hope I get down from my loom,
Pausing, then pacing up the east lane:
The moon comes out, travellers are few.

YÜ YEN

The one I love, one poem

Mauve wistaria brushes blossoming trees.
Golden orioles pass through green boughs.
Longing for you I whisper one sigh.
Stinging tears by whispers prompted trickle down.

SHEN YÜEH

Three poems

White-brass-shoes, from Hsiangyang

We let go hands on a peach grove slope,
I wished you goodbye on a steep hilltop.
If ever I want to send you word,
Han river flows towards the east.

324

Out early I met my former mistress and presented her with this poem from my carriage

Traces of scarlet still show faint,
A touch of powder still shows in smudges.
Where did you stay over last night
That this morning you come home brushing dewdrops?

For a neighbour to whom I felt strongly attracted, but who didn't come to me

A shadow creeps up with the slanting moon,
Perfume drifts in on a distant breeze.
Your promise true I know now is false.
My dawning smile turns into a sob.

SHIH JUNG-T'AI

Poem on Wang Chao-chün

With drooping silks she comes down from pepper galleries,
Lifts her sleeve to flick barbarian dust.
'Oh! Oh!' she touches her heart and sighs.
Moth eyebrows cast a deadly spell on men.

KAO SHUANG

Poem on the Girl pouring wine

Long cushions lie at angles, not close,
The honoured guest can't get near the charmer.
She hands back his winecup without glancing round,
Turns her back with a look so prim and proper.

?THE FAIRY OF WUHSING

A poem presented to Prefect Hsieh Lan

My jade hairpins are sliding down from nowhere;
My gold flower's sheen is going to wilt.
Alone I weep farewell to the spring wind,
In the orphaned night I'm wounded by the bright moon.

CHIANG HUNG

Seven poems

Two poems on picking caltrop

No. 1

Winds spring up, green leaves gather,
Waves stir, purple stalks part.
Laden with bloom, and then laden with fruit,
Just waiting for a handsome one to come!

326

No. 2

The white sun tones in with the pure breeze,
Light clouds dapple tall trees.
Suddenly, just at that very moment,
I pick caltrop and meet you once again.

The 'Green river' melodic song, two poems

No. 1

Lapping, splashing white and clean,
Light and fresh, such fun!
Perversely, a lovesick bird is lured
To its reflection, and then cruel widowhood.

No. 2

My grimy face I cannot bear to beautify.
I lean over the pool longing for my guest to come home.
Who can take green water in her hand,
Wash silk robes in a tedium of despair?

Autumn winds, two poems

No. 1

Living as a widow I hate the four seasons,
Especially in my autumn bedroom.
Frigid leaves flicker with last glints,
An empty garden pokes out cold vegetables.

No. 2

Against the north window winds crush a tree.
By the south fence cold crickets chirp.
Throughout the garden boundless moonlight.
A pining woman bangs her night pounder.

Poem on a 'Beautiful woman repairing her make-up'

In her carriage she dreads not being alluring,
Peers sideways, then right round at herself;
Furious at her painted eyebrows' length,
She keeps on saying, 'My face looks even worse!'

FAN CHING'S WIFE [SHEN MAN-YÜAN]

Three poems

The sighs of Wang Chao-chün, two poems

No. 1

If only I'd believed sooner in the art of green and cinnabar,
I'd have heavily bribed that Loyang painter!
With a thousand gold I'd buy my cicada sidecurls,
For a million he'd sketch my moth eyebrows.

No. 2

This morning she is still on Han soil,
Tomorrow dawn she'll enter the Hun pass.
The high hall's song and piping will recede,
Yet in her dreams this wanderer will be going home.

Reflections in the water, a melodic song

Her fluffy sidecurls are fashioned as floating clouds,
Her twin moths are modelled on new moons.
Where water's smooth she straightens slipped hairpins,
Where duckweed parts she tidies tumbled hair.

Five poems

South Park

Park gates throw wide their thousand wings.
Park doors open ten thousand leaves.
In mansion and hall are heard pearl slippers,
Bamboo and trees screen filmy clothes.

Bedroom frustration

By her bedroom door passers-by cease.
Across her room's lattice the moon's shadows slant.
Who can go near the north window
And face rear garden flowers all alone?

For someone's pining wife

Swallows play homing towards the eaves.
Blossoms fly landing before my pillow.
My inch of heart you'll never see.
Wiping the tears, I sit and tune my strings.

Poem on the Spring wind

Audible yet invisible,
May be strong and may be light,
Before the mirror it whirls spilled powder,
Across a lute sounds echoing notes.

Autumn bedroom frustration

Bamboo leaves rattle on south windows,
Moonlight shines upon the east wall.
Who knows at night I wake alone
Shedding twin tears beside my pillow?

WU CHÜN

Four chüeh-chü *poems*

No. 1

The noon cicada knows the pain of memory.
Night dew once more soaks a dress.
Parting from me long ago, what did you say
To make the glow-worm start its flight?

No. 2

On her brocade waist are 'embracing bough' knots,
On her broidered collar 'joy of love' blooms slant.
Though in my dreams I swear I see them,
My vision ends in a blur of blooms.

No. 3

Spiders dangle from the eaves,
Grasshoppers wail by the well.
When will I get to see my man?
When the mirror shines bright in east and west windows.

No. 4

I weep to hear songs of the night we part,
I grieve to savour wine of our farewell.
From this day on when you have left,
You must think of me still – won't you?

WANG SENG-JU

Two poems

Spring longing

The snow has stopped; the twigs are quite green.
The ice has cracked; the water is quite emerald.
Once more I hear the golden oriole's voice –
It makes me write a song of loving you.

Written for Deputy Director of the Department of State Hsü's singer

It's late in the day – he ought to be going back home,
The honoured guest is a terrible dawdler.
I slowly sense my jade pins weigh heavier,
See my silk tunic gradually grow cold.

HSÜ FEI'S WIFE [LIU LING-HSIEN]

Three poems

Kuangchai Pagoda

In long verandas I delight in letting my eyes see you off.
In spacious halls I enjoy our chance meetings.
But when will I live in cloistered rooms
Dark and gloomy without the sound of humans?

Attached to a banana-leaf to show someone

Crying at dusk is not uncommon now,
Weeping in dreams is really rather frequent.
Only my night pillow knows,
Otherwise no one suspects.

Picking a twin-stemmed gardenia, I presented it to Hsieh Niao with this poem attached

Even if I offer two sprays as a gift,
They'll never serve to show our mutual love.
Sweethearts are everywhere at freedom,
But these twin stems capture me completely!

Three poems

Poem written for Ch'en Ch'ing-chih's lovely lady

Leaning over her make-up she's on the brink of tears.
But afraid and shy her family might know
She puts her puff in white powder
And dabs her tears to stop them trickling down.

In a dream I saw my old lover

I woke with a start, then knew such hatred!
Human hearts are really not alike.
Who can face a pillow of horn
All night long completely on her own?

I had a date who didn't come

By yellow dusk the messengers cease,
I choke back remorse, my heart aching, aching,
Swivel the lamp, move towards my bed-stool,
Turn my face away to weep in the dark.

WANG HUAN

A poem for the Lord of West Feng's lovely lady

Up till now I've avoided party talk –
It reminds me how I wept at separation.
I've no way of following northern geese
That fly straight down towards the Yellow river.

EMPEROR WU OF THE LIANG, HSIAO YEN

Twenty-seven poems

A Border guard poem

The autumn moon rising mid-sky,
Whether near or far has no favourites,
But radiates one equal brilliant light
Upon all pining separated lovers.

Poem on the Candle

In the hall are fine silken people.
On the floormats are girl singers and dancers.
They all wait for my waves of splashing light
To shine glancingly for you.

Poem on the Pen

Once I heard of fragrant orchid months,
Only this is peach and plum time of year.
In case the heart in spring has not yet been described,
May this feast of love shine just for you!

Poem on the Flute

At Aspen Pavilion there are bamboos most rare,
They throb with passion in high and low key,
Sublime sounds pour from jade fingers,
Dragon music echoes with phoenix song.

Poem on the Dance

Arms delicately drop then lift,
Her body light keeps twirling.
If you mean this to tell of your own desire,
Come now and join your heart-throb!

A linked verse poem

She who destroys cities is not of human beauty,
In a thousand years you'll never meet her twice! [the man]
Though I long for your 'love in a carriage',
I'm ashamed of my far from lovely hairdo! [the woman]

Spring song, three poems

No. 1

Scent on the stairs invades my breast,
Flowers in the garden shine in my eyes.
Spring love is always like this:
Comes desire – I can't resist!

No. 2

Orchid leaves start filling the ground,
Plum blossom has fallen from the bough.
Taking this to be a sweet thought,
I scoop some up to send him who knows my heart.

335

No. 3

Crimson sun glinting on white ice,
Yellow blooms reflected on white snow.
I break plum sprays to send my pretty one,
We'll meet together in sunny months of spring.

Summer song, four poems

No. 1

South of the River lotus blooms have opened,
Their red sheen covers jade-green water.
Of like flush and in hearts alike,
Of different roots, their hearts won't differ.

No. 2

Flowers in her bedroom seem to be embroidered,
Dew on the blinds seems to be pearl.
Do you want to know if there's one she loves?
She stops her weaving and starts fidgeting.

No. 3

A jade dish laid with crimson plums,
Golden goblets brimming with white wine –
I'm just about to bring them closer to her,
Then I'm afraid her lips won't find them sweet.

No. 4

A day of laden peach-trees dropping blossom,
The hour for golden oriole's busy flight.
Stop, my lord, for now your horse is weary,
But I must go – the silkworms will be hungry!

Autumn song, four poems

No. 1

Her sash is broidered with 'joy of love' knots,
Her brocade dress has an 'embracing boughs' design.
Full of passion she goes in with the night moon,
Full of laughter comes out with dawn clouds.

No. 2

By a copper-gilt pillar of seven hues,
Under white-jade rafters with nine-bloom carvings,
She sings solo song that fades not even in clouds,
That leaves a trace of scent as she breathes out.

No. 3

Pipes fortissimo can't stop yet!
Strings in finale must start up again!
Both are making true-love harmonies,
Each is playing sweetheart melodies.

No. 4

You must believe my vow to 'clasp the bridge-post',
Don't listen to whirlwind rumour!
On my mirror are two heads of hair –
It's very clear our hearts aren't torn in two.

Girl of the Night song, two pieces

No. 1

Trusting his love she makes as if to draw near;
Bashful, she's still not willing to come up to me.
Her crimson mouth breathes sultry songs,
Jade fingers play flirtatious strings.

No. 2

Morning sun shines on silk-coin windows,
A flickering breeze sways gossamer silk.
Expert smiles dimple her 'two melons',
Lovely eyes beam beneath twin moths.

A Top-key song

She is more flowery fair than apricot or peach,
Her name is richer than gold or jade.
Celebrity songs she sings are not the country catch.
She makes top-key tunes full of laughter.

Rejoice to hear song, two pieces

No. 1

Svelte, svelte girl in the golden house,
Her heart is like jade-pool lotus.
With what to repay her lover's tenderness?
A promise to have fun in paradise together.

No. 2

Down south there is a 'loving you' tree
Full of passion and where hearts become one.
A girl of pleasure I cannot court,
So who to rest with in its airy shade?

A Round fan song

In her hand a white round fan
Is pure like the round autumn moon.
Clear breezes born from its movement
Release seductive perfume bearing love.

A song of Jasper

Apricot rafters the sun starts to brighten
Before pleasure nears its peak on orchid mats.
A jasper jewel, she offers a golden goblet,
Its green wine enhancing her flowery allure.

Three 'White-brass-shoes' songs from Hsiangyang

No. 1

At the top of the lane a soldier departs,
In her room a girl gets down from her loom.
Full of emotion she cannot speak:
Farewell has soaked her silk gown.

No. 2

'Plants and trees are not of one fragrance.
Flowers and leaves have a hundred different colours.'
I send these words to my former lover
To let him know my heart remembers him.

No. 3

Their dragon steeds have copper-gilt saddles,
Their kingfisher plumes in white-jade harness
Sparkle and glitter near the twin portals –
And I know they are Hsiangyang boys.

Twenty-one poems with miscellaneous titles

Cold bedroom

My quilt is empty, I often wake from sleep,
The cold gets keener, night winds blow.
The silk curtains aren't a river's swell –
So how can I cross to him who once knew me?

Falling rain

I come from the mountain of Wu,
No one has glimpsed my appearance –
Except the king of Ch'u's courtier
Who once said he knew me in a dream!

Rafter dust

Clinging to curtains it mottles to a deep kingfisher hue,
Soaked in sunlight it collects a pale redness.
It must have risen from the sound of singing,
Not from a round fan's breeze.

Florescent moon

A night when hare's shadow looms through clouds,
The hour Ch'ang O's form appears in Han.
Please carry him my thousand-league message:
Don't shine ten years' sorrow down on me!

Night after night, a melodic song

The Dipper star meanders away,
Night after night my heart suffers alone.
Horizontal moonbeams hit my pillow,
Lamplight half conceals my bed.

Back from camp I go to the south city wall

Parted for a while we both had doubts,
But I open your blinds, old love rekindles,
As if we'd never loved before,
Like falling in love all over again.

Spring river, a melodic song

Travellers thinking of our homeward path,
We race to ford the estuary.
We don't know the person on the dyke
Wiping away tears, waving hands in vain.

The new swallows

New birds return in response to the season,
All flying towards the house of piping.
They enter the blinds startling bangles ajingle,
They come through the windows colliding with dance dresses.

I play my zither

I play my zither beside the northern window,
The echoes of night are clear tones sad.
The key is raised, a string easily snaps.
My heart aches, the melody's power is lost.

Sending the one at home back at night by the tail-boat

The brocade-draped barge pushes from its mooring,
Orchid oars stroke the waves in gliding,
Receding torches still dapple water,
Haunting perfume floods our boat still.

Poem on the Prince of Wuling's [Hsiao Chi] pageboy, Wu Hao, passing the pledge-cup

His hair on top is parted like two topknots,
And with long hairpins signals his bound-hair puberty.
He takes the pledge-cup, seems as if about to pass it on,
But, anxious about the lees, he holds it back.

The one I ache for, three poems

No. 1

I can sigh but cannot think,
Or can think but cannot see.
The remaining string is broken on my guitar bridge.
A smudge of crimson stains my concert fan.

No. 2

Soft, soft are the echoes from twilight eaves.
Dark, dark are the colours of drawn curtains.
There's only moss upon the floor tiles,
And I seem to see a spider spinning.

No. 3

I'm going through the grove to view the bumpy buds –
Spring can't be long in coming.
When can I see him, just for once?
That's come to be like plum blossom!

Pleasure-seekers

Pleasure-seekers flirt in Longwillow Park;
They hold hands through Cloudy Terrace.
Their joy's delight is still not exhausted
As the white sun goes down on western hills.

A chüeh-chü *poem presented to a beauty*

Your waist and limbs are natural wonders,
Your eyebrows and eyes just amaze me!
I'm convinced there's no one else like you –
And yet, there *is* Lo river goddess!

Watching from a distance

Loosely her red shawl is draped,
Slantwise her jade hairpins are fixed.
So pretty, there's no one else like her –
I'd guess this one's worth a thousand gold!

In her sad bedroom she looks in the mirror

Long since we parted I've looked haggard;
Other people are amazed at my appearance.
Except there's my mirror in its case.
I hold it again and recognize myself.

Floating clouds

How prettily the wisps of cloud are born!
One moment banked, then thinning out again.
If you want to have the king of Ching's dream,
You must visit me in White Emperor city.

343

Cold bedroom

Green leaves yellow dawn by dawn,
Red cheeks change day by day.
Comparing them figuratively together,
I can't help my thoughts growing sadder.

Harmonizing with someone's poem, 'Fording the river'

Elegantly chic is her new chignon,
In her fresh, clean skirt she goes out to have fun.
To her belt front she ties scented herbs,
In her wig pins a pomegranate bloom.

HSIAO TZU-HSIEN

Two poems

Love in a spring boudoir

With golden harness her gallant knight is roving.
At her silk loom his parted wife is pining.
Spring is passing, but no one has come home.
She watches blossom all turned to leaf.

Poem on Someone strolling in a park

In the second month of spring her heart excited,
She strolls around to see the early peach blossom,
She turns her body, screens the sun with her fan,
Then steps back and straightens her windblown skirt.

Two poems

From a distance I watch a beauty picking lotus

Caltrop stems sometimes curl round her bangles,
Poked water now and then splashes her powder.
She doesn't care if red sleeves get soaked,
So long as she can savour green leaf scent.

Poem on Children picking caltrop

'Picking caltrop isn't *Picking beans*!'
'It's sundown, let's fill the boat!'
She dawdles, not daring to move closer,
Afraid he might compare her to 'leftover' peach.

YÜ CHIEN-WU

Four poems

Poem on the Dance, a melodic song, by royal command

Singers' voices lilt over painted galleries,
Dancers' sleeves emerge from fragrant woods.
Stone City certainly seems far away,
Ch'iench'i must be very deep.

345

Poem on the Master's girl singers, by royal command

Last year they all had ponytails,
This spring half wear their hair up.
How can I tell their bridegroom is a fine fellow?
They see fit to dismiss this 'prefect' hanging around!

Poem on the Grass at Eternal Trust Palace

Fading kingfisher tints seem to sense the season,
Heavy with scent it appears to feel emotion:
Just because slippered footprints are rare,
It seeks to spread on steps everywhere.

Shih Ch'ung's girl entertainer at Golden Vale

In orchid halls honoured guests arrive,
On silken mats clear strings are stroked.
He himself composes *Ming-chün's farewell*,
And asks Green Pearl to dance it once more.

WANG T'AI-CH'ING

*Two poems harmonizing with Drafter of State Documents
Hsiao's set of* Ten thematic poems

Moon over the house of a wastrel's wife

Moon idly skimming my tall house,
You're not even a moon of the three-fives time of year!
What's the point of shining into my bed?
There'll just be a person sleeping single after all!

346

Separating from a lovely person at South Bank

My frowning face sees you off as we separate;
Once it frowns, it will never relax again.
All it must do is wait to see you –
Then its smiles will smooth out my eyebrows!

LIU HSIAO-I

Two poems

Poem on the Weaver Girl

Gold floral pins now flash and glint,
The white sun has not yet tumbled.
She longs to wait till after the gloaming
To ford the shallow river radiantly.

Poem on Rock-lotus

Lotus, your name is worth a million,
Rock, your surname, richer than a thousand gold.
I don't understand how insensate things
Get to be so like the human heart.

LIU HSIAO-WEI

Harmonizing with one of the Marquess of Tinghsiang's [Hsiao Chih] set of eight chüeh-chü *poems, 'Her coming-of-age hairpin'*

Bound into braids it's still her familiar hair,
Teased into curls they're the strands of silk they used to be.
But from this day on a single comb through is over:
There'll be no more times when I wind and rewind them.

CHIANG PO-YAO

Harmonizing with one of the Marquess of Tinghsiang's [Hsiao Chih] set of eight chüeh-chü *poems, 'Her gown from Ch'u and Yüeh'*

It lies cut and stitched in its bamboo case.
Its incensed velvet nap bears a hint of scent.
She opens it and looks, hasn't the heart to wear it,
And from one glance a thousand streaming tears.

LIU HUNG

Poem on the Gay

How pretty! He stands out easily from the crowd:
His pallor, pallor is quite remarkable,
His elegant eyebrows arch smooth over twin eyes,
And mellifluous flows his murmuring voice.

348

A poem for Hsü Ling mourning his wife

Slow, slow his robe soaks with tears,
Piteous, piteous regret wreathes his breast.
No more days in her private room,
He hopes still he'll meet her down the hill.

HSIAO LIN

Poem on the Petticoat

Pale, pale glistens the gold voile clear,
Bit by bit her precious seams fall apart.
Her slender waist is not the Ch'u model –
Her loose belt is from longing for him.

CHI SHAO-YÜ

Poem on the Guttering lamp

The guttering lamp still not dead
Now goes out then rekindles its flame.
Only one or two remaining flickers –
Barely enough to slip her silky clothes off.

WANG SHU-YING'S WIFE [?LIU LING-HSIEN]

Chill at dusk

Plum blossom gives out a natural gleam.
The shrike welcomes the spring come early.
The colder it gets, the thinner my dress feels.
He no longer wants to hug my waist.

TAI HAO

Poem on Going to bed

She dusts the pillow, perfumes her red coiffure-net,
Swivels the lamp and then slips off her clothes.
Her maids know the night will be long,
But no call means they may go home.

LIU HSIAO-WEI [ENCORE]

A miscellaneous reverie in the old poetic style

At daybreak there's a gale and frost.
My business makes us both suffer.
Leaves fall, boughs hang still.
I'm forever getting up to stretch my legs.

Poem on a Lovely lady

She's adorable, well worth remembering . . .
Well worth remembering? She cost a thousand cash!
But I must say I do have one regret –
I regret it's not this man's heart she's after!

NOTES

A crow weeps, or *A crow weeps in the night*: the name of a ballad associated with the themes of wandering men, illicit love or grass widows.

'a plug of mud': in the reign of Emperor Kuang-wu (AD 25–58) of the Han Dynasty, a military officer called Wei Hsiao (d. AD 33) was occupying T'ienshui commandery (in modern Kansu province). His junior officer told him that during that occupation he himself would go and blockade the Hanku Pass for Wei Hsiao with a plug of mud. The term is synonymous with an act of stupidity.

A-chiao, consort of the Han Emperor Wu (r. 141–87 BC): her official title was Empress Ch'en (q.v.), A-chiao being her childhood name. When they were both young, Emperor Wu fell in love with her and exclaimed that he would build her a House of Gold and treasure her there if she became his wife.

Airs: One of the sections of *The Book of Songs*, comprising 160 poems of the total of 305 poems. The airs were generally lighter verse than the odes and hymns, and many were love-songs traditionally believed to have been gathered from the various states or kingdoms of ancient China. See *Book of Songs*.

alga: a feminine image in love relations, signifying woman's dependence on man, as the alga clings to the surface of water.

'always love you' (*ch'ang hsiang ssu*): pun for the silk floss padding of quilts and clothes, especially of marriage-bed quilts. The padding was a pun for never-ending love.

Angler's south: the name of a piece of music based on the name of a Han district in modern Hopei.

Anling: see Lord Anling.

Antares (*Shang*): a star associated in folklore with Orion (*Shen*), believed to be quarrelling brothers who never meet. These two stars are in equinoctial opposition. They symbolize estranged lovers or friends.

aquarian nature: an oblique reference to the Yin cosmic principle signifying the female, water, north, dark, cold, the moon, and softness.

art of gold-and-cinnabar: the alchemical arts.

autumn moon: on the fifteenth night of the eighth lunar month it is a full moon. Its circular shape gave rise to a pun in Chinese, *huan*, meaning a ring, which was a homophone for to come home. That time of the year was when people traditionally celebrated family reunion at the mid-autumn festival.

Autumn river: a reference to a tune, it is unclear which, perhaps *Green river*, or *Lu river*, an old lute melody.

autumn's nine: the week in antiquity was ten days long, each lunar month having three weeks, and each season three months, making a total of nine lots of ten-day weeks per season, or ninety days.

axe-print: in antiquity an emblem of high office; later it became a fashion motif for wealthy houses. In some contexts the axe-print denotes a matchmaker.

'baby-snatching': a reference to the anecdote about a girl from Yüeh state who was

353

the mistress of King Mu of Chou (trad. r. 1001–946 BC). When his consort, Queen Chiang, gave birth to a child, the king's mistress stole her baby from the parturition bed and claimed it as her own. The king was very angry with her for this.

bamboo leaf: a popular motif denoting frailty because of its slender leaves, constancy because it is evergreen, and long life because it is durable.

banana leaf: a motif denoting frailty because it is easily torn in rough weather.

Beanleaves in my patch: an allusion to poem 186 of *The Book of Songs*, in which a woman expresses her desire to keep her lover near her, likening this to tethering a white colt in her vegetable patch to nibble beans.

Black Gate: the east gate of the ancient city of Ch'angan, the western capital of the Former Han Dynasty. Ancient place names were often used in poems instead of modern ones or together with them to impart an aura of historical romance.

black ox: the Taoist philosopher, Lao Tzu, is said to have ridden a black ox, so it became part of reclusive hagiography, and, as here, a fashion design.

blue clouds: one meaning of this image is the soaring ambition of a man in politics.

bluebird: the mythological messenger of the legendary figure, Queen Mother of the West, who ruled the paradise of immortals in the western mountains, thought to be the K'unlun range between Tibet and Sinkiang.

bluebottles, blueflies: an allusion to poem 219 of *The Book of Songs*, in which these insects are associated with gossip.

Book of Songs, The (Shih ching): one of the *Confucian Classics*. Traditionally thought to have been compiled by Confucius from an earlier collection of over 3,000 folk-songs gathered from the different feudal states of Chou China. The present collection consists of 305 poems, of which 160 are *Airs*, and 145 are *Odes* and *Hymns*. The material is believed to date from about the early Chou era, perhaps between the ninth and seventh centuries BC. One section of this collection is devoted to songs from different regions, 160 from fifteen northern states, and contains many love poems, quoted often in the love poems of later periods. As a *Confucian Classic* it formed part of the basis for education, and young people were expected to be able to recite from it by heart.

bound hair: at the age of puberty boys and girls bound their hair. The phrase comes to mean marriage. It is sometimes used with another ritual, the first wine of marriage.

Bridge of Stars: see Chang Ch'ien for the anecdote.

bright bird: according to legend, the sun has a bright bird in it.

Bright Cloud Terrace: a reference to the royal pleasure spot of the ancient kingdom of Ch'u mentioned in *Sir Fantasy*, a prose poem by the Han poet, Ssu-ma Hsiang-ju.

bright moons: round pearls of a great size.

Bright Valley: a mythological place where the sun rises, home of the immortals upon whom the sun never sets.

Brilliance Vast: an esoteric book written by Liu An, Prince of Huainan (c. 170–122 BC), but no longer extant.

Broadbank: place near the mouth of the Yangtze river where courtesans and entertainers made assignations.

Broken willow: the name of a flute tune. See willow.

broken-melon age: see melon.

(Bronze) Sparrow Terrace: the name of a Loyang royal building erected in AD 210 by the statesman and poet, and founder of the Wei Dynasty, Ts'ao Ts'ao (AD 155–220). It was famous for the magnificence of the banquets held there. In his last testament Ts'ao Ts'ao instructed that his concubines and entertainers should live in this building as if he were still alive, bringing him food twice each day to his bedroom. On the fifteenth of every month they were to perform dances before invited guests. His sons, Ts'ao Chih and Ts'ao P'ei, and his grandson, Ts'ao Jui, were also ordered to contemplate his tomb from the top of this terrace.

Bronzebridge: the name of a mountain in the old kingdom of Shu, west China, in modern Szechwan.

Bushy Terrace (also translated as Shrub Terrace): a place in Hantan, capital of the ancient state of Chao, famous for the custom of lovers to meet there. It was built by a king of Chao in the Warring States era.

calendar: a man called Ling Lun made twelve bamboo pipes and fixed their pitch according to the notes of male and female phoenixes. He paired these pipes with the calendrical months.

caltrop, or water chestnut: its flower was very pale, a quality admired in a woman's complexion. Women usually picked the caltrops, and this imparts an erotic connotation to them.

candle stub: see Hsü Wu.

capitals: the most popular capitals mentioned in the poems are Hsienyang of the Ch'in Dynasty, Ch'angan of the Former Han, Loyang of the Later Han and of the Wei Dynasty, and Chienk'ang of the Liang Dynasty.

capstrings: used as a metonym for a man's official rank. To untie them was a ritual gesture, either implying retirement or political opposition. The phrase 'ripped capstring' refers to an anecdote about a guest at the court of King Chuang of Ch'u (r. 613–591 BC), who tweaked the dress of a palace lady when the candles went out at a banquet. In retaliation she ripped off his capstring in order to identify him later. The king, not wishing to disgrace his guest, ordered all his courtiers to remove their capstrings before lights were restored. A man's capstring might be offered to a woman as a love-token.

cardamom: its seeds form clusters, suggesting fertility and abundance. Used as an erotic motif with grapevines.

carp: in the old poems a letter was sometimes carried in a container shaped like a fish, which was said to be 'cooked' when opened. The carp is a prolific fish, and the double carp is probably an emblem of fertility, or wedded bliss.

Carp winds: the name of the wind of autumn in the ninth month of the lunar calendar.

carved litter: a reference to Lady Pan, the favourite concubine of the Han Emperor Ch'eng (r. 33–7 BC), who was invited by him to sit in his royal carriage as a mark of special favour. She refused on the grounds that her status was too lowly for such an honour.

cassia (kuei): a pun for come home. Its brilliant red in springtime is a metaphor for happy love, while its autumnal leaf-fall is a metaphor for blighted love. Known as a tree that flowers without bearing fruit, it is a poignant image. The cassia was also thought to grow on the moon, a symbol of immortality.

Cassia Forest: a region in Kwangsi province.

Cassia Lodge: the name of a palace in the Ch'in Dynasty.

Cassia Palace, Yellow Mount Lodge, P'ingling, Hsinfeng: all sumptuous buildings and fashionable places near the capital city of Ch'angan.

Cassia river: in Kwangsi province; it shares a joint source with the Hsiang river which flows south, while the Cassia flows north.

catalpa: a tree invested with grand and noble qualities, especially in the context of music. Expressive lutes were made out of this wood, and often such instruments were *objets d'art*. The best trees were said to grow at Dragon Gate (q.v.), one hundred feet tall and branchless, and favoured by phoenix. The catalpa features in the poems at a wellside, an amorous scenario.

cauldrons, a warrior who lifted: a reference to Hsiang Yü, who became king of Ch'u (233–202 BC). He fought Liu Pang for the empire and lost. He died at Kai-hsia.

Central Hall: name of an imperial harem.

Central Plains: the old name of the ancestral heartland of China prior to partition in AD 317 into north and south. It is situated in the basin of the Yellow river in Honan.

Chang Ch'ien: a minister (d. 114 BC) of the Han Emperor Wu sent to explore the regions of west China and beyond. Legend has it that he was ordered to discover the source of the Yellow river, believed to flow from the River of Heaven, or the Milky Way. One version of this legend has it that Chang Ch'ien sailed up the Yellow river and eventually reached the River of Heaven where he met a girl spinning, Weaver, and a boy leading an ox to drink, the star Herdboy. Weaver star gave Chang Ch'ien her loom-stone and told him to tell the astrologer, Yen Chün-p'ing of Ch'engtu, about it when he returned to earth. The astrologer had in fact noted a strange star at the very same time as the voyager's visit.

Chang Fang: when the Han Emperor Ch'eng used to leave the palace incognito to visit Ch'angan's pleasure quarter, he used to leave via Ch'i Gate with Chang Fang and masquerade as one of Chang's servants. Chang's title was the Marquess of Fup'ing.

Chang Heng: see *Background to Poets and Poems*. Wrote *Prose Poem on the Western Capital*, which has a line similar to that of Hsü Ling's *Preface* about gates and doors.

Chang Hua: see *Background to Poets and Poems*.

Ch'ang O: wife of the legendary figure, Yi the Archer, who had saved the populace from disaster by shooting down the suns when ten suns appeared together in the sky. In one myth, when the people rose against him, his wife decided to flee their palace, taking with her Yi's elixir of immortality. She took with her her pet hare, and after eating some of the elixir was assumed into the moon as an immortal. But, according to some legends, she was turned into a toad. When the moon is in eclipse the toad is said to swallow it.

Chang of the capital, i.e. Chang Ch'ang (d. 48 BC): a distinguished Han scholar and official, whose weakness for putting kohl on his wife's eyebrows was gently criticized by Emperor Yüan.

Chang Pi-ch'iang: son of Chang Liang (d. 187 BC), who had been ennobled as the Marquess of Liu as a reward for helping Liu Pang win the empire in 202 BC. His son, Pi-ch'iang, had a special status at court.

Chang river: in Hopei.

Chang-nü: it is not clear to whom this name refers, but the context indicates that she was a beautiful person.

Ch'angan: capital of the Former Han Dynasty, situated near the Wei river in north-west China, and known as the western capital. It was near the present site of Sian.

Ch'angsha: one of the southern kingdoms of ancient China, situated in the Yangtze river valley. In the second century BC Prince Ting of Ch'angsha came up to the Han court as the guest of Emperor Ching. At a court banquet the emperor cordially invited the prince to dance and sing. He did so, but only flapped his sleeves by way of dancing. Everyone tittered. The emperor asked him to explain himself. The prince said that his kingdom was so narrow that it was impossible to turn round in it. The emperor took the hint and increased the size of his territory.

Changt'ai: name of a pleasure quarter in Ch'angan.

Changt'i tree: mentioned in *The Book of Songs*, no. 174, which has the topos of brothers as the mainstay of a united family.

Ch'angyang Palace: a pleasure spot in a royal park of the same name in Ch'angan.

Chao: a state in ancient China (area of modern Shensi), which was famous for its beautiful women and skilled lutenists. It is usually linked with Yen state of similar fame.

Ch'ao: the name of a state in antiquity, modern Anhwei.

Chao Feiyen: Feiyen means Flying Swallow (d. 6 BC); she was the daughter of a musician. She was attached to the household of the Princess of Yang-a in Ch'angan, the sister of Emperor Ch'eng of the Han. She and her sister were discovered in the princess's household by the emperor on one of his incognito visits from the palace, and he brought them into his harem. Feiyen ousted his current favourite, Lady Pan, and eventually became consort. After the emperor's death Feiyen was driven to commit suicide by enemies at court, who rumoured that she was to blame for his death. She bore him no son. She was such a good dancer and so light that the saying was coined that she could dance on the palm of a man's hand.

Chao Hua jade: the name of a jewel given by the legendary Emperor Yao to his successor, Shun, when Yao gave him his two daughters in marriage. Yao's daughters were Nü-ying and O-huang according to a late myth.

Chaoyang Palace: the name of the palace where Chao Feiyen lived when she entered Emperor Ch'eng's harem.

Cheng: the name of an ancient state in the region of modern Honan, famous for its new kind of music in the sixth century BC. The 'tunes of Cheng' were abhorred by Confucius (551–479 BC), not because they lacked beauty, but because they 'corrupted classical music'. Other people did not think the music decadent, but erotic and lively, such as the Marquess of Wei, Wen (r. 424–387 BC), who said that he would never tire of the music of Cheng, whereas the classical music of the former kings used almost to make him fall asleep. In these poems they are considered for the most part to be love-songs, or erotic music.

Cheng Chiao-fu: the name of a man of the ancient state of Cheng who lived in the Chou dynasty. One day he was walking along the Han river when he met two lovely girls. He flirted with them and they gave him egg-sized jewels from their belts. He put the jewels in his robe against his bosom and went away. Later he found that the jewels and the girls had vanished. These were the sprites of the Han river.

Ch'engtu: capital of the old kingdom of Shu in west China.

Ch'i: the name of an ancient state in the region of modern Shantung and Hopei.

Ch'i and Wei rivers: in the ancient states of Wei and Cheng (modern Honan), respectively. The rivers were associated with trysting-places for lovers, especially in poems 39, 48 and 58 of *The Book of Songs*. Ch'i river is particularly associated with remembrance of past love, because poem 58 tells of a divorced wife who forded it on the way to her wedding and the full waters of the river soaked her carriage blinds, a good omen.

Ch'i Chiang: the name of a lady of the royal Chiang house of Ch'i state in the Spring and Autumn era, who was famous for her beauty and virtue. Poems 83 and 138 of *The Book of Songs* refer to a lady of this name who is much sought after in marriage.

Ch'i Liang: the name of a man of Ch'i state who was killed in battle in 550 BC. His wife is believed to have committed suicide by drowning in the Tzu river. She composed a plaintive song before she died, which is said to have made the city wall collapse. Tzu river is in the region of modern Shantung.

Chi Pavilion: in Kiukiang, near Mount Chiuli.

Chia I (201–169 BC): a statesman and poet of the Former Han. His early career at court was brilliant. Famous in his native Loyang for his ability to recite *The Book of Songs* and to compose works in different literary styles at the age of eighteen, he was made a scholar and palace counsellor by Emperor Wen. Later he was disgraced and exiled to the then foreign kingdom of Ch'u, considered by the Chinese as barbarous. There he wrote his famous *Prose Poem on the Owl*, which foretold his death.

Ch'iang: a tribe to the west of China, considered barbaric by the Chinese.

Chiangtung: the same as Chiangnan, South of the River (Yangtze).

Chiao-fu: see Cheng Chiao-fu.

Chiehshih: a place on the Gulf of Chihli.

Chienchang Palace, or Palace for Establishing Statutes: built in 104 BC by the Han Emperor Wen. It was a magnificent structure. To be appointed as its supervisor was considered a prestigious post. Empress Wei's (Wei Tzu-fu) brother, General Wei Ch'ing, was so honoured.

Ch'iench'i: a river in the region of Chekiang.

Chienhsing Park: built by the Liang Emperor Wu (Hsiao Yen) in AD 505 in the capital city of Chienk'ang.

Chienk'ang: capital city of the Liang Dynasty. Originally named Moling, it was renamed in the Three Kingdoms era as Chienyeh, then named Chienk'ang in the Chin Dynasty to avoid a taboo name. Near the modern city of Nanking by the Yangtze river.

Ch'ient'ang: modern Hangchow, made famous in poetry by the singer, Su Hsiao-hsiao, who lived there in the Chin and Southern Ch'i dynasties in the fifth century AD.

Chienyeh: capital of the Liang, renamed Chienk'ang.

Chin (Brocade): a river flowing past Ch'engtu city, the old capital of Shu kingdom.

Ch'in: the name of a short-lived dynasty (221–207 BC) before the Han. Its capital was Hsienyang. Originally a small state in the north-west of China (Shensi area), it gradually conquered and annexed the various states of feudal Chou by its superior military force and social discipline. When used in the sense of the earlier small state of Ch'in, this refers to the remote border region of north-west China.

Ch'in Lofu: the daughter of the Ch'in clan, which came from Hantan, capital of Chao state. She married a man called Wang Jen. One day the king of Chao caught sight of her from the pillars and parapet of his palace terrace when she was picking mulberry up the lanes. He was so attracted to her that he asked her to drink with him, hoping he could make love with her. She eluded his advances by composing a song for the lute, *Mulberry up the path*, in which she praised her husband and rejected the casual love of a passing official. The king then desisted from his efforts to seduce her. This song appears in Chapter One of this anthology under the title *Sunrise at the south-east corner*. The name of Ch'in Lofu occurs in another poem in this anthology, also in Chapter One, where she is said to be the eligible daughter of a family who could become the second wife of Chiao Chung-ch'ing. This poem appears here under the title *An old poem written for Chiao Chung-ch'ing's wife*. Ch'in often refers to Ch'in Lofu.

Ching (chou): the Hsiangyang region of modern Hupei. In early times it meant the area of the ancient state of Ch'u in south China.

Ching and Wei rivers: allusion to poem 35, *Valley wind*, of *The Book of Songs*, in which a divorced woman compares herself to the Ching river and her former husband's new wife to the Wei river. She says that the Ching itself is clear enough, but when it is seen in comparison with the Wei it seems to be muddy. There was a proverb that although the clear Ching river and the muddy Wei river (both in Shensi) flow together for a hundred miles of their course, they never become intermingled or confused.

Ching and Yang: regions of modern Hupei and Kiangsu.

Ching Mountain: in the old kingdom of Ch'u, which is often called the Ching region.

Chishe: an exotic perfume.

Ch'iu Hu: the name of the husband of a chaste wife, who came from the state of Lu. Five days after his marriage, he has to go to Ch'en state as an official. Five years later he goes back home, and on the way sees a pretty girl picking mulberry. He falls in love with her and tries to seduce her with some of his gold. She refuses his offer. He goes home, and gives the gold to his mother. Later his wife comes back from her work and goes in to meet her husband. To his dismay he finds that she is the woman he propositioned before. She rebukes him and commits suicide by drowning. She is one of the women praised for their virtue in *A Gallery of Good Women* (*Lieh nü chuan*), attributed to Liu Hsiang (77–6 BC). This was a popular narrative theme and has been treated by Fu Hsüan, Yen Yen-chih and Hsiao Lun here.

Cho girl: see Cho Wen-chün.

Cho Wen-chün, also called the Cho girl (second century BC): a recently widowed young woman, the daughter of a wealthy man called Cho Wang-sun who lived in Linch'iung. When the Han poet Ssu-ma Hsiang-ju lost his literary patron, he travelled to Linch'iung and was a guest at the Cho house. He played on his lute and sang, and Wen-chün, who was looking at him from the doorway, fell in love with him. He sent her gifts through her maids, and they eloped that night. Her father disowned her. Later they were reduced to selling wine in the market and Wang-sun was so ashamed that he finally gave his daughter her dowry. The poet's songs appear in Chapter Nine.

Chou: the name of the ancient dynasty (trad. 1111–256 BC), and also the name of the royal state to which the other feudal states owed allegiance. The name is used sometimes to mean China in general. With the Hsia and Shang was considered the Golden Age of antiquity.

Chou: the pageboy Chou, Chou *Hsiao-shih*, praised by the poet Chang Hua in the third century AD in a couplet similar to Hsiao Kang's.

Ch'u: the name of a state in south China in antiquity. In the early BC era it was considered barbarous, peopled by an uncouth tribe called the Man. For a long time it was felt that for a cultured Chinese to be posted there was virtual exile. Later Ch'u aroused considerable interest, especially in the literary sphere, since such works as *The Songs of Ch'u* (*Ch'u Tz'u*) originated there. Sometimes Ch'u is used with the southern state of Yüeh to mean a hostile region, and in abstract terms, estrangement between lovers. Ch'u is associated with slender waists because the fashion for slim waists was such that courtiers starved themselves to look thin.

Ch'u and Yüeh: the region of modern Hupei and Chekiang. See Ch'u.

Ch'u Ming-kuang: the name of a famous official in the reign of King Chao of Ch'u, and presumably a virtuoso musician.

Ch'ü Yüan (?332–?295 BC): a statesman and nobleman of Ch'u in the reigns of King Huai and Ch'inghsiang. Historical accounts vary, but he was generally believed to have been a favourite minister of King Huai, but later fell from grace and was banished under his son, King Ch'inghsiang. In his place of exile south of Ch'u he is believed to have committed suicide by drowning in the Milo river, a tributary of the Yangtze. It was also generally believed that he wrote a number of poems in *The Songs of Ch'u*, the rest being by his disciples and later imitators. The Ch'ü Yüan literary style is associated with the poem *Encountering sorrow*, an allegedly autobiographical narrative, telling of how he was slandered at court, of the misguided rule of his king, and of his futile search for the ideals of truth and beauty.

Chuang Chou, or Chuang Tzu: a famous philosopher of Meng state, one of the fathers of Taoist thought, who lived *c.* 399–295 BC. A passage from his writings describes how his friend, Hui Tzu, found Chuang Tzu beating a pot after his wife had died. When Hui Tzu asked him why he was not mourning her, Chuang Tzu replied that he looked on his wife's death as a slumber in the great house of the universe whither her bodily form had been transmuted into its prenatal state. He felt it would be wrong to object to her return to her natural abode by expressions of grief.

Chungchou: the same as the Central Plains.

Chungshan: the name of an important commandery in the Han, in modern Hopei. See Empress Yin.

Chungt'ai: an exotic perfume, probably taken from a place name, of which the place is now unknown.

Chuyai: formerly part of Kwangtung in the far south of China.

cinnabar: a red mineral used in elixirs of immortality. Used as an adjective it sometimes means a lover's faithful heart. 'Cinnabar and green' is a general term for paint.

cinnabar court: the general term for the long courtyard of red sandstone leading to the entrance of a palace.

city tumble, a: see city-destroyer.

city-destroyer: a reference to a woman so lovely that she has the power to destroy a city and a kingdom. The earliest extant mention of this occurs in poem 264 of *The Book of Songs*, which is actually derogatory. A later source for this phrase comes from the biography of Lady Li, concubine of the Han Emperor Wu, and in this context the phrase is one of praise. Before Lady Li entered the imperial harem, her brother, a court musician named Li Yen-nien, sang her praises to the emperor. This song appears in Chapter One here.

clasping the bridge-post: a reference to the romantic hero, Wei Sheng, of the sixth century BC, from Lu state. He promised to meet his sweetheart by Lan bridge in Ch'angan, but she failed to come. He waited for her there, even though the tide rose, and eventually he drowned. He was also known as Wei-sheng Kao.

Clear Note of autumn, or clear-tone autumn: the note called *shang*. According to an ancient theory of correspondences in the universe, the autumn season was associated with the second musical note in the pentatonic scale.

clear wine: said to be the drink of autumn, the clear wine like flowers. (Also see wine.)

clock, i.e. waterclock: one of the devices by which time was told in ancient China. It worked by a drip mechanism from a jar of water, and had a day cycle and a night one. When the jar dripped it gradually emptied out into another which tilted when it was full, restarting the drip cycle.

clothes perfumer: a silk-covered bamboo frame placed over a censer. Clothes were laid on top of the frame to be perfumed.

Cloud Gate: the name of the music of the legendary emperor Huangti, or the Yellow Emperor.

Cloud Terrace: a ceremonial edifice in the capital built in the Han Dynasty, so tall it was said to reach the clouds.

cocoon: has several connotations: (1) an early book of marvels tells of a mulberry tree of enormous size. In its top branches silkworms spun cocoons three feet long each holding twenty-one ounces of silk thread. This prolific cocoon is an erotic motif of abundance and fertility. Its silk was said to make a happy marriage quilt; (2) a woman's eyebrows are often likened to cocoons, and more frequently to the moths that emerge from them; (3) clustered cocoons are also an emblem of fertility.

Cold Dew Terrace: built by the Han Emperor Wu at the Palace of Sweet Springs in Shensi on a north-west mountain of the same name. It was the royal summer resort.

cold region: it is a convention of these love poems that an absent lover is often said to be on military duty in the northern border region, where the climate is much harsher than in the heartland of China. The coldness of the region acts as a metaphor for the cooling of a man's love in his absence.

'cold season' infidelity: the pine tree in winter traditionally symbolizes fidelity, staying green throughout the cold weather.

Cold Valley: in the ancient state of Yen. The statesman Tsou Yen of Ch'i state was assigned there in the fourth century BC. When he found that millet would not grow there, he blew on his bronze musical pipes to warm the valley, so that millet then grew and flourished.

cold winds: signal the arrival of autumn, with high clouds.

coming down the hill: see *Sweet herbs*.

'cook the carp': see carp.

cork: has a bitter taste (*k'u*), a pun for bitter in emotional terms.

Crested Wave: one of the emanations of the Goddess of Lo river, as she was described by Ts'ao Chih in his prose poem on the goddess.

cricket: a symbol of poignant suffering and likened to a woman's emotional distress when her lover deserts her. One of the earliest references to the cricket occurs in poem 114 of *The Book of Songs*: 'The cricket is in the hall, / The year draws to a close. / If we don't take pleasure now, / Days and months will pass by.'

Crossriver: a place in Sinkiang, a remote region.

crows: sometimes refer to the anecdote about Chu Po when he became a censor. Several crows perched at dusk on a cypress near the censorial office where he worked, and then at dawn they flew away.

crows turn white: a reference to the heir-apparent of Yen state, Prince Tan (d. 226 BC), when he was taken hostage in Ch'in state. He lamented in despair that he would only be freed when crows' heads turned white, when the sky rained grain and horses had horns. All those marvels happened and Tan did escape. But his father executed him in order to placate the Ch'in desire for vengeance.

Cypress Rafter Terrace (Poliang): where the Han Emperor Wu held a famous banquet; as such it stands for happy banquets of great magnificence in any time or era.

daddy-long-legs and wild plum: it was the custom at (lunar) New Year to put these in wine and dumplings. The name for the insect is *hsi-tzu*, a pun for happiness. Plum is the first tree to bloom in spring, the season of love.

dagger hilt: literally dagger ring; the word for ring, *huan*, is a pun for return, or come home.

Dagger Road: in Shu kingdom.

dagger-coin: money was made in different shapes and of different substances in ancient China. One such design was a knife or dagger shape made of metal with a hole for threading into sums of cash.

dance: one of the skills of a singing-girl, or entertainer, or courtesan, was the performance of a repertoire of dances, besides playing various musical instruments and singing. The gown worn by a female dancer had long wide sleeves that were used expressively to convey different emotions and actions, such as joy or a bird's soaring flight. There were set movements to some dances and a series of theatrical poses. During certain performances, such as at banquets, the female dancer could direct her interest in one of the guests or clients through her dance gestures and through eloquent eye movements.

Dark Dragon: probably the Hsüanyüan stars (Leo), also the place name by which the Yellow Emperor was known (in modern Honan).

Dark Gates: one of the names for the Gates of Heaven.

Dark Tower: one of the names for the Gates of Heaven, which like their counterpart on earth were topped with watchtowers.

daughter of Ch'in: see Nung Yü.

dawn clouds, dusk rain: the natural manifestations by which the Goddess of Mount Wu is known. She is said to have told this to an ancient king of Ch'u when she appeared to him in an erotic dream. The phrase 'clouds and rain' later came to mean sexual intercourse.

Dawn Wind: the name of a bird, the peregrine falcon.

day-lily: see flower of forgetfulness.

dew: an image that presages in some contexts autumn, since it turns to frost. It also acts as a metaphor for the transience of life. Heavy dew may serve as a metaphor for sexual favours, from a man to a woman, in some contexts.

'*Dew will not dry*': a refrain from *The Book of Songs*, no. 174: 'Soaking, soaking is the dew, / Without the sun it will not dry. / Content, content we drink at night; / Unless we're drunk we won't go home!'

Dewdrops: the title of poem 17 of *The Book of Songs*, in which a woman declares that she will not submit to marriage, no matter how influential her suitor's family is.

dewy mallow broth: fare conventionally offered by a woman to a man in the context of a professional courtesan and her client. The image of the mallow is often used elsewhere to suggest through its tendency to lean towards sunlight a woman's emotional need of a man.

Dipper star: see Northern Dipper.

Divine Flight and *Titular Six*: Taoist classics. The Titular Six were divinities of the Taoist pantheon whose names were formed from compounds of the Ten Celestial Stems and the Twelve Branches, numerical systems used in the calendar. A court lady is said to have locked her copies of these books in a jade box.

divorced woman skilled at plainweave: an allusion to the first poem in the anthology, *Sweet herbs* (q.v.). This reference varies depending on the context. In some poems the divorced woman featured in *Sweet herbs* is a pathetic person; in others the phrase denotes the sexual attraction of women who conventionally appear to be weaving.

do, re: lit. *kung* and *shang*, the first two notes of the ancient pentatonic musical scale.

dodder: a plant that grows by clinging to a tree or some other natural support. It is used as an image suggesting woman's emotional dependency on man.

dogwood: the same as oleaster in these poems, it has two contradictory meanings. One derives from a passage in *The Songs of Ch'u*, in which the poet compares the plant unfavourably with cassia and orchid, and in this sense I have translated the plant as dogwood to suggest its derogatory meaning. The other is a vaguely erotic emblem – perhaps the oleaster was used as an ingredient in aphrodisiacs? As such, the emblem appears on several items of women's clothing, and is translated as oleaster.

Double Ninth: a festival held on the ninth day of the ninth lunar month when it was customary for people to go on an excursion; they would climb a height, drink wine with chrysanthemum petals, and compose poetry.

double-body creature, or thing: a fabled creature which is an amalgam of two inseparable creatures, the *ch'iung-ch'iung* or the *chü-hsü* and the *ch'üeh*. The first ones are swift, horse-like animals that cannot feed themselves, so they have to have another beast, the *ch'üeh*, to help them. The *ch'üeh*, on the other hand, cannot run, so in times of danger the other beasts carry it away on their back to safety. As such this mutual dependence is an emblem of conjugal love.

dragon: a mythological creature with several different connotations: (1) its body is an assemblage of various animal forms, bird-like claws, serpentine body, carnivorous teeth; (2) an auspicious creature, the harbinger of rain and moisture to ripen the crops; (3) a courser of the skies, often described as the steed of the legendary star, Weaver; (4) in spring the dragon rises into the sky, in autumn it disappears into watery depths; (5) interlocked dragons are an emblem of sexual intercourse; (6) a symbol of the emperor; (7) the emblem of the east; (8) with the tiger it is the steed of the legendary Queen Mother of the West, ruler of the land of the immortals.

Dragon Gate: name of a mountain in Shensi. See catalpa.

Dragon Tower: Blue (or Green) Dragon Tower Gate in Loyang city.

drapes: often it is not specified whether these are on the door, window or bed of a woman's apartment. All three or just one is possible. Also, they might mean the flimsy curtains, or heavy brocade drapes, or tapestried hangings.

dried meat: the customary way to preserve meat was to process it so that it was dried out; not a derogatory term, it meant that the recipient was eating well.

drum: there was a custom of hitting a drum to call attention to one's grievances, such as crippling levies expended on extravagant buildings.

ducks and geese, or ducks and swans: a reference to an anecdote told in a Former Han sourcebook about a minister called T'ien Jao. He advised the Duke of Lu in the fifth century BC that though a cock had many virtues it should be eaten because it was locally raised and common fare, whereas certain ducks and swans or geese should be allowed to live in the royal ponds because they were rare imports.

Duke Highnose: the nickname of Emperor Kao-tsu, Liu Pang, founder of the Han dynasty.

Duke Wen of Chin: late seventh century BC. Also see Nanwei.

Dusk Shadow: a street in Ch'angan.

dust: flying dust or bright dust on the highway are two images signifying a man's exciting life in the world of politics. Its counterpart is the image of mud in a ditch, or thick river mud, to denote a woman's lowly, immobile position out of the public gaze. Dust sometimes refers to a woman's white cosmetic powder. 'Dust the pillow' is a term meaning to enjoy the sexual favours of one's lord and master.

Dust on items of furniture belongs to a complex of neglect images signifying a man's neglect of a woman. Dust flying on the rafters is an image suggesting that a woman's song is so sublime that the rafters resound joyously (see rafter dust).

dust-and-mop: metonymy, in a favourable sense, for a wife or mistress.

earrings: often of large pearls, 'bright moons', they are sometimes said to be behind a woman's ears, rather than on the lobe. A single earring might be thrown by a man to a woman by way of a love-token while she was performing a dance.

East Mulberry: see Leaning Mulberry.

east neighbour: a literary reference to an attractive woman who followed her amorous inclinations, without recourse to a matchmaker.

East Wall star: in the last days of the tenth lunar month this star might appear in the south sky, denoting a rare occurrence. Its western equivalent is Gemini.

eight: a propitious number.

'embracing boughs': an erotic emblem of mutual love.

Emperor Ch'eng (r. 33–7 BC): of the Former Han, named Liu Ao. Of his concubines Lady Pan was his favourite, until she was ousted by Chao Feiyen.

Emperor Wang: said to be a descendant of the legendary Yellow Emperor, he was the king of Shu. His name was Tu Yü. When his minister Pieh Ling was away from court, the emperor had an affair with his wife, and when this came to light Tu Yü died of shame. It was believed that when he died he turned into a cuckoo which in late spring weeps and sheds tears of blood, its cry making travellers homesick because it sounds like the words 'Better go home!' Another version of this legend goes that his minister went away on flood control and on his return discovered the affair. The emperor made amends by abdicating in his minister's favour. Sometimes the bird he was metamorphosed into is thought to be the nightjar.

Emperor Wu of the Han: see A-chiao.

Empress Ch'en: also see A-chiao, consort of the Han Emperor Wu. When she lost his favour she retired to Eternal Gate Palace. Her rival was Wei Tzu-fu, and she became Empress Wei. Empress Ch'en had not borne the emperor a son.

Empress Shen: consort of King Yü of Chou (r. ?781–770 BC), deposed by Paossu, a woman of exceptional beauty. See Paossu.

Empress Teng: said to have received instruction from the lady scholar, Pan Chao (d. 116 BC, sister of the Han historian, Pan Ku), in the *Confucian Classics*, of which *The Spring and Autumn Classic* was one text.

Empress Yin: this name and title could refer to two historical persons: (1) Lady Yin, a beauty of the Warring States era in the kingdom of Chungshan, who became the king's consort, Chungshan being a small kingdom between the northern states of Yen and Chao; (2) Feng Chao-i, who bore a son to Emperor Yüan of the Han (r. 49–33 BC), and was promoted to the fiefdom of Chungshan with her son. She is famous for having protected the emperor from a charging bear which had escaped from its cage, putting herself between them.

erstwhile carriage: see Mi Tzu-hsia.

Eternal Gate Palace (Ch'angmen): where Empress Ch'en retired when she lost the affection of Emperor Wu.

Eternal Joy Palace (Ch'anglo): built by the Han Emperor Kao-tsu in 200 BC in Ch'angan. Later it became the residence of the empress dowager. See reference to Wei Tzu-fu, under wardrobe mistress below.

Eternal Springs: see Yellow Springs.

Eternal Trust Palace (Ch'anghsin): the residence of the empress dowager in the reign of the Han Emperor Ch'eng to which Lady Pan retired when she lost imperial favour.

eye to eye fish: a mythical creature having two fishy bodies and sharing one pair of eyes, their symbiosis denoting marital devotion.

Fair Maid star (Wunü): the name of a star; not much is known of its legend.

Fairy Radiance: see O-huang.

falcon: an allusion to poem 132 of *The Book of Songs*: 'Swift is the falcon, / Dense the northern wood. / Not seeing my lord, / My sad heart is full of longing.'

'fallen colt' and 'chirping cicada': the names of hairstyles for women. See Lady Liang.

Falling Rain: see Goddess of Mount Wu.

fan: usually round, made of sheer white silk, and painted with amorous scenes. Its whiteness and roundness are likened to the full moon. Fans were kept in a person's sleeve or bosom. Used in summer and put away in winter, fans are a frequent metaphor for discarded love, for a woman deserted by a man. These love poems often quote the poem on the fan ascribed to Lady Pan which appears in Chapter One here, entitled *A poem on regret*, and popularly known as the *Round fan poem*.

Feiyen, lit. Flying Swallow: see Chao Feiyen.

Feng: east of Ch'angan, known as Hsinfeng.

Feng Tzu-tu: a slave in the household of General Huo Kuang (d. 68 BC). The general rose to high office under Emperor Wu.

Fenyin: a place in Shansi south of Fen river near the border between China and the nomadic tribes of the north-west in antiquity.

fifteenth, night of, or moon of: usually a full moon, especially in autumn (see also autumn moon).

firewood and feed: a reference to an anecdote about Chi An (d. ?108 BC), who told Emperor Wu that the emperor's method of selecting ministers was like gathering sticks for firewood – he put the last ones on top.

fish's belly: it was customary to send a message in a letter-container shaped like a fish (see also carp).

fish sport: an echo of an old folk-song about fish playing in all directions around lotus leaves (a pun for passion) in the area of South of the River (Yangtze).

Fishing rod: the name of an old song for the lute.

five days: according to an ancient book of rites, a husband must make love with his wife at least once every five days until she reaches the age of fifty. This custom is alluded to in *The Book of Songs*, no. 226: 'Five days he promised! / Six days and I still don't see him!'

Five Elements Theory: in the Han Dynasty, writers such as Tung Chung-shu evolved a system of cosmology relating different categories of natural and celestial phenomena to affairs in the human world. This system drew from many earlier philosophical sources. The five elements were wood (related to east, spring, the number eight, green, note E), fire (related to south, summer, seven, red, note G), metal (related to west, autumn, nine, white, note D), water (related to north, winter, six, black, note A), and earth (related to centre, five, yellow, and note C). Different systems created other sets, but this one is typical.

five horses: a team of five horses indicated the rank of a prefect, or similar status in early China. Sometimes this refers to the rebuffed prefect of the narrative poem in Chapter One, *Sunrise at the south-east corner*.

Five Lakes: a general name for the lake district of Wu in modern Kiangsu and Chekiang.

five wives: according to legend a king of ancient Ch'in offered five beautiful women to the king of Shu, who sent five strong men to greet them. On their way home the men saw a giant snake and tried to pull it out from the mountain cave, but as they did the mountain collapsed, killing them and the Ch'in beauties.

Flaming Cinnabar: see Huo Tan.

Fleetfox Pass: in the north-east border region, modern Chihli.

floral yellow: see yellow.

flower of forgetfulness, flower of oblivion: a drug that induces amnesia, taken to forget painful events. The earliest reference to it occurs in poem 62 of *The Book of Songs*, in which a woman says she suffers so much from pining for her lord that she wants to plant the herb by her north room, if only she could get it.

flowerboys: some sort of insect, such as a large species of butterfly or bee, probably the former since this appears as a popular motif in love poetry.

flowing yellow: raw silk or unbleached silk thread.

Flying Chestnut: the name of the famous steed of the legendary Yellow Emperor.

Flying Swallow (Feiyen): see Chao Feiyen.

foot of silk: a foot length of silk was the typical means for writing letters. Paper was invented in the second century AD.

Forbidden Palace: the imperial palace.

Forest Gleam, Linkuang: the name of a Ch'in Dynasty palace.

Four Clans: the four most prominent non-imperial clans of the Later Han were the Fan, Kuo, Yin and Ma.

four points: north, south, east and west.

four-width: four panels of material making a double-size quilt.

Fufei: the name of the Goddess of Lo river.

Fufeng: a commandery in Shensi. The place name marks an allusion to Su Hui's romantic woven poem. See palindrome.

fulling cloth: the process of pounding the fibres of silk after it had been woven, using a block and a beater of stone. This work was done by women in autumn in preparation for winter clothes. There are many conventional aspects to fulling in these love poems: it is done by elegantly dressed women; it is outside or near the city wall; the sounds are said to be mournful, reminding the women working of their absent lovers; and the words for pounder and silk were puns for a male lover and love or pining, respectively. Fulling is a popular folk-song theme.

General Li: Li Kuang-li, a military commander under the Han Emperor Wu who was sent to Ferghana to obtain a tribute of horses. He captured the city of Erh-shih. He was ennobled for his exploits. Eventually he was killed in captivity after being disastrously defeated by the Hsiungnu in 94 BC. (He was Lady Li's brother.)

girdle: besides a long embroidered sash a woman wore a jewelled girdle. When these were untied, her dress would fall open, and so the gesture comes to imply sexual intercourse. The girdle or its jewels might be offered as a love-token. See Cheng Chiao-fu.

girl of Jasper Terrace: Chien Ti, a legendary figure, the lovely daughter of the Lord of Sung. She was shut away in this building, but a hero, the mythical figure Ti K'u, sent her a swallow. Chien Ti ate its egg and became pregnant. She became the ancestress of the Shang with Ti K'u as its first ancestor.

Girl of Night, Tzu-yeh: believed to have been the name of a professional singer in the Eastern Chin Dynasty in the fourth century AD. A cycle of 42 songs is attributed to her, and they belong to a category of Southern Dynasties folk-songs. Bold and direct in style, they are love poems full of erotic puns and emblems. It is thought that they were originally arranged in a dialogue sequence between two lovers, and that the sequence was disturbed.

girl of Ying: see Nung Yü.

god's palm: see Welcome Dew Terrace.

Goddess of Hsiang river: the Hsiang is the second main river of south China, flowing north into the Yangtze, and is one of the rivers of Ch'u. In *The Songs of Ch'u* there is a cycle of shamanistic songs of which the third and fourth are addressed to the Princess of this river and to its Lady. Sometimes these two nymphs are confused with the two daughters of Emperor Yao, O-huang and Nü-ying, because another legend describes how they drowned in the Hsiang when their husband, Emperor Shun, died.

Goddess of Lo river: Fufei. The Lo ran by the old capital city of Loyang. Fufei appears in *The Songs of Ch'u*, in which the poet tells of his unsuccessful courtship of her. She is also the subject of Ts'ao Chih's famous prose poem quoted in these love poems. Her emanations are a crested wave or driven snow, as Ts'ao Chih describes her.

Goddess of Mount Wu: also known as the divine woman, she haunts the clefts in the rocks of Mount Wu. Traditionally this was believed to be above the Yangtze river in Szechwan. She is said to have met former kings of Ch'u in erotic dreams, leaving them in disappointment. She is also associated with Kaot'ang, a holy hill in Ch'u, and with Sunny Terrace, where King Hsiang of Ch'u saw her emanations as he walked with the poet, Sung Yü. Her emanations were dawn clouds and dusk rain, or falling rain.

gold: currency and a precious metal. Southern gold was considered the finest in quality; it was mined in Chingchou and Yangchow. There was a saying that one thousand gold would buy the fragrant season, or the pleasures of youth.

Gold stars, Musk moons: see yellow.

Golden Vale: a park belonging to the poet and official, Shih Ch'ung, and situated on the outskirts of Loyang in Honan. It was a pleasure park famous for the wealthy poet's extravagant parties. His favourite singer, Green Pearl (Luchu), would perform before his guests there. In about the year AD 296 he held a famous banquet for General Wang Hsü who was on his way back to Ch'angan.

goose, geese: often referred to as carriers of messages between lovers, particularly the wild goose which migrates from the northern region, where men are sent to fight, to the south where the wives and mistresses live. The goose is usually described as a lone bird, a pathetic image.

Goose Gate Pass (*Yenmen*): a military outpost in Shansi so named because when the geese migrated from the north to the south they seemed to fly through this natural pass.

goose-letter: see Su Wu.

Grand Plains (Kaop'ing): the name of a place in Shantung, suggesting somewhere far from the centre of China.

grapevines: first brought into China by Chang Ch'ien (q.v.) on one of his voyages to the western regions. Vineyards were laid out near the palace. Wine from grapes was not the usual alcoholic beverage in China, but a spirit fermented from rice. The grapevine was used as a decorative motif on women's clothing and furniture, suggesting abundance and fertility through its clustered flowers and fruit.

Great Curve bow (Tach'ü): the name of an archery bow in antiquity.

Great Mound: the name of a suite of music derived from the name of the capital city of Ch'u in the reign of King Huai.

Greater Ch'in: the far-flung provinces of the Roman Empire in the Roman Orient. It is recorded that this region was rich in gold, silver, rare gems, night-shining jade and bright moon pearls.

Green Chain Gate: the small gate leading to the imperial palace.

Green Jade (Piyü): the name of a concubine of the Prince of Junan in the Chin Dynasty, famous for her flute playing.

Green Pearl (Luchu, third century AD): the famous concubine of the poet and official Shih Ch'ung. She was very beautiful, and was a fine dancer and musician. She is remembered for her performances of dance and music at Golden Vale. Prince Lun of Chao was attracted to her and expected Shih Ch'ung to give her to him. On his refusal, and for other, political reasons, the prince had him executed. Green Pearl committed suicide by throwing herself from a tall building.

Green river (Lu shui): the name of a tune to which poems were set. 'Green' could refer to the name of the river or to the colour of the river.

Greensilk lute: the name of the famous lute belonging to the Han poet Ssu-ma Hsiang-ju.

gulf of heaven, or Gulf of Heaven: used figuratively or to denote a constellation.

hairpins: long, elaborately jewelled hair ornaments fixed at chic angles to hold the chignon in place. A popular design was a sparrow, or a peacock, or grains of seed. A dangling hairpin was an allusion to a poem by Sung Yü describing a woman attaching her hairpin to an official's capstring as a love-token.

half-forehead eyebrows, half across the forehead: an allusion to the anonymous song, *A children's rhyme of the Han era*, which appears in Chapter One, satirizing country girls for their extravagant aping of city fashions.

Han, celestial river: the counterpart of the Milky Way in the West. It is also called Starry River, Long River, Long Han, Sky River, River of Heaven or Cloudy Han. It was believed that the Yellow river on earth flowed from the Han river in the sky. Usually this reference conjures up ideas of the legend of Weaver and Herdboy stars (q.v.). The Han river is seen as an obstacle between these stellar lovers since it is in full flood every night of the year except the Seventh Night of the Seventh Month (q.v.). On that night the waters ebbed, allowing the lovers to meet. Weaver is sometimes called the girl of Han river.

Han: one of the names for China, derived from the Han Dynasty.

Han (Chung): one of the sorcerers of the first Ch'in emperor, Ch'in Shih Huangti (r. 221–210 BC), sent to find the elixir of immortality. He never returned from his quest, and was believed to have become an immortal. He is associated with the Taoist pantheon.

Han Hsin: see Huaiyin.

Han river, terrestrial: rises in Pochiung Mountain and flows into the Yangtze. It was one of the rivers of the old state of Ch'u and was believed to be the dwelling of a water goddess, or two nymphs, known as the Han woman, or the two sprites of Han river. (See Han river sprites.) The course of the Han is in modern Hupei.

Han river sprites: the terrestrial Han river is associated with various legends. One of these concerns two nymphs who rove the banks in human guise, and one day meet Cheng Chiao-fu (q.v.).

Hanku Pass: a natural pass fortified in the Ch'in Dynasty. Sited west of Loyang near the Yellow river, in modern Honan. An important military outpost for the defence of China's northern border against hostile northern tribes.

Hann: name of a feudal kingdom in ancient China, south of the Yellow river and south-east of Ch'in.

Hantan: capital city of the ancient state of Chao in north China, famous for lovely girls and skilled women musicians. Ch'in Lofu, heroine of the influential ballad, *Sunrise at the south-east corner*, or *Mulberry up the lane*, came from there.

Hanyang: in modern Kansu province, far north-west of China, signifying the remote borderlands.

hard and soft: see *Yin/Yang*.

Heaven's towers: twin towers on the Gates of Heaven.

hemp, hempen pledge: a love-token of hemp was picked by the shaman-poet in *The Nine Songs* section of *The Songs of Ch'u*: 'I pick the glistening bloom of Holy Hemp / To give to one who lives far away.'

Herb poem, or *Sweet herbs* poem: the first poem in this anthology. It tells of a divorced woman who meets her former husband when she has come down from a hill where she picked *miwu* herbs. It has been conjectured by some scholars that this herb might be a fertility drug, implying that the woman was divorced by her husband because she bore him no children. Also called the *Homespun* lyric.

Herdboy: a legendary star, the equivalent of Altair in Aquila, or Capricorn. Generally called Herdboy, but literally his name is Draught Ox. See Weaver and Seventh Night.

Herdboy bridge: built by Cheng, First Emperor of the Ch'in Dynasty, over the river Wei, south of the Ch'in capital in Hsienyang.

hibiscus (*mutabilis*) (*fuyung*): usually identified as a hibiscus or cotton rose; it is a brilliantly blooming plant of the mallow family, but sometimes also identified as the lotus when it is in bloom. Both plants have red blooms, some double, and are known for their vigorous growth. An erotic emblem because of its colour and prolific nature.

high notes: music has long had allegorical associations in Chinese thought. In the context of love, the analogy is made between the strings of the instrument, such as a lute, and the human heart, and the notes produced are compared with human emotions. Thus when the strings of a lute are tightened and produce a high-pitched sound, this is likened to the tense emotions of a person suffering from the pangs of love. Similarly, as the string of a lute may be broken by excessive tightening and violent playing, so the heart may break from excessive anguish.

Hillside bough: an allusion to the anonymous *Song of the Yüeh boatman*, which appears in Chapter Nine, in which a boatman in love with a nobleman compares himself to a branch of a tree on a hill.

History: *The Book of History*, one of the *Confucian Classics*.

Hochien: an ancient province in the state of Chao, modern Hopei. It became a kingdom in the Han and was ruled by members of the royal family. It was the fiefdom of the young Emperor Ling while Emperor Huan was still on the throne. Emperor Ling's mother, or in some versions Tu Nü (q.v.), amassed a huge fortune at Hochien and built an extravagant palace, so the rumour went. Hochien is also associated with the birthplace of Lady Chao, concubine of Emperor Wu of the Han and mother of Emperor Chao. She was discovered by a man who divined strange phenomena at her home in the form of a violet vapour. She was found to have both fists clenched, which the emperor unfolded, finding a jade hook.

homespun, or *Homespun* lyric: an allusion to the first poem of this anthology. See *Sweet herbs*.

Honei: the old name of a province in the region of modern Honan where the Shang Dynasty had its capital. It was called one of 'the legs of a tripod in the centre of the empire'.

hook: literally a jewelled brooch worn by a woman, or a hooked pole used for raising window drapes, or for drawing down branches of a mulberry tree. It also serves as a metaphor for a woman's curved eyebrows, or for the crescent moon.

Hop'u pearl: Hop'u was a famous pearl centre and a trading place as early as the Han era, and a pearl of this name means one of the finest quality; situated in the south-west, modern Kwangtung.

horizontal (*hengch'en*): one of the few references to lovers lying in bed.

horn: rhinoceros horn is believed to be an aphrodisiac.

horned beasts (*chiaotuan*): described in the ancient texts as a creature looking partly like a pig, partly like an ox, with a horn in its nose which could be used as an archer's bow.

House of Gold: a reference to a remark Emperor Wu made when he was still a boy about A-chiao with whom he had fallen in love. See A-chiao and Empress Ch'en, and Eternal Gate Palace.

How few: an allusion to poem 36 of *The Book of Songs*, in which, according to the traditional interpretation, those few who return from an expedition are mourned.

How slow she comes!: see Lady Li.

Hoyang: the name of an old province in the region of modern Honan. It may have associations with the pleasure park of Shih Ch'ung near Loyang where his beautiful entertainer, Green Pearl, used to perform for his guests. (See Golden Vale.)

Hsi Shih (fifth century BC): a beautiful girl from the countryside who was trained in the arts of entertainment and seduction by the state of Yüeh in order to distract their enemy, Wu state. This stratagem was devised by Kou Chien, King of Yüeh, who had been defeated by Fu Ch'ai, King of Wu, in 494 BC. In 473 BC Yüeh conquered Wu. Both states are in the area of modern Kiangsu and Chekiang. Hsi Shih was noted for the pertness of her sulky face, and later women imitated her frowns in order to appear beautiful like her.

Hsiang river: one of the rivers flowing through Ch'u. Many legends are associated with it; see Goddess of Hsiang river and Hsiao-Hsiang river.

Hsiang Yü: military leader who rebelled against the Ch'in Dynasty, and fought for the restoration of the ancient kingdom of Ch'u. He contested for supremacy with the future founder of the Han Dynasty and died at the battle of Kai-hsia (202 BC).

Hsiang-ju: personal name of the Han poet, Ssu-ma Hsiang-ju. He changed his name to this because he admired the famous statesman of Chao, Lin Hsiang-ju.

Hsiangyang city: in modern Hupei, famous for its knights-errant, and for a certain kind of song sung by women, generally known as Hsiangyang Music.

Hsiangyang Music: according to a record of music, this was a type of music compiled by Tan, Prince of Sui, in about the middle of the fifth century AD, when he was Governor of Hsiangyang. This account says that one night he heard women singing various popular songs and he wrote them down. Music called Tat'i tunes also belongs to this type of song, which appears to be characterized by a local, popular style rather than a formal, metropolitan style.

Hsiao Niang: a girl singer loved by Fan Ching. See *Background to Poets and Poems*, Shen Man-yüan entry.

Hsiao Tzu-hsien: see *Background to Poets and Poems*.

Hsiao-Hsiang river: the general name for two rivers that flow into lake Tungt'ing from the south in the region of Ch'u, modern Hunan. These rivers conjure up ideas of water-sprites, especially the Goddess of Hsiang river (q.v.), and O-huang and Nü-ying. The Hsiao is a tributary of the Hsiang and rises in north Kwangtung.

The two rivers are linked because the main Hsiang carries the waters of the Hsiao into lake Tungt'ing.

Hsiaop'ing ford: this may refer to a ford on the Yellow river north of Loyang city.

Hsiats'ai: a place in Ch'u made famous in literature by being mentioned as a city of alluring beauties by a poet in his prose poem *The Lechery of Mr Tengt'u*. It is in the region of modern Anhwei.

Hsieh T'iao: see *Background to Poets and Poems*.

Hsien pool: the legendary pool in which the ten suns (or the sun) were rinsed after their diurnal journey through the sky. In the shamanistic section of *The Songs of Ch'u* the shaman-poet says he will rinse his hair with a deity in Hsien pool.

Hsien-Ch'in: i.e. Hsienyang, capital city of the Ch'in Dynasty.

Hsientu: lit. Suspension Crossing, the name of a kingdom on the western border of the Han empire, east of modern Afghanistan. In Han travelogues it was described as inaccessible because of its sheer mountains and dangerous creeks. To journey through this area travellers had to use rope bridges over the mountains and rivers.

Hsienyang: capital of the Ch'in Dynasty, north of Wei river. The heartland of the old state of Ch'in before it conquered the whole of China was surrounded by natural defences of passes, mountains and rivers, and was called 'within the passes'. The first Ch'in emperor had magnificent palaces built there, the finest being completed in 212 BC. It was said to be one of the wonders of the world, measuring 2,500 feet wide and 500 feet long, and could accommodate thousands of people. Around Hsienyang 270 smaller imperial palaces were built with a network of covered, walled paths.

Hsinch'eng: this place name may refer to a town near Hsienyang, which, according to one commentator, used to be called Weich'ing. There is a group of tunes going by the title Weich'ing Tunes. This place is in the Shensi area.

Hsiu Shang-jen: see *Background to Poets and Poems*.

Hsiungnu, usually translated as Huns: a nomadic tribe on the northern border of China. Periodically they threatened the peace and stability of China, making incursions into the heartland. The Chinese pacified them by war or appeased them by marriage with members of the Chinese royal family, or by tribute.

Hsü Fei-ch'iung: the name of a fairy.

Hsü Mien: see *Background to Poets and Poems*, Hsü Fei entry.

Hsü Wu, a girl from Ch'i state who was so poor that she had to spin by night using reflected light from a neighbour's house, or other people's candle stubs.

Hsüanyüan: another name for the Yellow Emperor (Huang-ti), the supreme deity of the Taoist pantheon.

Hsün Feng-ch'ien: a man in antiquity who prided himself on his romantic conquests.

Hu and Yüeh: tribes of the north and south, respectively, they come to represent the north and south. The Hu tribe were nomadic horsemen; the red bird is a symbol of the south; so the Hu horse and the Yüeh bird act as polar opposites when used as dual images.

Huai river: the central river of China between the Yellow and Yangtze rivers of the north and south. It flows eastwards through the region of Ch'u into the Yellow Sea. There was a popular belief that at one point in the Huai river the incoming tide and outgoing tide met, suggesting the idea of a reunion between lovers.

Huainan: famous in the Han Dynasty as a place where exciting dances originated.

Huaiyin: in the region of modern Kiangsu, famous for its military hero, Han Hsin (d. 196 BC). A man of humble origins, he was ennobled for his bravery. He made a statement about political life, to the effect that when soaring birds have all been killed the hunter's bow is laid aside. Later, when he was executed, he compared himself to such a bird.

Huang O: mother of Shao Hao, son of the legendary Yellow Emperor. Sometimes such mythological references constitute polite flattery of a reigning monarch.

Huang-Lao: see Yellow Emperor.

Huanglung: one of the various Hsiungnu tribes whose territory was in the region of modern Jehol.

Huayang: the name of a favourite concubine of Lord Ankuo of Ch'in. It has been suggested by some scholars that this might be a confusion with the name of Lord Lungyang, the homosexual lover of a king.

Huhsiang: a place in Honan not far from the old capital city of Loyang. It was the site of several cities in antiquity having different names. This reference might be intended to evoke the idea of the golden age of antiquity, besides the more recent splendour of the city of Loyang.

Hun: a general translation for the Hsiungnu or the Hu tribes, meaning in general the northern tribes.

Hung city: name of a palace-gate building in the Han where books were stored.

Hung Yai: the name of the music master of the legendary emperors Yao, Shun and Yü.

Huo Ch'ü-ping (d. 117 BC): the illegitimate son of Wei Ch'ing's elder sister, and brother of Huo Kuang (q.v.), he rose to the rank of supreme commander of the Ministry of War. In 123 BC he won decisive victories over the Hsiungnu and was ennobled. Miracles and feats of valour are associated with his name.

Huo Kuang (d. 68 BC): brother of Huo Ch'ü-ping (q.v.), he rose to high office under the Han Emperor Wu. When the emperor died, General Huo promoted a royal grandson as his successor, who reigned as Emperor Hsüan.

Huo Tan, Flaming Cinnabar: seems to be the name of an immortal woman. Cinnabar (q.v.) was one of the ingredients for concocting the elixir of immortality.

Huona: the name of an exotic perfume, perhaps patchouli.

I pick beans, or *Picking beans*: an allusion to poem 226 of *The Book of Songs*, which tells of a woman unable to do her work of picking beans and indigo because she is pining for her lover.

'In the north there is a lovely woman': the opening line of a song performed by Li Yen-nien before Emperor Wu of the Han, in which he described his sister. She later became the favourite concubine of the emperor, and was given the title Lady Li (q.v.). His song appears in Chapter One.

Inaction: a reference to one of the meditation practices of the Taoists, in which one attempts to rid the mind of extraneous matters and achieve a measure of mental equilibrium.

incense candle: see sinking incense.

Indigo Field: a mountain in Shensi where fine jade was quarried.

Iyang: in the region of modern Honan.

jade coffer, or jewel box, or jade in a jewel box: a reference to the halcyon days of Wang Chao-chün (q.v.), before she was sent to be a bride of a Hsiungnu chieftain.

jade disc: a badge of office in antiquity for rulers or high officials, having a religious and political significance. Later it became a token of wealth, and even later was used as a design motif in the interiors of grand mansions. A cryptic jade was a jade tablet shaped like a colt, according to one interpretation, and inscribed with a secret message.

Jade Gate Pass (Yümen): in the north-west border region, west of Tunhuang, modern Kansu, where Chinese guards maintained border patrols against hostile tribesmen of the north.

Jade Girl: reference to the legendary game between the Lord of the Eastern Kings and Jade Girl, in which there were 1,200 throws.

jade jar: a waterclock, see clock.

Jade Scales: the central star of the Northern Dipper constellation, the eighth of the twenty-eight traditional constellations. The Dipper and Scales were considered auspicious stars because they were associated with the tools for scooping and weighing grain in times of a good harvest. Northern Dipper is the equivalent of some stars in Ursa Major.

Jade Tree: grows on K'unlun mountains in the west according to legend. In *The Songs of Ch'u* there are references to breaking off a branch of this tree.

jasper bloom: an echo of *The Songs of Ch'u*: 'A jasper bloom I cannot bear to pick', it expresses the poet's fear of ageing and losing his beauty. Sometimes, however, this merely refers to the artificial flower in a woman's tiara.

Jo: a place name, in the region of modern Hupei.

Jo river: according to legend it runs through the K'unlun mountains, home of the immortals in the west and realm of Queen Mother of the West (q.v.), a goddess.

Jo tree: a fabulous tree, which was red with bright green leaves and red blooms, the branches of which gave off a brilliant red glow.

'joint grave' poem: reference to *The Book of Songs*, no. 73.

'joy of love' (*ho-huan*): an erotic emblem appearing on fans, quilts and curtains. It is identified with the tree *Albizia julibrissin*, a deciduous tree of the pulse family with a tall trunk. Its leaves are like wings, formed as they are from double leaves. At night they close. In summer small flowers emerge with numerous long, red stamens which later turn to fruit. The ideas of double joining, redness and fruit are all present in the emblem.

jujube (*tsao*): a tree which is also a pun for the word 'soon', meaning 'better not delay', or hurry up and get married and have children.

Junglefowl: the name of a plaintive and romantic song.

Jutzu: the name of the favourite concubine of Prince Ching of Chungshan. He had another favourite called Ping.

Kaoliu: Tallwillow (q.v.).

Kaot'ang: a mountain associated with the Goddess of Mount Wu (q.v.), who appeared to former kings of Ch'u in erotic dreams. Wu means shaman, shamanka, a sorcerer or witch, male or female.

keys: the harem doorkeys were emblazoned with emblematic features, such as a crane (symbol of longevity) or a fish (symbol of fertility).

Kiangnan: the name of a region in modern Kiangsu and Anhwei south of the Yangtze given to a type of song, a love-song.

Kiangtung: the region south of the Yangtze.

kindling: traditionally different kinds of wood were used for making a fire, depending on the season. Willow was used in spring, jujube in summer, pagoda-tree in winter, and a species of oak in autumn, besides other kinds of trees for various seasons.

king of Ching: reference to King Ch'ing-hsiang of Ch'u. See Sung Yü, Goddess of Mount Wu.

king of Ch'in's daughter: see Nung Yü.

King Mu of Chou (trad. r. 1001–946 BC): built a terrace of layered ceremonial discs for his favourite concubine.

kingfisher: the actual bird does not figure *per se* in these poems, so much as its main attribute, glossy blue-green plumage. The plumes of a kingfisher were prized for ornaments in women's tiaras. Gathering the plumes is a conventional activity of love poetry, associated with the Goddess of Lo river as portrayed by Ts'ao Chih. The word 'kingfisher' came to be used as an epithet for a woman's eyebrows, either their natural green-black sheen, or the blue-black-green colour of kohl.

K'ot'ing: a place in Kweichi, Chekiang.

Kuangchai: the name of a Buddhist temple used by Hsiao Yen, Emperor Wu of the Liang.

K'unlun: see Mount K'unlun.

K'unming lake: south-west of Ch'angan, made by the Han Emperor Wu for naval exercises.

ladies of Ch'i: allusion to *The Book of Songs*, no. 39, 'How lovely are the ladies of Ch'i!'

Lady Fan: concubine of the king of Ch'u, she became a model of virtue when she refused to eat meat by way of protesting against the king's excessive love of the hunt.

Lady Hsü, or Lady Hsü Shu: wife of the poet, Ch'in Chia, she was a poet in her own right. Translations of their romantic correspondence in poems appear in Chapter One.

Lady Ju: favourite concubine of the prince of Wei state (north of the Yellow river), in the Warring States era. Not to be confused with Jutzu.

Lady Li (second century BC): sister of the court musician, Li Yen-nien, she became the favourite concubine of the Han Emperor Wu. Li Yen-nien composed a song praising her beauty, which is translated in Chapter One. Lady Li died prematurely and the emperor became distraught with grief. One night a magician from Ch'i attempted to bring her spirit back, and the emperor thought he glimpsed Lady Li's shadow. He is said to have composed this poem: 'Is it she, is it not? / I stand and stare. / Swish, swish of her silk skirt – / How slow she comes!'

Lady Liang (second century AD): named Sun Shou, the wife of Liang Chi, whose sister became consort to Emperor Shun of the Han. Lady Liang started a fashion in women's coiffure called 'twisting fall' or 'fallen colt', which other women tried to copy.

Lady Lu (second century AD): an imperial concubine, she entered the Han harem at the age of seven, and was transferred to the Wei harem when Ts'ao Ts'ao supplanted the Han. Later she married a man called Yin Keng-sheng.

Lady Lu: either a palace lady in the Wei Dynasty (Lady Lu above), or Lu Mo-ch'ou (Nevergrieve), a girl from Loyang who married into the Lu family at the age of fifteen. See Nevergrieve.

Lady Ming: see Wang Chao-chün.

Lady of Ch'u, or lady of Ch'u: either a possible reference to Lady Fan (?), or a general reference to a Ch'u palace lady.

Lady of Han: ? Lady Li (q.v.).

Lady of Letters: see Ts'ai Yen.

Lady Pan (first century BC): her first name is not known, but she goes by the name of her rank, *chieh-yü*, meaning Beautiful Companion, the highest among palace ladies. She was the favourite concubine of the Han Emperor Ch'eng. An anecdote illustrating her virtue is told in her official biography: once she had the honour of being invited to ride with the emperor in his carriage, but she refused saying she was not exalted enough for such an honour. Later she was displaced in the emperor's affections by Chao Feiyen (q.v.), and retired to serve the dowager empress at Eternal Trust Palace. Her biography contains a long autobiographical poem attributed to her telling of her sorrows, and a poem attributed to her, called *A poem on regret*, appears in Chapter One. It also goes by the popular title of the *Round fan poem*.

Lady Wen: wife of the statesman Wen Ch'iao (AD 288–329). He gave her a mirror-stand as a wedding gift.

Lady Ying: Nung Yü (q.v.). Ying was the family name of the rulers of ancient Ch'in.

Lant'ien: Indigo Field (q.v.).

latest catch: see Lord Lungyang.

'lead her chicks': reference to *Lunghsi, a folk-song*, in Chapter One, line 6.

Leaning Mulberry: the fabled tree where the sun rested after being rinsed in Hsien Pool following its journey through the sky. Most early texts place this tree in the east, providing a mythical explanation for the rising of the sun. Some versions of the sun myth relate that there were ten suns, and a black bird in its disc. 'Mulberry-Elm time' means the sunset years of life, or the twilight time of day.

'leftover peach': a reference to the anecdote about Mi Tzu-hsia (q.v.), favourite of the king of Wei. One day the two men were strolling in the orchard when Mi Tzu-hsia found a peach, and after eating some of it, found it was delicious. He offered it to his lord to enjoy, and the king was pleased with him, saying that he had denied himself the pleasure of finishing the peach so as to give pleasure to his lord. Later, when Mi Tzu-hsia's beauty faded, the king remembered this incident, but in an unfavourable light. Mi Tzu-hsia was executed.

lettuce: windblown leaves of the lettuce or the double heart of the lettuce were erotic emblems.

Li's city: a reference to Li Yen-nien. See *Background to Poets and Poems*.

Liang: in the Warring States era this was the name of a city in Honan, known as Taliang. In the Wei Dynasty it became the capital city, near the present site of K'aifeng, in Honan.

Liaohsi: in the old kingdom of Chao, the northern region of Shensi.

Liaotung: a remote province in the far north-east of China which was administered by the Wei Dynasty. It used to be part of the ancient state of Yen. In modern times it is part of Liaoning.

Lich'iu: a solid perfume, concocted from white honey and scents, which was pressed into a robe for lasting fragrance. The location of Lich'iu is not clear.

light: a metaphor for the radiant love a man bestows on a woman, be it natural light like sunlight, or artificial light from candles or lamps.

Lin Hsiang-ju (third century BC): prime minister of Chao state under King Hui Wen. He was noted for his bravery. The king of Chao possessed the famous Pien Ho jade and the king of Ch'in coveted it. He tried to win it by a ruse, but Lin Hsiang-ju foiled his plan.

Linch'iung: south of modern Ch'engtu, a town in the old kingdom of Shu, modern Szechwan. It was the birthplace of Cho Wen-chün, who was courted by the poet, Ssu-ma Hsiang-ju (q.v.).

Liu Piyü: Liu Green Jade (see Green Jade).

Liu Yün: see *Background to Poets and Poems*.

Lo river: associated with the legend of the Goddess of Lo river, and Loyang the eastern capital of the Han which was built on its banks.

Lofu: Ch'in Lofu (q.v.).

Lone stork: the name of a plaintive song.

Long River: one of the names of the celestial Han river (q.v.).

Long Wall, or Great Wall of China: constructed in the Chou Dynasty. Several hundreds of miles of walls were built as defences against northern tribesmen. Their construction, maintenance and surveillance were carried out by corvée labour. In the Ch'in Dynasty these sectional walls were joined to form one long barrier.

Longwillow (Ch'angliu): the name of a pleasure spot in Ch'angan.

Lord Anling: the favourite of King Kung of Ch'u (r. 492–462 BC). Once when the king was out hunting, he asked Anling who his lover would be when the king died. Anling replied: 'I will die with my lord!' The king gave him a generous fiefdom.

Lord Chang: see Chang Fang.

Lord Lungyang (third century BC): the catamite of the king of Wei, perhaps King Anhsi. One day Lord Lungyang went fishing with the king and when more than ten fish had been caught he started to weep. The king asked him the reason. Lord Lungyang replied, 'When I see you prize the latest catch to such an extent that you throw your first catch back into the water, I realize I am just like the first catch. That's why I'm sad.' From that time on the king penalized anyone daring to mention favourites.

Lord P'ingyüan (d. 250 BC): a nobleman, prime minister of Chao, and also known as the Prince of Chao, he was famous for his generous treatment of retainers, numbering 3,000 men in all. His retainers were so well dressed that even their shoes were embroidered with pearls. He was also famous for his humble recognition of the ability of men inferior in rank to himself.

Lord Sui: owned a fabulous pearl given to him by a wounded snake he had cured. Lord Sui pearl (or jade) is said hyperbolically to be used as a catapult pellet.

Lord Yang of Lu's lance: when the sun started to set while Lord Yang was still battling with Wei state, he hurled his lance at the sun to hold it back.

lotus: an erotic emblem. Its brilliant red colour is the colour of passion, its name, *lien*, is a pun for sexual love, and its other name, *ho*, means sexual union. Lotus leaves are also an erotic emblem, denoting passion. The roots, *ou*, are a pun for mates.

Lotusleaves, or lotus leaves: either a place name in the south, or a general term. The phrase often suggests an echo of the old folk-song about fish sporting around lotus, an erotic image of lovers' pleasure.

'love in a carriage': see Wei Tzu-fu s.v. wardrobe mistress.

loving you (*hsiangssu*): the name of a tree associated with the legend of a wife who pined to death for her husband while he was away from home in Wei state fighting against the Ch'in in the Warring States era. It is identified as the *Abrus precatorius*. According to legend this tree grew on the wife's grave, its branches stretching forward towards the place where her husband had gone to war. These outstretched branches figure as an erotic motif on women's clothes, boudoir objects and utensils such as a winecup.

Loving you: the name of an old love-song.

Loyang: the ancient capital of the Eastern Chou, then of the Later Han and a major city or capital of the Wei and Western Chin dynasties. It was built on the banks of the Lo river, which had legendary associations.

Lu: the name of a state in antiquity, modern Hupei.

Lu river: see *Green river*.

Luchiang: the home of the Chiao family whose story is told in the anonymous narrative poem translated in Chapter One, *An old poem written for Chiao Chung-ch'ing's wife*. Its site is in the region of modern Anhwei.

Lulu: the name of a dagger. Its hilt was shaped like the pulley of a well. The word for the ring of the pulley was a pun for return, or reunion (*huan*). One of the romantic scenarios of the love ballad was a well, usually under moonlight, and embellished by a silver well-curb, silver bucket and silk rope.

Lung: the name of a mountain range west of the region of modern Kansu. The Lung hills were guarded by Chinese border patrols, and had beacons for military alarms.

Lungyang: see Lord Lungyang.

lute medley: reference to a composition by Liyü, the wife of a Korean who told her the story of how a crazy old man tried to cross the river with a jug of wine, but sank and drowned, and then his wife, who had tried to stop him, sang a song accompanying herself on the lute, and afterwards committed suicide by drowning. Liyü preserved the dead woman's song in her *Lute medley*. Ts'ao Chih (see *Background to Poets and Poems*) composed a folk-song with the same title, but different content.

magpie: allusion to the legend about two lovers who kept half a mirror each as a love-token when they had to part. Later the woman fell in love with another man. Her half of the mirror turned into a magpie and flew off to her former lover and told him what had happened.

Magpie Lodge: a tower for viewing the panorama around Sweet Springs Palace (q.v.), the summer resort of Han emperors in the north-west.

mallow: usually an allusion to poem 1 of *The Book of Songs*, in which culling water mallow is a metaphor for finding a good wife: 'In patches we grow water mallows, / To left and right we must seek them.'

Man of Pa: the name of a piece of music, classified as coming from the state of Cheng. The poet Sung Yü told King Wei of Ch'u that in the capital city a thousand people were singing lyrics to such music, whereas only a few tens of people were singing lyrics for classical tunes such as *Sunny spring*.

man of Western Shu: Liu Yen, who taught a large number of slave girls to recite the poem, *Prose Poem on Lu Ling-kuang Palace*, composed by Wang Yen-shou of the Later Han. Emperor Yüan was so fond of one poem when he was crown prince, he made his harem ladies recite it; it was a poem by Wang Pao (fl. 58 BC), probably his eulogy on Sweet Springs Palace.

man of Yüeh: a reference to the *Song of the Yüeh boatman*, see Chapter Nine.

mandarin ducks (*yüanyang*): *Aix galericulata*, frequently mentioned in love poetry and serving as a symbol of conjugal fidelity because the birds stay together until they die, or pine to death if separated. Their brilliant plumage is often used to describe something glossy. These birds feature on such items as a marriage-bed quilt or drapes. Mandarin Duck Palace was the name of a royal building in the Han, perhaps part of the harem complex.

Mao Ch'iang (fifth century BC): a woman of legendary beauty, she was the favourite concubine of the Prince of Yüeh. The philosopher Chuang Tzu wrote that all creatures fled from her beauty – satirizing conventional concepts of beauty and ugliness.

Master Shu, Pan of Lu state: a craftsman in antiquity who devised a 'skyscraping ladder' to attack a city in Sung state.

mat: the usual name for a bed. The word also signifies a seat, or a floor for performance of dance and song.

Mayi: a place in the far north, modern Shansi, which was subject to invasion from northern tribes.

meet a minister: a phrase which occurs in a collection of stories about virtuous women, *A Gallery of Good Women* (*Lieh nü chuan*), implying that honest work in the mulberry fields is not so good as the lure of marrying a minister.

melon: in poem 57 of *The Book of Songs* a lovely girl is said to have teeth like melon seeds. 'Two melons' is a flattering term for the two rows of teeth. 'Broken-melon age' means sixteen, melon being an anagram in Chinese for that number. The numerous seeds of the melon denote fertility.

men of learning: a reference to the gathering of scholars and poets around their patron, Ts'ao P'ei, who ruled as Emperor Wen of Wei in the third century AD.

Meng Chu: probably the name of a female singer of around the fifth century AD, who is said to have come from Tanyang, part of Yangchou in the region of modern Anhwei.

Meng ford: north-east of Loyang city.

Meng Isle: probably near Yünmeng, a place in the Tungt'ing lake area.

metal, metallic: according to the Five Elements Theory (q.v.), autumn is associated with the element of metal because it is a season of harsh weather.

Mi Tzu-hsia: a favourite of the king of Wei in the Warring States era. The king promulgated a law that no one should use his royal carriage under any pretext. Mi Tzu-hsia, however, relying on the king's favour, appropriated the carriage when his mother fell ill. The king admired his courage. Later, when Mi Tzu-hsia lost the king's favour, this incident was recalled in an unfavourable light and Mi Tzu-hsia was executed. See leftover peach.

Mien Chü and Wang Pao: cultured men of antiquity famous for bringing their skills to different parts of China. Mien Chü settled in Kaot'ang and gave the people of Ch'i the art of song. Wang Pao settled by the Ch'i river and gave the people there his technique in song.

Millet thick: an allusion to poem 65 of *The Book of Songs*, in which the heavy ears of ripe millet contrast with the feelings of someone suffering from love.

Ming-chün: see Wang Chao-chün.

mirror: the early Chinese mirror was a bronze circular object, flat and shiny on one side, and elaborately decorated on the other. Fixed on a stand, usually made of jade and elaborately decorated with motifs such as twin dragons and phoenixes, it was an *objet d'art*. Its shiny surface had to be kept polished to prevent it from becoming tarnished or dirty. It is a frequent metaphor for the full moon, while a broken mirror stands for a waning moon. The mirror could also be hung at a window for the application of morning make-up. A dusty mirror is a typical metaphor for a woman neglected by her lover. See also magpie, paradise bird.

moon: a protean image in Chinese literature. It can denote (1) a mirror, (2) a round fan, (3) the legend of Ch'ang O, (4) a woman's eyebrow, (5) a boudoir curtain hook or hook brooch, or (6) reunion, based on a pun for circle (return). The single source of light at night, the moon acts as a focal point of communication between parted lovers. See autumn moon.

moth eyebrows: thick, dark eyebrows were a mark of feminine beauty. To accentuate this feature, kohl was applied in a broad line over and beyond the natural line of the eyebrow. In some cases the eyebrows were described as 'cocoon-emerging', meaning the moth that emerges from the cocoon, or, more precisely, the wings of the moth.

Mount Chungnan (South Mountain): occurs early on in *The Book of Songs*, poem 172, where the blessings of long life and happiness are invoked. It became a symbol of longevity. It stood south of Ch'angan.

Mount Heng: a mountain south of Ch'angsha in Ch'u, modern Hunan. One of the five holy mountains of China.

Mount Hua: has two connotations: (1) the name of the holy mountain in Shensi, (2) a mountain in Luchiang, Anhwei.

Mount K'un (K'unlun?): in the far west of China; see Mount K'unlun.

Mount K'unlun: believed to be the land of the immortals in the far west of China, upon whom the sun was said never to set. See also Queen Mother of the West.

Mount Sung: the highest of the five holy mountains, in Honan.

Mount T'ai: one of the five holy mountains, in Shantung. Mount Liangfu is a small mountain nearby.

Mount T'ang: said to contain vast stores of cinnabar (q.v.), the precious mineral used for concocting the elixir of immortality. Believed to be where the immortals lived.

Mount Wu: the home of the Goddess of Shamanka Mountain, traditionally believed to be above the Yangtze in Szechwan. See Goddess of Mount Wu.

moving a mountain: allusion to the story in the *Lieh Tzu*, a collection of Taoist writings dating around AD 300 based on earlier materials. Master Simple decided when he was almost ninety to remove two mountains which were blocking the road. He and his family started moving the mountains one by one, stone by stone, clod by clod. He reckoned it would be done in time after several generations. The gods intervened in this huge endeavour and had the mountains shifted for him.

Mr Pan's poem: although this title appears to indicate that the Han historian Pan Ku (AD 32–92) was its author, a poem attributed to him, *Poem on History*, bears no resemblance to the content of the poem entitled *Mr Pan's poem*. The latter has as its subject a dutiful wife, whose husband, Ch'iu Hu, is unfaithful.

Mr Sung: see Sung Yü.

mulberry: one of the traditional symbols of a woman's life was the mulberry grove where she picked leaves to feed silkworms, and women were often called 'mulberry girls'. In *The Book of Songs* the lanes where mulberry grew were a rendezvous for lovers.

Mulberry up the lane: an anonymous ballad which had an important influence on the development of love poetry. It was imitated by poets frequently, and there are many versions in this anthology. The original appears in Chapter One under the title *Sunrise at the south-east corner*. It is a narrative poem about a girl called Ch'in Lofu who is courted by a prefect while she is picking mulberry. She rejects his advances, saying she already has a fine husband.

Mulberry-Elm time: a phrase meaning twilight, when the sun sinks, or the last years of life.

Nanp'i: in the area of modern Tientsin, Hopei, it is a place where Ts'ao P'ei used to go on excursion with his literary coterie.

Nanwei, or Nanchihwei: the name of a beautiful woman, the favourite concubine of Duke Wen of Chin during the Warring States era. The duke was very much in love with her, but kept her at a distance for fear that her beauty would cause him to neglect affairs of state.

Nanyang: a region south of the Yellow river in modern Honan which produced a fine cosmetic powder.

narrow lane: a euphemism for the brothel district of a city.

needle: often associated with the celebration of Seventh Night (q.v.), when the legendary Weaver star met her lover, Herdboy (q.v.). Girls would compete on this night with embroidery patterns, using double needles and seven-colour thread. Double needles and threading needles, besides silk thread, were all erotic emblems.

needle and drugs: acupuncture and elixirs.

Nevergrieve (Mo-ch'ou): seems to refer to two separate people. One is mentioned in the poem, *The water midstream*, translated in Chapter Nine as no. 2 of *Two song lyrics*, either anonymous or attributed to Hsiao Yen. She comes from Loyang and is unhappily married to a rich man called Lu. She is sometimes called Lady Lu. She had wanted to marry the boy next door called Wang Chang. The other is the name of a female singer from Stone City, whose name appears in the title of a song in Chapter Ten.

Ngo: in Ch'u state, the region of Wuch'ang in modern Hupei. See *Song of the Yüeh boatman*, Chapter Nine.

night of the fifteenth: usually refers to the eighth lunar month when the autumn moon is full. See autumn moon.

Nine autumns: the name of a tune.

nine-blooms: the legendary Queen Mother of the West (q.v.) is said to have lit a nine-branched lamp when she met the Han Emperor Wu. The many lights of a candelabra or the nine-flowers of a woman's jewelled tiara probably derive from this mythical source.

Nine chord: the name of the music of the legendary Yellow Emperor (q.v.).

'nine death' sorrow: an allusion to poem 1 of *The Nine Laments* of *The Songs of Ch'u*, which describes the exile of the Ch'u courtier, Ch'ü Yüan: 'My bowels in a single night turned nine times over', as he longed to return to his capital city Ying. He was believed to have committed suicide by drowning in the Milo river.

nine heavens: the number nine is associated with paradise in some contexts. Sometimes it merely denotes a vast distance.

nine-barred: a palace gate or door closed with heavy bars.

nine-flower: used as an epithet to suggest something decoratively splendid, similar to nine-blooms.

Nineflower Hall: the name of the palace built in Loyang during the Wei Dynasty, and associated with the founder of the Wei, Ts'ao Ts'ao, who used to hold magnificent banquets.

Ninth Blaze: the name of the fabled torch lit by the legendary Queen Mother of the West (q.v.) when she met the Han Emperor Wu.

north: traditionally related to the female principle known as *Yin*, the cosmic force operating with *Yang*, the male principle. (See *Yin/Yang*.) The women's apartments were situated in the north part of the family complex of buildings. The north also has connotations of hostility in reference to the invading nomads such as the Hsiungnu.

Northern Dipper: eighth of the twenty-eight traditional Chinese constellations. See Jade Scales.

'not a mat': a phrase from poem 26 of *The Book of Songs*, in which a girl declares: 'My heart is not a stone, / You cannot roll it away. / My heart is not a mat, / You cannot roll it up.' The term comes to mean constancy, or to stand for the heart.

'not a stone': see 'not a mat'.

Nü-ying, Maiden Bloom: one of the two daughters of the legendary Emperor Yao of high antiquity whom he gave in marriage to Emperor Shun, his successor. When Shun died, his two wives drowned themselves in the Hsiang river. Sometimes they are identified as the nymphs of the Hsiang. The tears they shed when Shun died fell on a bamboo and speckled the leaves, and this species of bamboo was named after them.

Nung Yü (seventh century BC): daughter of Duke Mu of Ch'in. She was taught by Hsiao Shih, the master flautist, to copy the phoenix cry. She married him and the duke built a phoenix terrace for them. One day when Nung Yü and Hsiao Shih were playing the flute, the phoenixes that used to perch in their home flew away with them, and they disappeared.

O-huang, Fairy Radiance: one of the two daughters of the legendary Emperor Yao; see Nü-ying.

oatcakes: food conventionally served by a girl to her client in a brothel.

Odes and *Hymns*: see *Book of Songs, The*.

office swagger: a phrase echoing the last quatrain of *Sunrise at the south-east corner* (Chapter One), used to describe in flattering terms the husband of the folk heroine Ch'in Lofu.

Old Man of Heaven: his name features in one of the earliest recorded handbooks on sex listed in the Han Dynasty, *The Erotica of the Old Man of Heaven and Other Experts*.

oleaster: see dogwood.

orchid: a sweetly scented, gorgeous flower, noted in love poems for its vulnerability in autumn frost. It is a metaphor for a lovely girl. The name of the tragic heroine of the anonymous narrative poem, *An old poem written for Chiao Chung-ch'ing's wife*, is Lanchih, *lan* being the word for orchid. The word is also used as a general epithet like jade to mean lovely and fragrant.

Orion (*Shen*): a constellation associated in mythology with Antares (q.v.).

Pa: the name of an ancient state in the region of modern Szechwan.

palindrome brocade: Su Hui (*c.* AD 350) was the wife of Tou T'ao, an official. She was jealous of her husband's favourite concubine and refused to go with him on a new assignment to a remote region. Later she sent him a palindrome brocade she wove herself which formed an apologetic poem. Her husband forgave her.

palm-dancing girl: see Chao Feiyen.

P'an Yüeh: see biography of this poet under *Background to Poets and Poems*.

Paossu (eighth century BC): the favourite concubine of the king of Yu in the Chou Dynasty. She displaced the queen. The king was so entranced by her that he would do anything she asked. Being of a sulky nature, she refused to smile unless something extraordinary happened. The king was anxious to amuse her, so he permitted the beacons to be lit. This did effect a smile. Later when they were lit in earnest during an invasion, people just thought it was Paossu's tricks, so they ignored it. The king's realm was eventually ruined.

paradise (Fant'ien): one of the names of a Buddhist paradise, based on the name of Brahmadeva, a Buddhist deity.

paradise bird: one legend tells of a king of ancient Kashmir who found such a bird. It refused to sing, so his wife told him to do something to stop it pining for its mate. They set a mirror up in front of the bird, hoping it would sing to its reflection. The bird did sing, but its song was so sad that it died of a broken heart. It was believed that a pair of these divine birds (*luan*) danced and sang in happy times. Sometimes this bird also represents the female of the male and female phoenix, or lovebird.

Parted paradise bird: the name of a tune for the lute.

Parted stork: the name of a tune for the lute.

'pat my back': see wardrobe mistress.

Peachleaf (T'ao-yeh): the name of a concubine of Wang Hsien-chih, a painter and poet of the fourth century AD. Their poems appear in Chapter Ten.

Peak Cap: the name of a district in Ch'angan city.

pearl: see Cheng Chiao-fu, bright moon, Lord Sui.

pearl shot: see Lord Sui.

pebbles: possibly an image denoting constancy and integrity.

P'en city: in the region of Kiukiang in north Kiangsi.

peony blooms: Hsin Hsiao, the wife of Fu T'ung of the Chin Dynasty, wrote a poem called *Paean to the peony*. The flower was given as a love-token.

pepper: the bedroom walls of a palace lady were impregnated with a species of pepper plant, making them fragrant and conveying the idea of fertility.

pheasant: in pairs denote conjugal harmony.

phoenix: a mythological bird denoting love, especially when a pair is mentioned, the *feng-huang*. It responds to the sound of a flute when played exquisitely, and often features in the legend of Nung Yü (q.v.), or the poems entitled *We met in a narrow alley*. The phoenix was particularly attracted to the catalpa tree. The word is sometimes used to refer to the bedchamber of an imperial concubine or empress, and has as its male counterpart the dragon.

Phoenix and chicks: the name of a tune, symbolizing a happy family.

phoenix court: the imperial court.

phoenix fluting: see Nung Yü, or the poems in the series *We met in a narrow alley*, or phoenix.

phoenix-mate: see Nung Yü.

phoenixboys: either an insect, such as the huge brilliantly coloured butterfly, or a young bat.

Picking beans, or *I pick beans*: an allusion to poem 226 of *The Book of Songs*, which tells of a woman unable to do her work of picking beans and indigo because she is pining for her lover.

Picking caltrop: a popular song title, see caltrop.

Picking lotus: the title of a love-song, see lotus.

pictures: erotic illustrations of sex manuals.

Pien Ho jade: Pien Ho (eighth century BC) was from Ch'u. He found a piece of jade of very fine quality and wished to present it to the king, according to custom. His jade was judged to be inferior, so he suffered the penalty of having his left foot cut off. When another king came to the throne, Pien Ho submitted his jade again, but was once more punished by having his right foot amputated. Later, when another king came to the throne and Pien Ho offered the jade again, he wept tears of blood because his jade had been misjudged. This time his jade was found to be indeed of the finest quality and was accepted by the throne.

pillow: a hard object made of horn, tortoiseshell or some other expensive material, with a concave niche for the neck. For a double bed two pillows were put together, making a felicitous six-angled arrangement. 'Pillow and mat' was a phrase meaning a bed in general. 'To dust pillow and mat' was a phrase used of a woman or catamite to mean service to their lord.

P'ingch'eng: in the reign of the Han Emperor Kaotsu (202–195 BC), the Hsiungnu tribe north of China besieged P'ingch'eng near the border. The emperor was advised to offer the portrait of a beautiful Chinese girl from the palace to the wife of the Hsiungnu chieftain. This he did. When she saw the painting, she reasoned to herself that if the siege were not lifted, lovely girls such as the one in the painting would become the booty of her husband, and she would be sure to lose his favour. So she urged her husband to lift the siege. This traditional account is probably apocryphal.

Po Hill censer: hill-shaped censers date from as early as the Chou Dynasty. The typical Po Hill censer was of bronze, conical in shape to represent a holy mountain, studded with jewels, and decorated with fabulous fauna. Po Hill was a mountain in the region of Shantung. For the *double entendre* of Po Hill, see 'sinking-in-water'.

pole-star: it was customary for people to make an oath on the pole-star because it was fixed in the firmament, symbolizing fidelity to one's vow.

pomegranate: red and full of seeds, this was a symbol of love and fertility. The word is also used to describe the colour of red clothes. Pomegranate wine is occasionally mentioned.

pounder: an instrument used for beating silk fibres and softening them. One word for pounder was an elaborate pun for a lover, or mate, and silk fibre was a pun for love.

pounding block: an object used with a pounder for fulling cloth.

prefect: see *Mulberry up the lane*.

Prince of Ch'en, Ts'ao Chih: see Goddess of Lo river.

Prince of Ch'in's daughter: Nung Yü (q.v.).

Prince of Huainan, Liu An (d. 123 BC): a prince of the Han royal family. He dabbled in elixirs to attain eternal youth.

Princess of Ten Thousand Years: title of the Chin emperor's daughter. When she died, the emperor requested his concubine, Tso Fen, who was an accomplished literary woman, to compose a lamentation for her.

Princess's brother: see Wei Tzu-fu who first served in the household of the Princess of P'ingyang, sister of the Han Emperor Wu, and later became his consort.

Princess's mansion: see wardrobe mistress.

purple: the imperial colour, and used as an adjective to mean imperial.

Queen (Mother) of the West: mythological ruler of the land of immortals in the western region of the K'unlun mountains. She grew peaches which conferred immortality, but the trees bore fruit only once every 3,000 years. Originally, she was depicted as a wild creature with dishevelled hair, tiger's teeth and the tail of a leopard. Later she was made more civilized, and the only remaining suggestion of wildness was her long, unbound hair and serpentine lower body. She figures in a legendary account of a banquet she gave in honour of King Mu of Chou (trad. r. 1001–946 BC), at which she sang for him. She also gave a banquet in honour of the Han Emperor Wu, at which she gave him five peaches of immortality. Her guardians were the tiger and dragon.

quilt: a padded bed cover, sometimes made into a double, fitted garment. The padding was of silk floss, a pun for everlasting love. The cover was usually decorated with erotic motifs, such as mandarin ducks or lotus.

quince: in poem 64 of *The Book of Songs* the poet says a woman he desired threw him a token of a quince, then of a peach, and then a plum, and he requited her with different kinds of precious stones.

Racedog Terrace: part of a Han Dynasty palace.

rafter dust: an image of good fortune deriving from a legend about a woman called Han O who sang so marvellously that the echo circled the ridge-pole for three days, making the dust on the rafters leap. Sometimes the poems refer to a male listener in this context; he says he must leave his seat before the rafter dust leaps, meaning that he cannot bear to experience such sublime music.

rafters: usually described as being of some rich wood like apricot and carved with erotic motifs, such as a lotus, and gilded. Also see rafter dust.

rain: often suggests the legend of the Goddess of Mount Wu (q.v.).

rear: the location of the women's quarters in a family house.

red: the colour of passion. A bride wore red at her wedding. See hibiscus, lotus, pomegranate.

red rouge: metonym for female copy editors in Hsü Ling's *Preface*.

Reincarnation scent: a Buddhist term used in a secular way as a name for a perfume that was fashionable in the Southern Dynasties.

ripped sleeve: see Tung Hsien.

River: sometimes this refers to the celestial Han river, or the Yellow river.

River of Heaven: see Han, celestial river.

river sprites: see Han river sprites.

robe-changing: see wardrobe mistress.

rock-lotus: two puns are involved here: rock was often used to suggest constancy, and lotus was an emblem for passion.

rock-the-boat: a reference to the anecdote about the Lady of Ts'ai who went boating with Duke Huan of Ch'i (d. 643 BC). She started to rock the boat and refused to stop, even when the duke clearly was not amused. He finally grew so enraged, he sent her back to Ts'ai state, in modern Honan.

roots of the lotus, *ou*: their interlocking growth suggests the intimate bonds of love and entwined lovers.

rose of Sharon: a flower that blooms at dawn and is dead by dusk.

Round fan poem: ascribed to Lady Pan (q.v.), translated as *A poem on regret* in Chapter One, also referred to as the *Torn silk poem*. (See fan.)

Royal Forest: see Shanglin park.

same heart: a recurring phrase meaning lovers of one mind and heart, that is they are so close that they do not see things differently. Difference, it is suggested, leads to quarrels, and then to estrangement. This idea is conveyed by such motifs as 'same heart' lettuce, flowers and so forth. Often translated as sweetheart.

Saso Palace: pleasure resort of Han emperors.

Scales star: see Jade Scales.

Scarlet Crane, Bronze Clam: see keys.

Secret orchid: the name of a tune. A lovely girl is often called an orchid, and she is generally described as living in seclusion, or in a secret room.

Secretary Han: Han Shou of the Chin Dynasty responded to the amorous attentions of Chia Wu, daughter of his employer, the general and president of the imperial secretariat, Chia Ch'ung, by meeting her illicitly one night. As a love-token he gave her some rare palace perfume, said to last for three months without fading, which he had stolen. Eventually, Han Shou married Chia Wu. For Chia Ch'ung's love-poems to his wife, Lady Li, see Chapter Ten.

seven removes: a phrase occurring in poem 203 of *The Book of Songs* (q.v.) which describes Weaver star. It is taken by some commentators to mean that Weaver's movement through the firmament is like a shuttle passing the weft through the warp of other stars, and that she makes such a move once a month, or seven times a year. The number is clearly linked to Seventh Night, when Weaver is permitted to see Herdboy. Sometimes this phrase is taken to mean that Weaver rolls up her sleeves to weave seven times. See also Herdboy, Seventh Night, Weaver.

Seven spirals: the name of a dance.

Seventh Night, or the Seventh: the night of the seventh month when Weaver star was allowed to meet her lover, Herdboy. Also see Weaver. Women celebrated this night by embroidery competitions in honour of Weaver, using double needles threaded with seven-colour silk thread.

shadow and echo: a double metaphor for intimate love and friendship, or estrangement. Shadow may be bound to form, or separated; echo may be bound to sound, or separated. Usually woman is represented as shadow and echo, man as form and sound.

Shanghuang: place in Chingchou, Ch'u.

Shanglan: a Han Dynasty palace in the Royal Forest.

Shanglin park: the Royal Forest in Ch'angan where Han emperors used to hunt. The park had an imperial zoo. Several handsome lodges were built in the park.

Shansi general: there is a proverb that goes: 'Shansi produces generals, Shantung produces ministers.'

Shanyin: a place in the region of modern Chekiang.

Shanyü: the title of the chieftain of the Hsiungnu tribes.

Shen: see Empress Shen.

Shih Chi-lun: see Shih Ch'ung.

Shih Ch'ung (d. AD 300), courtesy name Chi-lun: a statesman and poet of enormous wealth. He had a pleasure park called Golden Vale near Loyang where he held lavish parties. His favourite singer used to perform there, delighting his guests with her dance and music. See Shih Ch'ung's biography in *Background to Poets and Poems*; also Green Pearl and Golden Vale. His famous poem on Wang Chao-chün appears in Chapter Two.

Shih-Yu gale: reference to the anecdote about a certain Mr Yu who married a Miss Shih. When he had to leave home on business she pined so much that she died. As she was dying she vowed she would become a contrary gale and stop boats from sailing away from wives at home.

shrike: there was a saying that the shrike calls in spring and then flowers will grow; it calls in autumn and then flowers will die.

Shrub Terrace: see Bushy Terrace.

Shu: an ancient kingdom in south-west China, part of modern Szechwan. It has many associations. Ssu-ma Hsiang-ju, the Han poet and wooer of Cho Wen-chün, came from its capital, Ch'engtu. The astrologer who divined the sky voyage of Chang Ch'ien also came from this city. Tu Yü, Emperor Wang, ruled the kingdom and turned into a cuckoo (or nightjar) when he died.

Shuiheng: the name of an office that was in charge of the Royal Forest Park during the Han Dynasty.

silk: sericulture was originally the task of women. It has acquired many erotic associations. Women used to pick mulberry leaves for hungry silkworms, a sexual metaphor. The silk thread of the cocoon was a pun for pining love. After spinning, women would weave cloth, often said in these poems to be clothes for their lover who was away fighting, and so forth. If a man loved a woman, he would show this in a visible way by wearing the clothes she prepared for him. Many of the poems contain several stages in the process of sericulture and tailoring: silkworm care, weaving, fulling, cutting material, sewing, embroidering, wrapping and perfuming the garment.

silkworm: in spring, the season of love, the silkworms grow quickly and feed hungrily on mulberry leaves. Girls tending them are called 'silkworm girls'. Also see cocoon, mulberry, silk.

single glance beauty: a reference to Lady Li, a phrase taken from the song her brother sang to Emperor Wu describing her beauty. See Lady Li, and 'A Song poem' in Chapter One.

sinking incense: a reference to a type of incense candle, often decorated with jewels such as pearl bands, used for perfume and for marking the time. When the candle burned down, the jewels would slip, appearing to sink.

'sinking-in-water': the name of a fragrance from aloes wood; this is a heavy wood which sinks in water, thus giving rise to the double meaning, in an erotic context, of a man's desire to lie with a woman, to which her response is 'Po-Hill', or, her desire to go to bed too.

Sip Dew Terrace: probably another name for Cold Dew Terrace.

sky and earth separate: the myth of the creation of the world, when the fused matter of ether and earth separated to form the sky and the earth, and then all living things.

Sky River: see Han, celestial river.

Sky Trails: in popular mythology this was a constellation which led to outer space.

Small Longbank: probably a region near Chienk'ang (modern Nanking), capital of the Liang Dynasty.

smoke: often associated with mountain mists and the Goddess of Mount Wu, it has erotic overtones.

Sobbing crow: a tune, perhaps the same as *A crow weeps*.

solar-ray: see speculum.

songhouse: the usual euphemism for a courtesan's residence. She was called a singing girl, a singer, or artiste. Originally a green-painted house indicated the residence of a nobleman, but later this fashion was adopted by courtesans. The phrase, songhouse, is also translated as the house of song.

Songs: Book of Songs, The (q.v.).

Songs of Ch'u: anthology of seventeen poems compiled in second century AD; its earliest pieces date from the fourth century BC, and contain mythic and literary material which greatly influenced writers of amatory verse.

Sop'an dance: either a transliteration of a Central Asian word, or a descriptive term meaning a gyrating type of dance.

south: when contrasted with the north (q.v.), it may denote a male image, compared with the feminine image of the north, or else the north in a hostile relationship with the south. Sometimes the south suggests an exotic region. When birds migrate south, the image conveyed is one of homecoming, or the pursuit of warmth. See also *Yin/Yang*.

South Mountain: see Mount Chungnan.

South of the River: the region south of the Yangtze river, especially associated with love-songs and amorous music.

South Park: an amusement park for city people in Chienyeh, or Chienk'ang, the Liang capital.

Sparrow Terrace: see (Bronze) Sparrow Terrace.

speculum: a highly polished bronze mirror used as a reflector to catch solar rays in order to generate fire.

Spread Scent Hall (P'ihsiang): a harem residence in the Han.

spring's three: the three months of spring.

Ssu-ma Hsiang-ju: the Han poet famous in the literature of love for his courtship of Cho Wen-chün and elopement with her. He courted her with two songs, featured in Chapter Nine. For his biography, see *Background to Poets and Poems*. He is believed to have written an entreaty on behalf of Empress Ch'en with the result that her estranged husband, Emperor Wu, felt affection for her again.

stars: in the ancient Chinese astronomical system, the sky was divided into four 'palaces', namely Green Dragon in the east, Vermilion Bird in the south, White

Tiger in the west and Black Tortoise in the north. The sky was further subdivided into twenty-eight 'mansions', or constellations, conceived of as resting-places for the sun, moon and planets. The planets moved in a sequence of 360 degrees. Of the constellations, the most popular in love literature were Herdboy, Weaver, Three Stars, Antares, Orion, Warp, Tzu-wei, Troubled Star, Northern Dipper and Jade Scales. It was also believed that the earth was patterned on the heavens, and that each locality had its counterpart in the sky. Thus Shu kingdom was the earthly equivalent of Wall star. Pole-star, being fixed, was often used as an emblem of constancy for swearing oaths.

'step-quiverer': see tiara.

steps: usually described as being of jade, connected with a palace or palatial ambience, and leading to a woman's bedroom. They are often featured with a film of heavy dew or coated with frost, showing clearly the absence or presence of footprints. They are an erotic image, connected with the erotic appeal of the foot. A poem by Hsieh T'iao (Chapter Ten) made this image famous, and set the style for many later imitations. Usually a woman is pictured waiting near the steps for her lover on an autumn night.

Stone City (Shihch'eng): a place in Hupei, which gives its name to a type of popular music. A girl called Nevergrieve (q.v.) is said to have come from here.

storax (suho): a perfume, originally imported from Rome and Parthia, it was scented resin, a dark purple in colour.

stork: a symbol of longevity, often also called a crane, and linked in this context with the tortoise. The cry of a stork was thought to be particularly plaintive, and usually considered to be of a bird parted from its flock or mate. This meaning derives from poem 156 of The Book of Songs: 'A stork cries on the ant-hill, / A wife sighs in her bedroom.'

straight as a bowstring: a simile from a ditty circulating in the reign of the Han Emperor Shun (r. AD 126–144): 'Straight as a bowstring, / You'll die by the wayside. / Crooked as a hook, / You'll be dubbed a duke!'

strange star: reference to the legend of a Han voyager who sailed up to the river of stars, Han river, and met the star Herdboy, who told him to contact the astrologer, Yen Chün-p'ing of Ch'engtu, when he got back to earth. He did so, and was told that the astrologer had observed a strange star in the sky at the time of the voyager's travel in space.

stuff, material: lit. a bolt of cloth, p'i, a pun for a mate.

Su Hsiao-hsiao: a singer of the fifth century AD who made a pact to be true to the grave. She died young and her spirit was said to hover around her grave waiting for her lover to join her. See this entry in Background to Poets and Poems.

Su Wu (first and second centuries BC): a Chinese envoy captured by the Hsiungnu in the reign of the Han Emperor Wu. After many trials and tribulations during nineteen years of captivity, he was released and returned to China. It was believed that while in captivity he wrote his wife at home a letter of sorrowful pining, and a poem on the same theme; the latter is featured in Chapter One. He is also believed to have sent his love poem by a goose's foot.

sulky pertness: see Hsi Shih.

Sumen: in the ancient state of Yen, north-east China.

Sun Terrace (Yangt'ai): where the Goddess of Mount Wu is believed to have appeared to a king of ancient Ch'u in a dream, telling him that this was her abode at dawn and dusk. It was thought to be located in the region of Szechwan or Hupei.

Sung Jung-hua: the name of a woman singer at the time of Ts'ao Ts'ao in the late Han and early Wei eras.

Sung Yü (? third century BC): a courtier poet of Ch'u, perhaps during the reign of King Ch'ing-hsiang. He is thought to have been a literary disciple of the semi-legendary poet and statesman, Ch'ü Yüan. Tradition has it that Sung Yü was a romantic and a flirt. A number of prose poems are attributed to him: *The Lechery of Mr Tengt'u*, *Mount Kaot'ang*, *The Goddess* and others. The first piece is supposed to have been occasioned by a counsellor called Tengt'u denouncing Sung Yü at court as a lecher. The poet responded by saying that while he himself had lived chastely next door to a really lovely girl, Tengt'u had sired five children by his unbelievably ugly wife. The last two pieces are on the theme of the Goddess of Mount Wu. Sung Yü's name is also connected with two tunes, *Man of Pa* and *Sunny spring*.

Sunny spring: a classical tune on the theme of love.

supreme commander, Huo: see Huo Ch'ü-ping.

Sweet Dew Gate, Lamp of Wisdom: Buddhist terms denoting the stage of enlightenment, when earthly cares have been left behind and sorrow no longer pains the human heart.

Sweet herbs, or sweet herbs: both the name by which the first poem of the anthology is generally known and a herb called *miwu*, the purpose of which is not understood. Some commentators suggest it might be a fertility drug, arguing that the person featured in that first poem was divorced because she bore no children. This important poem contains several features which later poets developed: (1) an encounter between a divorced woman and her former husband; (2) the suggestion that as the first wife she was more honest and down-to-earth than his second wife; (3) she wove more homespun cloth than the second wife, who wove a fancier cloth, much quoted in love poetry in general; (4) the idea that the first wife was still in love with her former husband.

Sweet Springs Palace (Kanch'üan): a summer resort of the Han emperors situated on a mountain of the same name in Shensi. Built in the Ch'in Dynasty, it was reconstructed by Emperor Wu in 121 BC. When his favourite concubine, Lady Li (q.v.), died, Emperor Wu enshrined her portrait there.

sweetheart string: string tied in a knot suggesting the bond between two lovers.

sword spirit: see swords.

swords: a pair of magic swords; a reference to the story about the third-century AD astrologer, Lei Huan, who was asked by Chang Hua, the poet, statesman and scholar, the meaning of a purple vapour in the sky. Lei Huan explained that it was the spirit of a magic sword in the Ch'u city of Fengch'eng. Sent there as a governor he found two swords, one marked 'Dragon Fount' and the other marked 'Tai'a' made by Kan Chiang for the Ch'u king. Lei Huan put one sword in his belt and gave Chang Hua the other. Hua commented that because the swords were magic the time would come when they would reunite. When Hua died, his son wore his magic sword, but one day it vanished into a river without a trace, leaving two dragons in its place. The colour purple was imperial, and one meaning of dragon was also imperial.

Ta Chi (twelfth century BC): a famous beauty, concubine of Chou Hsin, last ruler of the Shang Dynasty, who was condemned as a tyrant. She was said to have been so beautiful that she caused the downfall of the dynasty. At the end when the Shang was in ruins, no one dared to execute her, except for one aged counsellor on the victor's side who was immune to her charms.

T'ai Yung: master of music to the legendary Yellow Emperor.

T'aiyüan: the region of modern Shansi.

Tallwillow (Kaoliu): a place in the region of modern Shansi. Represents the border region where the Chinese had to mount patrols to guard against invasion from northern tribesmen.

Tanyang: part of the region of Yangchou, modern Anhwei.

Tat'i city: associated with Hsiangyang music, situated in modern Hupei. The city gave its name to a collection of popular local tunes.

thorn-tree halls: official name of the Shanglin Palace. The leaves of the tree were used for feeding silkworms.

Three Chancelleries: imperial offices of the Han.

thread: see silk.

Three Gods: the three spheres of Heaven, Earth and Human Life.

Three Hills: an allusion to poem 110 of *The Book of Songs*, which describes a man on military campaign pining for his family as he looks homeward from three types of hill: a tree-covered hill, a bare hill and a ridge.

Three Lights: the sun, moon and stars.

Three Rivers: the Yellow, the Lo and the Yi, which flow near Loyang, and come to represent that city.

Three Sparrow Terrace: see (Bronze) Sparrow Terrace.

three springtimes: the usual meaning of this phrase is the three months of spring, but it may also mean three spring seasons, or three years in some contexts.

Three Stars, or Triad: usually involves an allusion to two poems in *The Book of Songs*, either poem 21, in which a nobleman's concubines complain that just as the small stars fade at dawn, so they have to leave their lord early, whereas his senior wife like the Triad star may stay with him until late morning. Or the allusion may be to poem 118 in which a nobleman rejoices to see the charming concubines, like the Three Stars, whom he receives on his wedding night together with his senior wife.

thundercloud: an ancient art motif featured on ritual bronzes of the Shang and Chou dynasties, it later became a fashion detail on such objects as a winecup. A symbol of good fortune signifying fructifying rain.

Tiaoling: an allusion to the philosopher Chuang Tzu, who is said to have shot 'a peculiar magpie' there.

tiara: a woman's jewelled headdress; called a 'quiverer' because its delicate assemblage of kingfisher plumes, pearl pins and gilt artificial flowers would quiver as she walked. Also called 'step-quiver'.

tigers roar: a propitious image deriving from the fact that in mythology the tiger was the guardian and steed of Queen Mother of the West (q.v.), ruler of the land of the immortals.

toad and hare: two of the mythical creatures on the moon. When Ch'ang O (q.v.) fled to the moon with her husband's elixir of immortality, she took with her a pet hare, and, having taken a dose of the elixir, she changed into a toad. The hare is sometimes depicted holding a magic herb. The toad is one of the emblems of immortality. It was believed that an eclipse of the moon was caused by the toad swallowing the moon. Also, when the moon wanes, the toad and hare disappear.

top-key: name of a musical mode; contrasted with rustic songs, the term suggests a metropolitan, fashionable style of music.

Torch Dragon (Chulung): according to a sourcebook of myths, *The Classic of Mountains and Seas (Shan hai ching)*, this was a deity with a human face and a snake's body which dwelt on the Changwei hills beyong the north-west seas. It controlled wind and rain and lit up the Nine Darknesses. Its eyes were so bright that when they were open it became as light as day, and when they were shut it became as dark as night. Its name was used to describe intense or brilliant light.

Torn silk poem: see *Round fan poem*.

tortoise and stork: emblems of longevity.

Trinity Prayer: in legendary antiquity a guard is said to have met Emperor Yao on the border of Hua and prayed that he would have long life, wealth and many children.

Troubled Star: the first star in the handle of the Northern Dipper. It was believed to herald autumn when it pointed south-west.

Ts'ai Yen (*fl. c.* AD 190): the daughter of the famous literary figure, Ts'ai Yung (AD 133–192), she was captured by the Hsiungnu and married to one of their chiefs. When she died, she married her first husband's son by another wife, a custom of that tribe. Eventually, she returned to China. A long narrative poem ascribed to her tells of her ordeal in captivity. She is generally known by the title *Wen-chi*, or Lady of Letters.

Ts'ai Yung (AD 133–192): a famous man of letters. He wrote a poem called *A blue dress*. His biography appears in *Background to Poets and Poems*.

Ts'angchou: one of the places known as the land of the immortals.

Ts'ao Chih (AD 192–232): one of the poets translated in this anthology, he is quoted in many love poems in connection with his *Prose Poem on the Goddess of Lo River*, a fanciful evocation of the deity as she appeared to him in a vision.

Tu Nü: the name of a girl mentioned in a ditty circulating in the reign of the Han Emperor Huan (r. AD 147–168): 'Tu Nü of Hochien cleverly amassed a fortune.'

t'uchih ink: it is not clear what this name means; perhaps it is a transliteration of a Central Asian word. The context in which it is mentioned indicates that an exotic ink is meant.

Tuliang: the name of an exotic perfume, probably deriving from the name of a place the site of which is not known.

Tung Hsien: the catamite of the Han Emperor Ai (r. 7–1 BC). One night as they lay sleeping together, the emperor's sleeve got caught under the boy's body. When the time came for the emperor to go to the dawn court ceremony, rather than waken the boy, he ripped his sleeve off and slipped away quietly.

Tung Sheng: this may refer either to Tung Yen or Tung Hsien, but in any event both lovers were famous for their handsome features.

Tung Yen: the name of the catamite of the Han Emperor Wu.

Tung-men Wu: a man named Wu from the Tung-men area in the Wei era was so stoical that even when his son died he showed his fortitude by refusing to grieve.

Tunghsia: the old name for a region in modern Shantung, famous for the manufacture of silk thread.

Tungt'ing lake: in the kingdom of Ch'u, modern Hunan. It formed a confluence for several important Ch'u rivers which were associated with various legends, namely the Han, Hsiang and Hsiao, besides the Yangtze. It is mentioned in two of the shamanistic songs of *The Songs of Ch'u* addressed to or about the deity of the Hsiang river. Elsewhere in that anthology it is associated with sad journeys undertaken by men in the vain pursuit of happiness.

Tungyang: the old name of a region in modern Chekiang.

turrets: in popular mythology the sky was divided into different palaces, each having gates with turrets above them. The mythical Gates of Heaven is a general name given to a region of the sky, and these are also said to have turrets, or flying turrets.

T'ushan: when Yü saw the daughter of the T'ushan clan, he left for a tour of the south before marrying her. She longed for him and sent a messenger with her song of love. Yü was the legendary founder of the Hsia Dynasty.

twentieth: the moon of that night.

'twin disc': see Two Discs.

twin hearts: an emblem of good fortune, of devoted love; a typical example is a double-flower plant.

'twisting fall' hairdo: see Lady Liang.

two boys: an allusion to the anonymous ballad, *We met in a narrow alley*, translated in Chapter One. It tells of two youths whose carriages get stuck in a narrow lane, and who start chatting to each other about where one of them lives.

Two Discs: sun and moon, symbols of constancy for their supposed regular motion in the skies. A sun and moon motif, or Two Disc motif, was fashionable in the Southern Dynasties for items of clothing and furnishing.

two pleasure-seekers: the Han river sprites (q.v.).

Tzu river and Sheng river: an allusion to an anecdote about Yi Ya (seventh century BC) who was head cook to Duke Huan of Ch'i. His sense of taste was so subtle that he is said to have been able to distinguish between the waters of these two rivers. When the duke said he had tasted everything except a boiled baby, Yi Ya served him his own baby on a dish.

Tzu Tu: a good-looking man in antiquity.

Tzu-wei star: the name of a constellation, and a general name for an imperial palace, partly deriving from the word for purple in its name (*tzu*).

Unicorn Gallery: a Han building for storing archives.

'Unless we're drunk why go home?' and 'The dew will not dry': refrains from *The Book of Songs*, no. 174: 'Soaking, soaking is the dew. / Without the sun it will not dry. / Happy, happy we drink at night; / Unless we're drunk why go home?'

untidy hair: allusion to *The Book of Songs*, no. 226: 'My hair is untidy, / I go home and wash it.'

Upper Palace (Shang kung): a trysting-place for lovers, and an allusion to poem 48 of *The Book of Songs*, which tells of a man's assignations with lovely women among the mulberry near Upper Palace and along the Ch'i river.

upstairs girl's powder: an allusion to lines 3 and 5 of 'Green, green riverside grass', no. 5 of *Nine miscellaneous poems* in Chapter One.

Vast Wave (Hungpo): the name of a Ch'in Dynasty terrace, a pleasure spot of Chao Chien-tzu.

Vermilion Bird Window: probably denotes a south-facing window; the emblematic bird of the south was vermilion in colour. It carries an allusion to the Han courtier Tung-fang Shuo, who wrote that he peeped through such a window when the legendary Queen Mother of the West (q.v.) made her mythical visit to the Han Emperor Wu.

vermilion pillows: pillows were hollow and could be used for putting private things in; vermilion was the imperial colour.

'vow unto death': an allusion to *The Book of Songs*, no. 45: 'Unto death he swore to have no other', and also no. 31.

Wan-shan: a place in Hsiangyang.

Wang Chao-chün (first century BC), courtesy name Chao-chün, given name Ch'iang: her name was changed from Chao to Ming because it violated the taboo name of Ssu-ma Chao, posthumously entitled Emperor Wen of the Chin (AD 211–65). She was a palace lady in the harem of Emperor Yüan of the Han. Because she refused to bribe the court painter, Mao Yen-shou, he depicted her with a blemish. Later, when the Hsiungnu demanded a Chinese bride, Emperor Yüan picked out Wang Chao-chün's portrait and sent her off in marriage to the tribal chieftain. When the emperor saw her leaving the palace he realized that hers was no flawed beauty and deeply regretted her departure. She had to leave China, however, and in due course married the chieftain, bearing him a son. When he died, she married his son by another wife. Her story is told in Shih Ch'ung's long narrative in Chapter Two.

Wang Ch'iang: see Wang Chao-chün.

Wang Mang: usurped the Han throne and set up his Hsin Dynasty for a short-lived interregnum AD 9–23. He took as his emblematic colour yellow, symbolizing the earth (see Five Elements Theory).

Wang Pao: see Mien Chü and Wang Pao.

Wang (Tzu-ch'iao): called by his other name of Wang Tzu-chin (sixth century BC), son of King Ling of the Chou Dynasty. He studied the occult arts for thirty years and then, according to legend, flew away on a white stork, the symbol of longevity, and became an immortal. Other versions of the legend say that Wang was a sorcerer or a Taoist immortal, who changed into a rainbow serpent, then into a shoe, and then into a great bird. He figures frequently in *The Songs of Ch'u*, riding the clouds as a divinity.

wardrobe mistress: a reference to the career of Wei Tzu-fu (second century BC), who was originally employed in the household of the Princess of P'ingyang, the sister of the Han Emperor Wu. One day when the emperor was returning from an outing, he visited his sister and she showed him her ladies-in-waiting. He was only interested in Wei Tzu-fu. Later she helped him change his robes, and the emperor made love to her in the corridor. He gave his sister 1,000 weights of gold, so she offered him Wei Tzu-fu. As the latter was about to enter the carriage taking her to the imperial palace, the Princess patted her back encouragingly and told her not to forget her benefactress. Eventually Wei Tzu-fu displaced Empress Ch'en who bore no son. As Empress Wei she bore the emperor a son and he became the heir-apparent.

Warp stars: the seven luminaries of the sun, moon and five planets move on the woof of the other stars' trajectories.

washing clothes in Nanyang: allusion to Chang Lü's daughter, who used to wash her clothes at the bottom of a hill south of Han river, beating them clean with a stone. Later, she gave birth to two dragons. When she died, her hearse suddenly ascended to the top of the mountain, and she was buried there. It was called Mount Maid, with a Maid Peak, and at the bottom was Maid Shrine with her washing stone.

waterplant: see alga.

Weaver: stars in Vega and Lyra, associated in folklore with the wife of Herdboy. The legend goes that when they married they were so happy they would not work. The king and queen of Heaven were so angry with them that they separated them. The queen drew her silver hairpin across the sky and created the Han river, or River of Heaven, to divide the lovers. But the king was moved by their plight and allowed them to meet once a year on the Seventh Night of the seventh month of the lunar calendar. Then the water of the river would abate, and Weaver could cross in her divine carriage to Herdboy. The sky would form their boudoir with clouds forming thick bedcurtains. During the rest of the year Weaver is shown fidgeting at her task of weaving, never completing her pattern because she is pining. She is the patroness of embroidery, and on Seventh Night (q.v.) girls compete in embroidery patterns using double needles (probably to represent the two stellar lovers) and seven-colour thread. Sometimes Weaver is called the girl of the river Han in the sky. Most poems on this theme stress the brevity of the joy of Seventh Night.

Wei: the name of the dynasty founded by Ts'ao Ts'ao in AD 220 and ruled until 265 by the Ts'ao family with their capital at Loyang.

Wei and Cheng: names of ancient states and of sections of the 160 regional songs of *The Book of Songs*. The songs and music associated with these states were traditionally considered to be licentious, or enjoyable, according to the listener's point of view. See also Cheng.

Wei Hsiao (d. AD 33): a military man who once occupied T'ienshui. See 'a plug of mud'.

Wei river: a traditional rendezvous for lovers, often coupled in this context with the Ch'i river. It flowed north of Ch'angan.

Wei Sheng (sixth century BC): see clasping the bridge-post.

Wei Tzu-fu: see wardrobe mistress.

Weich'eng: the name of a city near Hsienyang, capital of the Ch'in Dynasty, north of Ch'angan.

Weiyang Palace: a Han palace, residence of royal ladies.

Welcome Breeze Lodge: a Han summer residence in Sweet Springs, Shensi.

Welcome Dew: a reference to the bronze pillar built by the Han Emperor Wu, on the top of which he had erected an image of an immortal holding its palm up to the sky to receive dew. Dew was believed to be the nectar of immortals.

Welcome Dew Terrace: a terrace where the bronze pillar was built bearing the same name.

Well Path: the name of a district and of a mountain north of Hantan, capital of Chao state.

Wen-chün: personal name of Cho Wen-chün (q.v.).

West Mound: a place west of Ch'ient'ang river, modern Hangchow area.

West Park: in Yeh city during the Wei Dynasty.

West Willow: a mythological tree in the west where the sun sets. Called Hsi-liu, a pun for Slim Willow.

Western: usually means Central Asia in the context of traditional China.

whistle, whistling: has a romantic connotation in these poems, sometimes expressing wistfulness or deep feeling. In the context of reclusion, whistling summons a wizard or an immortal.

white courser: simile for the swift passage of human life.

White crest song: the name of an anonymous folk-song, also entitled *White as snow on the hills*, translated in Chapter One as *White as mountaintop snow*.

White Elm star: its location in the sky is not certain.

White Emperor city: in Kweichow, Szechwan, founded by Kung-sun Shu (d. AD 36).

White Gate: the south-west gate of Chienk'ang, formerly Hsüan-yang Gate.

White Girl (Sunü): the name of a goddess entrusted with the arcane mysteries of sexual techniques. She is linked in this context with the Dark Girl.

White hemp dance: considered a modern tune in the fifth century AD. Possibly performed by youths wearing white hempen robes. White was the colour associated with autumn. Hemp was usually worn in summer.

white horse(s): a traditional image of time's swift passage, usually described galloping past a crack in the wall. White is the emblematic colour of death.

White snow: the name of a melody.

'white sun vow': an oath sworn by pointing up at the sun (and / or the moon), symbolizing constancy and fidelity to one's vow. Poem 73 of *The Book of Songs* contains the couplet: 'You thought I had broken faith; / I was true as the bright sun above.'

White-brass-shoes: it is not clear if this is a place name in Shansi in the Han era, or refers to an object. Attached to a song, the name seems to indicate a traditional air.

Whitehorse ford (Paima): near the Yellow river.

willow (*liu*): a pun for to detain, to keep someone from going away on a journey. Since the Han Dynasty it was the custom for a person escorting a traveller part of his journey to give him a twig of willow. 'Broken willow' or 'Breaking willow' denotes a parting theme. The willow was also an image of feminine grace and slenderness. The willow, like the plum, heralds the spring with its green fronds and fluff. Its silky strands are often compared with silk thread, a pun for love.

'wind-flow' (*feng-liu*): a phrase meaning romantic, following from the use of natural imagery such as wind, flowers, moon and snow in amatory literature.

window: the panes of early Chinese windows were of silk. The frame was wooden. Sometimes there was a wooden fretwork or lattice, a pun for cage, *lung*. In a woman's sheltered life the only time she might be seen by outsiders was at her window, where she applied her make-up, sewed and stared into the distance.

wine: although the grapevine was introduced to China during the Han Dynasty, wine from grapes was not the usual alcoholic drink. Fermented rice wine was more usual. This is sometimes described as white or green. Sometimes wine is generally said to be 'orchidaceous', meaning fragrant. Mulled wine was served in wineshops by women. 'First wine' meant the first ritual sharing of wine by bride and bridegroom at their marriage, and came to mean marriage itself, like the phrase 'bound hair'. There was an old song which said that clear wine like flowers was the drink of autumn, wine sweet like milk was the drink of spring. Lovers pledged with wine, the male or master offering a cup of wine from which he had drunk the first half. The cup was supposed to be drained.

Wu: see Mount Wu, and the Goddess of Mount Wu. Wu is often linked with Lo, meaning Lo river and its goddess.

Wu: the name of an ancient state in the region of modern Kiangsu and Chekiang. In some poems the region is mentioned in connection with the production of tailoring shears, for which it was famous. Also, the region is associated with Hsi Shih (q.v.). Wu music was associated with the region of the Southern Dynasties capital, Chienk'ang, modern Nanking.

Wu-ling (Five Mounds): burial place of Han emperors; situated in the outskirts of Ch'angan. There were five famous burial mounds in antiquity for the Han emperors Kao-tsu, Hui, Ching, Wu and Chao, who reigned between 202 and 74 BC.

Wuwei: the name of a place in modern Kansu.

Yang city: in the old kingdom of Ch'u, modern Honan. Sometimes used as a general place name for lovely women, deriving from the poet's mention of it in *The Lechery of Mr Teng'tu*, in the same way as Hsiats'ai (q.v.) is mentioned.

Yang clan: reference to Yang Yün of the Han Dynasty; he was from Chao state and was a skilful performer on the *se*, a large stringed instrument.

Yang Hsiung (53 BC–AD 18): poet and philosopher of the Han Dynasty, his courtesy name was Tzu-yün. Though poor, he was a man of honour and integrity, preferring to live quietly and modestly, rather than pursue fame and fortune.

Yang-o: a place in Shansi. Probably a reference to Chao Feiyen, who came from there. See Chao Feiyen.

Yangchow: in the Southern Dynasties era this place name was synonymous with Hsiangyang, modern Hupei.

Yeh valley: a very long valley in Shensi.

Yehchung: capital city of the Wei Dynasty in the third century AD, it was taken over by Shih Hu of the Chieh tribe of the Hsiungnu.

yellow: it was a cosmetic fashion in the Southern Dynasties for a woman to attach a beauty-spot of different shapes and colours to her brow. The usual colour was yellow, and the shape varied between a mountain, flower, moon or star.

Yellow Emperor: Huang-ti, legendary sage-king of ancient China, believed to have bestowed upon mankind various benefits, including sericulture (invented by his wife). The philosophical school of Taoism is often referred to as the Teaching of the Yellow Emperor and Lao Tzu, or Huang-Lao. The titles of many arcane texts bear his name.

Yellow river: the northern river of China, the basin of which formed the central heartland of ancient China, known as the Central Plains. The capital cities of Hsienyang, Ch'angan and Loyang were all situated in this region. The river is often mentioned in love poetry as an insuperable obstacle for one seeking to follow a beloved traveller. The Yellow river was believed to be a continuation of the Han river in the sky. Another popular belief was that the normally muddy Yellow river flows clear once in a thousand years, a symbol of rare good fortune. The river is also used to symbolize the flow of time.

Yellow Springs: the afterlife, considered as a lower world beneath the world of men. Also called Eternal Springs.

Yellow stork: the name of a song composed by a girl called T'ao Ying from Lu state when her husband died and her relatives tried unsuccessfully to make her remarry.

Yen: see Chao Feiyen. (Yen means a swallow.)

Yen: the name of an ancient state in north-east China annihilated in the third century BC by Ch'in state. It was famous in its heyday for its lovely women, and is linked in this context with Chao state. A Yen song is about parted lovers.

Yen Ssu: a man who served the Han emperors Wen, Ching and Wu, who successively ruled 180–87 BC. He lived so long that he became a symbol of decrepitude.

Yen-chih: title of the consort of a Hsiungnu chieftain. See P'ingch'eng.

Yi city: on the River Han, south of Hsiangyang, which was the capital of Yung province. Hsiao Kang was Governor of Yung in Hupei, AD 523–6.

Yi river: in the region of Hupei.

Yih river: perhaps south-east of Shantung (different from Yi river).

Yin/Yang: one of the earliest cosmological ideas in ancient China was that the universe operated according to the interaction of two primeval opposing forces in a complementary way, *yin* and *yang*. *Yin* stood for the feminine cosmic force, being dark, cold, north, submissive, weak, soft, negative, woman, and the moon. *Yang* stood for the male cosmic force, light, hot, south, dominant, strong, hard, positive, man, and the sun. Their interaction was believed to cause the phenomena of the universe. Also see Five Elements Theory.

Ying: capital of the kingdom of Ch'u, usually associated with the rhapsodies and shamanistic chants of *The Songs of Ch'u*. Sung Yü was sometimes called 'the man from Ying'.

Ying Gate: the main south gate of a palace.

Ying-ch'uan: a river in Honan. Said to be so pure that the legendary sage Hsü Yu rinsed his ears in it after the sage ruler Yao sullied them with his offer to make him minister. Also an area famous for beautiful women.

Yingchou: one of the names for fairyland in the east, thought to be one of the three sacred mountains in the Gulf of Chihli, the other two being P'englai and Fangchang.

Yingchow: a place in the region of Ch'i, the eastern state of ancient China, modern Shantung.

Your collar: the title of poem 91 of *The Book of Songs*, in which a girl imagines the blue collar and belt jewels of her lover who has gone away.

Yü: a place in the region of modern Szechwan.

Yü: a princess, daughter of King Fu Ch'ai of Wu in the fifth century BC.

Yu and Chi: names meaning the north in general.

Yü Ch'ing (third century BC): a minister in the court of King Hsiao-ch'eng of Chao.

Yü Gulf: a mythological place where the sun sets.

Yu Yü: was asked by the ruler of the Jung territory in the west to visit the court of Duke Mu of Ch'in state (r. 658–619 BC), which he criticized for its extravagance, noting that such wastefulness could cause popular unrest.

Yüeh: the name of an ancient state in the region of modern Chekiang.

Yükuan: in modern Suiyüan, north of the bend of the Yellow river.

Yüling bookworms: allusion to Emperor Mu of the Chou Dynasty, whose books became riddled with bookworms when he was on his travels.

Yünchung: in the Pingchou region of Shensi, the border area where military defence was regularly maintained.

Yungchou: ancient name of the region west of the Yellow river.

BACKGROUND TO POETS AND POEMS

Anonymous, *A children's rhyme of the Chin Emperor Hui's era* (r. AD 290–307).

Anonymous, *A children's rhyme of the Han era*, late first century AD. This originally appeared in 'The Biography of Ma Liao' in *The History of the Former Han* by I'an Ku (AD 32–92). Its other, more popular title was *The city rhyme*.

Anonymous, *A Modern Miscellaneous Poem*, fifth century AD.

Anonymous, *An old poem written for Chiao Chung-ch'ing's wife*, third or fourth century AD. A long narrative poem, rare in Chinese literature, it has 355 lines. The poem goes by another title, *A peacock south-east flew*. The formulaic opening of the narrative contains an image popularly used in the folk-song tradition, that of a bird which becomes separated from its mate or its flock. The theme of separation is echoed in the closing section of the story when Chiao Chung-ch'ing commits suicide on a 'south-east' bough of a garden tree.

Anonymous, *Eight Old Poems*, middle of the Later Han, around AD 100. The first poem in this set is one of the most influential of the early love poems. Refrains from it appear in many poems in this anthology, imitating the bittersweet theme of a reluctant divorce. The fifth poem was also popular among later imitators, having the theme of a gift sent from a lover to his lady. Poems 2, 3, 4 and 5 are the equivalent of poems 16, 8, 17 and 18, respectively, of *The Nineteen Old Poems*. The old poem, or *ku-shih*, is a five- or seven-syllable verse form. The last word of each couplet usually rhymes. The rhyme category may be the same throughout, or it may change in the course of the poem.

Anonymous, *Five Modern Western Melodic Songs*, ? fifth century AD. 'Western' in this context means the region of Hsiangyang, modern Hupei. Stone City gave its name to a certain kind of folk music and song to accompany dance, but later lost the association with dance. The third poem in this set was believed to have been composed by Liu I-ch'ing, Prince of Linch'üan (AD 403–44), the famous author of *New Tales of Society* (*Shih-shuo hsin-yü*). The fifth in the set is said to be a children's rhyme, and refers to the story that in AD 494 of the Ch'i Dynasty Yang Min, the son of a shamaness, was the Empress's lover.

Anonymous, *Four old chüeh-chü poems*, ? third century AD. From their position in Chapter Ten, prior to poets of the third and fourth centuries, these four poems appear to belong to the third century, or slightly earlier. As such they would be the earliest prototypes of that verse form. The *Chüeh-chü* began as a short song in the popular tradition, linked to the folk-song, having four lines, with five or seven syllables per line. The name itself means 'cut-off lines'.

Anonymous, *Nine Miscellaneous Poems*, ? first or second century AD. Traditionally attributed to Mei Sheng (d. 149 BC), they are now, except for poem no. 6, classified as anonymous poems in *The Nineteen Old Poems*. Poems 1–5 and 7–9 appear as poems 5, 12, 1, 6, 2, 9, 10 and 19 respectively of *The Nineteen Old Poems*. These are all seminal poems in the development of medieval love poetry, and attracted many later imitations.

397

Anonymous, *Nine Modern Wu Songs*, fifth century AD, from the region of Nanking. Wu was the name of the old kingdom on the south-west coast, south of the Yangtze river, in the region of Chekiang and Kiangsu. Such songs are sometimes also called 'Chiangnan Songs' or 'South of the River [love] songs'.

Anonymous, *Six Old Folk-songs*, ? c. AD 100. The first is the famous narrative poem about Ch'in Lofu, of which refrains occur in many later love poems. It goes by several other titles: *Sunrise from the south-east corner suite*, *The Lofu love-song suite* and *Mulberry up the lane*. 'Suite' means a series of related stanzas linked to make one long poem. The second poem in this set is another favourite. Its theme is of marital harmony in a wealthy household. The fifth poem was traditionally thought to have been composed by Cho Wen-chün, wife of the Han poet Ssu-ma Hsiang-ju, when he tried to take another girl as his new bride. 'Folk-song' is used as a general term for the poetic form called *yüeh-fu*. Originally this term meant the Bureau of Music revitalized by the Han Emperor Wu c. 120 BC. It then came to mean those anonymous folk-songs collected by officials attached to this bureau. Later still the term meant folk-songs in general, whether they were genuine folk pieces or polished imitations by named poets. They are characterized by narrative, formulaic and musical elements, by simple diction, bold imagery and punning devices. The earlier type of *yüeh-fu* was metrically irregular, while the later version was metrically inseparable from the old poem or *ku-shih*.

Anonymous, *Song of the Yüeh boatman*, first recorded in the first century BC by Liu Hsiang, it derives from an earlier oral tradition of Yüeh, and was then transcribed into the Ch'u dialect. It has in its present form elements of the *sao*-song style, similar to some poems in *The Songs of Ch'u*. This poem is often quoted in later love poems having a homosexual theme.

Anonymous, *Three Modern Miscellaneous Songs*, fifth century AD. They are songs for accompaniment by percussion, bells and wind instruments, but not for strings.

Anonymous, *Two children's rhymes of the Han Emperor Ch'eng's era* (r. 33–7 BC). The first of the rhymes appears at the end of Chao Feiyen's biography in *The History of the Former Han*, where it is implied that she was instrumental in causing the death of Emperor Ch'eng. That version ends with the couplet: 'The princes died, / Swallow pecks their turds.' Similarly, another version of *Cassia* starts with the couplet: 'Crooked paths ruin fine fields, / Gossiping tongues confuse honest men.' Such rhymes were believed to be prophetic and were often incorporated by historians into their biographies of the famous or infamous. Despite the historian's censure in her biography, Chao Feiyen enjoys the status of a romantic heroine in the pages of these love poems.

Anonymous, *Two children's rhymes of the Han Emperor Huan's era* (r. AD 147–68). During the years AD 151–3 the Ch'iang tribe of Kansu rebelled and invaded Szechwan and Shensi, inflicting great damage. Chinese punitive expeditions against them failed. Because of all this military activity, the seasonal labour of harvesting was neglected and the work had to be carried out by the womenfolk. Local officials requisitioned all forms of transportation, making farming even more difficult.

Anonymous, *Two song lyrics*, ? Han Dynasty, or ? Liang Dynasty. Their position at the beginning of Chapter Nine prior to a poem datable from the first century BC suggests that they are of that era or slightly earlier. Their form, however, the regular seven-word metre, clearly indicates that they are much later. One popular theory is that they belong to the sixth century AD and were put in the wrong chronological section. Another theory is that they were written by Hsiao Yen.

Chang Heng, courtesy name P'ing-tzu, AD 78–139, from Honan. A poet, astronomer and mathematician of the Later Han era, he wrote famous prose poems on the twin capitals of Ch'angan and Loyang. His poem in Chapter One is entitled *Like sounds*, a phrase originating in *The Book of Changes (I ching)*, one of the *Confucian Classics*. The original passage is: 'Like sounds accord with each other, / Like minds seek each other out.' His four poems in Chapter Nine called *Four sorrows* were based on the *tristia* of *The Songs of Ch'u*, and were themselves imitated by later poets.

Chang Hsieh, courtesy name Ching-yang, *fl. c.* AD 295, from Shantung. Younger brother of Chang Tsai. Known with him and Chang Hua as the 'Three Changs' of literature. Ranked as a major poet in the Southern Dynasties, but only twelve poems survive.

Chang Hua, courtesy name Mao-hsien, AD 232–300, from Hopei. Rose from poverty to wealth and status through literary talent. (See Chang Hsieh.) Served as minister of state in the Chin Dynasty. Became a famous scholar and was appointed as junior tutor to the heir-apparent. He wrote the *Treatise on Investigating Phenomena (Po wu chih)*, which survives in a reconstructed fragment. Executed for espousing the cause of Empress Chia against the Prince of Chao. The first line of the first of his series of five love poems echoes that of Li Yen-nien in Chapter One.

Chang Shuai, courtesy name Shih-chien, AD 475–527, from Kiangsu. Served the Liang as deputy of the imperial chancellery and later became a prefect of Hsinan. Transferred for irresponsibility, he became an official for Hsiao Kang in AD 509 for a decade. His poetry won the admiration of Hsiao Yen, Emperor Wu. He was a prolific writer and his lifetime compositions amounted to thirty tomes. His first poem in Chapter Six is an imitation of the old ballad which appears in Chapter One as *We met in a narrow alley*.

Chang Tsai, courtesy name Meng-yang, *c.* AD 289, from Hopei. Brother of Chang Hsieh and Hua, also poets. He attracted the attention of the Chin Emperor Wu by his moral inscription on a mountain pass in Szechwan. He served the heir-apparent as secretary, but retired early from politics. His four imitative poems may be compared with those by Chang Heng and Fu Hsüan in Chapter Nine, entitled *Four sorrows*.

Chen Ku, ? *fl.* early sixth century AD. Biographical data scant. One of his poems is modelled on one by Hsiao Kang, suggesting a possible connection with the Liang court.

Ch'en Lin, courtesy name K'ung-chang, d. AD 217, from Kiangsu. One of the 'Seven Masters of the Chien-an Era' (196–220). He held office with Yüan Shao and Ts'ao Ts'ao as secretary. The poem by him in Chapter One is not in the regular five-syllable metre featured in this part of the anthology, but in a mixed metre. Because it belongs to an early period *vis-à-vis* the Liang, and because it comes immediately after one having the same title by Ts'ai Yung (?), it remains here rather than in Chapter Nine, which features irregular metres.

Chi Shao-yü, courtesy name Yu-ch'ang, *c.* AD 535, from the area of Chienk'ang, the Liang capital, modern Nanking. While Hsiao Kang was Crown Prince, he became an erudit in the Eastern Palace, the heir-apparent's official residence, in AD 541. He also served other Liang princes, such as Hsiao Chi and Hsiao Lun, also poets. The theme of Chienhsing Park in the capital city was popular, and Chi's treatment of it may be compared with that by Yü Chien-wu in Chapter Eight.

Chia Ch'ung, courtesy name Kung-lü, AD 217–82, from Shansi. He inherited the title of Marquess. He served the Ssu-ma family and helped them defeat the last Wei emperor, thus inaugurating the Chin Dynasty. Enfeoffed as the Duke of Lu and made prime minister. Said to have died from shame when the Chin attack against the kingdom of Wu, which policy he had vetoed, met with great success. Branded as a traitor in some later histories. His wife, Lady Li, was the daughter of Li Feng, who had been executed for a crime.

Chiang Hung, c. AD 502, from Honan. Served the Liang Dynasty, but died because of his involvement with a political scandal. His name was linked with the poet Wu Chün, and the few details known of his life mostly appear in the latter's official biography.

Chiang Po-yao, ? mid-sixth century AD. Biographical data scant. Invited by Hsiao Kang to become one of the 'Ten Scholars of the Lofty Studio' to work on the imperial library.

Chiang Yen, courtesy name Wen-t'ung, AD 444–505, from Honan. Probably a poor orphan, he rose to high office because of his wide scholarship. Served the last Ch'i emperors and Hsiao Yen, the first Liang emperor. He was one of the 'Eight Comrades', a literary group whose patron was Hsiao Yen. Ennobled as the Marquess of Liling. His poetry, prose poems, essays and so forth amounted to over a hundred volumes, two volumes of which survive. He admired the poet Ssu-ma Hsiang-ju. The second of his poems in the old style in Chapter Five is modelled on *A poem on regret*, attributed to Lady Pan in Chapter One, and the fourth, *Resentment in separation*, is modelled on the poet T'ang Seng-chi, also known as Hsiu Shang-jen.

Ch'in Chia, courtesy name Shih-hui, *fl. c.* AD 147, from Kansu. Later editors tacked a preface on to his three poems to his wife (in Chapter One) to provide a biographical context for them. Lunghsi is in Kansu. Prose letters linked to the poems survive. Ch'in Chia died young.

Ch'iu Ch'ih, courtesy name Hsi-fan, AD 464–508, from Chekiang. He served the Ch'i Dynasty and then the Liang under Emperor Wu, Hsiao Yen. He was a favourite at court. One volume of his work survives.

Ch'iu Chü-yüan, *fl. c.* AD 457, d. *c.* 484. Little is known about him. He served under the Liu-Sung Emperor Hsiao-wu, the poet Liu Chün.

Emperor Hsiao-wu of the Liu-Sung Dynasty, Liu Chün, courtesy name Hsiu-lung, AD 430–64, from Kiangsu. Third son of Emperor Wen of the Liu-Sung Dynasty. He acceded to the throne in AD 454. Depicted in the histories as a pleasure-seeking spendthrift. One of his poems imitates the latter part of Hsü Kan's *Bedroom longing* which appears in Chapter One; Liu Chün's version appears in Chapter Ten.

Emperor Ming of the Wei Dynasty, Ts'ao Jui, courtesy name Yüan-chung, AD 204–39. Acceded to the Wei throne on the death of his father, Ts'ao P'ei, in AD 226. His mother, Empress Chen, was deposed and committed suicide in AD 221, so he temporarily forfeited the right to succession. Later he was reinstated. The three imperial Ts'ao – Ts'ao Ts'ao, Ts'ao P'ei and Ts'ao Jui – are known in literary history as the 'Three Imperial Ancestors'. His poem, the second of *Two folk-songs* in Chapter Two, is elsewhere listed as an anonymous old lyric entitled *Song of anguish*.

Emperor Wen of the Wei Dynasty, Ts'ao P'ei, courtesy name Tzu-huan, AD 187–226. Acceded to the Wei throne in AD 220 as the first Emperor Wen on the death of his father, Ts'ao Ts'ao, founder of the Wei. He established his capital at Loyang. Patron of the arts, he gathered a select group of writers to his court called 'Seven

Masters of the Chien-an Era'. He wrote *Essay on Literature* (*Lun wen*), one of the earliest pieces of Chinese literary criticism. His brother, Ts'ao Chih, and son, Ts'ao Jui, are also represented in this anthology. There is some controversy about the authorship of the poem entitled *Empress Chen* listed either under his name or after his name in Chapter Two. In some collections this poem is attributed to his wife, Empress Chen, or to Ts'ao Ts'ao, or treated as anonymous. Similarly, the next two poems attributed to Wang Sung are also ascribed to Ts'ao P'ei, who is believed to have written them on behalf of Wang Sung.

Emperor Wu of the Liang Dynasty, Hsiao Yen, courtesy name Shu-ta, AD 464–549, from Kiangsu. Founder of the Liang Dynasty, reigning from AD 502 until 549, the longest reign in the Southern Dynasties era. Though a distant relative of the Ch'i royal family, he took up arms against the last Ch'i emperor because he had executed Hsiao Yen's eldest brother. Shen Yüeh advised Hsiao Yen to found his own dynasty. A devout Buddhist, he became a monk twice, retiring to a monastery three times in his lifetime. He was a man of great learning and considerable poetic ability, as were two of his sons, Hsiao T'ung, compiler of *Anthology of Literature*, and Hsiao Kang, poet and patron of *New Songs from a Jade Terrace*. Hsiao Yen formed a literary group called the 'Eight Comrades of Chingling', consisting of himself, Shen Yüeh, Hsieh T'iao, Wang Yung, Fan Yün, Hsiao Ch'in, Jen Fang and Lu Ch'ui, the first three of whom are poets represented in this anthology. Some of the poems listed under his name in Chapter Ten are elsewhere attributed to other authors: some of his *Spring*, *Summer* and *Autumn Songs* belong to the poems entitled *Tzu-yeh Seasonal Songs* (Girl of the Night, a professional singer, fourth century AD). Another source lists some of Hsiao Yen's poems as compositions by Wang Chin-chu. Also, some *Tzu-yeh songs* ascribed to Hsiao Yen are elsewhere listed among the cycle of forty-two songs believed to have been composed by the singer Tzu-yeh, Girl of the Night, herself.

? Fairy of Wuhsing, early sixth century AD, from Chekiang. Probably the name of a professional female entertainer. She presented a love poem to Hsieh Lan, perhaps when he was a senior official in Wuhsing.

Fan Ch'in, courtesy name Hsiu-po, ? d. AD 218, from Honan. Served under Ts'ao Ts'ao, founder of the Wei Dynasty.

Fei Ch'ang, *fl. c.* AD 510, from Hupei. Little is known about him today, but he was appreciated as an important poet in his own time.

Fu Hsüan, courtesy name Hsiu-i, AD 217–78, from Shensi. Rose from poverty and obscurity to wealth and fame through his literary talent. Served as censor and lord chamberlain under the Chin Emperor Wu. All that survives of his *oeuvre* of one hundred volumes are sixty-three poems, mostly folk-songs. His poem, *A poem harmonizing with Mr Pan's poem*, is traditionally thought to refer to a poem by the Han historian, Pan Ku (AD 32–92), to whom several other works are spuriously ascribed. But the historian did not write a poem on the theme of Fu Hsüan's poem, which is about a chaste wife and her unfaithful husband, Ch'iu Hu. Perhaps an earlier, unidentified narrative poem was the model? Later editors dubbed some of Fu Hsüan's folk-songs 'northern' because they were meant to contrast with the southern style that emerged after the partition of China into north and south after AD 317. One of his so-called imitations of northern folk-songs in Chapter Nine, translated under the title *Past autumn's nine*, is subtitled *The 'Tung flees' ballad*, which is the name of a children's rhyme dating from the Later Han which tells of the eventual defeat of Tung Cho, who sacked Loyang in AD 190. But this subtitle bears no relation to the content of his poem.

Heir-apparent, Emperor Chien-wen, Hsiao Kang, AD 503–51. Became heir-apparent in AD 531 when his brother Hsiao T'ung died. He was the third son of Hsiao Yen, and succeeded his father in AD 549 as Emperor Chien-wen of the Liang. He was assassinated two years later by the Tartar general, Hou Ching. A statesman of great erudition and literary talent, he was interested in philosophy, religion, literary theory and composition, and surrounded himself with the outstanding literary personalities of the day. He was a believer in Buddhism. Hsü Ling's father was his tutor, as was Yü Chien-wu, a famous poet and father of the poet Yü Hsin. Hsiao Kang is credited with the development of a new form of love poetry called 'Palace Style Poetry', featuring a noblewoman languishing from unhappy love in a richly furnished boudoir. Its main characteristics, however, are now generally thought to have been elaborated by several poets in his entourage, including Hsü Ling's father, Hsü Ch'ih, and Yü Chien-wu. It is traditionally believed that Hsiao Kang commissioned Hsü Ling to compile *New Songs from a Jade Terrace* in order to immortalize the new type of love poem with the finest examples of his day. His own poetry reveals great artistry and a sensitive, individual imagination. The title *Night after night* in Chapter Ten is elsewhere listed as a composition by Shen Yüeh.

Ho Man-ts'ai, ? mid-sixth century AD, biographical data scant.

Ho Ssu-ch'eng, courtesy name Wu-ching, ? AD 481–?534, from Kiangsu. Served the Prince of Nank'ang and the Prince of Wuling, the poet Hsiao Chi. His poem on Lady Pan in Chapter Six, commissioned by Hsiao I, may be compared with that of K'ung Weng-kuei, similarly commissioned and in the same chapter.

Ho Sun, courtesy name Chung-yen, d. *c.* AD 517, from Shantung. Served the Liang as the secretary of the Prince of Luling. The poet Shen Yüeh particularly admired his poetry, and contemporaries ranked him with Liu Hsiao-cho. Over one hundred of his poems survive. His imagination and artistry mark him as one of the major poets of the Southern Dynasties.

Ho Tzu-lang, courtesy name Shih-ming, b. *c.* AD 479, d. *c.* 522, from Shantung. With Ho Ssu-ch'eng and Ho Sun, he was called by the group name of 'The Three Ho of Tunghai'.

Hsiao Lin, ? *fl.* mid-sixth century AD, biographical data scant.

Hsiao Tzu-hsien, courtesy name Ching-yang, AD 489–537, from Shantung. Grandson of the founder of the Ch'i Dynasty, Emperor Kai, and related to the Liang royal house. Enfeoffed as the Marquess of Ningtu. He wrote *The History of the Southern Ch'i Dynasty*, spanning the years AD 479–501. He became head of the Board of Civil Office and later served as governor of Wuhsing in Chekiang. His imitative folk-song, *Sunrise at the south-east corner*, in Chapter Eight, may be compared with the original folk-song in Chapter One. His other poem there may be compared with the same title by Ts'ao Chih in Chapter Two, *A beautiful woman*.

Hsieh Hui-lien, AD 397–433. Younger cousin of Hsieh Ling-yün, from Honan. Served the Liu-Sung Dynasty as a top official in the judiciary under Prince I-k'ang of P'engch'eng. His poem in Chapter Three, translated as *In the manner of old verse*, is based on the early anonymous folk-song appearing in Chapter One, *Eight Old Poems*, no. 5, and may be compared with Pao Ling-hui's version in Chapter Four entitled *In the style of 'A traveller came from a far place'*.

Hsieh Ling-yün, AD 385–433, from Honan. Came from a noble and famous family of distinguished statesmen, and was entitled Duke of K'anglo. At the fall of the Chin Dynasty he pledged support for the Liu-Sung in AD 419. Exiled because of envious enemies, he was forced to live in obscurity on his estate. He became a Buddhist convert and wrote religious treatises. While in Chekiang and Kiangsi he was influenced by the splendid scenery of hills and lakes, brilliantly describing them in his poems. With T'ao Ch'ien he is ranked as the earliest nature poet in Chinese literature. Admired by Li Po and Tu Fu. He was executed in Canton on false charges. Over a hundred poems survive.

Hsieh T'iao, courtesy name Hsüan-hui, AD 464–99, from Honan. Served the Ch'i Emperor Ming as head of the Bureau of Civil Offices. Later he was imprisoned for failing to support the rebellion of Lord Tung-hun, and died in prison. He was a distant relative of the Hsieh family famous in the annals of literature with such names as Hsieh Ling-yün and Hsieh Hui-lien. Shen Yüeh said in admiration of Hsieh T'iao's poetry, 'We have not had poetry like this for two hundred years!' He was one of the 'Eight Comrades', Hsiao Yen's literary group. He was also admired by Li Po. About 150 poems survive, mostly lyrics.

?Hsin Yen-nien, second century AD. Nothing is known of him. His poem in Chapter One, *The Imperial Guards officer*, apparently refers to the cavalry brigade patrolling the imperial palace called the *Yü-lin*, but the man featured in the poem is a slave.

Hsü Chün-ch'ien, courtesy name Huai-chien, early sixth century AD, from Shantung. Was administrative adviser to Hsiao I, when the latter was a general.

Hsü Fei, courtesy name Ching-yeh, d. AD 524. Second son of Hsü Mien who held high office under the Liang. He died eleven years before his father. He was a page to the heir-apparent and later served as his equerry. Was a friend of Hsiao I. His wife was Liu Ling-hsien, younger sister of Liu Hsiao-cho, and a poetess in her own right. Examples of their letter-poems appear in Chapter Six.

Hsü Kan, courtesy name Wei-chang, AD 171–218. One of the 'Seven Masters of the Chien-an Era'. He came from Shantung. He served under Ts'ao Ts'ao. His set of six pieces entitled *Bedroom longing*, which appear in Chapter One, was greatly admired by generations of poets, and the third piece's last quatrain beginning with 'Ever since you went away' was frequently imitated. He was famous in his day for rendering Nâgârdjuna's *Pranyamûla Shâstra Tîkâ* into Chinese as *Essay on the Middle Way*.

Hsü Ling, courtesy name Hsiao-mu, AD 507–83, from Shantung. His father, Hsü Ch'ih, was tutor to Hsiao Kang while he was a young prince, and he introduced Hsü Ling to the prince's court. He showed a penchant for scholarship and literature from an early age. He served Hsiao Yen as a minister of state. He enjoyed Hsiao Kang's patronage, being included in his literary circle with many leading literary lights of the day. Between AD 534 and 545 – the precise date is not known – Hsiao Kang is traditionally believed to have commissioned Hsü Ling to compile *New Songs from a Jade Terrace*. He was one of the poets identified with the new form of love poetry known as 'Palace Style Poetry', which he well represented in his anthology. Later in his career, which outlasted the Liang Dynasty, he was sent as an envoy to the north and temporarily captured during dynastic upheavals. He eventually returned south to serve the new Ch'en Dynasty which had replaced the Liang in AD 557.

Hsü Shu, *fl. c.* mid-second century AD. Ch'in Chia's wife. One of her poems, *A poem in reply* in Chapter One, answers one of his letter-poems to her. Written in the *sao*-song metre (four syllables with an intervening *hsi* sound carrier particle), it barely qualifies as a poem for inclusion in that chapter, otherwise devoted to pentasyllabic poetry, but appears there alongside her husband's poem.

Hsü Yao, courtesy name ? Yao-chih, ? late fifth century AD. Little is known about him.

Hsün Ch'ang, courtesy name Mao-tsu, *c.* AD 420, from Honan. Became deputy head of an imperial secretariat under the Liu-Sung in the mid-420s. His two folk-songs in Chapter Three, *We met in a narrow alley* and *Green, green riverside grass*, imitate the same titles among the anonymous series in Chapter One.

Juan Chi, courtesy name Ssu-tsung, AD 210–63, from Honan. Popularly known by his official title, Pu-ping, or chief of infantry. He was one of the 'Seven Sages of the Bamboo Grove', a literary-philosophical group given to discussing intellectual matters. He was a gifted poet, thinker and musician. He is reputed to have drunk excessively, partly as a critical gesture against the political authorities. His literary legacy includes eighty-two poems in a series called *Poems from my Heart (Yung huai shih)*, nos. 2 and 12 of which appear in Chapter Two here. He was very much in vogue during the T'ang Dynasty.

Kao Shuang, *c.* AD 502, from Kiangsu. Served under the Ch'i and Liang Dynasties.

K'ung Weng-kuei, *fl. c.* AD 539, from Kweichi. Served as secretary to the Prince of Nanp'ing.

?Lady Pan, *fl. c.* 48–6 BC. Her first name is not known. Her official title, *chieh-yü*, or Beautiful Companion, indicates that she was a high-ranking lady in the palace. She entered the Han harem, becoming a favourite concubine of Emperor Ch'eng. Both her sons died in infancy. Later she was discarded by the emperor in favour of a girl dancer called Chao Feiyen. It was traditionally believed that Lady Pan composed *A poem on regret*, popularly known as the *Round fan poem*, when she lost imperial favour. It has many imitators. Although she was a noted poetess in her day, none of her work survives. *A poem on regret* may date from as late as the third century AD, for this may be when round fans were invented.

Li Ch'ung, courtesy name Hung-tu, *fl. c.* AD 323, from Hupei. Served the Eastern Chin Dynasty as an imperial documents editor. Later he became a privy councillor. He was a noted calligrapher. Author of miscellaneous works, including poetry, a treatise on Buddhism and Taoism, and a satire on excessively bookish scholars.

Li Yen-nien, *c.* 140–87 BC. Court musician and entertainer in the reign of the Han Emperor Wu. He had a beautiful sister whose praises he sang in *A song poem*, Chapter One, before the emperor. She was introduced to the emperor and became his favourite concubine. She received the title of *Fu-jen*, translated as 'Lady'. He was promoted to the rank of Harmonizer of the Tones. His poem is considered to be the earliest example of the five-syllable metre, and belongs to the *ko-shih*, sung poem, category.

Liu Hsiao-cho, courtesy name Hsiao-cho, AD 481–539, from Kiangsu. He enjoyed the patronage of both Emperor Wu of the Liang and of Hsiao T'ung while the latter was the Crown Prince Chao-ming. He held different governmental posts.

Liu Hsiao-i, courtesy name ? Hsiao-i, ? early to mid-sixth century AD. Younger brother of Liu Hsiao-cho and brother of Liu Hsiao-wei. Was well received by Hsiao Kang while he was crown prince. His short poem in Chapter Ten entitled *Poem on the Weaver girl* is elsewhere attributed to Liu Hsiao-wei, his brother.

Liu Hsiao-wei, courtesy name Hsiao-wei, d. AD 548. Younger brother of Liu Hsiao-cho, and Liu Hsiao-i's brother. He enjoyed the patronage and friendship of Hsiao Kang, while he was crown prince, and of Hsiao I, the Prince of Hsiangtung. His two poems at the very end of Chapter Ten are clearly 'encores' added by later editors, since Liu appears earlier in that same chapter.

Liu Huan, courtesy name Han-tu, *c.* AD 549, from Shantung. Served Hsiao I as secretary. One of his poems was written in honour of a man called Liu who was a senior official in Hsiao I's service, and three others are modelled on Hsiao I's poems, all four poems appearing in Chapter Eight.

Liu Hung, ? mid-sixth century AD. Little is known about him.

Liu Ling-hsien, Hsü Fei's wife, ? from late fifth century to early sixth century AD. She was the sister of Liu Hsiao-cho, Liu Hsiao-i and Liu Hsiao-wei. Of Liu Hsiao-cho's three sisters, Ling-hsien was the most literary. When her husband, Hsü Fei, died prematurely in AD 524, she married again to Wang Shu-ying. At Hsü Fei's funeral his father, the man of letters and top official Hsü Mien, decided to compose a funerary oration, but when he saw Ling-hsien's funerary prayer he is said to have thrown down his pen in a gesture of defeat. Two of her poems in response to her husband appear in Chapter Six, where his to her also appear somewhat earlier. She also seems to be the author of the last poem in Chapter Six, which was written, according to some commentators, to her late husband's mistress named T'ang Niang. Either this was added by a later editor as another example of her poetry, or another example of Hsü Fei's, or else it is by neither of them, but by an unknown author. The same kind of confusion exists with poems tacked on to the end of Chapter Eight, where they clearly do not belong in chronological terms.

Liu Miao, ? mid-sixth century AD, from Kiangsu. It seems he was taken prisoner by the Tartar general, Hou Ching, perhaps in AD 552 when the Liang capital of Chienk'ang had been captured.

Liu Shuo, courtesy name Hsiu-hsüan, AD 431–53, from Kiangsu. Fourth son of the Liu-Sung Emperor Wen. At the age of nine he was enfeoffed as the Prince of Nanp'ing. By the time he was twenty he had composed more than thirty imitations of old poems, a source of wonder among his contemporaries. He served as a general of the Army of the Centre, but was killed in his early twenties during the closing years of his father's reign. His poems at the end of Chapter Three are imitations of several of the anonymous old poems appearing in Chapter One.

Liu Tsun, courtesy name Hsiao-ling, d. AD 535, from Kiangsu. He was a cousin of Liu Hsiao-cho. While Hsiao Kang was still the Prince of Chinan (from AD 506 to 531), he was in his service as his secretary. Later, when Hsiao Kang became crown prince, he enjoyed a position of trust and favour at his court. Some of his poems were directly commissioned by Hsiao Kang, for example *Gay* in Chapter Eight.

Liu Yün, courtesy name Wen-ch'ang, AD 465–511, from Shantung. Held office under the first Liang Emperor as a senior official, and then as prefect of Wuhsing. His name is linked with that of Shen Yüeh in the formulation of the new tonal rules in poetry. His poems on fulling are based on a popular folk theme which many poets in this anthology imitated, such as Ts'ao P'i and Hsieh Hui-lien in Chapter Three, and Hsiao Yen in Chapter Seven.

Lu Chi, courtesy name Shih-heng, AD 261–303, from Kiangsu. His grandfather had helped to found the Wu kingdom, and when it was later conquered by the Chin Dynasty in AD 280, Lu Chi went into hiding. He went to Loyang ten years later and served the Chin. He was sponsored by the poet Chang Hua at the Chin court. Accused of treason, he and his two sons and brother were executed. His brother, Lu Yün, was also a famous poet. Hsiao T'ung included over one hundred of his poems in his *Anthology of Literature*. He is famous for his *Prose Poem on Literature*, a discursive, evaluative piece written in metaphorical language. His poems in Chapter Three are imitations of the anonymous *Nine Miscellaneous Poems* in Chapter One, followed by letter-poems written for a man called Ku Yen-hsien who also came from Wu. Lu Yün also composed letter-poems for this same Ku.

Lu Chüeh, courtesy name Han-ch'ing, AD 472–99, from Kiangsu. When his father and brother were executed, he was so heartbroken that he pined to death.

Lu Yün, courtesy name Shih-lung, AD 262–303. Younger brother of Lu Chi. He also went to Loyang and served Ssu-ma Ying of the Chin royal house. Chang Hua was his sponsor, too, and secured a post for him at court. He was executed with his brother on charges of treason. They are known in literary history as 'the Two Lu'.

Meng Chu, ? fifth century AD, from Tanyang in the region of Anhwei. Meng Chu was the name of a professional female singer.

P'an Yüeh, courtesy name An-jen, ? AD 247–300, from Honan. Served the Chin Dynasty as equerry and archivist to Grand Marshal Chia Ch'ung, and later served in the central secretariat. Famous for his poetry and his good looks. It was said that when he drove through Loyang women used to mob him, offering him peaches (the emblem of immortality, or eternal youth). He was a dominant figure in the literary group called 'Twenty-four Fellows'. Charged with treasonous involvement in the revolt of the Prince of Ch'i, he was executed. Of his fifteen extant poems those lamenting his dead wife are considered the finest. He was ranked in the Southern Dynasties as a major poet.

Pao Chao, courtesy name Ming-yüan, AD ?412–?66, from Kiangsu. Served in several posts under the Liu-Sung Emperor Hsiao-wu, the poet Liu Chün. He was assassinated by rioting soldiers when his patron, Liu Tzu-hsü, the Prince of Linhai, was forced to commit suicide for rebellion. Traditionally ranked with the poets Hsieh Ling-yün and Yen Yen-chih, he was esteemed by the T'ang poets, Li Po and Tu Fu. He is now generally regarded as a major poet of the Southern Dynasties, especially for his ballads and innovative developments in the folk-song genre. Of his surviving *oeuvre* of about two hundred poems, one-third are ballads, the best-known ones being eighteen poems in the series *It's hard travelling the road*, four of which appear in Chapter Nine. Many other poets wrote on this theme, such as Shih Pao-yüeh, Wu Chün, Fei Ch'ang and Wang Yün, all four of whom are also represented in Chapter Nine. One of Pao Chao's imitations of old ballads may be compared with the original, *White as mountaintop snow* in Chapter One and *The white head lament* in Chapter Four. His two poems in Chapter Four entitled *To my former love* go by the title *To Ma Tzu-ch'iao* in other editions. It is not clear who this person was, but it would be a man rather than a woman, and if this is the correct title, then Pao Chao probably wrote it for the man's wife, or former mistress.

Pao Ch'üan, courtesy name Jun-yüeh, d. AD 552, from Tunghai. Served Hsiao I when he was the Prince of Hsiangtung, and when he became Emperor Yüan continued in the imperial employ.

Pao Ling-hui, *fl. c.* AD 464. Younger sister of Pao Chao. Little else is known about her. Many of her poems imitate earlier models, particularly the anonymous old poems featured in Chapter One.

Pao Tzu-ch'ing, early sixth century AD. Little is known about him.

Prince of Hsiangtung, Hsiao I, AD 507–55. Enfeoffed as the Prince of Hsiangtung. He proclaimed himself Emperor Yüan of the Liang in AD 552, a year after his older brother, Hsiao Kang, had been assassinated. He moved the capital from Chienk'ang to Chiangling. He was the seventh son of Hsiao Yen. While still a prince, he was served by several Liang poets, and many poem titles in this anthology are addressed to him as patron. He was well known not only as a poet, but also as a fine painter. His brother, Hsiao Kang, called him 'my Tzu-chien', a eulogistic reference to a great poet of the third century, Ts'ao Chih, whose courtesy name was Tzu-chien. Two years after becoming emperor, Hsiao I was asphyxiated with a heavy sack of sand.

Prince of Shaoling, Hsiao Lun, AD 507–51. Enfeoffed as the Prince of Shaoling in AD 519. Younger brother of Hsiao Kang, sixth son of Hsiao Yen. In the histories he is presented as a base tyrant. In AD 532 he was temporarily reduced to the status of a commoner for his involvement in a brutal murder. Like many members of the Hsiao family, he participated in Buddhist ceremonial and attended services in many different Buddhist temples. His poem on Ch'iu Hu, translated in Chapter Seven, may be compared with poems treating the same theme by Fu Hsüan in Chapter Two and by Yen Yen-chih in Chapter Four.

Prince of Wuling, Hsiao Chi, AD 508–53: eighth son of Emperor Wu of the Liang, Hsiao Yen. Enfeoffed as the Prince of Wuling. In AD 552 he proclaimed himself emperor, but within a year was assassinated by his brother, Hsiao I, who had meanwhile proclaimed himself Emperor Yüan.

Shen Man-yüan, c. AD 540. She was Fan Ching's wife and Shen Yüeh's granddaughter. Her husband served the Liang Dynasty.

Shen Yüeh, courtesy name Hsiu-wen, AD 441–512, from Chekiang. Served three successive dynasties, the Liu–Sung, the Ch'i and the Liang, achieving the rank of head of the imperial secretariat. Because his grandfather and father before him had been executed, he pursued a career in politics with utmost caution. He was one of the 'Eight Comrades', Hsiao Yen's literary group. He is credited with classifying, together with Liu Yün, the four tones of literary Chinese and of evolving a system of tonal harmony which was fully developed into basic prosodic rules in the T'ang. He was a great scholar, reputedly owning a library of 20,000 books, including works on Confucianism, Buddhism and Taoism. He wrote histories of the Chin (no longer extant), of the Liu–Sung and of the Ch'i Dynasties. He developed the art of love poetry, capturing with sensitivity the feelings of lovers. His poetry was very popular in his own day. Two hundred or so of his poems survive.

Shih Ch'ung, courtesy name Chi-lun, AD 249–300, from Hopei. He was ennobled for his service to the Chin Dynasty, and was a favourite of Emperor Wu. He became extremely wealthy through maritime trade, and lived ostentatiously, having a well-known rivalry with Wang K'ai as to who could be more extravagant. He owned a magnificent park north-west of Loyang called Golden Vale where he used to entertain with lavish banquets. He was a member of the literary group called 'Twenty-four Fellows'. He had a concubine named Green Pearl, a beautiful entertainer who used to perform dance and music for his guests. Prince Lun of Chao wanted her for himself, but Shih Ch'ung refused to surrender her. Because that literary group was patronized by Chia Mi whose clan was purged, Shih Ch'ung was implicated and executed. His family was exterminated, and Green Pearl committed suicide by leaping from an upper storey of their mansion.

Shih Jung-t'ai, ? late fifth century AD. Little is known about him.

?Shih Pao-yüeh, late fifth century AD. A fine musician and poet in the reign of the Chin Emperor Wu. Biographical data are scant. Some commentators think that his poem in the middle of Chapter Nine was composed by Ch'ai Lang, based on information given by Chung Hung in his *Classification of Poets* (*Shih p'in*) in the sixth century AD.

Ssu-ma Hsiang-ju, courtesy name Ch'ang-ch'ing, c. 179–117 BC, from Ch'engtu, the old capital of Shu in modern Szechwan. Was very poor until his literary talent was recognized by the Han Emperor Wu. Author of several famous prose poems, a genre popular in the Han era, the best-known being *Sir Fantasy*, which includes *Shanglin Park*. Once when he travelled to Linch'iung he was invited to the home of a wealthy man called Cho Wang-sun. At a banquet there he sang songs of courtship intended for the ears of Cho's recently widowed daughter, Wen-chün, who was listening behind the door. She fell in love with the poet and they eloped that night. The courtship songs appear in Chapter Nine.

Su Hsiao-hsiao, fifth century AD, from Ch'ient'ang, modern Hangchow. She was a professional singer of the Chin and Ch'i Dynasties. A beautiful courtesan, she vowed to be true to her lover to the grave, beneath the 'pine and cypress'. She died young, and the legend arose that her spirit waited for her lover to join her in the next world.

?Su Po-yü's wife, ? third century AD. This attribution is given by one of Hsü Ling's eighteenth-century editors, Chi Jung-shu, who cited an earlier source-book on poetry, appearing to derive mainly from information given in the poem itself. Su Po-yü is said there to have lived in Shu, modern Szechwan, his wife in Ch'angan, the Han capital further in the north.

?Su Wu, 142–60 BC. The poem translated as *A poem on the wife I left behind* in Chapter One is traditionally attributed to him, partly because the theme of separation fits his historical life. The title appears to provide a biographical context, but it may be spurious, and not by the hand of Su Wu. The historical Su Wu was an envoy sent to the Hsiungnu by the Chinese court, but was held captive by them for nineteen years. Later he was sent back to China, partly as the result of a ruse: the Hsiungnu were informed that a letter sent via a goose's foot had reached the Han court telling the emperor that Su Wu was still alive. The Hsiungnu, who had told the emperor that Su Wu had died, were so amazed by this feat that they set him free. Similarly, the belief arose that he had sent his wife a letter from captivity. The poem here is one of a set of four attributed to him.

Sun Cho, courtesy name Hsing-kung, AD 301–c. 380, from Shansi. For ten years he roamed the mountains and lakes of Chekiang. Later he served the Chin Dynasty in important posts. He was considered a major poet in his own day. Two of his poems were written on Green Jade, a favourite concubine of the Prince of Junan in the Chin Dynasty: *Two songs for my beloved Green Jane*, Chapter Ten.

Sung Tzu-hou, from late second to third century AD. Probably lived in the Later Han and Wei Dynasties. Biographical data are scant. His poem in Chapter One translated as *A poem on Graceful Tung* may be the name of the girl speaking in the poem. The poem title, *Graceful Tung* (*Tung Chiao-jao*), may have originally belonged to an old folk-song text which is now lost.

Tai Hao, ? mid-sixth century AD. Biographical data are scant.

T'ang Seng-chi, ? personal name Hsiu, also called Hsiu Shang-jen and Yang Chi. The title *Seng* in a man's name meant that he was connected in some formal way with Buddhism, and *Shang-jen* is a similar religious title. His poem translated as *Poem on the title, 'In a stagnant well I found a golden hairpin'* in Chapter Eight, expresses the theme of the vanity of human cares and also a certain misogyny which might be construed as Buddhist attitudes. The poet lived in the fifth century, his birth date probably being AD 464.

T'ao Ch'ien, courtesy name Yüan-ming, AD 365–427, from Kiangsi. In his youth the family wealth was diminished. Much of his early adult life was spent in unsuccessful efforts to secure a post at court or in an office at the capital. Later he retired to the country, still only in his forties. Much of his poetry reflects a philosophical view of life. He is admired as a nature poet and, though rated in the Southern Dynasties as a second-rank poet, was fully recognized in the T'ang and is acknowledged today as one of China's major poets.

?T'ao-yeh (Peachleaf), *fl.* fourth century AD. Favourite concubine of the painter and writer Wang Hsien-chih, son of Wang Hsi-chih, the famous painter and calligrapher. Her three poems on a round fan were written, it is thought, in answer to Wang Hsien-chih's letter-poems. They appear in Chapter Ten.

Teng K'eng, *c.* AD 502. Enfeoffed as the Marquess of Sung-tzu. His father was from Hupei. Biographical data are scant.

?Ts'ai Yung, courtesy name Po-chieh, AD 133-92, from Honan. Was a well-known poet, musician and calligrapher. He was well versed in astronomy and musical theory. He wrote the authorized version of the *Six Classics* (the five *Confucian Classics*). Later he incurred the displeasure of the authorities and was condemned to death, sentence being commuted to having his hair pulled out. He became a recluse, but when the warlord Tung Cho challenged the Han Dynasty he summoned Ts'ai Yung to court, inviting him to take office and ennobling him as a marquess. When Tung Cho was defeated, Ts'ai Yung was again imprisoned for an indiscreet remark, and he died in jail. Known as Drunken Dragon for his drinking bouts. He was the subject of a play by the fourteenth-century playwright Kao Ming, who portrayed him in less than flattering terms; the title of the play is *The Lute*. His poem in Chapter One is elsewhere listed as anonymous, and its attribution remains doubtful.

Ts'ao Chih, courtesy name Tzu-chien, entitled the Prince of Ch'en, and also known as the Prince of Yung-ch'iu (he was enfeoffed ten times), AD 192-232. Third son of Ts'ao Ts'ao. He was passed over as heir to the Wei throne in favour of his brother Ts'ao P'ei. The bitter rivalry in power and in love between the two brothers is legendary. Ts'ao Chih wrote in a variety of styles and adopted many different, sometimes contradictory, literary poses, such as a Confucian statesman, a Taoist immortal, or bon viveur. The view that persists of his tragic life is partly fictional. Efforts to reconstruct a chronology of his poems, arguing a descent from happy youth to tragic manhood, are erroneous. Ts'ao Chih was the most gifted of a family of literary men. He was particularly successful in using existing folk-song themes in new ways, and in establishing the new five-word metre as an expressive art form. His *Prose Poem on the Goddess of Lo River* was greatly admired, and is frequently referred to in the poems of this anthology.

Ts'ao P'i, courtesy name Fu-tao, *fl. c.* AD 317, from Anhwei. Related to the Ts'ao family of the Wei Dynasty. Served the Eastern Chin as a scholar in the Grand Academy, holding several minor posts and rising to the rank of Great Officer of Brilliant Favour. His cycle of songs to Orchid Fragrance, a nymph, were greatly admired in his day, but have not survived.

Tso Ssu, courtesy name T'ai-ch'ung. b. ? AD 250, d. ? 306, from Shantung. Ridiculed by local girls because he was ugly and stammered. Devoted himself to scholarship. Served as secretary to Chia Mi, nephew of Empress Chia, but retired from office when the Chia clan was purged. His sister became an imperial concubine, which rank brought wealth and status to his family. Famous for his *Three Prose Poems on the Three Capitals*, a literary endeavour that took him ten years to complete. It was so popular that paper was scarce in Loyang when it was circulated. His poems often contain colloquialisms which may have been erroneously copied and misinterpreted in transmission, making some passages very problematical.

Wang Chien, courtesy name Mao-kao, *c.* AD 277-322, from Kiangsu. Served the Eastern Chin Dynasty as secretary to the heir-apparent. Said to have become the son-in-law of the imperial family. The last few lines of his poem are construed by some as his flattering reference to the empress, mother of his wife the princess; *A poem on watching Weaver star on Seventh Night*, it appears in Chapter Three.

?Wang Hsien-chih, courtesy name Tzu-ching, AD 344–88, from Kweichi in Chekiang. Son of the famous painter and calligrapher Wang Hsi-chih (AD 321–79). Hsien-chih was also a famous calligrapher, scholar and writer. He served the Eastern Chin Dynasty in the archive department. He had a concubine called T'ao-yeh, Peachleaf, for whom he is thought to have written two songs, which appear in Chapter Ten. In some anthologies, however, his poems are attributed to Peachleaf herself.

Wang Hsün, courtesy name Huai-fan, AD 511–36, from Shantung. Became a head of a department in the imperial chancellery, and served Hsiao Kang when he was crown prince. His literary talent was considered exceptionally fine, and he attracted a number of devotees. One of his poems in Chapter Eight is modelled on Hsiao Kang's *Extempore composition* in Chapter Seven.

Wang Huan, from late fifth to early sixth century AD. Little is known of his life.

Wang Seng-ju, courtesy name Seng-ju, personal name unknown, AD 465–522, from Shantung. Devoted himself to literature and scholarship from early youth. Though from a poor family, he rose in office to serve the Liang as prefect of Nanhai, and later became a deputy of the Board of Censors. The title *Seng* in a man's name meant some formal connection with the religious life of a Buddhist, either as a monk or lay religious. His poem *Spring regrets* in Chapter Six is listed elsewhere as a composition by Wu Chün.

Wang Seng-ta, AD 423–58, from Shantung. Served one of the Liu-Sung princes as an administrator, prefect and departmental head of an imperial secretariat. He was eventually thrown into prison for his blunt memorials and he died there.

Wang Shu, ? from late fifth to early sixth century AD. Biographical data scant. One poem title indicates that his poetry had attracted the attention of Hsiao Yen's brother. Another title shows that he attended a banquet given by a ministerial head, probably the illustrious Hsü Mien, all of which suggests that he moved in the top circles.

Wang Shu-ying's wife: see Liu Ling-hsien.

Wang Su, courtesy name Hsiu-yeh, AD 418–71, from Shantung. When his mother died, he became a recluse and lived in the country. On the accession of the Liu-Sung Emperor Hsiao-wu, Wang Su was often summoned to court. The emperor was the poet Liu Chün.

?Wang Sung, wife of General Liu Hsün, ? from late second to early third century AD. A favourite official of Ts'ao Ts'ao, her husband was later killed. There is some doubt about the attribution of her poems. Some ascribe them to Ts'ao P'ei.

Wang T'ai-ch'ing, courtesy name T'ai-ch'ing, ? from late fifth to mid-sixth century AD. Served the Liang administration and was well received by members of the royal family.

Wang Wei, courtesy name Ching-hsüan, AD 415–43, from Kiangsu. (Not to be confused with the T'ang poet Wang Wei.) He served the Liu-Sung Dynasty as administrative adviser to the Army of the Right for Prince Shuo of Nanp'ing. Disliking official duties, he retired on the grounds of ill health. He died young.

Wang Yün, courtesy names Yüan-li and Te-jou, AD 481–549, from Shantung. Grandson of Wang Seng-ta. Admired in his day for his literary talent, especially by Shen Yüeh and Hsiao T'ung. He died from misadventure, leaping into a well to escape from rebels. His six poems in Chapter Eight harmonize with Master of Records Wu's poems (probably Wu Chün the poet). Thirty-nine of his poems are extant.

Wang Yung, courtesy name Yüan-chang, AD 468–94, from Nanking. He was Wang

Seng-ta's grandson. Served the Ch'i Dynasty in the departments of astronomy and receptions. Because his personal name was the same as the taboo name of the Ch'i Emperor Ho, his courtesy name was used instead. He was imprisoned for political intrigue and seems to have died in captivity.

Wen-jen Ch'ien, personal name Ch'ien, ? *fl.* mid-sixth century AD. Biographical data are scant.

Wu Chün, also known as Wu Yün, courtesy name Shu-hsiang, AD 469–520, from Chekiang. Prince Wei of Chien-an appointed him as his secretary and as governor of Yangchou. Later he attended court with the honorary title *Ch'ao-ch'ing*, by which he is sometimes known. He did some editorial work on the *Annals of the Ch'i Dynasty*, but was dismissed for inaccuracies. He also worked on a general history, but died before its completion. His poetic artistry was generally acclaimed and there were many imitators of the 'Wu Chün style'. He is one of the earliest poets to have used the term *chüeh-chü* for a short, four-line verse.

Wu Man-yüan, *fl. c.* AD 471. Biographical data are scant. His poem *There came flying a pair of white swans* in Chapter Four is based on the old folk-song in Chapter One.

Wu Tzu, ? sixth century AD. Little is known about him.

Wusun Princess [Hsi-chün], 110 BC: daughter of Liu Chien, the Prince of Chiangtu, and related to the Han Emperor Wu. She was sent in marriage to a chieftain of the Wusun tribe in the region of modern Lake Balkash (Kazakhstan) and Sinkiang. Her poem, *A song poem* in Chapter Nine, features the *hsi* sound-carrier particle in each line, reminiscent of the *sao*-song style of *The Songs of Ch'u*.

Yang Fang, courtesy name Kung-hui, *fl. c.* AD 317, from Chekiang. Served the Western Chin Dynasty in various prefectural posts, and finally retired to the countryside. His five epithalamia which appear in Chapter Three have attracted different theories concerning their composition: (1) all five are love-songs or wedding songs; (2) the first two are wedding songs, the last three miscellaneous poems; (3) all five are on the *ho-huan*, or 'joy of love' flower; (4) all five are allegorical, two describing deep devotion, one estrangement and two unrequited love; (5) all five are letter-poems between a man and a woman, of which the sixth is missing.

Yao Fan, ? *fl.* early sixth century AD. Little is known about him.

Yen Yen-chih, courtesy name Yen-nien, AD 384–456, from Shantung. Orphaned and impoverished in his youth. Given to drink. Became a page to the heir-apparent and was promoted to deputy head of an imperial secretariat. Served the first four Liu-Sung emperors. Demoted to governor of a district in Chekiang. Nicknamed Yen the Clown for being outspoken and bibulous. Was protected by the Liu-Sung Emperor Wen's bemused favour. His poetry is often compared with that of Hsieh Ling-yün. His narrative poem, *A poem on Ch'iu Hu*, in Chapter Four, in nine stanzas of ten lines each, with a change of rhyme in each stanza, may be compared with Fu Hsüan's version in Chapter Two.

Yü Chien-wu, courtesy name Tzu-shen, AD 487–550, from Honan. From a poor family. Father of the famous poet Yü Hsin. While Hsiao Kang was Prince of Chinan, he and Liu Hsiao-wei, together with eight others, were known as the 'Ten Scholars of the Lofty Studio'. At the age of twenty he served Hsiao Kang the infant and stayed with him when he became the Crown Prince, enjoying over thirty years of royal favour. Enfeoffed as the Marquess of Wuk'ang. Both Yü and later Hsü Ch'ih shaped Hsiao Kang's literary taste. Both men, and others, are identified with 'Palace Style Poetry', but Hsiao Kang is more popularly accredited with immortalizing this new verse form. Almost a hundred of Yü's poems survive, many of which illustrate the new poetic style.

Yü Hsin, courtesy name Tzu-shan, AD 512–80, from Honan. His father was Yü Chien-wu, who was tutor to Hsiao Kang. During his lifetime the Tartar general Hou Ching captured Chienk'ang. The Liang ruler moved his capital to Chiangling. The Liang foundered in AD 556, and was replaced by the Ch'en Dynasty. When Yü Hsin was sent as an envoy to the north, the northern dynasty of the Western Wei invaded the south and captured Chiangling. Western Wei was in turn defeated by the Northern Chou Dynasty. The poet was in virtual exile during all these upheavals, and while still in the north wrote a famous prose poem *Lament for South of the River*, meaning the old southern region of the Yangtze of his birth. He was greatly admired as a poet in his own time, especially by his conquerors. Later Tu Fu expressed the highest praise for his verse.

Yü Tan, ? from late fifth to early sixth century. A scholar. He served as governor of a district in Kwangsi, and as secretary to Hsiao Wang.

Yü Yen, *fl. c.* AD 488, from Kweichi in Chekiang. A contemporary of Shen Yüch. Served in a military capacity.

SELECTED BIBLIOGRAPHY

Birrell, Anne, *Chinese Mythology: An Introduction.* Johns Hopkins University Press, 1993.

Birrell, Anne, 'Courtly Love Poetry in Early Medieval China', in *Agenda*, 20:3–4 (1982–3), pp. 109–121.

Birrell, Anne, 'The Dusty Mirror: Courtly Portraits of Woman in Southern Dynasties Love Poetry', in Robert E. Hegel and Richard C. Hessney (eds.), *Expressions of Self in Chinese Literature* (Studies in Oriental Culture, no. 19), Columbia University Press, 1985, pp. 33–69.

Birrell, Anne, 'Erotic Decor: A Study of Love Imagery in the Sixth Century AD Anthology: "Yü-t'ai hsin-yung" (New Poems from a Jade Terrace)', Columbia University, Ph.D. thesis, 1978.

Birrell, Anne, 'Mythmaking and Yüeh-fu: Popular Songs and Ballads of Early Imperial China', in *Journal of the American Oriental Society*, 109:2 (1989), pp. 223–35.

Birrell, Anne, *Popular Songs and Ballads of Han China* (1988), University of Hawaii Press, 1993.

Chao Chün (ed.), *Yü-t'ai hsin-yung* (New Songs from a Jade Terrace), Ming edn 1633; facsimile of a Sung edn of AD 1215 by Ch'en Yü-fu, reprinted in *Chung-kuo wen-hsüeh ming chu*, Wen-hsüeh ku-chi, Peking, 1955.

Chi Jung-shu (ed.), *Yü-t'ai hsin-yung k'ao-i* (Critical Text of *New Songs from a Jade Terrace*), Ts'ung-shu chi-ch'eng edn Commercial Press, Shanghai, 1935–7.

Davis, A.R., *T'ao Yüan-ming (AD 365–427), His Works and Their Meaning*, 2 vols. (Cambridge Studies in Chinese History, Literature and Institutions), Cambridge University Press, 1983.

Diény, Jean-Pierre, *Les Dix-neuf poèmes anciens* (Bulletin de la Maison Franco-Japonaise, n.s. 7:4), Presses Universitaires de France, 1963.

Diény, Jean-Pierre, *Aux Origines de la poésie classique en Chine, étude sur la poésie lyrique à l'époque des Han* (Monographies du T'oung Pao, no. 6), Brill, Leiden, 1968.

Diény, Jean-Pierre, *Pastourelles et magnanarelles, essai sur un thème littéraire chinois*, Librairie Droz, Geneva, 1977.

Evans, Marilyn J., 'Popular Songs of the Southern Dynasties: A Study in Chinese Poetic Style', Yale University, Ph.D. thesis, 1966.

Frankel, Hans H., 'The Abduction, the War, and the Desperate Husband: Three Early Chinese Ballads', in *Ventures*, 1:5 (1965), pp. 6–14.

Frankel, Hans H., *The Flowering Plum and the Palace Lady: Interpretations of Chinese Poetry*, Yale University Press, 1976.

Frankel, Hans H., 'The Formulaic Language of the Chinese Ballad "Southeast Fly the Peacocks"', in *Bulletin of the Institute of History and Philology*, 39 (1969), pp. 219–44.

Frankel, Hans H., 'The Problem of Authenticity in Ts'ao Chih', in Chan Ping-leung (ed.), *Essays in Commemoration of the Golden Jubilee of the Fung Ping-shan Library (1932–1982)*, Fung Ping Shan Library, Hong Kong, 1982, pp. 183–201.

Frankel, Hans H., 'The Relation between Narrator and Characters in Yuefu Ballads', in *Chinoperl Papers*, 13 (1984–5), pp. 107–27.

Frankel, Hans H., 'Yüeh-fu Poetry', in Cyril Birch (ed.), *Studies in Chinese Literary Genres*, University of California Press, 1974, pp. 69–107.

Fusek, Lois, 'The Poetry of Ts'ao P'i (187–226) [Ts'ao P'ei]', Yale University, Ph.D. thesis, 1975.

Graham, William T., Jr, *'The Lament for the South': Yü Hsin's 'Ai Chiang-nan fu'* (Cambridge Studies in Chinese History, Literature and Institutions), Cambridge University Press, 1980.

Hawkes, David, *The Songs of the South: An Ancient Chinese Anthology of Poems by Qu Yuan and Other Poets* (Penguin Classics, 1959), rev. edn, Penguin Books, Harmondsworth, 1985.

Hightower, James Robert, *The Poetry of T'ao Ch'ien* (The Oxford Library of East Asian Literatures), Clarendon Press, Oxford, 1970.

Hightower, James Robert, 'Some Characteristics of Parallel Prose', in Soren Egerod and Else Glahn (eds.), *Studia Serica Bernhard Karlgren Dedicata*, Ejnar Munksgaard, Copenhagen, 1959, pp. 69–91, reprinted in John L. Bishop (ed.), *Studies in Chinese Literature* (Harvard–Yenching Institute Studies, no. 21), Harvard University Press, 1966, pp. 108–39.

Holzman, Donald, *Poetry and Politics: The Life and Works of Juan Chi, AD 210–263* (Cambridge Studies in Chinese History, Literature and Institutions), Cambridge University Press, 1976.

Hsü I-min, Huang K'o and Ch'ai Chien-hung (eds.), *Yüeh-fu shih ming p'ien shang-hsi* (A Critical Analysis of the Main Yüeh-fu Poems), Shih-yüeh wen-i, Peking, 1988.

Karlgren, Bernhard, *The Book of Odes*, Museum of Far Eastern Antiquities, Stockholm, 1974.

Knechtges, David R., *Wen Xuan, or Selections of Refined Literature*, 2 vols. (Princeton Library of Asian Translations), Princeton University Press, 1982–7.

Li Po-ch'i, *Ho Sun chi chiao-chu* (Annotated Edition of the Collected Works of Ho Sun), Ch'i-Lu shu she, Chinan, 1988.

Marney, John, *Chiang Yen* (Twayne's World Authors Series, no. 629), Twayne Publishers, Boston, Mass., 1981.

Marney, John, *Liang Chien-wen Ti* (Twayne's World Authors Series, no. 374), Twayne Publishers, Boston, Mass., 1976.

Martin, François, 'Le Yutai Xinyong et la nouvelle poésie: une anthologie de poésie galante en Chine au VIe siècle', Université de Paris, Ph.D. thesis, 1979.

Mather, Richard B., *The Poet Shen Yüeh (441–513): The Reticent Marquis*, Princeton University Press, 1988.

Mather, Richard B., *Shih-shuo hsin-yü: A New Account of Tales of the World by Liu I-ch'ing with Commentary by Liu Chün*, University of Minnesota Press, 1976.

Mayhew, Lenore, and William McNaughton, *A Gold Orchid: The Love Poems of Tzu Yeh*, Charles E. Tuttle, Rutland, Vermont and Tokyo, 1972.

Mu K'o-hung, *Yü-t'ai hsin-yung chien-chu* (Annotated Edition of *New Songs from a Jade Terrace* [the edition of Wu Chao-i and Ch'eng Yen]), 2 vols. (Chung-kuo ku-tien wen-hsüeh chi pen ts'ung-shu), Chung-hua, Peking, 1985.

Obi Kōichi and Takashi Chikao (eds.), *Gyokudai shin'ei sakuin* (Concordance to *New Songs from a Jade Terrace*), Yamamoto, Tokyo, 1976.

Paper, Jordan David, 'The Life and Thought of Fu Hsüan (AD 217–278)', University of Wisconsin, Ph.D. thesis, 1971.

Prynne, Jeremy H., 'China Figures. *New Songs from the Jade Terrace: An Anthology of*

Early Chinese Love Poetry. Translated with Annotations and an Introduction by Anne Birrell', review in *Modern Asian Studies*, 17:4 (1983), pp. 671–88.

Suzuki, Torao, *Gyokudai shin'ei shu* (The New Songs from a Jade Terrace), 3 vols. (Iwanami series, 32–010 (1953–6)), reprinted Iwanami, Tokyo, 1970.

Uchida, Sennosuke, *Gyokudai shin'ei* (New Songs from a Jade Terrace), 2 vols. (Shinshaku kambun taikei, 60–61), Meiji Shoin, Tokyo, 1974.

Waley, Arthur, *The Nine Songs: A Study of Shamanism in Ancient China* (1955), reprinted City Lights, San Francisco, 1973.

Wang Yün-hsi, *Yüeh-fu shih lun-ts'ung* (A General Discussion of Yüeh-fu Poetry), Ku-tien wen-hsüeh, Shanghai, 1958.

Watson, Burton, *Chinese Rhyme–Prose: Poems in the Fu Form from the Han and Six Dynasties Periods* (UNESCO Collection of Representative Works, Chinese Series), Columbia University Press, 1971.

Wu Chao-i (ed.), *Yü-t'ai hsin-yung chien-chu* (Annotated Edition of *New Songs from a Jade Terrace*), 1675 edition; revised by Ch'eng Yen, 1774, reprinted in Ssu-pu pei-yao edn.